The 100 Best Resorts of the Caribbean

The 100
Best Resorts
of the Caribbean

by Kay Showker

A Voyager Book

The
Globe
Pequot
press

Old Saybrook, Connecticut

The prices and rates listed in this guidebook were confirmed at press time but under no circumstances are they guaranteed. We recommend that you call establishments before traveling to obtain current information.

Photo credits: P. xiv: U.S. Virgin Islands Division of Tourism; p. 8: Round Hill Hotel and Villas; p. 13: Cap Juluca; p. 115: Hyatt Regency Grand Cayman; p. 123: Avila Beach Hotel; p. 130: Ramada Renaissance Jaragua Resort, Casino & Spa; p. 148: photo by Joe Petrocik; p. 155: Photo by Alan Montaine; p. 188: photo by Joe Petrocik; p. 208: El San Juan Hotel & Casino; p. 226: Photo by Fernando Marquez, courtesy Puerto Rico Tourist Board; p. 243: The Old Gin House; p. 256: Anse Chastanet Beach Hotel; p. 277: photo by Vignelli; p. 311: © Carol Lee/St. Croix.

Library of Congress Cataloging-in-Publication Data

Showker, Kay.
   The 100 best resorts of the Caribbean / by Kay Showker. — 1st ed.
      p. cm.
   "A Voyager book."
   Includes index.
   ISBN 1-56440-066-2
   1. Hotels, taverns, etc.—Caribbean Area—Guidebooks. 2. Resorts—Caribbean Area—Guidebooks. 3. Caribbean Area—Guidebooks. I Title. II. Title: Hundred best resorts of the Caribbean. III. Title: One hundred best resorts of the Caribbean.

TX907.5.C27S56 1992
647.9472901—dc20
                                                      92-32520
                                                      CIP

Manufactured in the United States of America
First Edition/First Printing

Contents

Contents

A Word of Thanks

When a book covers one hundred resorts on forty islands, it goes almost without saying that the author needs the help of many people to complete the task. I am certainly no exception. This book has required an incredible amount of research, discussions with knowledgeable people, and follow up. Dozens of people were tireless in their effort to help me. I only wish I could name them all, but I would be remiss not to mention some.

First, I would like to express my everlasting gratitude to Marcella Martinez of Marcella Martinez Associates, New York, and her staff, who helped me every step of the way from obtaining information, giving me advice, and editing copy to helping me find photographs at the last minute to replace mine, which were lost in transit en route to my publisher.

Adrianne Rice of Pisa Brothers, Inc., New York, and Lynn Hochberg of Landmark Travel, Weston, Massachusetts, are among the most knowledgeable travel agents in the country with intimate, first-hand experience on Caribbean resorts. Their advice was invaluable. I am also grateful to Raymond Kane, president of Pisa Brothers, Inc., who generously allowed me to use the agency's library whenever I needed it.

The questionnaire for the "Green Leaf" awards was based on months of discussions with environmentalists, experienced hotel managers, architects, and others working in the conservation field. But none of it would have been possible without the help of Stan Selengut, the proprietor of Maho Bay Camps and a recognized authority and advisor to governments and tourism officials around the world on ecotourism, and Peggy Bendel of Development Counsellors International, whose work for the U.S. Virgin Islands formed the basis of my questionnaire.

Others whose generous efforts on my behalf are Claire Devener, Suzanne Seitz, and Martin Flaherty, Anquilla; Carmen Tuttle, Villa Banfi, New York; Steve Kravitz, New York; Barbara Daley, Brown and Powers, Grand Cayman; Leslie Cohen, Pace Advertising, New York; Marilyn Marx and Rose Abello, Karen Weiner Escalera Associates, New York; Myron Clement and Joe Petrocik, Clement-Petrocik, New York; Cecile Graffin, French West Indies Tourist Board, New York; Alison Ross, Peter Martin Associates, New York; Mariam Trokan, The Rowland Company, New York; Tim Benford, Tim Benford Associates, Mountainside, New Jersey; Joan Bloom and Jill Solomon, Hill & Knowlton, New York; Patrick Arton and Sharon McCoy, The Keating Group, New York; Deborah Weintraub, D. Weintraub Communications, St. Thomas; and Deborah Weinstein, Hyatt Hotels, New York.

Text Contributions

Because the time constraint in writing this book made it impossible for me to revisit every resort prior to my deadline, as I had wanted to, I called on my writing colleagues for help. Some contributed specific material written for this book, others allowed me to use material from articles that had been published recently elsewhere. In every case, they are writers who specialize in the Caribbean and are as qualified as I to write this book. Indeed, several have written books on the Caribbean.

Several entries are based on articles that first appeared in *Caribbean Travel and Life*, and I am particularly grateful to the publisher, Patricia Fox, and the editors, Veronica Stoddart and Sharon Jaffe Dan, as well as the authors for their generous cooperation in allowing me to use the material.

Specifically, these are the *Cotton House* (Mustique), *K Club* (Barbuda), and *Sapore di Mare* (St. Barts) by Susan Pierres; *Boscobel* (Jamaica) by Amy McAllister; *The Horned Dorset Primavera* (Puerto Rico) and *Casa San Jose* (Puerto Rico) by Suzanne Murphy; *Royal St. Lucian* (St. Lucia) by Sharon Jaffe Dan; and *Caneel Bay* (U.S. Virgin Islands) by Veronica Stoddart.

Young Island by Jennifer Quale is based on an article that originally appeared in the Miami *Herald* (April 5, 1992). Suzanne McManus advised and helped me with the research on all the resorts in Jamaica; Gail Knopfler worked with me on St. Maarten; while Joan Scobey gathered material for me in the Abacos.

Katharine Gordon Dyson not only helped me edit much of the material in the book but she also contributed *Pineapple Beach* (Antigua) and *Sandcastle* (Jost Van Dyke, B.V.I.); Joan Iaconetti researched most of the resorts in the Grenadines and contributed *The Frangipani* (Bequia), *Petit St. Vincent* (Petit St. Vincent) and *Salt Whistle Bay* (Mayreau).

In addition to her articles, I am deeply grateful to Susan Pierres for sharing her extensive knowledge of Caribbean resorts with me.

Kay Showker

UNITED
STATES

Freeport

Nassau

BAHAMAS

T
AND

CUBA

CAYMAN
ISLANDS

GRAND
CAYMAN

Montego
Bay   Ocho Rios

JAMAICA   Kingston   Port Antonio

HAITI

Caribbean
Sea

White indicates island represented in this book.

The Caribbean Islands

Atlantic Ocean

BRITISH
VIRGIN
ISLANDS

PUERTO
RICO

TORTOLA

San Juan — VIRGIN GORDA

Santo
Domingo

ST. THOMAS

ANGUILLA

ST. MAARTEN

ST. CROIX

ST. BARTS

U.S.
VIRGIN
ISLANDS

SABA

ST. EUSTATIUS

ST. KITTS

ANTIGUA

NEVIS

MONTSERRAT

GUADELOUPE

DOMINICA

MARTINIQUE

ST. LUCIA

BARBADOS

ST. VINCENT

GRENADINES

BEQUIA

ARUBA

CURAÇAO

BONAIRE

GRENADA

MARGARITA
ISLAND

TOBAGO

TRINIDAD

Introduction

Ask any ten Caribbean frequenters to name the best or even their favorite resort in the Caribbean and you will probably get ten different answers. You will certainly start an argument.

In the twenty years or so that I have written about the Caribbean, the questions I am asked most often are "What's your favorite place?" and "What's the best place to stay in . . . ." It is not surprising, since the choice of a hotel is usually a traveler's first concern. But the best resort, like beauty, is in the eye of the beholder. And resorts, like people, differ. Not every resort suits everyone's needs and style.

Any of us can recognize high quality and good service. We all appreciate good architectural design and interior decor. But to be the best, a hotel or resort must have that "something special" that is almost impossible to define and strikes each of us differently.

Then, too, there was a time not long ago when the choices in the Caribbean were clearer, as good resorts were few. But now, after more than a decade of steady building throughout the region, the number has more than doubled. (The Caribbean Hotel Association's reference guide lists almost 1,500 entries.) The choice is more difficult, but, happily, the selection is more interesting.

Consider, too, that these hotels, inns, and resorts are spread over more than forty separate islands, or island groups, and you will see that the task is daunting. *The 100 Best Resorts of the Caribbean* is meant to make the choice easier. Most people do not want or need the standard long list of options with brief descriptions that appear in many Caribbean guidebooks; they prefer some selectivity, and selectivity is precisely the aim of this book.

Since standards vary so much from island to island, it is difficult to set up arbitrary rules or criteria to apply across the board. What passes as the best in Guadeloupe may be only acceptable in Anguilla. What has some travelers turned on in St. Barts would be turned down in Jamaica. A great deal also has to do with an island's tradition—British, French, Dutch, Spanish—and the kind of tourists it attracts.

The Caribbean "best" are recognized by the same attention to detail and quality of service, food, care, comfort, and facilities that distinguish the best hotels and resorts around the world. But in judging the Caribbean one has to be generous. There are many problems in trying to operate a top-quality resort in the tropics. This, coupled with the region's high operating costs, means that the "best" tend to be equated with the most expensive.

Yet it would have been a mistake to include only the most expensive resorts. The selection would have been easy, but you don't need me to tell you which are the 100 most expensive hotels in the Caribbean. Any good travel agent can tell you that. What's more, being expensive is no guarantee of being the best—or even good—and there are some real dogs out there. Rather, consideration was given to ambience, historic setting, management style, uniqueness, and other elements that make some resorts the best for other than traditional reasons.

What impresses me, even after twenty years, is the enormous variety that the Caribbean offers. I wanted the 100 resorts in this book to reflect that variety and to represent a broad range of establishments: large and small, beachside and hillside, modest and deluxe, homey and elegant.

I made a conscious effort to provide diversity, choosing the resorts I considered the best in each category across the broadest possible spectrum on as many islands as possible. The selections run the gamut from rustic retreats to private island hideaways to large, full-service layouts. They range in their degree of luxury from minimal to extravagantly luxurious. That's why you will find such widely differing entries as back-to-nature Maho Bay Camps in St. Johns, U.S. Virgin Islands, at one end of the spectrum and posh Malliouhana in Anguilla at the other.

What Is a Resort?

But first, what is a resort? Because my selection covers such a broad range, readers may wonder how I define a "resort," and they will certainly want to know the criteria I used.

Webster defines a resort as a place providing recreation and entertainment, especially to vacationers. Roget's *Thesaurus* and Rodale's *The Synonym Finder* list as synonyms *hotel, inn, club, lodge, spa, watering place, camp.* This book has places fitting all these appellations, along with *haven, hideaway,* and *retreat.*

But let me make it simple. I define a resort as *a place to go for a vacation.* It is a broad definition, but it reflects a reality, namely, that vacationers are an extremely diverse group whose ideas of a vacation differ as much as their interests, needs, and expectations. What is paradise for one person might be hell for another.

For some people, the ideal resort is a pleasure palace by the sea, the more luxurious, the more pampering, the more exclusive, the better. For others it is the exact opposite. They willingly trade creature comforts to be close to nature with as few manmade intrusions as possible.

Then there are the honeymooners, golfers, divers, birders, hikers; those who want action, those who want serenity, those who care about cuisine, those who take family vacations; those who want to be directly on the beach, those who want a vacation in the mountains; those who select a resort by the variety of sports and recreation available; those who care little about activities. All of these people will find resorts in this guide to suit them. Yet, the traveler's "need" did not guide my initial selection—only the fine-tuning. My first concern was the quality of the resort itself.

Criteria

So what were my criteria? To be the best a resort needs a combination of factors based on location, setting, layout, service, appearance, ambience, dining experience, sports facilities, management, and staff. But then it must have something beyond these—the intangibles—that *je ne sais quoi.*

Maybe it's warmth, maybe it's style. It is a certain quality, a feeling that is hard to define but that you know instinctively when you find it. When I described my dilemma to a fellow writer, he replied instantly, "Yes, I know what you mean. Would you want to spend a week there?"

"That's it." I replied. "That's it." Would you want to spend a week there? And perhaps more important, at the end of the week, do you long to return? Every entry in this book was put to that test. There were other tests, too. Does the resort live up to the goals it designed for itself? Does it fulfill its role—whatever the style, price, category—better than any other?

Another important criterion: The resort had to have been in business for at least one year. Most of those included here have been around much longer than a year; they have stood the test of time. A few, which barely got in under the time requirement, were included because the owners have established track records for running outstanding hotels and because the inn or resort is of such quality and distinction that it merits early recognition.

On the Horizon, a section that appears at the end of some island chapters, includes resorts that have opened in the last year or are due to open soon and hold the promise of being among the best.

Certainly, some testing was influenced by my personal likes and dislikes. When I go to the Caribbean I want to know I'm in the Caribbean. I want to feast on its beauty as well as its bounty, to feel the balmy air and hear the sea. My ideal resort takes advantage of its location, lets the tradewinds cool the air and blow away the sand flies. Its rooms and restaurants are open to the sea, with breezy balconies and splendid views. Architecture to me is as important as ambience—the two work together to make a place special. Good architectural design fits its environment and helps to create the ambience. I also care a great deal about the Caribbean's heritage—natural, historic, cultural—and have more to say about this later in the Green Leaf Awards section.

I like places that make me feel good as soon as my taxi pulls up to the front door. I like places that look as though they are expecting you, from an alert doorman to a friendly check-in desk to a bellhop who tells me everything I need to know about my room and points out the features of the hotel that I am likely to need soon after my arrival. I appreciate one who takes the time to find the luggage rack and place my suitcase on it, who checks the ice bucket or water in the fridge to insure I can have a cool drink of water after my long trip.

Little things mean a lot: good reading lights, firm mattresses, efficient bathrooms with a place for toiletries; fresh flowers; lit footpaths or flashlights to light the way. I like omnipresent but unobtrusive managers and I want to shake hands with the person minding the store.

Although I let my experience guide me, I sought the opinions and advice of many others—travel agents and other writers who specialize in the Caribbean, hoteliers with long Caribbean experience, friends who live in the Caribbean part or all of the year, and most important, dozens of vacationers I met along the way. They gave me their overall impressions and were particularly helpful in highlighting the features that had made their visit to a particular resort memorable. But in the end the choices are mine. So, too, are the comments and criticism.

The Goal

My principal objective in the resort profiles was to define a resort's personality and stress the elements that make it different and distinctive from other resorts to enable readers to identify with those best suited for them. But defining a resort's personality is not an exact science. Sometimes it is the history of the structure that helped to shape the resort's character, sometimes the owner and/or manager whose imprint is indelible, sometimes the setting, the staff, the ambience, or a specific feature—or all of the above.

In the beginning, I thought finding 100 different ways to describe 100 different resorts would be the hardest part about writing this book. I found, instead, that the resorts have such distinctive personalities, the descriptions almost wrote themselves. In a way, the ease of writing about them further confirmed my choices.

Small Versus Large

Those who know the Caribbean well will not be surprised to learn that out of the total 100 resorts in this book, more than half have fewer than fifty rooms and forty-one have fewer than thirty rooms. Less than a third are large resorts with 100 or more rooms. This was not a deliberate decision. In fact, I had not even analyzed the numbers until after I had written all the entries.

There's no mystery about the results. Big resorts are better known because they have the muscle to market and promote themselves, but small ones of under fifty rooms are more typical of the Caribbean and are its strength, providing a more authentic Caribbean experience.

Small hotels have a personality—that's what makes them worthy of attention—while large ones tend to be homogenized. Let me quickly add, however, that the large resorts included here run counter to the norm; they, too, have strong character.

The size of a hotel makes a difference in the type of Caribbean holiday you have. Large hotels have a greater array of activities and facilities, a busier atmosphere, and more round-the-clock staff and services than a small hotel, where the atmosphere is usually quiet and very relaxed.

At the smallest ones you get more personal care and attention from the manager, who is often the owner, and from the staff who will call you by name and learn your preferences from the first day of your visit. Usually you feel as though you are a guest in a friend's home or at a weekend house party. The service may not be as polished as at large resorts, but it is warm and genuine.

Commitment

The Caribbean is full of wonderful stories about people with a dream. Owning a small hotel in the Caribbean is a popular fantasy that's right up there with buying a boat and sailing around the world. So irrepressible is the idea that many, many people have done it and continue to do it. Most give up after a few years when they learn how difficult it is to run a really good hotel in the Caribbean. The innkeepers in this book are people who made it; invariably, they reflect the high degree of personal commitment it takes to succeed.

Amenities

Many small hotels, including some of the most expensive, do not have air-conditioning, television, or phones in the rooms. Not having a phone is a blessing to some people, an inconvenience to others. The Calabash in Grenada has the ideal solution: All guestrooms have telephones—along with a printed note that says, "the phone will be removed if you find it a nuisance."

As for air-conditioning, you may be surprised (I was amazed) to discover how many resorts do not have air-conditioning—and don't need it. Ceiling fans and natural breezes do a better job. Generally, the absence of air-conditioning in a good hotel says the structure was built architecturally sensitive to its setting.

In the past, Caribbean hoteliers believed they could not attract guests, particularly Americans, if they did not have air-conditioning. But during the oil crises of the 1970s, when skyrocketing fuel bills almost put them out of business, many returned to Mother Nature out of necessity. The response from guests was so positive, more and more have followed suit. Architects with Caribbean experience have long abandoned the concrete square block hotels in favor of styles that suit the natural environment, stressing open-air dining, louvered windows and doors, shaded terraces, and tile and terra cotta floors. What a joy!

Paradise Isn't Perfect

Even the best resorts aren't perfect. Where I feel it's warranted, I point out weaknesses. And, you may notice, I save my toughest judgment for the posh corners of paradise where prices unhappily have risen to heights as heavenly as the pleasures. To me, expensive resorts have a greater responsibility to deliver what they promise than those that keep rates low and don't try to be fancy. Higher rates, however, are usually justified as the degree of luxury increases, since almost everything is imported and catering to Americans—a demanding lot—is costly. Nonetheless, people who seek luxury still want their money's worth.

Maintenance in the tropics, government taxes, and service charges also drive up costs. High labor costs and restrictive policies—often more politically than economically motivated since hotels are usually the island's largest employers—are contributing factors, too. Which brings us to the matter of service.

Service

The Caribbean offers service at a stroll. Swift, at-the-snap-of-a-finger, professional service is unusual. If that's your yardstick for judging service, you will be disappointed even in the best of the best places. If you require this kind of service to be happy, the Caribbean is the wrong place for you.

Caring, cheerful, and thoughtful service by a friendly staff, not speed or polish, are the ingredients on which to make a judgment here. Turn off your motor, leave your watch at home, relax. This is not a cop-out or apology for service in the Caribbean. Rather, it is said to help readers enjoy their holiday by knowing the parameters with which Caribbean resorts operate.

Careers in service industries are only now getting the respect they deserve from people who, having only recently passed from colonialism to independence, equated such work with servitude. Fortunately, this attitude is fading as islanders have come to recognize their need for tourism and local ownership in hotels has broadened. Professionalism, too, is increasing as training and opportunities grow, and the hospitality profession, as it matures, offers meaningful advancement to young people.

Cuisine

The time has come for travelers and travel writers to stop saying "you can't get a good meal in the Caribbean." It simply isn't true. I've enjoyed wonderful meals from the Bahamas to Trinidad. It may be difficult, but not impossible; too many restaurants and hotels have demonstrated otherwise.

Instead, it's time to hold hotels to higher standards. In judging a resort, I gave cuisine a great deal of attention. Some places have brought a new dimension to the quality and creativity of their cuisine not associated with the Caribbean in the past. Many have young imaginative chefs who are turning out great dishes.

Trouble in Paradise

Idyllic places today must be more than pretty to get our attention and gain our loyalty. They must be reasonably efficient, if not always convenient, and secure. Trouble in paradise is troubling whenever it rears its ugly head, but with the exception of a few islands—ironically those that have the most tourists—crime is less of a problem at hotels in the Caribbean than in any major city in the United States.

We who live by security systems and double bolted doors have forgotten what it's like not to worry about security. But imagine! There are still Caribbean islands where people don't lock their doors. And there are still resorts where you are not given a room key because they don't have them—they don't need them. When I visit some of my favorite places where there are no locks on the doors, I find it unsettling at first, until I realize I can shed those city fears. The freedom is exhilarating.

Crawling Critters

Welcome to the tropics. If this is your first visit, we have some explaining to do. If you have been to Florida or the Mississippi Delta, you already know about bugs and other creatures that thrive in warm humid climates. Ninety-nine percent are harmless. They may not be cheering to see, but they won't hurt you. "I saw a roach two inches long," I've heard visitors new to the tropics say. And I reply, "Yes, I see them often."

It's true, even in the best Caribbean resorts. Recently, at one of the very best, most expensive resorts in this book, I opened a drawer, and there it was—a huge waterbug flat on its back, dead.

You'll also see geckos or chameleons and, after the first shock, you'll get to liking them, like pets. They are wonderfully interesting to watch; some have great color, too.

At certain times of the year, mosquitos can be fierce, particularly after a rain. I know; they love me. I never go anywhere without insect repellent. Most good hotels provide a can of repellent in their guest rooms and will

Round Hill Hotel and Villas, Montego Bay, Jamaica

usually have a can on hand at the bar. People with allergies may have a problem using repellents and should consult their doctors. Needless to say, in air-conditioned places you are less likely to be bothered. It's the best reason I know for air-conditioning.

How the Book Is Organized

The 100 Best Resorts of the Caribbean covers forty separate islands in twenty-five island groups arranged alphabetically by island and within its group. For example, under the U.S. Virgin Islands, you will find St. Croix, St. John, St. Thomas, in that order. Each island or island group starts with a profile intended as no more than a quick introduction. We have made the assumption that readers have been to the Caribbean or have other guidebooks by me or other writers with the nitty-gritty details for planning a vacation.

At the end of each entry, you will find an information block providing standard information on the resort that is not included in the text, such as where to make reservations or how much local tax or service charges are levied. Other information, such as room amenities like television and air-conditioning or sports facilities such as tennis and water sports, are also listed for quick reference. If, however, a resort is known for a particular sport like golf or diving, more information on its special features is provided in the text.

Seasons and Symbols

There is absolutely *no* uniformity in designating the beginning and ending of high season and low season in the Caribbean. The dates differ from island to island, hotel to hotel. Unless specified to the contrary, the definitions throughout this book are those used generally in the region: High season is the winter months from mid-December to mid-April; low season comprises the balance of the year when hotel rates are reduced by 30 percent or more. More and more, resorts are adding a third one, known as the shoulder season (mid-April to late May and/or September–October) when rates are also reduced substantially.

Rates peak during holiday periods, particularly during Christmas and New Year's and in February, when most resorts require a week or longer stay. When your priority is a winter vacation, paradise can be pricey, but you can often save a bundle by shifting slightly from March to mid-April or by going in November instead of December. And do not overlook packages. Even the fanciest resorts have them, particularly in the shoulder and low seasons. They usually represent meaningful savings and have additional bonus features.

Rates found at the end of each resort indicate the resort's price range rather than the the rates for each different type of accommodation. All rates are subject to change, and if the past is prologue, they *will* change. Consult the resort's U.S. representative provided at the end of each resort or a travel agent who can get the most current information.

The symbols used are as follows:

EP (European Plan): Room only, no meals
CB (Continental Breakfast): Room with continental breakfast
FAB (Full American Breakfast): Room with full American breakfast
MAP (Modified American Plan): Room with breakfast and dinner
AP (American Plan): Room with three meals daily
FAP (Full American Plan): Room with three meals; full American breakfast daily
AI (All inclusive): The rate includes accommodations, all meals, on-premises sports and entertainment, drinks, tax, and service. Readers should know that many resorts call themselves all-inclusive or say they have all-inclusive packages when in fact they do not. The hotel's brochure spells out what is and is not included. It is important to *read the fine print.*

Facilities

Almost any of the resorts in this book can arrange those sports not available at their property and island tours or boat trips to nearby islands. Most have tennis and beachside sports, but it is important in comparing prices to factor in these additional costs when the use of facilities is not included in room rates.

Dress Code
Specific guidelines are given under each resort, as the code does vary, but generally throughout the Caribbean, dress during the day and evening is casual and informal. This, however, does not mean sloppy, tacky, or tasteless. West Indians are often quite offended by the way some tourists dress. Hotel owners are also. They ask that beachwear be kept for the beach. Many resorts require a jacket for dinner in the winter season, but only a very few still require ties for men. Some of the smallest, least pretentious hotels have the strictest dress codes for evening.

Children
More and more couples are vacationing with their children. Most Caribbean resorts welcome children, but a few do not or they limit the age or the time period. The policy is provided for every resort in this book. Those that welcome families often have special rates for children; some have special meals and supervised activities. All that take children can arrange babysitters, although some resorts request that you notify them in advance.

Meetings
Almost all resorts now take meetings, but some small ones are likely to take them only at certain times of the year. Alternatively, you can book the entire hotel—not a bad idea for small groups.

Star Gazing
Since I have already selected 100 resorts out of the 1,500 hotels in the Caribbean, you may wonder why I added stars. I'm wondering, too, since it will probably cause me nothing but grief, from readers who will tell me I overrated this or that resort, from hoteliers who will think I've underrated them. I agonized over each one, but I don't claim that I always got it right.

The distinctions are as follows:

◙◙◙◙◙	A league of their own. They stand out not only as the best on their island, but they stand up to each other as well.
◙◙◙◙	Close to the top but not quite in a league all their own
◙◙◙	All-around good but not quite in the top league
◙◙	All-around good but on a modest scale
◙	Small, very modest

N/S/T: A few resorts were not given stars because they are (N) too new to be judged, (S) too specialized to be classified in the usual manner, or (T) in transition under new owners or management.

Green Leaf Awards

Protecting the environment is not a fad but a concern that we must have day in and day out. In no place in the world is this more essential than the Caribbean, where the natural environment is its number one asset and protecting it must be its number one priority. The need is as great, if not greater, for the people who live there as for visitors. Without it, they have nothing.

More and more, people are becoming aware of their role as travelers, and many (myself included) want to support those who demonstrate an environmental awareness and are making an effort to protect this heritage through their daily actions.

In researching this book, I created an environment profile that I asked every resort to complete; their participation was entirely voluntary. To my knowledge it is the first time a guidebook has made such an attempt in any part of the world. My purpose was not to serve as critic, since there are, as yet, no internationally recognized standards by which to judge and I do not consider myself an expert, only a concerned citizen. Rather, I wanted to survey this group in particular to learn if the 100 that are the best at operating their resorts treat their environment with the care they give their guests and to award "green leaves" to those who demonstrate an ongoing concern through their conservation policies and practices.

I was surprised and pleased by the results. Out of the 100 resorts, 75 responded. Environmental awareness and conservation among these hotels is at a much higher level than I had realized. This being the first time anyone has made such a selection, I limited the Green Leaf Award to twenty resorts. I would be pleased to send a copy of the questionnaire to readers who request it and would welcome their suggestions for future editions.

Author's Postscript

I want to assure readers that there was no charge for a hotel to be in this guide—a practice not uncommon for books of this kind, particularly in Europe. Nor did I incur any obligation *whatsoever* in the course of researching the resorts and making my selections.

The choices are entirely my own. I sought opinions often and listened to advice. I tried to cast myself into the mold of the people for whom a resort was designed. But in the end, the process was subjective. I don't claim to be all-knowing, nor do I expect everyone to agree with all my selections. However, I can say without hesitation, there is no entry in this book that I wouldn't be happy to return to many times. Indeed, I believe that sentiment is the most valuable criterion a writer can use.

About the Author

Kay Showker is a veteran writer, photographer, and lecturer on travel. Her assignments have taken her to more than one hundred countries in the Caribbean and around the world. She is the author of *Caribbean Ports of Call, A Guide for Today's Cruise Passengers* (Globe Pequot, 1990); *Eastern Caribbean Ports of Call* (Globe Pequot, 1991), which was a finalist in the Benjamin Franklin Awards for 1992; *The Outdoor Traveler's Guide to the Caribbean* (Stewart, Tabori & Chang, 1990) which won first runner-up as travel guidebook of the year in the Lowell Thomas Travel Journalism Awards; and two Fodor guides—*Egypt 1993* and *Jordan and the Holy Land*. She also writes regularly for *Travel and Leisure, Caribbean Travel and Life, Cruise Views,* and other publications. She served as senior editor of *Travel Weekly,* the industry's major trade publication, with which she was associated for eleven years.

A native of Kingsport, Tennessee, Ms. Showker received a Master's degree in international affairs from the School of Advanced International Studies of Johns Hopkins University in Washington, D.C. She was the 1989 recipient of the Marcia Vickery Wallace Award, given annually by the Caribbean Tourism Organization and the Government of Jamaica to the leading travel journalist on the Caribbean, and the 1990 Travel Writer of the Year award of the Bahamas Hotel Association. She was the first recipient of the Caribbean Tourism Association Award for excellence in journalism and has served as a consultant to government and private organizations on travel and tourism.

Anguilla

Cap Juluca

Sea, sand, and serenity—these are the assets of this tranquil hideaway in the northeastern corner of the Caribbean. Anguilla (pronounced Ann-GWEE-la), 5 miles north of St. Martin, is a dry, low-lying coral island with only 35 inches of rainfall per year.

What Anguilla lacks in mountains and tropical foliage it makes up for in powdery white beaches, which you can have almost to yourself, and fantastically clear aqua and cobalt blue waters that have attracted yachtsmen for decades and fishermen for centuries. More recently the spectacular waters have been luring snorkelers and scuba divers to the large reefs that lie off Anguilla's coast.

Yet, until it burst on the scene in the 1980s with some super-deluxe resorts, Anguilla was the best-kept secret in the Caribbean. Since then trendsetters have been flocking to this little-known spot to learn what all the fuss is about. A beachcomber's island at heart, Anguilla even now is so laid-back that you might need to practice doing nothing to enjoy its tranquillity. The island has no golf courses, casinos, or shopping arcades, and all but a few small cruise ships pass it by. If you want a change of pace, though, Anguilla is only a twenty-minute ferry ride from the casinos and duty-free shopping of St. Maarten.

Traditionally among the region's most skilled boatmen and fishermen, the Anguillans supply the markets and restaurants of St. Martin with much of their fish. You can watch the fishing boats come in at Island Harbor on the east end. They also make boats, including an unusual racing vessel that gets tested during Anguilla's annual Race Week in August. Sleek yachts and humble fishing boats are available to take you to nearby atolls for a picnic and a day of snorkeling.

For a destination whose total number of guest rooms is less than that of a midsize hotel, Anguilla has a surprising range of accommodations, from guesthouses to posh hotels.

Information

Anguilla Tourist Information and Reservations Office, c/o Medhurst and Associates, 271 Main Street, Northport, NY 11768; (800) 553-4939, (516) 261-1234.

Cap Juluca (T)

Casablanca by the sugary shores of the Caribbean . . . I must be dreaming, you will say to yourself. But this Arabian Nights fantasy is no mirage, although there is enough deep sand around it to make you think you got lost in the Sahara.

Splashed across the glossy pages of every fashionable magazine from New York to New Caledonia, Cap Juluca has gotten so much attention since it opened in 1988, that if I had not included it here, many readers would think I didn't know what I was talking about.

Let's start with the good news. Cap Juluca could win any contest for being the most beautiful resort in the Caribbean, if not the world. It is sensual, romantic, glamorous. It also has the potential for being the best, but it has not yet reached that potential.

Situated on Anguilla's leeward shores on 179 acres at Maunday's Bay, with St. Martin in the distance, Cap Juluca is a villa resort stretching for a mile along the curve of a magnificent beach. The posh resort comprises super-deluxe villas in Moorish style, complete with arches, domes, turrets, and keyhole doorways, in a fairyland of colors in which the blue skies, azure sea, magenta bougainvillea, and green gardens seem all the more intense against the snow-white villas. Cap Juluca is fittingly named for the Arawak god of the rainbow.

Guest rooms, in two-story "hotel" villas and pool villas with up to five bedrooms, provide a bewildering variety: from a bedroom with kitchenette and bath with shower only to a large villa with a private pool. Bedrooms and suites are rented separately, as in a hotel, and the pool and sundeck are shared. Or take an entire villa, and you can have a pool to yourself.

The sumptuous interiors vary, but they all have Italian tile floors and louvered doors of Brazilian walnut. Generally, those east of the pool have built-in banquettes of white masonry with colorful cushions and pillows that give the interior a clean sophisticated look. Moroccan artifacts and design elements inspired by colorful Moorish motifs are set against pure white walls, conveying the impression of a palace in Morocco. The newer villas are furnished in rather grand fashion in European colonial style, which seems to this writer's eye a bit heavy and pretentious for the airy, dreamy ambience that Cap Juluca is meant to convey.

The huge, luxurious bathrooms found in some suites are second to none. They are fabulous if not downright decadent. They have a king's ransom of Italian marble and mirrors, oversize bathtub, double sinks, separate shower, and bidet. Some even have a double bathtub with leather headrests and a private solarium.

You can sink into the mile of soft, deep white sand at your doorstep, or loll about the large freshwater pool of the Azzamour complex, added in 1991. The space along each side of the pool is separated by hedges for private tanning and relaxing. Each enclosure has a bell with which to summon an attendant.

A continental breakfast served in your room is part of the luxury at Cap Juluca. But if your room does not have a terrace from which to enjoy an early morning sea view, you can have breakfast and lunch at the pool terrace and refreshments at the Beach Pavilion under its onion-shaped dome. A beverage buggy patrols the beach; you signal it by planting a red flag in the sand.

The eastern end of the beach is anchored by Pimm's, the main restaurant. Named after a refreshing drink popular with the British in the days of the raj, Pimm's has an enchanting setting directly by the sea looking across the sweep of Cap Juluca by the bay. In the evening the candlelit tables and the sound of the water lapping at the rocks make it even more romantic.

Pimm's lunch and dinner menus offer light, refined fare created by French chefs and often based on the island's supply of fresh fish. Another restaurant, Chatterton's, has a more eclectic menu with Cajun, West Indian, and pasta selections.

Should you care to leave your villa or hideaway by the pool, Cap Juluca has three Omni-turf tennis courts (two lit) and a pro shop. The use of Sunfish, snorkel gear, windsurfers, and Hobiecats is included in the rate.

Entertainment at Cap Juluca is light. A manager's cocktail party is held on Monday evenings and there is dancing at Chatterton's nightly. Cable television is available in the Beach Pavilion, as are VCRs and cassettes on request. The main building near the entrance has a library and boutique. Cap Juluca has no "front" desk or reception room; check-in is done in guest rooms.

Cap Juluca has been designed as a secluded, stylish retreat for sophisticated travelers and is meant to have a mystique and air of illusion and exotic, erotic luxury about it. But when you must drive through sand as deep as the Saudi desert to get to your room, or wait in the hot sun for a shuttle that never comes, or walk a mile to get to dinner, the fantasy disappears faster than the genie in Aladdin's lamp.

Perhaps because the resort has not lived up to the goals it set for itself and the expectations raised by all the publicity—not to mention its prices— I am inclined to judge it more critically than other resorts with less promise or pretension.

So—go if you can lower your expectations. If you prefer to see the genie, wait until Cap Juluca has its act together.

Address/Phone: P.O. Box 240, Maunday's Bay, Anguilla, B.W.I.; (809) 497–6666; Fax: (809) 497–6617

Owner: Cap Juluca Partners

General Manager: Charles F. Ingalsbee

Open: Year-round

Credit Cards: American Express

U.S. Reservations: Cap Juluca/New York, (212) 425–4684; (800) 323–0139

Deposit: 3 nights; 21-day cancellation

Minimum Stay: 7 nights during Christmas/New Year's

Arrival/Departure: Guests met at airport by hotel representative. Complimentary transfer service in packages.

Distance from Airport: (Wallblake Airport) 5 miles; taxi one-way US $18, via ferry from Marigot, St. Martin (15 minutes): 4 miles, $15.

Distance from The Valley: 5 miles; taxi one-way, $18

Accommodations: 85 rooms, 13 suites in 12 hotel villas and 6 pool villas; most with terraces or interior patios, all have king-size beds; some suites with extra queen-size daybed

Amenities: Air-conditioning, ceiling fans, refrigerator/ice maker, and stocked mini-bar, telephone; some baths with tub, some with solarium and double tub, and some with shower only; hairdryer, deluxe toiletries, bathrobe; nightly turndown service; room service as requested; bottle of rum and fruit in room; kitchen in villas.

Electricity: 110/220 volts

Sports: Freshwater swimming pool, 6 villa pools, tennis, Sunfish, Hobiecats, snorkel gear, waterskiing free. Scuba, fishing, golf in St.
Maarten arranged for charge.

Dress Code: Casual by day; casually elegant in the evening; no jackets or
tie required

Children: All ages, but for those under 3, advance inquiry requested; cribs,
baby-sitters

Meetings: Up to 40 persons

Day Visitors: None

Handicapped: No facilities

Packages: Honeymoon, Romantic Retreat, weddings

Rates: Per person, daily, CP. *High Season* (mid-December–mid-April):
$195–$750. *Shoulder Season* (mid-April–May 31 and November 1–mid-
December): $147.50–$500. *Low Season:* $127.50–$440.

Service Charge: 10 percent

Government Tax: 8 percent

Coccoloba ▣▣▣

Perched on a small promontory between Barnes and Meads bays—two
coves with gorgeous beaches on Anguilla's northwest coast—Coccoloba
Plantation has had almost as many lives as a cat. The most dramatic
changes happened in 1987 following a multimillion-dollar transformation of
an earlier hotel. The latest came at the end of 1991 with new British owners
and managers who have left well enough alone—just made it better.

The canopied entrance to Coccoloba (the Latin word for seagrape)
leads into the lobby of the central building, which has a high pointed roof
that reminds me of a chalet in the Swiss Alps. But the high ceilings do create a pleasant breezeway into the huge Main Pavilion, all freshly painted
and refurbished by the new owners.

The vast space, decorated in bright yellow and white with green accents and cheerful chintzes, is broken up by white louvered shutters into
interconnecting lounges, a boutique, an exercise room and sauna, library
with VCR and videos, and a dining room with a fabulous 200-degree
panoramic view. To one side is a large swimming pool with a swim-up bar,
surrounded by several gazebos that seem to float on the water. The hotel
calls them "tea houses," and indeed they are delightful spots to enjoy tea or
a sundowner.

Most of the guest rooms are located in seafront white-stucco cottages
with patios shaded by trellises of West Indian gingerbread trim laden with

bougainvillea. The cottages are staggered in zigzag fashion along a walkway edging a bluff that overlooks a mile-long crest of sand that sweeps west from the central pavilion.

The guest rooms are big, split-level junior suites, which seem all the larger and airier for their cathedral ceilings, huge bath and dressing rooms, sitting rooms, and patios. They are fitted with two *double* beds on an upper level behind a waist-high bookshelf (filled with books) that serves as a room divider. It provides privacy from passersby, yet is low enough for you to have an unobstructed view, sitting up in bed, of the seascape or a dramatic Anguillan sunset.

At the far end of the beach, Coccoloba Residence is a secluded two-story villa, ideal for a wedding party or small group. Built as a private home, it has four bedrooms on the ground floor and three suites upstairs with a private pool and patio and dining area overlooking the gardens and sea.

Steps in front of the cottages lead down to Coccoloba's biggest attraction, the beach. It's so long that it is never crowded, even when the hotel is full. Thatched umbrellas are placed along the sand; the staff manning the Beach Hut sets up chairs and provides snorkel gear, Sunfish, and windsurfers, as well as instruction in their use. Every fifteen minutes or so, an attendant strolls along the beach delivering sodas, ice water, and tea. If you want something stronger, they'll bring that, too.

You set your own pace here. Breakfast, a full American feast, is served in the open-air dining room. You can read or laze away the morning on a float board until lunchtime, when a waiter will bring a picnic-basket lunch to your chaise under your umbrella, or you can take lunch in one of the tea houses by the pool.

At sunset enjoy a drink on your patio, or wander up to the Main Pavilion, where complimentary predinner drinks are available at the poolside bar nightly under the stars while soft calypso music plays in the background. The manager's cocktail party is held here on Mondays.

Candlelight and the gentle sea breezes give the dining room an intimate, romantic ambience for dinner. The new chef, Paul Hackett, an alumnus of *Le Gavroche*—Michel Roux's famous three-star London restaurant—has designed new menus featuring sophisticated continental cuisine with a light touch and an emphasis on fresh ingredients. A new seaside terrace grill and fish restaurant is to be added.

Coccoloba's setting on twenty-eight acres draws an average of two weddings a week, and honeymooners love it. At the same time it is well suited for families with children, because the cottages are large and spaced sufficiently apart to be very private, and the beach is long, with lots for kids to do.

Coccoloba strikes a balance between the elegance that fits its accommodations, amenities, and price level and an informality that most people on a beach vacation prefer. The genteel and friendly staff is no small factor in creating the warm atmosphere that makes this small resort so appealing.

Address/Phone: P.O. Box 332, Barnes Bay, Anguilla, B.V.I.; (809) 497–6871; Fax: (809) 497–6332

Owner: Coccoloba Caribbean, Ltd.; Management, Delta Hotel Management, Ltd.

General Manager: Michael Longshaw

Open: Year-round

Credit Cards: All major

U.S. Reservations: Coccoloba Reservations, (800) 833–3559

Deposit: 3 nights; 30 days cancellation in winter; 14 days for balance of year

Minimum Stay: 10 days at Christmas

Arrival/Departure: Hotels not allowed by local taxi association to provide transfer.

Distance from Airport: (Blowing Point ferry dock) 8 miles; one-way taxi, US $16

Distance from The Valley: 9 miles; taxi one-way, $17

Accommodations: 51 seaside units with patios (40 junior suites in private cottages, 4 in 2 connecting cottages, 7 in two-story residence), most with 2 double beds, 6 with kings, 1 queen

Amenities: Air-conditioning, ceiling fans, telephone, mini-bar, safe, hairdryers, bathrobes, Neutrogena toiletries, dressing area with vanity; nightly turndown service, bath with tub and shower in 6 rooms, others with showers only; room service for continental breakfast, no television, radios, or keys.

Electricity: 110 volts

Sports: 2 freshwater swimming pools; 2 lighted Omni tennis courts and Peter Burwash pro; water sports with instruction included in price; sauna and massage rooms; gym with Universal equipment. Deep-sea fishing, scuba, golf in nearby St. Maarten arranged for fee. Putting green being added.

Dress Code: Casual by day; casually elegant in the evening; no jackets or ties required

Children: All ages, cribs, high chairs, baby-sitters

Meetings: Up to 25 people

Day visitors: Welcome on individual basis or small group

Handicapped: No facilities

Packages: Honeymoon, weddings, 4 and 7 nights

Rates: Per person, daily, FAB. *High Season* (December 19–May 31):

$180–$280. *Shoulder Season* (April 1–May 31): $142.50–$225. *Low Season* (June 1–October 31): $97.50–$197.50.
Service Charge: 10 percent
Government Tax: 8 percent

La Sirena ▣▣ ✿

Soothing to your mind, gentle on your pocketbook, this small, ridge-top resort refutes the ill-founded image that Anguilla is a hideaway only for the filthy rich.

Only a short slope—200 yards, maybe—from powdery sands, La Sirena gives you fabulous Mead's Bay Beach but at a third of the cost of Malliouhana, the pricey preserve of celebrities and moguls that anchors the beach's eastern end.

To be absolutely accurate and not to mislead, La Sirena has accommodations of two types in two locations. There are three villas near the shore; the walk to the beach for guests here takes about one minute. At the top of the rise is the main hotel, an attractive complex of two- and three-story buildings housing the restaurants, bar, lounge, and most accommodations.

Guests here take a three-minute walk along a landscaped path to the same fine beach—hardly an inconvenience. What's more, some rooms at Malliouhana are even farther away from the beach. Then, too, all the rooms at La Sirena have private patios or terraces facing the sea. But again, to be accurate, only those on the second and third floor get that dramatic view of the sea.

Designed by a Swiss architect, La Sirena combines Mediterranean tradition with Caribbean touches: white-stucco walls and arches, peaked ceilings, weathered red-tiled roofs, and balconies trimmed with latticework painted white and trimmed in the turquoise color of the sea around Anguilla.

The main building has guest rooms on three floors, each with a balcony overlooking the gardens and the large swimming pool. Rooms are modest and uncluttered. They have terra-cotta tile floors, tiled bathrooms, and are furnished with wicker, green plants, and fresh flowers. A wicker chest conceals a stocked mini-bar.

I would have been happy had the rooms been just a wee bit larger with a teeny bit more closet space (pack lightly). But I'll not be as unkind as one writer who called them "motel-style," for in fact, they do have style. Not much style, but some.

At any rate, they are functional and immaculate and even include single rooms—an almost unheard-of commodity in Caribbean resorts. The singles are small with a queen-size bed and a tiny terrace. The most desirable double rooms are the top-floor ones, which have high ceilings and the best views. Rooms 301 and 302 have access to a roof terrace and wraparound views.

The hotel lobby greets you with a cool, breezy lounge under graceful white arches and flows informally into the bar and open-air restaurant overlooking the swimming pool and gardens.

Recently, the hotel's two restaurants were redecorated and are now under the new management team of Peter and Frida Holleran, former restaurateurs from Dallas, Texas.

Top of the Palms, the more formal of the two restaurants, has a menu of New American cuisine to go with its new contemporary decor. Coconuts, the informal poolside restaurant, offers a light menu. A Sunday brunch, something of a tradition, is served here, and Thursday nights feature performances by the Mayoumba Folkloric Theater, a local dance group.

Stone pathways through the gardens lead to the three comfortable, but rather modest, villas and the mile-long beach. Two villas have two bedrooms with two baths, and one has three bedrooms, each with bath and separate entrances. The villas have lounges, fully equipped kitchens, private patio or rooftop sundeck, telephone, barbecue equipment, daily maid service, and their own freshwater pool and Jacuzzi. Dishwashing and cable television are available at extra charge. The villas are particularly well suited for families. La Sirena's owners have a small child of their own and welcome families with children.

Opened in 1989, La Sirena is owned and operated by a young, personable Swiss couple who have blended Swiss efficiency with a Caribbean ambience. They hold a manager's cocktail social on Tuesdays and usually join their guests for drinks or dinner in the evenings.

La Sirena may not have the panache of its ritzy neighbors, but many people would probably find its casual and comfortable digs far more suitable for a relaxed beachside vacation. The price of a villa equals a room in a pricey resort—and then some. You could use the money you might spend on an expensive room to splurge on dinner at Malliouhana or Hiberia, my favorite restaurant at the eastern end of the island.

Generally, La Sirena receives more Europeans, particularly Swiss, than Americans. Its low-key, friendly atmosphere is well suited to singles who want a quiet vacation, young couples, and families with children who are happy building sand castles on the beach and can go without a daily fix of television or Nintendo.

Address/Phone: P.O. Box 200, Mead's Bay, Anguilla, B.W.I.; (809) 497–6827; Fax: (809) 497–6829

Owner/General Manager: Rolf Masshardt
Open: Year-round
Credit Cards: All Major
U.S. Reservations: International Travel and Resorts (ITR), (800) 223–9815, (212) 251–1800; Fax: (212) 545–8467
Deposit: 3 nights; 10 days confirmation; 30-day cancellations
Minimum Stay: 10 days during Christmas/New Year's
Arrival/Departure: Transfer arranged upon request for fee
Distance from Airport: 9 miles; taxi one-way, US $14
Distance from Main Town: 9 miles; taxi one-way, US $14
Accommodations: 28 units with balcony or patio in three-story main building (16 doubles with queen, king, or twins; 4 singles with queen) and villas (9 with 2 queens)
Amenities: Ceiling fans, telephone, clock/radio, bath with shower only, hairdryer, basket of toiletries, mini-bar, no room service. Air conditioning and cable television in villas only.
Electricity: 110 volts
Sports: 2 freshwater swimming pools; free snorkel gear; windsurf equipment, bicycles for fee; tennis arranged.
Dress Code: Informal
Children: All ages, cribs; baby-sitters
Meetings: None
Day Visitors: Welcome
Handicapped: No facilities
Packages: Summer, pre-Christmas, winter
Rates: Per person, daily, EP. *High Season* (mid-December–mid-April): $95–$117.50. *Low Season*: $60–$75.
Service Charge: 10 percent
Government Tax: 8 percent

Malliouhana ◙◙◙◙◙

Located on the northwest coast, on a twenty-five-acre bluff overlooking two spectacular beaches, Malliouhana (the Arawak Indian name for Anguilla) is a sybaritic fantasy in Mediterranean design set in a garden of Eden.

Almost from the day it opened in 1983, the resort won rave reviews for its extraordinary interiors, style, refinement, gourmet cuisine, and attention to detail. It raised deluxe to a lofty new level that few can equal.

Before creating Malliouhana, British industrialist and well-traveled bon vivant Leon Roydon and his late wife, Lyane, had dreamed of building a Caribbean resort with the standards to which they were accustomed in Europe. Like most people, the Roydons fell in love with Anguilla when they visited it in 1980 for the first time.

There they met another English couple, Robin and Sue Ricketts, seasoned hoteliers who were already at work on their dream. It seemed a perfect marriage: experienced innkeepers with great flair and sophisticated builders with imagination, technical expertise, and deep pockets.

There are no signs pointing the way to Malliouhana. A driveway passes through landscaped gardens exploding with color and shaded by stately palms to a cluster of white-stucco buildings with arched galleries and red-tiled roofs that look more like palatial Mediterranean hilltop mansions than a hotel.

From the elegant lobby, you step through a series of tall, cool white arches that rise to cathedral ceilings of warm Brazilian walnut. They lead to terraced gardens and high-ceilinged, breeze-filled lounges with light terracotta–tile floors and upholstered rattan furniture.

Designer Larry Peabody sets off his stylish decor with brass sconces and hurricane lamps on heavy brass bases, lush foliage, and enormous panels of ethereal paintings by famous Haitian artist Jasmin Joseph. To one side a lounge/bar plucked from Andalusia overlooks three terraced swimming pools interconnected by waterfalls.

Malliouhana's accommodations all feature huge bedrooms with king-size beds; they are located in wings of the main building on the cliff and in villas with one- and two-bedroom suites directly on the beach. Junior suites have large bedrooms and dressing rooms; one-bedroom and two-bedroom suites have separate bedrooms, living/dining rooms, and covered patios. Guest rooms have marbled and mirrored bathrooms almost as large as the bedrooms and terraces overlooking Anguilla's peacock blue waters.

Exquisitely designed tropical furniture of the highest quality rush and bamboo, and rich Brazilian mahogany louvered doors and windows with solid-brass fittings contrast with the stark white bed covers, tiled floors, and walls adorned with subdued Asian prints and vibrant Haitian paintings.

The resort has a mile of powder-fine beach on one side and a small intimate cove, accessible only from the hotel (or by boat), on the other. There are four Laykold tennis courts (lighted) and Peter Burwash International pro; a water-sports center and fitness center. The hotel's launch is available for trips to nearby islets and reefs for snorkeling, picnics, and trips to St. Martin.

At cocktails guests enjoy light musical entertainment, but the evening's highlight is dining on haute cuisine in the casually elegant terrace restaurant overlooking the sea. Chef Alain Laurent has continued the tradition of his teacher, the late Jo Rostang of La Bonne Auberge—a two-star Michelin restaurant on the French Riveria—who developed Malliouhana's cuisine. In the winter season staff from La Bonne Auberge come to work with the Anguillian staff, some of whom have been given training in France. Malliouhana also has an outstanding wine cellar, stocked with thirty-five thousand bottles of fine wine selected and shipped by connoisseur Leon Roydon, mostly from France.

Roydon clearly understands the needs of his discerning guests. A staff-to-guest ratio of more than two-to-one and the high level of service by the resort's staff of two hundred Anguillians, more than half of whom have been with the resort since it opened, insure that those needs are met in a gracious atmosphere.

From the time it opened, Malliouhana has maintained the very high standards it set for itself and has attracted celebrities, film stars, and a loyal following of well-heeled, sophisticated travelers. Being splashed across the pages of every slick fashion and travel magazine in North America and Europe and featured on "Lifestyles of the Rich and Famous" hasn't hurt either.

Today Leon Roydon, his wife, Annette, and son Nigel manage the hotel with meticulous care. One of them is on hand to greet guests on arrival and to say farewell at the end of their stay. At other times, however, the managers keep their distance, believing that people come to Malliouhana for privacy. As a result, however, many people find Malliouhana cold.

Malliouhana's chic, sophisticated ambience is not for everyone, regardless of price. It might even seem pretentious if you prefer your beachside elegance to be barefoot.

Address: P.O. Box 173, Mead's Bay, Anguilla, B.V.I.; (800) 835–0796, (809) 497–6111; Fax: (809) 497–6011

Owner/General Manager: Leon Roydon

Open: Year-round except September and October

Credit Cards: None

U.S. Reservations: David B. Mitchell and Co., (800) 372–1323; (203) 655–4200; Fax: (203) 656–3475

Deposit: 3 nights; cancellation, 30 days

Minimum Stay: 7 days, December to March

Arrival/Departure: Transfers not available

Distance from Airport: 8 miles from airport and Blowing Point ferry terminal; cost of taxi one-way, $14

Distance from Main Town: 9 miles; cost of taxi one-way, $16

Accommodations: 54 rooms (34 double rooms, 8 junior suites, 8 one-bedroom and 2 two-bedroom suites), 20 in main building wings; others by the beach

Amenities: Air-conditioning, ceiling fans (also in bathrooms), telephone, stocked mini-bars, ample closet space, bathroom vanities with makeup lights; deep tub, shower stall, bidet, plush towels, bathrobes, and toiletries, television, VCR, and hairdryers on request, 24-hour room service, masseur, beauty salon, designer boutique, sundries shop

Electricity: 110 volts

Sports: Freshwater pool; tennis, snorkeling, fitness center with Universal equipment

Dress Code: Casual but chic sportswear by day; casually elegant in the evening

Children: All ages; baby-sitters available

Meetings: None

Day Visitors: No

Handicapped: No facilities

Packages: Honeymoon, June 1–August 31, 4 or more nights

Rates: Single or double, daily, EP. *High Season* (mid-December–March 31): $500. *Shoulder Season* (April 1–May 31; November 1–mid-December): $335. *Low Season* (June 1–August 31): $250.

Service Charge: 10 percent

Government Tax: 8 percent

Antigua and Barbuda

Curtain Bluff, Antigua

Shaped somewhat like a maple leaf, Antigua has protruding fingers that provide its coastline with sheltered bays, natural harbors, and extra miles of beautiful beaches—one for every day of the year, the Antiguans say—fringed by coral reefs. These assets have made Antigua one of the most popular beach and water-sports centers in the Caribbean. As a bonus, low humidity and year-round trade winds create the ideal climate for tennis, golf, horseback riding, and a variety of other sports and sight-seeing.

Antigua (pronounced Ann-TEE-ga) is the largest of the Leeward Islands. Barbuda, her sister island 32 miles to the north, is largely undeveloped. Located east of Puerto Rico between the U.S. Virgin Islands and the French and Dutch West Indies, Antigua is a transportation hub of the region and the home of LIAT (Leeward Islands Air Transport), the regional carrier of eleven Eastern Caribbean states.

After English settlers from St. Kitts established a colony near Old Town on the south coast in 1632, Antigua remained a British possession until 1981, when full independence was achieved. Today the island's British heritage and historic character are most evident at English Harbour, once the headquarters of the British Navy, where the buildings of the old wharf, now known as Nelson's Dockyard, have been restored to house shops, inns, restaurants, and museums.

This relaxed and quietly sophisticated island has been having a tourism boom that shows no signs of slowing. St. John's, the capital and once sleepy West Indian village, has become a popular tourist mecca with charming historic buildings of West Indian architecture housing attractive boutiques and restaurants.

Although there are a few large resorts and casinos, most of the island's hotels are small and operated by their owners—a feature that helps to give Antigua a less commercial atmosphere than some other Caribbean destinations.

Information

Antigua and Barbuda Department of Tourism, 610 Fifth Avenue, Suite 311, New York, NY 10020, (212) 541–4117.

Antigua

Blue Waters Beach Hotel ◙◙◙

The first time I visited Antigua in the early 1970s, I stayed at Blue Waters Beach. It was a small, cozy hotel on a quiet, secluded cove at Soldier Bay. It was owned and operated then by Desmond Kelsick, one of the true pioneers in Caribbean tourism. Over the years Kelsick developed the hotel, expanding as he could. The hotel got better and better and always seemed to feel right, like an old shoe.

In 1988 Kelsick sold the hotel to a group of British entrepreneurs who upgraded all the facilities and guest rooms and continued the expansion, perhaps sacrificing in the process some of the cozy quality of the past. Not to worry. Blue Waters' friendly, congenial atmosphere remains, and the setting gets prettier and more intoxicating with each passing year.

Tucked into a steep hill on fourteen acres of a cove trimmed with two white-sand beaches, Blue Waters is smothered in a jungle of brightly colored tropical flowers, fruit trees, and graceful palms. The hotel is approached by a steep circular, downhill driveway. From the lobby you step onto a tree-shaded terrace enveloped in lush gardens and overlooking the pool and beach. The central building is flanked by the two-story wings that house the guest rooms.

Next to the lobby is the Turtle Bar, as well as an air-conditioned lounge, library with television, video and game room, small gift shop, and two restaurants. The open-air Garden Terrace offers a casual setting for three meals and tea daily; a snack menu is available at other times. The stylish Cacubi Room, recently renovated and updated, is one of the island's leading restaurants for dinner. Both restaurants serve European cuisine and West Indian specialties.

The hotel hosts a barbecue on Tuesdays, preceded by the manager's poolside cocktail party; a West Indian buffet on Fridays; and the all-time favorite, curry brunch on Sunday. During the winter season, guests can enjoy live musical entertainment and dancing several evenings a week.

Guest rooms, all with terraces approached by sliding glass doors, are attractively furnished in wicker with soothing floral fabrics and rush throw rugs on cool tiled floors. There are roomy closets and tile bathrooms with separate tubs, shower stalls, and dressing areas.

To the north are the most deluxe rooms in eight two-story villas, which look out to the sea. Each villa has a living/dining room, fully equipped kitchen, and two or three bedrooms with baths. The master bedroom's bath has a Jacuzzi and a bidet.

Blue Waters offers tennis and water sports galore. The use of most equipment is included in the room rate. When the hotel's two small beaches get a bit crowded in high season, you can escape via a path over a knoll to a quiet secluded strand.

On the breakwater known as North Point, there's a tiny gazebo just for two. It's very romantic with the balmy Caribbean air, the waves lapping at the shore—you get the picture. Little wonder Blue Waters is a popular spot for weddings and honeymoons. But it's a delightful place, too, for anyone who simply wants to relax—in pretty, quiet surroundings.

I have heard Blue Waters described as a Caribbean country club with a lot of English accents—more now than ever. The British—Mick Jagger for one—are the majority and return regularly, followed by a loyal band of Canadians, Americans, and a sprinkling of other Europeans.

Address/Phone: P.O. Box 256, St. John's, Soldier's Bay, Antigua, W.I. (809) 462–0290; Fax: (809) 462–0293/0291

Owner: Carib Holdings Ltd.

Managing Director: Keith Woodhouse

Open: Year-round

Credit Cards: All major

U.S. Reservations: David B. Mitchell and Co. (800) 372–1323; Fax: (800) 446–1323

Deposit: 3 nights; 21 days cancellation

Minimum Stay: 10 days Christmas period; cancellation by November 1
Arrival/Departure: Transfer service arranged for a fee
Distance from Airport: 5 miles; taxi one-way, $10
Distance from St. John's: 4 miles; taxi one-way, $10; hotel runs daily morning shuttle to/from town for modest fee
Accommodations: 67 units (17 standard rooms; 29 deluxe rooms in two-story buildings, all with verandas; 21 deluxe rooms and suites in 8 two-story villas, some with kitchens)
Amenities: Air-conditioning, radio, telephone, safe, bath with tub and shower, hairdryer, basket of toiletries, stocked refrigerator; ice service daily; room service to 10:00 P.M.
Electricity: 220 volts; 110-volts outlets in room
Sports: Freshwater swimming pool; lighted Laykold tennis court; free use of windsurfers, Sunfish sailboats, pedaloes, kayaks, snorkeling gear, fishing rods. Charge for waterskiing. Scuba and fishing arranged.
Dress Code: Casual but chic; men asked to wear long trousers after 7 P.M.
Children: Accepted; early meals arranged; cribs, baby-sitters
Meetings: Up to 60 people
Day Visitors: Welcome with advance notice
Handicapped: Limited
Packages: Honeymoon, wedding
Rates: Per person, daily EP. *High Season* (mid-December–mid-April): $235–$285. *Low Season*: $140–$175.
Service Charge: 10 percent
Government Tax: 7 percent

Curtain Bluff ▣▣▣▣ ❧

Ideally located on a secluded promontory on Antigua's south coast, with Atlantic surf washing the beach on one side and the tranquil Caribbean lapping the shore on the other, Curtain Bluff is an exclusive enclave of tropical splendor spread across fifty beachfront acres against a backdrop of verdant hills.

The time-tested resort has been called Antigua's blue-chip address for conservative travelers by some and a tropical paradise with a country club ambience by others, but perhaps the best description was offered by a guest who said, "This is a place where you fall in love with your wife all over again."

Not a bad vote of confidence for a resort that set a new standard for the Caribbean when it was opened in 1961, watched a host of competitors blossom—and wither like dandelions—and is still going strong.

Whatever Curtain Bluff is, for sure it is a reflection of its creator, Howard Hulford, who is now chairman of the board. A legend in his own time, many have called him the "best hotelier in the Caribbean." Gruff, opinionated, love-me-if-you-dare Hulford is as famous for his silver handlebar mustache as he is for his manner.

He and his fine staff have made sure his standard of excellence has been maintained at Curtain Bluff for three decades. As a result the resort is usually booked a year in advance, primarily by repeat visitors: an affluent, well-traveled lot from Chicago, Boston, Washington, New York, and Europe—not an easy bunch to please.

Curtain Bluff operates as an all-inclusive resort. Included in the price are all meals and tea, cocktails and table wine, most sports, laundry, and even postage stamps. Room service is available for all meals and bar service is provided at no additional charge—an unusual amenity for an all-inclusive resort.

Accommodations include seafront double rooms with sitting areas as well as one- and two-bedroom suites in two-story, low-rise buildings, all with terraces and dreamy views. The tastefully appointed rooms have tile floors and wicker furniture dressed in pastels. The two-bedroom, two-level suites offer a breeze-cooled patio with a hammock just waiting to be used; the second bedroom can be rented as a single accommodation.

The newest accommodations are the most luxurious: deluxe suites perched in stair-step fashion near the top of the bluff. Each unit has a bedroom larger than most New York apartments, a spacious living room that opens directly onto a large terrace with spectacular views, five ceiling fans, and a well-equipped marbled bathroom. Rooms are furnished in wicker and rattan with cheerful fabrics that take their colors from the sea, sky, and flowers around you.

Your introduction to Curtain Bluff begins at the central building, approached by a circular drive and surrounded by a riot of flowers with a pretty white filigree gazebo in the gardens. Beyond the reception/concierge desk is a small patio shaded by a large tamarind tree and the dining terrace. To one side is a boutique and the Sugar Mill Bar, the gathering spot for predinner drinks and hors d'oeuvres.

Daytime activities are centered on the twin beaches. The calm, palm-fringed Caribbean strand is sporting a new Beach Club, where informal lunches are served; the Wednesday barbecue buffet is a beach party with steel band music. You'll find umbrellas, changing rooms, showers, and water-sports equipment.

Tennis is one of Curtain Bluff's main attractions for some of its most loyal fans. It has four all-weather championship courts (two lighted), practice court, viewing stands, resident pro, and pro shop. Courts and equipment are free; proper court attire is requested.

Meals are served in the main restaurant, tea in the Bar Terrace. The kitchen at Curtain Bluff, a member of Relais & Chateaux Hotels, has been under the eye of chef Reudi Portmann for almost three decades, garnering many kudos and culinary awards. Portmann, trained in the classic Swiss tradition, keeps his menus limited, changing them daily to maximize the use of fresh products. (Hulford has his own food import company to insure quality.) Visitors are welcome for lunch but not dinner.

Lunches are light, but dinners are the real treat with a choice of hot and cold soups, appetizers, salads, six different entrees, and too many yummy desserts each night. The wine cellar, with approximately twenty-five thousand bottles of the finest vintages, is Hulford's pride, second only to his fabulous gardens. You can take a guided tour of either.

Traditions abound at Curtain Bluff. Ten-year guests receive a silver tray; twenty-year ones, a gold tray. During the summer, when Curtain Bluff is closed, the resort undergoes a complete refurbishing and usually something new is added.

Hulford and his charming wife, Chelle, run the resort like a country club. They live in a lovely villa on the bluff, where they often entertain hotel guests.

Curtain Bluff is not for everyone, but it does not try to be. The ambience may seem a little staid, but it appeals to Curtain Bluff's loyal patrons who enjoy dressing for dinner and dancing under the stars to the sounds of the oldies, updated with a touch of reggae and calypso. If you like tradition, appreciate attention to detail, and are comfortable in a congenial, clubby ambience, you might easily become the newest member of Howard's fan club.

Address/Phone: P.O. Box 288, Old Road, Curtain Bluff Peninsula, St. John's, Antigua, W.I. (809) 462–8400/3; Fax: (809) 462–8409
Owner: Howard Hulford
General Manager: Calvert A. Roberts
Managing Director: Rob Sherman
Open: October 15–May 15
Credit Cards: American Express
U.S. Reservations: Curtain Bluff, (212) 289–8888
Deposit: 3 nights; 30 days cancellation except for December 16–January 1, which must be received before November 1
Minimum Stay: 2 weeks during Christmas period
Arrival/Departure: Hotel transfers not available due to local taxi regulations
Distance from Airport: 16 miles (45 minutes); taxi one-way, US $21
Distance from St. John's: 13 miles; taxi one-way, US $17

Accommodations: 61 double rooms and suites, all with terraces (21 double with double beds; 28 with king-size beds; 12 suites; 45 rooms have bath with tub and shower; 16 shower only)

Amenities: Ceiling fans, telephones (newest suites have them in bathroom), wall safes, bathrobes, fresh flowers daily; hairdryers available, full room service, suites have mini-bars; no television, radio, or airconditioning

Electricity: 110 volts

Sports: Excellent tennis facilities (see text); squash court, croquet court; putting green; Sunfish, snorkeling, waterskiing, and windsurfing. Scuba for certified divers only. 47-foot ketch for day sailing; another boat for deep-sea fishing. No swimming pool. Exercise room; aerobic classes. Hiking trips in the nearby hills available; the area offers some of the best birding locations in Antigua.

Dress Code: Casual by day; cover-up required in dining room. Dinner formal, with jacket and tie required for men after 7:00 P.M. in public areas 6 nights a week

Children: All ages, except from January 5–March 10, when only those 12 years and older are welcome; cribs, baby-sitters

Meetings: For up to 20 persons

Handicapped: Limited facilities

Day Visitors: No

Packages: Tennis Week, wedding

Rates: Two persons, daily, all inclusive. *High Season* (mid-December–mid-April): $525–$825. *Low Season*: $425–$725.

Service Charge: 10 percent

Government Tax: 7 percent

Galley Bay ◙◙

By the time you have made the long drive from the airport, through St. John's, and down the bumpy road to Galley Bay, you may be having second thoughts. But press on. It's worth it.

Galley Bay (not to be confused with Galleon Beach on the east side of Antigua) has one of the prettiest, away-from-it-all settings in the Caribbean. Tucked away on the west coast on forty tropical acres—some landscaped, some natural—the resort is bordered on one side by a half-mile of unspoiled, uninterrupted white-sand beach shaded by bowing palms and tangled seagrape trees and, on the other side, by a lagoon and bird sanctuary, banded by green hills.

Under its new British owner who took over in 1986, Galley Bay was upgraded extensively in 1989 and became an all-inclusive resort. It also acquired as manager the personable and energetic Peter Hoehm, who has added a certain Swiss efficiency to the tropical tempo.

Galley Bay offers two types of accommodations: beachfront rooms, only seconds from bed to sea; and thatched roof huts called, "Gauguin Cottages," resting under shade trees by the lagoon and in sight of the sea. The beachfront rooms, in two-unit cottages with patios, have terra-cotta floors, rush rugs, and a fresh look with white furniture covered with attractive prints and louvered windows that catch the breezes. Five of the rooms are more spacious and deluxe than the others.

The Gauguin Cottages turn out to be much more comfortable than you might expect upon first sight. In fact, they are two rooms whose masonry walls are covered with wooden strips and topped with thatched roofs made to look like huts; they are connected by a thatch-covered breezeway-patio. One "hut" is a spacious bedroom with a sitting area; the other has a bath/dressing room where you will find extra-plush towels and toiletries. The "huts" have whitewashed walls and peaked ceilings with a sort of South Sea–island feeling—if you use your imagination a little.

The resort has a hard surface tennis court, racquets, and balls; bicycles; and around the lagoon, a rough track for walking and jogging. Galley Bay's star attraction, however, is its splendid beach. Equipment for snorkeling, windsurfing, and Hobiecats and Sunfish is provided. There's good snorkeling directly off the beach.

Another of Galley Bay's distinctive features is the open-air beachside lounge and bar. It sits under a high pyramid of weathered wood and plaited palms and adds to the rustic, sand-between-your-toes ambience. Furnished with traditional planters' chairs and comfortable sofas, it is the gathering place for most activities—drinks, daytime chats, afternoon tea, and lots of doing nothing. By evening at cocktails, when folks have gotten dressed a bit fancier, there's something of a house-party atmosphere for after-dinner socializing and dancing.

To one side of the lounge is the covered, open-air pavilion, which extends to an outdoor terrace by the beach. Breakfast, lunch, and a weekly barbecue buffet are served on the outdoor terrace. Dinner moves to the pavilion where you dine in a romantic candlelight setting on Caribbean and continental selections created by the hotel's Swiss chef. There is piano music most nights, and live entertainment, featured three or four evenings a week, might be a calypso singer, a combo, or a steel band.

Galley Bay is a comfortable, laid-back, informal retreat. It was opened in 1962 by Pennsylvania native Edie Holbert, who gave it the funky, deserted-island atmosphere that attracted a loyal following. Some of her friends and fans are still coming, along with the next generation. Most guests in winter are British and European; in summer more are American. Galley Bay has the advantage of seeming to be on a remote island when, in fact, it is only about fifteen or twenty minutes by car (which you will need) from town and nightlife at nearby hotels. That should be ideal for active urbanites who are attracted to a totally relaxed life-style but are unaccustomed to vegging out and might get restless.

Address/Phone: Box 305; Five Islands, St. Johns, Antigua, W.I.; (809) 462–0302; Fax: (809) 462–1187

Owner: Richard Kendle

General Manager: Peter Hoehn

Open: Year-round

Credit Cards: All major

U.S. Reservations: Robert Reid Associates, (800) 223–6510

Deposit: 3 nights; 21 days cancellation in winter, 7 for summer

Minimum Stay: 7 nights, December 20–January 1

Distance from Airport: (Bird Airport) 8 miles; taxi one-way, US $15

Arrival/Departure: Transfer service is not provided

Distance from St. John's: 4 miles; taxi one-way, US $10

Accommodations: 30 rooms with patios (17 beachfront rooms; 13 thatched cottages) with twin, king-size beds

Amenities: Ceiling fans, hairdryer, bath with shower (5 deluxe beachside rooms have bathtubs), bathrobe, deluxe basket of toiletries; refrigerator, coffee maker; room service for breakfast, no television, radio

Electricity: 110 volts

Sports: Tennis, sailing, snorkeling, windsurfing, bicycles included in price. Scuba and golf arranged. No pool.

Dress Code: Casual by day; after 7 P.M. no shorts, jeans, or T-shirts in bar and restaurant areas.

Children: All ages, but none under 8 years in February and March, cribs, baby-sitters

Meetings: Up to 30 people

Day Visitors: No

Handicapped: No facilities

Packages: All inclusive

Rates: Two persons, daily, all inclusive. *High Season* (mid-December–mid-April): $355–$445. *Low Season:* $295–$355.

Service Charge: Included in rate

Government Tax: Included in rate

Jumby Bay ◙◙◙◙◙

Less than a mile off the north coast of Antigua is the ultimate private island resort, Jumby Bay, consistently ranked among the world's best. The tony hideaway so captivated Robin Leach of "Lifestyles of the Rich and Famous" that he built a palatial home to join the other well-heeled guests who have fallen under Jumby's spell.

Situated on a three-hundred-acre dot of land scalloped with pearly beaches, the exclusive resort was created in 1983 by real estate investor Homer Williams. Within a year he sold 80 percent of his holdings to the owners of New York–based Villa Banfi, vintners and wine importers who added several million dollars worth of improvements and changed the name, Long Island, to Jumby Bay.

Jumby Bay offers quietly luxurious facilities, amenities, and cuisine as fine as can be found in the Caribbean for one all-inclusive price. That means all meals; cocktails and wine with meals; afternoon tea; champagne, rum, and soft drinks in your room; all sports and recreational facilities on the property; transfers; and even laundry and postage stamps.

At the airport in Antigua, you are met by a Jumby Bay representative and whisked off to the nearby Beachcomber dock, where the Jumby Bay high-speed catamaran is waiting. Registration is completed during the ten-minute boat ride while you sip champagne. A manager is on the dock to welcome you and drive you in a golf cart to your room, orienting you en route.

Jumby Bay has three groups of accommodations, all near, but not directly on, the beach. Semi-rondavel villas, each with two suites, are set along paved paths leading from the main beach to a two-hundred-year-old plantation house, the resort's centerpiece. More junior suites are located in Pond Bay House, a graceful Spanish mission-style structure on a finger of land overlooking a long beach.

The beautifully appointed rooms, all with sitting areas, are furnished in custom-designed rattan with pillows and bed covers in designer fabrics of pleasing pastels. Another six super-deluxe villas inspired by traditional West Indian architecture are the most luxurious of the lot. Set alongside Pond Bay House, each villa has two spacious suites and a veranda facing the sea.

Each cluster of villas is different, but all of the resort's accommodations have walls of louvered doors and windows of Brazilian walnut, adding a rich accent to the decor and providing cross ventilation. High beamed ceilings create a sense of space and airiness. Bathrooms are unusually large and have separate showers, toilets, and dressing area with double vanities; those in the deluxe suites have garden showers. Some private houses are also available for rent.

The beautifully restored Estate House, with its red-tiled roof, white-washed arches, and delightful garden courtyard, is actually reminiscent of a Mediterranean palazzo. The courtyard opens onto a pretty indoor/outdoor dining terrace used for dinner. Courtyard steps lead to a second-floor lounge with a cozy bar and library.

Daytime activity is centered in the large, flower-bedecked beach pavilion near the entry dock and main beach. Breakfast, lunch, and afternoon tea are served on open-air terraces—and shared with a host of banana quits and hummingbirds.

Next to the beach pavilion are three Laykold tennis courts (lighted) with a full-time pro. The Beach Hut serves as the sports center. If you feel less ambitious, you can take up residence on a lounge chair beneath a thatched umbrella by the 1,800 feet of white-sand beach or in a hammock nearby. When you prefer privacy, try another of the bands of sand that trim the shoreline.

A more romantic setting than al fresco dining at the graceful Estate House would be hard to find. The candlelit terrace under beamed ceiling and graceful arches sits at the edge of the gardens under the spreading arms of an enormous mimosa. In the distance are the twinkling lights of Antigua.

Light music by a local combo combines familiar songs with just enough Italian and Latin tunes to give the setting a European aura. Diners chatting in a babel of languages—Italian, German, English—enhance the cosmopolitan setting. Werner, the attentive maitre d'hotel, and the extremely pleasant, well-trained Antiguan staff are the bubbles in the Banfi champagne.

The cuisine, directed by Enrico Derflingher, who has been the personal chef of Prince Charles and Princess Diana, is some of the finest in the Caribbean. A sophisticated blend of classic European and New American specialties with Caribbean inspiration, menus are changed daily with choices for each of five courses.

Jumby Bay maintains an impressive greenhouse and a large staff to grow an enormous variety of tropical plants. Except for the flower-festooned resort grounds, the island is covered with woods where nature trails and biking paths meander past sumptuous villas and lead to beaches. One path goes to Pasture Bay where the endangered Hawksbill turtle comes to lay her eggs from May to November. Under a watch directed by WIDECAST (Wide Caribbean Sea Turtle Conservation Network), Jumby Bay hosts marine biology students studying the endangered species during the nesting season.

Jumby Bay, with its gracious informality and aura of well-being, is made for honeymooners and romantics, but it appeals equally to families with teenagers and to those who simply want to get away from it all in spacious, sophisticated surroundings with a touch of Europe in the air.

From the day Jumby Bay opened, it seemed as idyllic as a resort could be. During my last visit, however, I saw that continued development could dilute the elements that have made the resort so special. Plans call for adding a marina, restaurants, palatial homes, and a total of sixty new villas. To be sure, Jumby Bay has not exactly invited in the world—villa lots alone go for a cool million. But more than doubling the size will certainly change it—for better or worse remains to be seen.

Address/Phone: Box 243, Jumby Bay, Long Island, Antigua, W.I.; (800) 421–9016; (809) 462–6000/2/3; Fax: (809) 462–6020

Owner: The Arawak Company, Ltd.

President/Managing Director: Paul Zuest

Resort General Manager: Ted Isaac

Open: Year-round except September and October

Credit Cards: Most major

U.S. Reservations: Direct to hotel, (800) 421–9016

Deposit: 3 days; 45 days cancellation

Minimum Stay: 10 days during Christmas/New Year's

Arrival/Departure: Transfer service is included

Distance from Airport: Under a mile (5-minute ride) to ferry dock, and 10-minute boat ride to Jumby Bay dock; Jumby Bay has its own scheduled water shuttle between resort and Beachcomber dock in Antigua

Distance from St. John's: 7 miles (15 minutes) from Beachcomber dock in Antigua; taxi one-way, $10

Accommodations: 38 junior suites in villas, all with verandas and either king-size or two double beds

Amenities: Ceiling fans, wall safe, hairdryers, basket of toiletries, bathrobes; plush towels changed twice daily; ice service daily; umbrellas, walking sticks; no air-conditioning, telephones, television; room service for breakfast on request; champagne and fruit basket in room on arrival

Electricity: 110 volts

Sports: Putting green; croquet court; equipment and lessons for tennis, windsurfing, snorkeling, Sunfish, waterskiing. No swimming pool. Scuba diving, deep-sea fishing, golf in Antigua arranged for fee.

Dress Code: Casual by day, slightly more formal for evening but no jacket or tie required for men.

Children: 8 years and older

Meetings: Pond Bay House or entire island can be rented in summer

Day Visitors: Welcome with advance reservations

Handicapped: Most facilities accessible

Packages: Honeymoon, wedding

Rates: Two persons, daily, all inclusive. *High Season* (mid-December–mid-
April): $895. *Low Season:* $595.
Service Charge: 10 percent
Government Tax: 7 percent

Pineapple Beach Club ◙◙◙ ∮

Few people took notice of the run-down resort on the beautiful northeastern coast of Antigua until Rob Barrett came along and changed everything
about it except the location. Today the Pineapple Beach Club enjoys a
year-round occupancy of 86 percent, thanks to a combination of features.

Pineapple is an all-inclusive resort. Guests who come here pay one
price: for accommodations, meals, all beverages (and they don't skimp on
the alcohol), water sports, tennis, airport transfers, tips, service charges, and
some excursions.

But the reason they keep returning may be less obvious. The resort
gives you the true feeling that you have vacationed on a tropical island.
Most of the guest rooms, located in low-rise buildings fanning out toward
the sea, are directly on the beach. I counted the steps from my veranda to
the sand: ten. And others were even closer. Villas, which are set into a rise
of 50 feet above the sea, afford great privacy.

The guest rooms range from standard to deluxe beachfront and villas;
they all have patio or balcony. Inside, the rooms are spacious and comfortable, with natural tile floors, rattan headboards, floral bedspreads, and large
windows opening to the sea. The rooms are kept meticulously clean by a
staff that really seems to care. You will not find a radio, television, or telephone here, but if you are the right person for Pineapple Beach you won't
miss them. (Just in case, there are telephone and fax facilities in the main
reception building.)

The white buildings, spread over twenty-five acres, are pepped up by
sunny yellow accents and red roofs and are surrounded by wonderful tropical foliage and flowers that come from Pineapple's own nursery. The resort
also grows much of its own fruits and vegetables.

Pineapple has good recreational and sports opportunities for guests
who want an active vacation. They can enjoy four tennis courts, water
sports with instruction in windsurfing, Sunfish sailing, snorkeling, and reef
fishing. There are two open-air fitness centers, in addition to table tennis,
croquet, and a game room.

Each afternoon the resort schedules a sight-seeing trip by boat to the
surrounding islands. Four days a week you can take a romantic cruise to

Bird Island, a sanctuary for the exquisite long-tailed tropic bird, for a picnic and snorkeling; five times weekly you can try your luck on a fishing expedition.

As evening approaches, guests gather for hors d'oeuvres and drinks at the bar and the open-air lounge before dinner. You dine at your own private table in one of the two restaurants. One is set on the hillside, the other is steps away from the beach. Pineapple employs young, eager-to-please chefs who have trained at the famous Culinary Institute of America. They prepare island specialties and continental dishes that look as good as they taste.

Pineapple has live musical entertainment in the evening for dancing and listening, but this is not really a late night scene. Here evening ends before midnight, but if you want to sample the local night action, you'll find inexpensive optional excursions that can be arranged through the hotel's service desk.

Above all, the pleasure of Pineapple is that all these activities are available at your fingertips if you want them. You can also decide to do nothing. You set your own pace; no one will push you.

Want to get your hair braided? Just ask. Two ladies on the staff will do it at no charge. Want to try a little gambling? Pineapple has an "electronic casino" called Pirates' Den. The resort's boutique has wonderful coral jewelry and stocks Pineapple logo items, gifts, and film. If you want to go into town for a shopping trip there is a free shuttle (one per guest during your visit).

Early risers don't have to wait for the dining room to open. As the sun comes up, take a stroll to the beachside bar, where you can help yourself to a cup of fresh hot coffee, juice, and a freshly baked muffin. One of Pineapple's staff is there to welcome you even at this hour. What a great way to start another day in the Caribbean.

Address/Phone: P.O. Box 54, Long Bay, Antigua, W.I.; (809) 463–2006
Owner: Robert Barrett
Manager: Stan Rose
Open: Year-round
Credit Cards: Most major
U.S. Reservations: Pineapple Beach Clubs, (800) 966–4737; Fax: (407) 994–6344
Deposit: 3 nights within 14 days of reservation
Minimum Stay: 4 nights
Arrival/Departure: Transfer service is available from Pineapple to airport, but, due to taxi regulation, the hotel cannot make airport/hotel transfer
Distance from Airport: 12 miles (30 minutes); taxi one-way, US $20 for up to 4 persons
Distance from St. John's: 14 miles; taxi one-way, US $20 for up to 4 persons

Accommodations: 134 rooms, all with patios and queen-size or 2 double beds, waterside, deluxe beachfront and one-bedroom villas have ocean views; others have limited beach or garden view.

Amenities: Air-conditioning, ceiling fan; bath with shower, some with tub

Electricity: 110 volts

Sports: Freshwater pool, 4 tennis courts; water sports with instruction. Walking trails.

Dress Code: Casual. In restaurants, shoes and cover-ups required; no tank tops or sleeveless shirts. After 6:30 P.M., no shorts.

Children: No children under 6 years of age; those over 6 are charged at regular rates.

Meetings: None

Day Visitors: None

Handicapped: Limited facilities

Packages: All-inclusive

Rates: Two persons, daily, all inclusive. *High Season* (December 18–March 31): $370–$420. *Low Season* (April 1–December 17): $270–$340.

Service Charge: Included

Government Tax: Included

Barbuda

The K Club (N)

The *K* stands for Krizia, one of Italy's leading high-fashion houses. Its owners, designer Mariuccia Mandelli and her husband and business manager Aldo Pinto, created this super-posh retreat on the escape island they discovered almost two decades ago. After a false start in late 1989, the eagerly awaited K Club opened a year later with anything but a flawless debut.

At the start of the 1991 winter season, however, the Italian couple brought in the Bel-Air Hotel Company, which operates some of the world's best hotels; before the season ended, the word was out that the K Club was on its way to becoming one of the Caribbean's top resorts. Without question, it has launched a new look for Caribbean luxury—Italian style.

Simple yet sophisticated, the K Club's sense of style is unparalleled in the Caribbean. To this add Mariuccia Mandelli's impeccable design sense, relentless perfectionism, and dedication to detail. Mandelli colored the whole in white and a delicate aquamarine reflecting exactly Barbuda's natural environment of sand and sea. She captured the color so perfectly, in fact, that a paint store in Antigua now sells the Mandelli-designed hue they call Barbuda Blue.

Designed by the celebrated Italian architect Gianni Gamondi, the K Club sits on 230 beachfront acres with villas and bungalows stretching along 1.5 miles of the resort's private 3.5 miles of white-sand beach. Lavish landscaping has transformed the brush-covered terrain, and great splashes of bougainvillea and other exotic flora decorate the vast public areas and cottages.

Just inside the clubhouse, the grand central building of the complex, is an open garden patio flanked by reception on one side and a Krizia boutique carrying a specially designed K Club line of resort wear on the other. The stunning snow-white square structure, trimmed in "Barbuda Blue" with high wooden ceilings and Krizia tiles, embodies the owners' taste for understated luxury and wide-open spaces; its pitched roof rests on 146 pillars. Oversized wicker armchairs and sofas striped in the signature aqua and white face the palm-fringed beach in vast *conversazione* areas, offering strategic views of unforgettable sunsets.

At the pool end of the colonnaded lounging area is the airy bar, where a charming barman whips up a mean "K-tail" to match the Barbuda Blue all around (Blue Curaçao mixed with coconut milk, lemon, and pineapple juice gives it its color; Cointreau and Antiguan rum its zing).

At the other end is the breezy restaurant, actually three open dining areas facing the water. The Krizia-designed tables are of dappled (blue!) ceramic, and each meal has its own colorful table service. Everything—glasses, napkins, even the swimming pool bottom—bears the Club's logo, with its distinctive K topped with a palm crown.

Lunch is an elaborate buffet; dinners of sophisticated cuisine are long, leisurely affairs masterfully presented and served by smiling Barbudans in uniforms bearing the Krizia label. There is light musical entertainment in the evening and a lounge with large screen cable television and video movie library.

A visit to the chilly wine cellars beneath the kitchen uncovers huge wheels of fragrant Parmigiano Reggiano, aged prosciutto, and virgin Umbrian olive oil awaiting transfer to a storage all their own, as well as extremely rare distillates of grappa and whiskey. Aldo Pinto, who has called the K Club "Mariuccia's folly," has a few follies of his own, which include old whiskeys and wines.

Pinto's favorite folly, however, is golf. On this desert island, shaping an oasis is no easy feat. K Club's power plant, hidden behind a man-made dune, produces seventy-thousand gallons of desalinated water a day. The first three holes of the golf course, designed by Luigi Rota Caremoli, are open; nine holes are expected to be completed in the coming year. The K Club has an impressive beachfront swimming pool; tennis and windsurfing and use of snorkel gear and Sunfish are included in the rate. A health center is to be added.

But a week of doing nothing at the K Club would be healthful enough for most, with long walks down the blissful beach, snorkeling over the coral heads just offshore. Or you could jog around your 20-by-20-foot room with its soaring ceilings in the trademark aqua and white, then luxuriate in the huge white shower, sampling the Krizia bath products (including a small bottle of Mariuccia's perfume), and don your personal Krizia-designed kimono to enjoy a room service breakfast on your spacious beachfront verandas, or prepare your own tea in your fully equipped terrace kitchen.

The resort has four types of rooms, including suites with a smaller bathroom and two-bedroom villas with a living room. All the bedrooms are the same: spacious with walk-in dressing rooms, large tile bathrooms, waterfront verandas and kitchenettes.

With its decidedly cosmopolitan appeal, the K Club seems to attract moneyed Europeans and other internationals as much as Caribbean *cognoscenti* from North America.

Address/Phone: Barbuda, Antigua, W.I.; (809) 460–0300/0304; Fax: (809) 460–0305

Owner: Mariuccia Mandelli and Aldo Pinto

Management: Bel-Air Hotel Company

General Manager: Frank Pfaler

Open: Year-round except June 1 to November 15

Credit Cards: All major

U.S. Reservations: Bel-Air Hotel Company, (800) 648–4097; Fax: (310) 474–5890

Deposit: 3 nights; 30 days cancellation, 45 days at Christmas

Minimum Stay: 10 days at Christmas

Arrival/Departure: Transfer from Antigua airport arranged in K Club private plane for $100 per person, round-trip; twice-daily LIAT flight, $33 round-trip to Barbuda

Distance from Airport: (Codrington/Barbuda Airport) 1 mile; from Antigua/Bird International airport, 40 miles (15-minute flight)

Distance from Codrington: 1 mile; Club's vehicle meets arriving guests for 15-minute bumpy ride to/from hotel

Accommodations: 42 guest rooms in 35 villas and bungalows, all with terraces and oversized twins together as oversized king

Amenities: Air-conditioning, ceiling fans, telephone, wall safe, kitchenette, bath with shower only, hairdryer, Krizia toiletries, bathrobe; ice service, nightly turndown service; 24-hour room service; concierge
Electricity: 110 volts
Sports: Freshwater swimming pool, Jacuzzi by pool; 2 lighted tennis courts; tennis pro. Free snorkel gear, windsurfing, Sunfish; driving range; golf additional. Deep-sea fishing arranged, birding; hiking.
Dress Code: Casual by day; elegantly casual in the evening
Children: None under age 12
Meetings: Up to 80 people in off season
Day Visitors: Welcome for dining
Handicapped: Limited facilities
Packages: None
Rates: Two persons, daily, FAP. *High Season* (November 15–April 15): $700; $1,300 and up, suites and villas. *Low Season:* to be announced.
Service Charge: 10 percent
Government Tax: 7 percent

Aruba

Hyatt Regency Aruba

Aruba was little more than a sleepy sandbar three decades ago when the gracious Arubans began to develop their tourism. Now they have created one of the most popular fun-loving playgrounds in the tropics. And they never stop. The Dutch island is booming with new resorts, marinas, smart boutiques, and more.

Fifteen miles off the Venezuelan coast in the Netherlands Antilles, this dry low-lying island has surprisingly diverse landscape and natural attractions for an island only 20 miles long. Similar to the American southwest, with rocky desert terrain and less than 20 inches of annual rainfall, the island has two totally different faces.

On the south coast tranquil beaches, sophisticated resorts, and glittering casinos line Palm Beach, a beautiful 5-mile band of sand where most of the hotels are located. In sharp contrast, the rugged north shore reveals moonscape terrain with pounding surf, shifting sand dunes, caves with prehistoric drawings, and strange gigantic rock formations sculpted by the strong winds. The countryside is dotted with tiny farm villages of Dutch colonial architecture. They're surrounded by cactus fields, which turn overnight from a lifeless gray to flowering green following a good rain, and the distinctive everpresent divi-divi tree. The outback can be fun to visit on horseback or by Jeep safari with a naturalist guide.

Aruba is ringed by coral reefs, making snorkeling and diving popular; deep-sea fishing is good, too. But the most popular sport is windsurfing; the strong winds that shape the divi-divi tree and keep the island cool have made Aruba one of the leading windsurfing locations in the Caribbean. In June an annual international windsurfing competition is held at Eagle Beach, where winds can exceed 25 knots. Another big June event is the Jazz Festival, which highlights famous Latin artists as well as North American ones.

In the capital of Oranjestad, a redesigned town center with a new shopping plaza showcases Aruba's Dutch colonial past in design. The Aruba Historical Museum, housed in Fort Zoutman and William III Towers, one of the island's oldest landmarks, reveals its ancient past. The fort was built in 1796 to protect Aruba's harbor from attack by pirates; the tower was added in 1868 as a lighthouse.

The museum and other historic preservation reflect Aruba's increased emphasis on its cultural and historic heritage. Folkloric shows presented regularly at hotels as well as new restaurants serving authentic Aruban dishes are still other reflections.

Information

Aruba Tourist Authority, 1000 Harbor Boulevard, Main Floor, Weehawken, NJ 07087; (800) TO–ARUBA; (201) 330–0800.

Divi Divi Beach Resort (T)

The inclusion of the Aruba Divi in this book is an act of faith combined with a large dose of nostalgia. Divi invented barefoot elegance. At a time when faceless air-conditioned high rises were beginning to mushroom on beaches from Miami to Margarita, Divi built its first hotel, which captured the essence of the Caribbean.

Set low under a forest of swaying palms, it made a happy marriage between modern innkeeping—stylish rooms, air-conditioning, full bath—and outdoor, easy living in a carefree ambience of tropical bliss that it called barefoot elegance. The restaurants and activities were centered around a pool and thatched open-to-the-breezes pavilion where people could mix and mingle only steps from the beach. The food and service were good, the people delightful, the ambience young, fun, and fabulous—and it all came at affordable prices.

For more than two decades, Divi continued to be one of the most popular resorts in the Caribbean. The Divi organization overexpanded and in the late 1980s got into the red. It was rescued by Doral Hotels, which is totally renovating the resort. My act of faith is based on confidence in Doral, which has a good track record of turning around hotels in New York City. Their goal is to make the Divi better than ever, and I expect them to succeed.

Immediately noticeable is the new entrance with a fabricated coral stone portico that leads into the inviting, open-air lobby, redesigned so that you can look through to pool and gardens, and the beach and sea beyond. Throughout the decor uses light woods, terra-cotta floors, scattered sisal rugs, colorful peach and turquoise fabrics—all with clean, simple lines to give it a fresh, new but not posh, look. The aim is to improve the Divi, not to change its category, remaining faithful to its basic concept.

Spread across eleven acres on Aruba's southwest coast, the Divi Beach and its neighboring sister hotel, Tamarijn Beach, with which it shares recreational facilities and amenities, enjoy 4,000 feet of palm-shaded, powdery white sand, one of the longest stretches of beach on the island.

Divi Beach accommodations, all to be refurbished by the end of 1993, come with patio or balcony and have ocean views. The ones in the two-story wings off the main building are large and have two double beds, tile floors, and small patios overlooking the gardens. A group of casitas are directly on the beach in a more secluded area offering more privacy. The lanais, among the newest and most expensive, look directly to the sea and have larger, more deluxe bathrooms and spacious tiled patios.

The newest rooms are in a building not directly on the beach, but these are the most luxurious accommodations. Most have king-size beds, and all have bathrooms with Jacuzzi, bathtub, and private balcony. At the center is a free-form pool with a small island center, accessible by a bridge. Throughout, the number of king-size beds is being increased considerably, in response to guests' requests.

At the center of the resort, a large elevated pool with a thatch-roof dining area is also the hub of action most of the time. The Pelican Terrace, the open-air dining room, serves a breakfast buffet and light meals. Red Parrot, an air-conditioned gourmet dinner restaurant with a slightly more formal atmosphere, is being refurbished from top to bottom. Updated menus reflect the nineties trend toward lighter fare with an emphasis on fresh seafood.

Nightlife at Divi includes a weekly manager's cocktail party and another for repeat guests, and the Eddie Samson Trio plays its mellow jazz six nights a week. Theme nights are big at the Divi: Monday is Pirates Night on the beach, with a sunset sail, barbecue, and music by steel band; Tuesday is Carnival with a buffet by the pool, a water ballet, Carnival show, and steel-band music. Saturday is the Divi signature, Barefoot Elegance, with a beach barbecue, a limbo show, and a fire show.

Night owls can also take in the Tamarijn and the Divi-operated Alhambra Casino and Bazaar, whose design is more Taj Mahal than Andalusian. You can try your luck on the slot machines, or take lessons if you don't know the games. Next door, Roseland, a nightclub named for its New York inspiration, has the latest dance music under high-tech lights, guest deejays, giant video screen, and special theme nights. The complex also has many shops, a New York-style deli and buffet restaurant. Golf carts shuttle guests between the sister hotels and the Alhambra Casino and Bazaar.

The full range of water sports is available at additional change. The priority is windsurfing, due to Aruba's fame as one of the Caribbean's leading windsurfing locations. Divi Winds, the windsurfing and water-sports center, can teach you the basics or help you become a champion. Other sports facilities include free tennis (lighted courts at Tamarijn); volleyball, shuffleboard, and board games.

Divi offers a vacation for the young and young at heart. It enjoys a high rate of repeat guests from all walks of life who appreciate the relaxed, tropical setting of barefoot elegance, where bikini and black tie are compatible.

Address/Phone: Druif Beach, L.G. Smith Boulevard 45, Aruba; (297) 8–23300; Reservations: (800) 367-3484
Owner: Doral Hotels & Resorts Management Corp and Divi Hotels, Inc.
General Manager: Tom Pas
Open: Year-round
Credit Cards: All major
U.S. Reservations: Doral Hotels (800) 22–DORAL
Deposit: 2 nights in summer, 3 nights in winter; 7 days cancellation in summer; 21 days in winter
Minimum Stay: 1 night
Distance from Airport: (Queen Beatrix International Airport) 4 miles; taxi one-way, $5
Arrival/Departure: Transfer arranged for fee
Distance from Oranjestad: 1 mile; taxi one-way, $3
Accommodations: 200 rooms with patios and ocean views in one-, two- and three-story buildings (90 superiors in main building; 60 deluxe in casita and lanais; 50 luxury, all with 2 doubles or kings
Amenities: Air-conditioning, ceiling fans, telephone, bath with tub and shower, cable television, radio-clock, ice machines, toiletry amenities; no room service
Electricity: 110 volts
Sports: Two freshwater swimming pools; tennis free. Snorkeling, windsurf-

ing available for fee. Deep-sea fishing, scuba, and other water sports arranged.

Dress Code: Casual
Children: All ages; cribs, baby-sitters
Meetings: Up to 25 persons
Day Visitors: No
Handicapped: Limited
Packages: Honeymoon, all inclusive, windsurfing, dive, return guest, weddings
Rates: Per room, single or double, daily, EP. *High Season* (December 19–January 2; February 9–23): $250–$375; (January 3–February 8; February 24–April 16): $225–$325. *Low Season* (April 17–October 29): $120–$170. *Shoulder Season* (October 30–December 18): $150–$200.
Service Charge: 11 percent
Government Tax: 5 percent

Hyatt Regency Aruba ⊡⊡⊡⊡

Located on Palm Beach along twelve beautiful beachfront acres on Aruba's southwestern coast, Aruba Hyatt proves that you can have your cake and eat it too. In other words, with good design it is possible to have a large full-service resort and still retain the warmth and grace of a small hotel.

Opened in 1990, the hotel's handsome design is inspired by Spanish-mission architecture. It consists of a nine-story tower flanked by two wings of four and five stories that overlook the hotel's centerpiece: a landscaped, multilevel pool and lagoon that starts as a waterfall by the open-air lobby and flows into a series of interconnected pools in flower-filled gardens and leads to a wide white-sand beach. You can slip quietly into the pool at one end, splash down a two-story winding water slide at the other, or swim up to the bar on another side.

In the public areas the decor plays on Aruba's gold mining days at the turn of the century with mock ruins, special carvings, textured and tinted concrete, and weather-beaten rocks in the gardens and around the pool to create the look of the old mines still found in several locations on the island. A rock wall by the Ruinas del Mar restaurant that seems to float in the lagoon near the center of the gardens is built of a native limestone called Aruba Rock, quarried on the island's north coast.

All guest rooms have water or garden views, and most have balconies. They are furnished in lively tropical prints of tranquil beige and aqua with brightly colored accessories and original art by local artists, commissioned for the hotel. The furniture in guest rooms and throughout the hotel blends bleached ash, wicker, and rattan, often with leather trim.

The Regency Club, Hyatt's executive rooms enhanced with more luxurious amenities, is located on the ninth floor and has a private concierge and a lounge where complimentary continental breakfast and evening cocktails and hors d'oeuvres are served daily.

There are several suites with one to four bedrooms, large living rooms with cathedral ceilings, stocked wet bars and guest baths, as well as rooftop terraces with wraparound views of Palm Beach and the Caribbean. One of the master bedrooms, furnished with a king-size bed, has a spacious bathroom with a whirlpool tub.

Low-key compared to other large Aruban resorts, the Hyatt has as many, if not more, services and facilities as its flashier neighbors. The Ruinas del Mar is an indoor/outdoor restaurant with a pretty setting by the lagoon. It serves breakfast, dinner (featuring Mediterranean cuisine), and a late-night menu. The more casual Palms is also a beachfront indoor and outdoor restaurant where lunch and dinner are available daily; it offers local seafood, salads, and sandwiches. The poolside Balashi Bar and Grill features grilled meat and seafood, sandwiches, and salads during the day.

In the evening you can take in a sunset cruise, a folklore show, comedy show, or the disco. The Casino Copacabana has a nightly live musical show and offers introductory clinics on casino games.

The resort offers a full range of water sports operated by Red Sail Sports, including free daily windsurfing clinics. It has cruiser and mountain bicycles for rent and arranges escorted biking tours of the island.

The resort's health club has state-of-the-art exercise equipment, including a multistation workout, stair climber, rowing machine, lifecycle, treadmill, and free weights. There is a sauna and steam room, massage rooms, men's and women's locker rooms and showers. A program of pool and beach aerobics, volleyball, pool basketball, and other activity is offered daily. In conjunction with the health club, the Hyatt maintains an arrival/departure lounge with lockers and showers, enabling early arrivals or late departures to have full access to hotel facilities.

While you are checking out the gym, you can check the kids into Camp Hyatt, a program of supervised day and evening activities for children ages three to twelve, or Rock Hyatt for ages thirteen to seventeen, available during the summer months, holiday periods, and on weekends year-round. Among the activities planned by the counselor staff are swimming and windsurfing lessons, games, and movies. Children get special menus and a frequent-stay program.

Casual and friendly, the Aruba Hyatt has a certain glamor and attracts a wide range of guests, mostly from the United States and Latin America. It appeals to couples, families with children, and water-sports enthusiasts.

Address/Phone: L. G. Smith Boulevard #85, Palm Beach, Aruba; (297) 8–31234; Fax: (297) 8–21682

Owners: Aruba government, Hyatt Aruba, Aruba Beachfront Resorts, and other investors

General Manager: Carlos Cabrera

Open: Year-round

Credit Cards: All major

U.S. Reservations: Hyatt Worldwide, (800) 233–1234

Deposit: Varies, depending on season; 14 days cancellation except 60 days at Christmas

Minimum Stay: 10 days at Christmas

Arrival/Departure: No transfer service

Distance from Airport: 7 miles; taxi one-way, $8

Distance from Oranjestad: 4.5 miles; taxi one-way, $6

Accommodations: 360 guest rooms and suites with twin or king beds, most with terrace

Amenities: Air-conditioning, ceiling fans, telephone, bath with tub and shower, basket of toiletries, hairdryer on request, bathrobe; stocked mini-bar, personal safe, television with CNN and other cable services, clock, radio; nightly turndown service, 24-hour room service; floor of nonsmoking rooms; concierge, business services, quality boutiques, hair salon

Electricity: 110 volts

Sports: 3-level pool with waterfalls and slide; wide white-sand beach; 2 tennis courts (lighted) free. Health club and sauna. Biking. Water sports; dive resort and specialty courses, PADI certification for fee; dive boat departs from beach on trips daily. Luxury catamaran with private-yacht amenities and glassbottom. Deep-sea fishing arranged

Children: All ages; cribs, high chairs, baby-sitters; Camp Hyatt for ages 3 to 12; Rock Hyatt for ages 13 to 17

Meetings: Up to 600 people

Day Visitors: Yes

Handicapped: Facilities fully accessible

Packages: Honeymoon, dive, family, summer

Rates: Per person, daily, EP. *High Season* (mid-December–mid-April): $270–$430. *Shoulder Season* (April 15–May 31; October 1–December 19): $170–$285. *Low Season* (June 1–September 30): $125–$240.

Service Charge: 11 percent on room

Government Tax: 5 percent

The Bahamas

Green Turtle Club and Marina, Abacos

An archipelago of more than seven hundred tropical islands stretches south from the eastern coast of Florida over 100,000 square miles of peacock green and cobalt blue seas. The Bahamas are so close to the United States mainland that many people hop to them in their own boats or private planes for the weekend.

Proximity, together with the foreign but familiar cultural influence of Great Britain, which ruled them for over two centuries, helps make this island-nation the tropical destination most visited by Americans—more than three million a year. The variety and range of activity are further attractions.

Most people's introduction to the Bahamas includes Nassau, the capital and commercial center, and Paradise Island across the harbor. Both bustle with activity day and night, but when you want to exchange the razzle-dazzle for tranquillity, you need only escape to the "other Bahamas," where life is so laid-back and serene, ten people make a crowd. The Family Islands, as they are known, offer lazy, sunny days of sailing, snorkeling, scuba diving, fishing, windsurfing, or doing nothing at all, and evenings dining on fresh fish and homemade island specialties.

But visiting the Family Islands can be a case of you-can't-get-there-from here. Fewer than three dozen islands and cays (pronounced *keys*) have hotels, and even fewer have regular air service. Unless you use a private plane or boat, you usually must double back to Nassau or Florida for connections.

The Abacos: At the northern end of the archipelago, a group of islands is strung in boomerang fashion for 130 miles around the Sea of Abaco, whose sheltered waters offer some of the Bahamas' best sailing. Marsh Harbour is the hub, and New Plymouth is a Cape Cod village with palm trees.

Andros: Directly west of Nassau, Andros is the largest of the Bahamas but one of the least developed. The interior is covered with forests and mangroves. The Barrier Reef, third largest in the world, and just beyond, the Tongue of the Ocean, a thousand fathoms deep, lie off the east coast and attract divers and sports fishermen from afar. The towns, hotels, and airstrips are also on the east coast.

Eleuthera: First-timers in search of the "other Bahamas" will delight in the quiet and beauty of this island paradise with three hundred years of history, comfortable hotels, and good dining and sports facilities. Eleuthera, 60 miles east of Nassau, is a 110-mile skinny slice of land never more than 2 miles wide except for splays at both ends. Historic villages and unpretentious beach resorts dot the entire length of the island and nearby cays.

Governor's Harbour, near the center of the island, is the main town and commercial hub. Harbour Island, almost touching the northeastern tip, is one of the Bahamas' most beautiful spots and site of Dunmore Town, its original capital.

Information

Bahamas Tourist Office, 255 Alhambra Circle, #425, Coral Gables, FL 33134; (800) 228–5173, (305) 442–4860; Fax: (305) 448–0532. Offices also in Atlanta, Boston, Chicago, Dallas, Detroit, Houston, Los Angeles, New York, Philadelphia, Washington, D.C.

Abacos

The Bluff House ◙

Casual and comfortable, this friendly hideaway is reminiscent of a weathered beach house far, far off the beaten path. It offers the kind of laid-back life where guests are welcome to borrow liquor from the office and replace it when next they visit the local liquor store.

Set in forty acres of palm, oak, and pine forests, The Bluff House is perched atop an 80-foot-high peninsula—the highest hill in the Abaco chain—that rises from a sheltered harbor and sandy beach. From the pool deck you see the Atlantic Ocean, the Abaco Sea, beautiful sunrises, and spectacular sunsets.

Originally opened in 1950, the modest, rustic hotel was acquired in 1987 by an English-born brother-and-sister team, Martin Havill and Barbara Bartley, who treat it as their home. They say they want you to feel that it's your home, too. You will be welcomed with a "Tranquil Turtle," the house specialty, and treated to cocktails nightly before dinner on the Clubhouse deck to accompany the sunset. There are no room keys at Bluff House and when the bartender is away, you write your own tab.

The L-shaped, low-slung main house opens onto a saltwater pool with a wooden deck at the edge of the hill sloping down to the beach. The house holds a comfortable lounge and dining room. It is the venue for breakfast and dinner. Lunch, a more informal affair, is available in the beach club, and the hotel arranges picnics.

The candlelit dining room is the festive setting for good cuisine created by Walter, a Bahamian and long-time executive chef who makes full use of the local bounty of fresh fish. Nightly you'll be asked to make your selection in advance from three entrees on the menu. Dinner at 7:30 P.M., with the owner arranging the seating, is served family style with complimentary wine. The dining room is also a favorite spot for visiting yachtsmen, who add to the house-party atmosphere.

Although television in the lounge has CNN and other cable services, it is plugged in only for special occasions like the Super Bowl.

The Bluff House offers three types of accommodations: split-level suites, tree houses, and small cottages, either tucked into the wooded hillsides or by the sea. The units are simply decorated. All units have balconies and views of the sea and are furnished with either twin beds or a queen-size bed.

The bilevel suites are by the water and have a bedroom and bath upstairs and a lounge with a refrigerator and a redwood deck downstairs. The tree houses have two bedrooms on one level, with steps up to them. The villas are basically one bedroom with a lounge/dining area and kitchen and adjoining bedrooms, and they can be rented therefore as a one- to three-bedroom unit. They are particularly suitable for families with children.

Guests come to The Bluff House to sun, snorkel, sail, and play tennis. There are jogging trails, and secluded beaches are a short walk or boat ride away. Shelling in the shallows and wandering on uninhabited cays with rod or camera are popular pastimes. You can go bonefishing or try reef and deep-sea fishing—and there's a hammock stretched between two palm trees waiting just for you.

The Bluff House has a loyal following, mostly from the United States. They are treated as friends more than as paying guests and have the pleasure of doing what they want at their own pace. They know the resort's charm and its faults, but they would not vacation anywhere else. The resort is ideal for couples or families, and the camaraderie is an invitation to those who travel alone. The pretty setting is popular for weddings, too. The Bluff House has a wedding package in which it makes all arrangements for a very simple wedding—the minister, photographer, flowers, cake, and even witnesses, if requested, for only $250. That's not only a romantic idea, it's a bargain.

Address/Phone: Green Turtle Cay, Abaco, Bahamas, (809) 365–4247; Fax: (809) 365–4247

Owners/Managers: Martin Havill

Open: Mid-October to mid-August.

Credit Cards: MasterCard, Visa, Discover

U.S. Reservations: International Travel Services, (800) 521–0643

Deposit: 3 nights except Christmas/New Year's when 5 nights required, 15 days cancellation, 30 days during holidays

Minimum Stay: 3 nights

Arrival/Departure: No transfer service

Distance from Airport: (Treasure Cay Airport): 3 miles; taxi to ferry dock, $3; boat from Treasure Cay to Green Turtle Cay/Bluff House Marina on White Sound, $8

Distance from New Plymouth: 5 minutes by boat, water taxi on demand; Bluff House's boat operates Tuesday, Thursday, Saturday, free to guests.

Accommodations: 25 rooms (10 suites; 7 bedrooms in cottages with kitchens; 4 tree houses all with decks or balconies)

Amenities: Air-conditioned bedrooms, most with ceiling fans, no telephones, some bathrooms have tub, most have shower only.

Electricity: 110 volts

Sports: Saltwater pool, private beach, bikes, tennis, racquets, snorkel gear, Sunfish sailing free. Marina with self-drive boat rentals; waterskiing, diving instruction, equipment and resort course for fee; fishing charters and bonefishing with guides arranged.

Children: All ages; cribs, high chairs; baby-sitter on advance request

Dress Code: Casual but neat. Shoes and shirts at meals; after 6:30 P.M. no bathing attire, cutoffs, or T-shirts in the dining room.

Meetings: Up to 50 people

Day Visitors: With reservations

Handicapped: No facilities

Packages: Wedding
Rates: Single or double, daily, EP. *Year-round:* $75–$85.
Service Charge: 10 percent
Government Tax: 8 percent

Green Turtle Club and Marina ◙◙

Set on a point overlooking White Sound and the Bluff House on the south, Coco Bay on the north, and surrounded by green forested hills, the Green Turtle Club has been a favorite of yachtsmen since it started as a boathouse bar three decades ago.

The British Charlesworth family, which owns the resort, came to the Bahamas originally in search of a family vacation house. When you see Green Turtle Cay, you will understand immediately why they decided to stay. It has one of the most idyllic settings in the Abacos, if not the entire Bahamas.

Old-timers will not recognize the place after the recent $2.7 million renovation of its spacious rooms and villas and the expansion of some facilities. The former slate gray wooden cottages are now a fresh yellow with white trim; inside, most have been completely renovated with new bathrooms and attractive mahogany, colonial-style furniture dressed in Meissen prints and oriental rugs.

There is a variety of accommodations. Some rooms and suites as well as cottages with kitchens for up to four people are located on a small rise by the swimming pool. Other villas directly on the water have private docks and can accommodate up to ten people.

The pine-paneled dining rooms with high-pitched ceilings and colonial-style furnishings have been expanded with the addition of another room to accommodate the many visitors, mainly boaters, who are not guests of the hotel. Menus are changed daily for dinner, and you are asked to make your selection by 5 P.M. each day. The fare is good quality and very traditional, if not a bit dated (and heavy on the sauce). Dinner is served promptly at an uncompromising 7:30 P.M., which might bother some free-spirited souls.

Green Turtle has the ambience of a club, but the name is something of a misnomer as it is not a club at all, although it is associated with the Birdham Yacht Club in England, the Palm Beach Yacht Club, and some other clubs in Florida. Most of their members are attracted here by the 33-slip marina, which is one of the most modern docking facilities in the Bahamas, and by the camaraderie of fellow yachtsmen.

The bar, with its dark wood and beamed ceiling, is in the original boathouse and is decorated with flags from yacht clubs around the world. Its walls are papered with one-pound British sterling notes, U.S. dollars, and other currency from a tradition begun in World War II when RAF pilots, about to depart on a mission, left money for a round of drinks in their memory, in case they did not return.

The bar is the social center in winter, but in summer the crowd moves out to the pretty new terrace by the marina. At sunset and after dinner it is probably the liveliest place in the Abacos, particularly on the three nights when Brendal, a versatile singer and guitarist (who is also the scuba instructor), performs. A lounge by the bar has cable television.

Tucked in the corner to one side of the terrace is a small quiet cove with a white-sand beach where lounge chairs and thatched umbrellas draw sun worshippers during the day. Up a small hill where the rooms and villas are located there is a pretty tiled lap swimming pool, which is solar heated in winter.

For those who are more energetic, a path behind the cottages leads to secluded Coco Bay, a beautiful white-sand beach where there is good snorkeling. A narrow dirt road to New Plymouth, the main settlement on Green Turtle Cay, is about an hour's walk away. Water sports, boats for fishing (including a Bertram for deep-sea fishing), and dive excursions are available daily.

Getting here is not half the fun, unless you arrive in your own yacht. The nearest airport is on Treasure Cay where you take a taxi ride to the ferry dock, a ferry to New Plymouth, and a water taxi to the club.

Celebrities such as Christopher Reeves, Kenny Rogers, and former President Jimmy Carter have already discovered this haven, and it's no telling who will show up after the recent visit by "Lifestyles of the Rich and Famous."

Address: Green Turtle Cay, Abacos, Bahamas; (809) 365–4271; Fax: (809) 365–4272
Owner: Charlesworth family
General Manager: William Rossbach; resident manager: Chris Farrington
Open: Year-round
Credit Cards: All major
U.S. Reservations: International Travel Services, (800) 521–0643
Deposit: 5 nights at Christmas, 3 nights balance of year; 3 weeks cancellation for holidays, 14 days balance of year
Minimum Stay: 5 nights during holidays; 3 nights balance of year
Arrival/Departure: No transfer service
Distance from Airport: (Treasure Cay Airport) 3.5 miles; taxi one-way $5; ferry one-way $8

Distance from New Plymouth: 2 miles; free water taxi daily

Accommodations: 28 rooms with deck or terrace in cottages and villas; some with kitchens (7 with twin beds; 21 with king)

Amenities: Air-conditioning, ceiling fans; 6 have bathroom with tub, 22 have shower only; small fridge; no phones, television, or room service

Electricity: 110 volts

Sports: Freshwater swimming pool. Boating, snorkeling, scuba diving, windsurfing, deep-sea fishing available for fee.

Dress Code: Casual

Children: All ages; cribs, baby-sitters

Meetings: Up to 50 people

Day Visitors: Welcome; advance reservations for meals

Handicapped: No facilities

Packages: Dive

Rates: One or two persons, daily, EP. *High Season* (December 20–April 15 and Race Week, late June/early July): $120–$160; villas $250–$365. *Low Season*: $100–$135; $195–$295.

Service Charge: 10 percent

Government hotel tax: 8 percent

Andros

Small Hope Bay Lodge ▨▨ ✿

The very antithesis of the glitz and glitter of Nassau and Paradise Island is Small Hope Bay Lodge, a rustic retreat in an idyllic setting on the east coast of Andros. Here friendly conversation replaces casinos and floor shows; and "natural" means not only an almost undisturbed landscape but genuine people and an ambience where guests blend into the "family" and love it— or quickly find they are in the wrong place.

When Dick Birch decided to give up cold Canadian winters and the fast track to create a resort on an undeveloped island, he found the ideal spot: on a white-sand beach on Andros, facing the third-longest barrier reef in the world, only an hour's flight from Florida. When he began in the 1960s, Andros had no roads, electricity, or running water, and only one telephone.

Hidden under pine and palm trees on the shallow bay from which it takes its name, Small Hope Bay Lodge has twenty bungalows for forty guests at the edge of a crescent beach. Birch, an engineer by profession, built the bungalows and lodge himself out of local pine and coral stone. The bungalows have large carpeted rooms decorated with colorful handmade batiks created at Androsia, the factory begun by Birch's wife and now a mainstay of the island's economy. Hammocks wide enough for two are in place outside each cabin.

Romantic? You bet. The debonair former prime minister of Canada, Pierre Trudeau, a repeat visitor, is said to have proposed to Margaret Sinclair here. He must have been only one of many people prodded by Cupid.

The lodge, the focal point of the resort, has a large living room rather than a hotel lobby. (Check-in means having your name hung on your cottage door.) The homey lounge has a large stone fireplace and walls lined with well-read books: everything from scientific treatises to science fiction. An old fishing boat, "Panacea," serves as the bar, which operates on the honor system.

Meals are informal in keeping with the resort's laid-back style. Breakfast and lunch are served buffet style. By early evening guests have gathered in the lodge to sample a Bahamas Mama or another cocktail at the bar, along with conch fritters and grouper fingers served every evening before dinner. A thatched-roof patio at the water's edge is another popular gathering place for cocktails.

Dinner is a communal affair with guests dining family style with the Birches, dive masters, and staffs. It is slightly—but only slightly—more formal than other meals, with table service. The chef, who has attended the Culinary Institute of America, specializes in Bahamian-style home cooking and favors fresh seafood supplied by local fishermen, with fresh vegetables from Small Hope's own farm.

Guests help themselves to tea or coffee, or perhaps to another glass of wine, and linger at the table. Entertainment after dinner might be an impromptu party or slide show in the lounge. On cool winter evenings guests settle on huge cushions by a warm fire to continue their conversations. Others play chess, backgammon, or Ping-Pong. Someone strumming a guitar might bring on song; records might inspire dancing.

Children are easily included in the informal atmosphere. There is plenty for them to do, but they must be fourteen years old to dive. Children under twelve have a separate dinner hour and are kept busy in the game room while the adults enjoy dinner. The Birches' own grandchildren are likely to be around. Their adopted Bahamian son, Peter, manages the lodge, and another son, Jeff, operates the resort's aircraft, which will ferry you from Florida.

The star attraction is the 142-mile long barrier reef, less than fifteen minutes from the lodge. A conservationist and record-setting diver, Birch convinced the Bahamian government to declare the Andros reef a national reserve. As a result the reef has a tremendous variety of coral and fish, and virgin dive sites are continuously being found. Conditions for diving are ideal: expert instructors and gin-clear warm water.

The dive center in front of the lodge has excursions several times daily, ranging from 10 feet on one side of the reef to "over the wall," a dive to 185 feet that looks down a sheer vertical 6,000-foot drop into the Tongue of the Ocean. You can have a personalized video of your dive made by the lodge's resident diver/photographer. Nondivers snorkel in shallow water or learn to scuba at no cost. Equipment is provided.

For Dick and Mona Birch, this unspoiled rustic paradise is not just a business but a way of life. It's like spending the weekend at a beach cottage with friends who come from all over the world. While diving continues to be the main attraction, nondivers in search of tropical bliss and beauty, good food, and good company will be happy here, too. "Rest, relax and rediscovery" is the resort's motto, and it delivers what it promises.

"Nobody puts on airs here—in fact, hardly anyone even puts on shoes," writes Mona Birch in her greeting to newly arriving guests. "Small Hope is home for us and for you as long as you are here. We want you to feel part of our family, meet our kids, pet our dogs, and share our lives."

Address/Phone: Fresh Creek, Andros Island; P.O. Box N1131, Nassau, Bahamas; (809) 368–2014; Fax: (809) 368–2015
Owner: Dick and Mona Birch
General Manager: Peter Douglass
Open: Year-round except, September and October
Credit Cards: All major
U.S. Reservations: Small Hope Bay Lodge, (800) 223–6961, (305) 359–8240
Deposit: 50 percent within 10 days of reservation
Minimum Stay: 5 nights during Christmas/New Year's
Arrival/Departure: Free transfer
Distance from Airport: 3 miles; Bahamasair or Lodge arranges prepaid plane from Fort Lauderdale; $200 per person, round-trip, 2-passenger minimum.
Accommodations: 20 doubles with twin beds or king (good mattresses), all with patios; singles in Family Cottage with private room/share bath or paying $45/night surcharge for regular cottage/private bath
Amenities: Ceiling fans; bath with shower, hot/cold water; oceanfront hot tub; turndown service nightly; room service on request; no phones, television, or locks on doors

Electricity: 110 volts/60 cycles
Sports: Scuba (see text); windsurfing (equipment free), Laser sailboat; bird-
ing, biking, hiking in woods with local bush doctor. No swimming
pool. Great bonefishing, $100 half day for 2 people, boat, guide, and
equipment. Reef fishing.
Dress Code: Informal resortwear, day and evening. Small Hope has only
one rule: no ties.
Children: All ages: cribs; playroom and supervised activities; baby-sitters
available
Packages: Scuba
Meetings: Up to 40 people when rent entire resort
Day Visitors: Welcome
Handicapped: Limited facilities
Rates: Two person, daily, all inclusive. *High Season* (mid-December–mid-
April): $280. *Low Season*: $260.
Service Charge: Included
Government Tax: Included in rate.

Harbour Island

Dunmore Beach Club 🌕🌕

This small cottage colony has not won the hearts of its many loyal fans and
the coveted Hideaway Small Inn of the Year Award for nothing, but to understand what it is and is not, let's step back briefly in time.

Three decades ago Long Islander Basil Albury converted a house on
the crest of the ridge overlooking Harbour Island's famous pink-sand beach
into a small inn and added some cottages. For twenty-five years he ran it
like a private club, preferring guests who were in the social registry and not
accepting anyone who was not recommended. Albury did not like tourists,
did not allow Bahamians, and was outspoken to a fault.

Still the resort garnered praise, loyal fans, and legions of repeaters—
more than 90 percent. Most say it was the outstanding food. So concerned
was Albury that it remain as it was that when he decided to sell, he looked
for and found buyers from among his previous guests.

Today under new owners some of the "our club" atmosphere remains,
but the young managers, John and Kathy Phillips, have introduced a more
open attitude and fresh spirit—not to mention some fresh paint and profes-

sionalism. The Club takes anyone, with or without recommendations, who fits. Fitting in has more to do with understanding what the Club is than with who you are.

Dunmore Beach is a small, quiet—very quiet—resort set high above the beach on eight well-manicured acres shaded by tropical trees and colorful flowers. The half-dozen guest cottages, each with two units, are spaced sufficiently apart from one another to provide a great deal of privacy.

The structures are nondescript square boxes devoid of any architectural merit—all the more noticeable since Harbour Island has so many historic gems. Another writer, more charitable than I, has described them as having "an agreeable New England summer house simplicity."

Nonetheless they are saved somewhat by being painted in pretty pastels, each one a different color. Each unit has a breezy porch with fabulous views where it is easy to spend hours reading, sipping a cool drink, snoozing, watching the changing colors of the beautiful sea, and feeling completely removed from the cares of the world.

The guest rooms are large junior suites with pickled-wood beam ceilings. Recently renovated, each is individually furnished in attractive—but not posh—cheerful, English country style with tropical touches and island paintings. Some units have a separate sitting room. The bathrooms are scheduled for major renovations.

The main house serves as clubhouse and social center. It has a large, comfortable living room with a library and a lounge with a bar and is invitingly furnished with white rattan and pretty prints. The lounge extends to an indoor dining room with an oceanfront terrace. A lacy gazebo by the dining terrace is another good perch for viewing the gorgeous beach and deep blue sea. The bar is open as a self-service honor bar all day, but is attended during prelunch and predinner cocktail hours, which quickly gain a house-party ambience.

The resort's reputation for having the best cuisine on the island is well deserved. Guests enjoy creative and imaginative interpretations of Bahamian dishes and international classics. The staff who serve it are also wonderful: attentive, caring, and delightful.

Breakfast and lunch are served on the outdoor terrace in full view of the pretty pink-sand beach and the sea, or in the rather spartan dining room with walls reaching to a high-pitched hip roof with a pickled-wood-beamed ceiling; the snow-white wooden tables, with white captain's chairs, are brightened with bouquets of fresh pink hibiscus.

At dinner the room gets much dressier and more formal as do the guests. Dunmore Beach is one of the few places in the tropics that still require coat and tie for dinner during the winter. Most of the guests would not have it any other way. The dining room tables are dressed in white linen and candlelight, and meals are served on fine china with crystal stemware and silver flatware. Dinner is served at one sitting at 8:00 P.M. When space is available nonresident guests are accepted if they have advance reservations. Occasionally there is musical entertainment in the evenings.

From the dining terrace steps lead down to the beach—as good for walking or jogging as for sunning and swimming. There are beach chairs and umbrellas for lounging. The resort offers tennis and snorkeling and other water sports; bonefishing and deep-sea fishing can be arranged.

Dunmore Beach has an informal, clubby atmosphere, and if you feel you belong to the club, you'll love it. Although the owners are from Locust Valley, New York, southern accents predominate. Guests are affluent, mostly professionals and CEOs. Families with children come frequently.

Address/Phone: Box 122, Harbour Island, Eleuthera, Bahamas; (809) 333–2200; Fax: (809) 333–2429

Owner: Dunmore Beach Club, Ltd.

General Manager: John and Kathy Phillips

Open: Year-round except September–October

Credit Cards: None

U.S. Reservations: Direct to hotel

Deposit: 2 days deposit; 30 days cancellation

Minimum Stay: None

Arrival/Departure: No transfer service.

Distance from Airport: (North Eleuthera Airport) 3 miles; from airport to ferry, 1 mile, $3; from dock to Harbour Island, 2 miles, $4; from Harbour Island to hotel, taxi one-way, $4

Distance from Dunmore Town: half mile; taxi one-way, $3

Accommodations: 12 units in 6 cottages, all with terraces; 5 with twins; 7 with kings

Amenities: Air-conditioned, ceiling fans; bath with tub and shower, basket of toiletries; refrigerator; ice service, nightly turndown service; no telephone, television, radio, or clock; room service during breakfast and dinner hours

Electricity: 110 volts

Sports: Tennis court, racquet and balls, and snorkel gear free use. Diving, fishing, waterskiing, windsurfing, sailing, glass-bottom-boat rides arranged. No swimming pool. Bikes, $10 per day.

Dress Code: In winter, men are required to wear jackets and ties for dinner; May to August, jackets requested.

Children: All ages; children under 12 dine separately. Cribs, high chairs, baby-sitters

Meetings: Up to 28 people
Day Visitors: No
Handicapped: Facilities, but beach access difficult
Packages: None
Rates: Per person, daily, FAP. *High Season* (November 1–May 31): $325. *Low Season* (June 1–August 31): $275.
Service Charge: 15 percent
Government Tax: 4 percent

Runaway Hill Club 🔲🔲

Getting there is *not* half the fun—nor any fun at all—and if what awaits at the other end weren't so utterly delightful, it might not even be worth the trip. It requires at least one, usually two, plane rides, a taxi ride followed by a short boat ride, and another taxi ride before you see Runaway Hill. Since it's sometimes harder to get a room here than at the White House, lots of people obviously think it's worth the effort.

On the last leg from the ferry dock in Eleuthera to Briland, as islanders call Harbour Island, Mr. Major or one of his nine children is likely to be on hand to transfer you in his boat. Someone will probably be waiting at the Briland dock to taxi you to Runaway Hill. If you had no luggage, you could walk, the island is so small.

A long driveway through the resort's seven wooded acres leads to a pretty, pink stone manor, reminiscent of a gracious old Bermuda house. When you walk through the front door, you will feel as though you are walking into a friend's home. The reception is something like that, too.

Depending on the time or the day, you might be greeted by Roger or Carol Becht, the managers and part owners, or by Charlie, the bartender and Mr. Everything. He will fix you a welcome drink and show you to your room. When he is not around to make you a drink, the honor bar system is in operation.

A New England-style inn with palm trees, the Runaway Hill Club is a small, intimate hotel overlooking the pink sands of Harbour Island. Built in the early 1940s as a private home, it was converted into a small inn in the early 1960s, when a second floor and a terrace, which is now the dining room, were added. A group of Brilanders headed by the Bechts took over the property in 1980, after it had been closed for two years, renovated it, and opened it as a hotel again the following year.

The house sits in a grove of casuarina trees on a bluff overlooking the Atlantic. It sits at road level on the town side but high above the beach on the ocean side, giving it the dual advantage of capturing balmy breezes and spectacular views.

There are guest rooms in three buildings: the main house which has three on the ground floor in the original building, and two on the second floor—all with patios or balconies and views of the sea; in the garden wing by the main entrance, and in one of the two new villas.

Each guest room is different and individually decorated, but all are furnished comfortably, like a private home rather than a hotel. Room 1, for example, is the size of a large suite. White bamboo and wicker furniture sit on ceramic tile floors patterned like a Spanish rug. The pink-tile bath has a tub and double sinks. There are lots of good lamps, and the rose curtains and bed covers and watercolors on the wall give the room a homey informality.

The cozy lounge with a fireplace for chilly winter evenings has walls of books, while the bar and dining room are in one large space, divided by furniture and flowers rather than walls and opening onto a breezy veranda looking out over the beach.

Breakfast and lunch are served on the ocean-view veranda, weather permitting, while dinner by candlelight is set in the indoor dining room. Outsiders with reservations are accepted for dinner when space is available.

The bar becomes the social center at cocktails and after dinner for guests who do not retire early. Tuesday evenings during the winter, Danny and the Dana-Lites, a local trio, are on hand in the lounge, and most nights one of the other resorts has entertainment featuring island musicians who play a range of music from calypso to easy-listening tunes.

From the veranda steps lead down the terraced bluff through tropical greenery to a freshwater swimming pool, set about midway between the main building and the beach. Lazy days are spent in shaded hammocks catching up on reading, with an occasional swim in the reef-protected waters or a walk along the magnificent, 3.5-mile beach. Diving and other water sports and fishing trips, particularly for bonefishing, can be arranged.

A surprising variety of people run away to this hideaway. Although most are from the States, they also come from Canada, Europe, Latin America, and now Japan. The ages and backgrounds vary greatly, too, from honeymooners to retirees, from a police captain to captains of industry. Many are repeat guests who first saw Runaway Hill while sailing by in their yachts. The friendly, family atmosphere appeals to people who travel alone, and its setting and tranquillity make romantics of us all.

Address/Phone: Box 31, Harbour Island, Bahamas; (809) 333–2150; Fax: (809) 333–2420

Owner: Dunmore Development Group

General Manager: Roger and Carol Becht

Open: Year-round except September and October
Credit Cards: All major
U.S. Reservations: Direct to hotel
Deposit: 4 nights; 3 weeks cancellation in winter; 3 nights, 2 weeks cancellation in summer
Minimum Stay: 1 week from mid-December to Easter
Arrival/Departure: No transfer service
Distance from Airport: 3 miles; taxi to ferry one-way, $3; ferry to island, $4; taxi to hotel, $3
Distance from Dunmore Town: half mile; taxi one-way, $3
Accommodations: 10 rooms in 3 buildings (5 rooms in main house, 3 with kings, 2 with twins; 3 in garden wing, 2 with twins, 1 king; 2 in villa with kings); all with terrace, patio, or balcony
Amenities: Air-conditioning, ceiling fans, hairdryer; 7 baths with tub and shower, 3 shower only; ice service, nightly turndown service, room service on request; no telephone, radio, or television
Electricity: 110 volts
Sports: Freshwater swimming pool, hammocks on beach, snorkeling gear available. Water sports and fishing arranged. Bike and moped rentals.
Dress Code: Casual; jacket requested for men in evening; shoes required in the bar and lounge.
Children: 16 years and older
Meetings: No
Day Visitors: With reservations
Handicapped: No facilities
Packages: None
Rates: Two persons, daily, EP. *High Season* (mid-December–mid-April): $160. *Low Season*: $130.
Service Charge: 10 percent
Government Tax: 8 percent

Valentine's Yacht Club and Inn ◙◙

You don't come here for pink beaches, plush rooms, or privacy. You come because you love to sail and enjoy spinning yarns with old salts; you want to learn to dive or to hone your skills; and you like to be at the center of the action; or all of the above.

It helps, too, that Valentine's has the friendliest atmosphere on this pretty little island of clubby, self-satisfied expatriates. Personable, energetic general manager Brendan Foulkes makes sure of it. But the main reasons to vacation at Valentine's are that it's fun and the price is right.

Valentine's is a yacht club with a hotel, rather than the other way around. It is located on the west side of the island facing Eleuthera, instead of overlooking Harbour Island's famous pink-sand beaches. The compensations for the lack of pretty beach views are calm waters, glorious sunsets, and a direct transfer from North Eleuthera, dock to dock. What's more, there is a direct path from Valentine's to the beach that takes eight minutes (ten if you're poky) to walk uphill and six minutes on the return—not exactly a hardship. The main building is across from the marina complex and houses the reception/lounge, bar, and inside dining room.

The accommodations at Valentine's are in several uninspired motel-style, two-story buildings amply obscured by big shade trees and gardens with masses of hibiscus, bougainvillea, and other tropical flowers. They lack the charm of the island's most celebrated inns, but they are comfortable and pleasant and were renovated and refurbished recently by the new owners. Most have a common terrace across the front of the building on each floor and look onto the gardens; the ones on the second floor get views of the sea and the sunset.

The guest rooms sit on two sides of a large freshwater swimming pool, used regularly to introduce first-time divers to the sport. There's also a hot tub, appreciated most by divers after a long day in the sea. Diving here is as much of an attraction as sailing. Use of the resort's one tennis court is free.

By the marina and ferry dock, the newly added open-air deck restaurant serves breakfast and lunch. If you are lucky, you will be aided in making your selection by Joseph, who just might be the best waiter in the Bahamas. Certainly, there are none more friendly and attentive.

The Reach, the marina bar popular with local folks and the yachting crowd, is a great perch for sunset. Special television broadcasts, such as the Super Bowl, are shown here.

Dinner is served by candlelight in the inside dining room of the main building. Menus are posted daily in the main office, and you are asked to make reservations. The tops of the dining tables are covered with laminated artificial gold coins, and antique ships' lanterns cast a gentle light from overhead. Oh, well, it's different.

The Bahamian and European cuisine is prepared by executive chef and sometime-pianist Ian McPhee. Dinner is usually preceded by drinks in the cozy wood-paneled bar, where the walls are covered with photographs of boats that have been berthed in the marina.

Valentine's bar usually draws a crowd in the evening, as it is something of the town's social center. Frequently there is live entertainment, and after dinner Chef Ian gives his renditions of Beethoven and other composers' music on the piano. Saturday is Bahamian night, featuring a local combo. At Valentine's the accent is on water sports. They all can be arranged; all are extras. In addition to sailing, you'll find windsurfing, fishing, and a large scuba center, managed by Bob Beregowitz, which offers a resort course, PADI certification, and other courses up to instructor level.

When you arrive by yacht, you might park your rig next to someone you have seen before: Barbara Mandrell or Mick Jagger, for example. Both have moored their vessels here. Valentine's marina has thirty-seven slips (up to 165 feet) and offers full service, including baby-sitting your yacht.

Valentine's is just a three-minute walk from Dunmore Town, the earliest capital of the Bahamas. The town is a tango of pretty pastel colonial cottages with gingerbread trim and bright flowers along narrow streets. Bahamians love Briland (as those in the know call Harbour Island) as much as tourists do for its tranquillity and simplicity.

Most guests come from the United States. Obviously, Valentine's appeals to boaters and divers, but singles, couples, families with children, and anyone looking for modestly priced, unpretentious digs in a fun and friendly, laid-back atmosphere could enjoy this no-frills waterside resort.

Address/Phone: Box 1, Harbour Island, Bahamas; VHF monitor channel 16; (809) 333–2142, (809) 333–2080; Fax: (809) 333–2135
Owner: Harbour Island Bay Holdings
General Manager: Brendan Foulkes
Open: Year-round except September and October
Credit Cards: All major
U.S. Reservations: Smarts Reservations, (800) 323–5655
Bahamas Reservations Service: (800) 327–0787
Deposit: 3 nights winter, 1 summer; total payment 14 days in advance, 3 days winter; 1-day summer cancellation
Minimum Stay: None
Arrival/Departure: No transfer service
Distance from Airport: (North Eleuthera airport) 3 miles; taxi to ferry one-way, $3; ferry to Valentine's dock, $4
Distance from Dunmore Town: ½ mile; taxi one-way, $3
Accommodations: 39 rooms in two-story buildings with verandas; 2 twin beds or 1 double
Amenities: Air-conditioning, ceiling fans, bath with tub and shower, ice machines; no phone, television, hairdryer, or room service
Electricity: 110 volts
Sports: Freshwater swimming pool, hot tub; free tennis (bring equipment). Marina with 37 slips. Dive shop with resort course, certification and in-

structor courses for fee. Snorkel, windsurfing, deep-sea fishing arranged. Bikes, scooters, golf carts for rent.

Dress Code: Casual
Children: All ages; cribs, baby-sitters
Meetings: Up to 15 people
Day Visitors: Welcome
Handicapped: Limited facilities
Packages: Dive
Rates: Two persons, daily, EP. *High Season* (mid-December–mid-April): $120. *Low Season*: $100.
Service Charge: 10 percent
Government Tax: 8 percent room only

Paradise Island

Ocean Club Golf and Tennis Resort ▢▢▢▢

Paradise in Paradise. In the ups and downs of the Bahamas' development, the posh Ocean Club on Paradise Island is the one resort that's kept its panache. Located on thirty-five acres along a white-sand beach across the bridge from Nassau, the tony Ocean Club is one of the most beautiful resorts in the tropics. It has style.

As soon as you turn into the long drive through gardens and manicured lawns to the main entrance, you know you have arrived at a special place.

Long a hideaway for the rich and famous, the estate began as the private winter home of a Swedish millionaire industrialist, who named it Shangri-La in 1939. In the 1960s A&P heir Huntington Hartford built the Ocean Club adjacent to Shangri-La, got government permission to rename the island (originally known as Hog Island) Paradise Island, and turned it into a premier resort for his wealthy friends.

Shortly after Resorts International acquired the majority interest in Hartford's holdings in 1966, the eastern section of the hotel (including Shangri-La) burned to the ground. The hotel was rebuilt and expanded. Paradise Island was transformed by the addition of hotels, a casino, golf, marina, sports, a 1,500-foot-long bridge connecting the island to Nassau, and an airport with direct service from Miami and Fort Lauderdale.

The Ocean Club remained secluded and exclusive—light years away from the glitter of Paradise Island Resort and Casino. In 1988, in a highly publicized deal with Donald Trump, showman/producer Merv Griffin bought Resorts International, which included the Ocean Club along with its other Paradise Island facilities.

The Ocean Club's style begins with check-in. While you complete registration formalities, you are served a rum punch or champagne mimosa in a crystal goblet presented on a silver tray. Already you feel special.

Guests are usually greeted by the manager, and if you have been a guest before, the staff will remember your name and probably your preferences for breakfast, newspapers, sports, and any special services you require. An attendant escorts you to your room, either in the main building, known as the clubhouse, or to one of the villas near the tennis courts and swimming pool.

The graceful clubhouse is a classic two-story colonial-style mansion with rooms set around a tropical garden courtyard with an ornamental pool and fountain at the center. The rooms to the north overlook turquoise waters edged by 2 miles of beach along expansive lawns where hammocks swing in the breeze under palms and giant eucalyptus trees. Rooms have verandas and are furnished in light woods and bleached rattan.

To the south of the clubhouse is the freshwater swimming pool, which you can have to yourself in the early morning. The pool has a wonderful setting overlooking the terraced Versailles Gardens, which flow for a quarter of a mile in seven tiers to a twelfth-century French cloister on the highest rise at the far south end.

The cloister, with its graceful arches and columns, was originally part of an Augustinian monastery and was brought, piece by piece, from France to the United States by William Randolph Hearst. Hartford purchased the stone structure, shipped it from Florida, and had it reassembled here. Beyond the cloister at the end of the garden by the water's edge, there is a pretty gazebo and a lovely view across Nassau harbor.

The club's nine Har-Tru tennis courts (four lighted) are available to guests without charge; a resident pro is available for games and lessons; and there is a pro shop. Two major tennis championships are held here annually.

Ocean Club guests have the best of both worlds: peace and tranquillity in a romantic setting and a glittering nightlife at the island's other facilities, as well as health club with spa, water sports, and an eighteen-hole golf course.

Breakfast and dinner are served al fresco daily at the lovely Courtyard Terrace. Local seafood and classic French fare are featured; meals are served on Wedgwood china, and tables are set with Irish linen and fresh flowers. The Terrace's garden setting is so pretty, it's even romantic at breakfast! And in the evening with candlelight and an overhead shower of stars, it's a setting even Hollywood couldn't improve. Service is pleasant and friendly, but usually at a stroll.

The Club House, which serves lunch and afternoon tea, is particularly popular for Sunday brunch. Lunch is also available at the Beach Bar and Grill. The lobby bar serves cocktails and hors d'oeuvres each evening. Ocean Club guests may choose dining plans at other Resorts International restaurants. Free shuttles run hourly to Paradise Island golf, casino, and other hotels, and every thirty minutes to hotels at dinnertime.

In addition to its romantic appeal, the fashionable resort is for people who like a quietly elegant and slightly Old World ambience. It attracts tennis and golf enthusiasts any time of the year, and honeymooners in the spring and summer when prices are 25 percent or more lower. The Ocean Club's well-heeled guests come mostly from the United States (some from Europe), and they return frequently. Among the list of famous guests here are Ronald and Nancy Reagan, who stayed for two weeks, and, of course, Mr. Showman himself, Merv Griffin.

Address/Phone: Box N-4777, Paradise Island, Nassau, Bahamas; (809) 363–2501, (800) 321–3000; Fax: (809) 363-2424.
Owner: Resorts International
General Manager: Brian Webb
Open: Year-round
Credit Cards: All major
U.S. Reservations: Resorts Representation International, (800) 321–3000, (305) 895–2922
Deposit: 2 nights
Minimum Stay: During holiday periods, inquire
Arrival/Departure: Transfer service available for fee
Distance from Airport: (Nassau International Airport) 30 minutes; taxi one-way, $22. 5 minutes from Chalk's Terminal on Paradise Island.
Distance from Nassau: 3 miles; taxi one-way, $6 + $2 bridge toll; water taxi between Paradise Island and Nassau, $2 one-way
Accommodations: 71 rooms (49 rooms and 4 suites, in main building; 5 two-bedroom/two-bath villas, each with terrace and whirlpool; and 12 lanai next to tennis courts); rooms have twin or king-size beds
Amenities: Telephones (including 1 in bathroom), stocked mini-bars, air-conditioning, ceiling fans, television, marbled baths with tub and shower, hairdryer, toiletries, and sundries; room service, towels changed twice daily, nightly turndown service; suites and villas have fresh flowers daily, fruit basket, terry robes.
Electricity: 110 volts
Sports: Tennis, golf, walking paths, bikes, water sports

Small Hope Bay Lodge, Andros

Children: All ages but not encouraged; baby-sitters; Camp Paradise, operated by Resorts International at its other hotels, has daily supervised activities.

Dress Code: Casual but always chic. Men required to wear jackets in the evenings.

Meetings: Small executive groups

Day Visitors: Not encouraged

Handicapped: Limited facilities

Packages: Golf, tennis, honeymoon, wedding

Rates: Per person, daily, EP. *High Season* (mid-December–mid-April): $112.50–$450. *Low Season:* $77.50–$225.

Service Charge: 15 percent plus a daily maid-gratuity charge

Government Tax: 8 percent on room rate only

Barbados

The bridal suite at Cobbler's Cove

Barbados is an elegant place in a quiet sort of way. Whether it is the three hundred years of British rule, the Bajans' pride and natural grace, or the bluestocking vacationers who return annually like homing birds to their roost, this Caribbean island feels something like "Masterpiece Theatre" in the tropics.

Independent since 1966, Barbados still seems as British as the queen. Bridgetown, the capital, has a Trafalgar Square with a statue of Lord Nelson. Bewigged judges preside over the country's law courts, hotels stop for afternoon tea, and a police band gives outdoor concerts.

The 166-square-mile island of green rolling hills even resembles the English countryside and is a pleasure to explore. On an island only 21 miles long, you can visit stately homes and gardens and more than fifty important historic sites, and the outstanding Barbados Museum.

A coral island 100 miles east of the Lesser Antilles, Barbados is the easternmost land in the Caribbean. Its west coast, fringed with attractive beaches, is bathed by calm Caribbean waters; the eastern shores are washed by white-capped rollers of the Atlantic. It is one of the main locations for windsurfing in the Caribbean and is often a venue for international competitions. The island is surrounded by coral reefs good for snorkeling and learning to scuba dive, and there is sailing, fishing, golf, tennis, horseback riding, and polo.

Barbados has one of the widest selections of accommodations of any island in the Caribbean, ranging from modest guesthouses to ultra-posh resorts with great style. Each is different and distinctive. Their ambience is often more European than in hotels in Caribbean islands closer to the United States, because the majority of Barbados's visitors come from Britain and other European countries.

Information

Barbados Board of Tourism, 800 Second Avenue, New York, NY 10017; (800) 221–9831, (212) 986–6516; Fax: (212) 573–9850; and 3440 Wilshire Boulevard, #1215, Los Angeles, CA 90010; (800) 221–9831, (213) 380–2198; Fax: (213) 384–2763.

Cobblers Cove ◙ ◙◙

A cozy complex of two-story cottages in gardens overlooking a gorgeous beach produces love at first sight in those who want a casual, romantic resort with just enough history to lend it charm—but with attractive, modern, spacious accommodations to boot.

The centerpiece of this quiet resort is a pale pink villa built in the early part of this century by a Bajan sugar baron as a summer home. The former living room, similar to an English country drawing room, serves as a reading lounge with daily United States and European newspapers.

The villa's open-air, seaside terrace doubles as the dining pavilion and bar, a favorite meeting place for hotel guests and local friends. During the winter season you'll hear a strong British upstairs accent, but in summer the voices are likely to have a more familiar American ring.

In the evening the pavilion and another terrace next to the lounge become romantic settings for candlelight dining on the best hotel cuisine in Barbados, created by French-trained English chef Leslie Alexander. Blending traditional European dishes with local fresh products, he has developed an innovative, sophisticated cuisine that has won the Barbados Gold Award on five occasions and wins accolades from diners every day. Because all dishes are cooked to order, guests give their selections to the head waiter while they enjoy a drink at the bar adjacent to the dining terrace. Cobblers

Cove, one of the seven Elegant Hotels of Barbados, has a dinner exchange with any one of the other member hotels.

The cottages, each with four suites, sit snugly in a V in three acres of tropical gardens alongside the main house and around a small pool overlooking the Caribbean. (The pool area can be crowded when the hotel is full, but you'll get plenty of solitude on the picture-perfect beach, one of Barbados's finest and most secluded, only 10 yards away.)

Refurbished in 1991, all accommodations are suites with large bedrooms, ample closets, and special drying racks for wet bathing suits and towels. Each suite overlooks the garden or sea and has a kitchenette and separate sitting room with louvered doors that, when folded back, open onto a furnished patio or balcony creating one large airy space.

The most sensational accommodation is the bilevel Camelot Suite, created in 1989 on the top floor of the main villa by architect Ian Morrison, known for his handsome design of nearby Glitter Bay and Royal Pavilion hotels. The posh love nest with ultimate privacy has marble floors, a king-size, canopied four-poster bed, and a lounge area with a settee, writing desk, and chaise longue—all in fresh blue-and-white decor. The Camelot Suite may well be the most heavenly honeymoon hideaway in the tropics. The price is heavenly, too.

The huge bathroom has a whirlpool tub, twin sinks, bidet, and "his and her" showers with twin shower heads. A spiral stairway leads to the upper deck with a private swimming pool, wet bar, and terrace overlooking a wonderful view of the sea.

Cobblers' sports facilities include complimentary water sports and day-and-night tennis. You can go snorkeling directly off the beach or enjoy excursions over the reef in the hotel's glass-bottom boat.

Life at Cobblers Cove is very low-key. There's the usual manager's weekly cocktail party and occasional live musical entertainment, but essentially the resort is a friendly, easy-living sort of place where guests meet and mingle or go their own way. It all happens under the watchful eye of Hamish Watson, a hands-on, wonderfully friendly manager.

The resort's informality is especially suited to families with children, while its cozy, romantic ambience attracts couples of all ages.

Address/Phone: Road View, St. Peter, Barbados; (809) 422–2291; Fax: (809) 422–1460
Owner: Hayton, Ltd.
General Manager: Hamish Watson
Open: Year-round except September to mid-October
Credit Cards: All major

U.S. Reservations: Robert Reid Associates, (800) 223–6510; Fax: (402) 398–5484

Deposit: 3 nights year-round except 7 nights Christmas; cancellation 28 days in winter, 14 days in summer

Minimum Stay: 10 nights during Christmas/New Year's

Arrival/Departure: Transfer service arranged for fee

Distance from Bridgetown: 12 miles (25 minutes); taxi one-way, $13.50; free shuttle weekdays to Bridgetown

Distance from Airport: 18 miles (45 minutes); taxi one-way, $21

Accommodations: 38 suites (24 garden view; 14 seaview) with twin beds in 10, two-story cottages, all with kitchenettes, terraces, and patios; 1 super-deluxe suite with pool

Amenities: Air-conditioning, ceiling fans, direct-dial telephones, individual safes, television (arranged on request), radio (at front desk), bath with tub and shower, hairdryer, terry robes, basket of toiletries, stocked mini-bar; ice service, room service from 8:00 A.M. to 9:00 P.M.

Electricity: 110 volts/50 cycles

Sports: Freshwater swimming pool; free waterskiing, windsurfing, Sunfish sailing, snorkeling, tennis, and glass-bottom boat. Special fees for golf at Sandy Lane. Scuba, parasailing, cocktail cruise, private yacht arranged.

Dress Code: Informal by day; elegantly casual in evening. Men wear slacks and open neck shirts. Jeans, shorts, and swimwear are not allowed in the bar area after 7 P.M.

Children: All ages except late January to late March when none under 12; cribs, baby-sitters

Meetings: None

Day Visitors: With advance reservations

Handicapped: Facilities available

Packages: Honeymooners and Lovers, gourmet

Rates: Per persons, daily, MAP. *High Season* (mid-December–mid-April): $240. *Low Season:* $85, EP.

Service Charge: 10 percent

Government Tax: 5 percent

Glitter Bay ◑ ◉ ◑ ◑

Upon entering the front gate that opens onto twelve beachfront acres of landscaped gardens and stately trees, you get the immediate impression that someone important once lived here. He did.

Glitter Bay, overlooking Barbados's Caribbean coast, was the former seaside retreat of Sir Edward Cunard of British steamship fame. In its heyday, when his passengers came to winter in the tropics, his guests were a glittering gathering of lords and ladies. In more recent times the retreat has attracted a sparkling array of Hollywood stars, Wall Street lights, and Washington luminaries, as well as a young English real estate tycoon, Michael Pemberton, who bought the property in the early 1980s.

If you want to make a dazzling arrival yourself, you can be transported from the airport by the hotel's stretch Mercedes (for $50). A glass of champagne awaits you on arrival, and on departure the concierge will arrange airport executive check-in.

Glitter Bay is a baronial spread of quiet grandeur with stately royal palms leading the way to flower-trimmed walkways, a split-level swimming pool with a waterfall and wooden footbridge, and a half-mile-long white-sand beach with a water-sports center that it shares with its neighbor Royal Pavilion, which Pemberton also owns.

Cunard's gracious coral-stone mansion serves as the centerpiece of the resort. As part of a $4 million facelift in 1991, the building was expanded with a new marble-floor wing that provides space for a fitness center, concierge desk, and a small courtyard of quality boutiques and a hair salon.

On both sides of the extensive gardens are clusters of three-story, white-stucco buildings with red-clay roofs and a cascade of terraces reflecting the Mediterranean design, which is architect Ian Morrison's signature. All units have private verandas overlooking the gardens and the sea. They are furnished like living rooms, making the accommodations very spacious. The standard rooms are interconnected to provide a second room for a one-bedroom suite.

In the recent renovations all units were redecorated with pretty pastel prints and the bathrooms, which have tubs, showers, and bidets, were markedly improved, helping to raise the hotel from a three- to four-star level. Rooms have refrigerators, and suites have kitchens. All accommodations are furnished with king-size beds; twin beds, rollaways, and cots are available on request.

Off to one side beyond the main complex are two beachside villas— one a replica of Cunard's Venetian mansion—with five super-posh suites, the most desirable of the lot. They offer the best of both worlds: the intimacy and privacy of a small resort with the facilities of a large one.

Beside the pool is the breeze-cooled restaurant, Piperade, serving international and local cuisine. Monday and Friday nights feature a buffet and barbecue with a local show.

Afternoon tea is served in the Residents Lounge of the estate house, which is also the center of indoor activity. It has a bar and television screen (with CNN and other cable channels) and a VCR. In addition to the manager's weekly cocktail party, guests are offered complimentary cocktails each evening.

Glitter Bay offers complimentary water sports, along with two Astroturf tennis courts (lighted) and a fitness center with Life Cycle equipment, treadmill, stair climber, weights, daily aerobics, and personalized training. And its guests have use of all facilities at Royal Pavilion.

Shared facilities do not mean, however, that the two resorts are similar. After Royal Pavilion opened in 1987, taking on a young, sophisticated image, Glitter Bay redefined itself to be more informal and family oriented. Its large apartment-type accommodations, space, and facilities are well suited to families. The mix of patrons, too, is different, with as many coming from the United States as from Britain.

Address/Phone: Porters, St. James, Barbados; (809) 422–4111 or 422–5555; Fax: (809) 422–3940
Owner: Pemberton Resorts, Ltd.
Acting General Manager: Peter Bowling
Open: Year-round
Credit Cards: All major
U.S. Reservations: Pemberton Hotels Travel Resources Management Group, (800) 283–8666 or (214) 556–1538
Deposit: Winter: 3 nights, 30 days cancellation; summer: 1 night, 14 days cancellation
Minimum Stay: 10 nights during Christmas/New Year's
Arrival/Departure: Limousine transfer service can be arranged.
Distance from Airport: 12 miles; taxi one-way, $20
Distance from Bridgetown: 8 miles; taxi one-way, $10
Accomodations: 33 double rooms and 41 suites with kitchens; 7 penthouses; all have balconies; most have seaviews or partial seaviews.
Electricity: 110 volts/60 cycles
Amenities: Air-conditioning, ceiling fan, direct-dial telephone, radio; bath with tub, shower, and bidet; hairdryer, bathrobes, basket of toiletries, stocked mini-bar; ice service, nightly turndown service, daily newspapers, 24-hour room service; concierge
Sports: Freshwater swimming pool, children's pool, fitness center; free tennis, waterskiing, Hobie and Sunfish sailing, snorkeling, and windsurfing. Scuba diving for fee. Golf, fishing, and horseback riding arranged.
Dress Code: Informal by day; casually elegant in the evening. Cover-ups requested in dining room for all meals; at dinner men are asked to wear trousers; no shorts, T-shirts, or jeans allowed in public rooms in evenings.

Children: All ages; children's pool and menus; cribs, baby-sitters
Meetings: Up to 50 people
Day Visitors: Welcome with advance reservation
Handicapped: Facilities available
Packages: 4, 7, and 14 nights; dive, honeymoon, wedding
Rates: Two persons, daily, EP. *High Season* (mid-December–mid-April):
$345–$525. *Shoulder Season* (November 21–December 17; April 3–30)
$250-$355. *Low Season* (May 1–November 20: $185–$265.
Service Charge: 10 percent
Government Tax: 5 percent

Royal Pavilion ◙◙◙◙

The Royal Pavilion, opened in 1987 by British real estate tycoon Michael
Pemberton, had a hand in getting Barbados back on track as the fashionable
winter resort it was in the 1960s. Adjacent to Glitter Bay, which Pemberton
also owns, and designed by the same architect, Ian Morrison, the Royal
Pavilion was aimed directly at today's younger affluent travelers. Although
grand luxe in the European tradition, it has made a point of being more contemporary in style and attitude than the grande dames of Barbados's hotels.

Set amid eight acres of manicured, tropical gardens directly on a white-
sand beach in a quiet cove it shares with its sister resort, the pastel pink
Royal Pavilion combines Spanish mission and Mediterranean elements in its
design. An imposing avenue of royal palms leads to the flower-encircled
portico of the main entrance. There you step into a marbled reception hall
with a concierge desk and a colonnaded Andalusian courtyard cooled by a
fountain.

As at Glitter Bay, if you wish to have your arrival match the hotel's
grand entrance, you can be met at the airport in one of the resort's stretch
Mercedes limousines (for $50). No matter how you arrive, a glass of cham-
pagne will be waiting.

The resort's accommodations, all facing the sea, are in two wings of
three-story buildings. All are junior suites with terraces designed and furnished to be part of the room—making the rooms all the more spacious.
One of the best features of the terraces is a built-in settee of white sculpted
masonry set off with colorful cushions that pick up the hues of the flowers
in the gardens and of the Caribbean Sea directly in view. All guest rooms are
attractively decorated in fashionable prints against pickled-wood furniture.

Four suites on the top floor can be combined into two-bedroom penthouses. Completing the roster is a villa with three junior suites. The de-

mand for these large accommodations has motivated the hotel to add a group of one- to three-bedroom super-deluxe suites in a separate unit located in the gardens between the Royal Pavilion and Glitter Bay.

Royal Pavilion's triumph is the Palm Terrace, an elegant, pink marble dining room by the sea. Here the romantic palm-court effect is enhanced by a skylight pavilion roof shaded by living palm trees that are part of the decor. The restaurant's gourmet cuisine is under the direction of British chef Guy Beasley, who trained with Michel Roux at La Gavroche, one of Britain's only two Michelin three-star restaurants. The Palm Terrace features dinner music nightly.

Adjacent to the restaurant is a spacious lounge with graceful arched doorways and windows opening onto views of the gardens and sea where guests enjoy afternoon tea, cocktails, and after-dinner drinks. The residents lounge has television with CNN and other cable services and videos.

On the north side of the resort, Tabora is a casual, open-air restaurant of confetti pink and white where breakfast and lunch are served. It is named for Fernando Tabora, a well-known Latin American landscape architect who designed the exquisite gardens for Royal Pavilion and Glitter Bay.

Tabora is flanked by the sea on one side, with the swimming pool and a large sunning deck on the other. The hotel has two Astroturf tennis courts (lighted) and shares the water-sports, fitness, and restaurant facilities of Glitter Bay next door. One of the courtyards has a cluster of fashionable boutiques.

Royal Pavilion is tony but not snobbish and enjoys a high number of repeat guests, mostly from Britain, Germany, and Italy—less than a quarter come from the United States. It is well suited for those who want a relaxing vacation in a stylish yet casual ambience where the emphasis is on pretty surroundings, a high level of comfort, and sophisticated cuisine.

Address/Phone: St. James, Porters, Barbados; (809) 422–4444, 422–5555; Fax: (809)422–3940
Owner: Michael Pemberton
General Manager: Peter Bowling
Open: Year-round
Credit Cards: All major
U.S. Reservations: Pemberton Hotels Travel Resources Management Group, (800) 283–8666; Fax: (214) 556–1538
Deposit: Winter: 3 nights, 30 days cancellation; summer: 1 night, 14 days cancellation
Minimum Stay: 10 nights at Christmas
Arrival/Departure: Limousine transfer service arranged for fee
Distance from Airport: 12 miles; taxi one-way, $20
Distance from Bridgetown: 8 miles; taxi one-way, $16

Accommodations: 75 oceanfront junior suites with king-size beds and private balconies in 2 three-story buildings; 1 three-bedroom villa (no sea
view)
Amenities: Air-conditioning, direct-dial telephone, radio, room safe, bath
with tub and shower, hairdryer, basket of toiletries, bathrobe; stocked
mini-bar, daily international newspapers; twice-daily maid service,
concierge
Electricity: 110 volts/60 cycles
Sports: Freshwater swimming pool, complimentary tennis and equipment
(lessons extra), Hobies and Sunfish, snorkeling, waterskiing, and windsurfing; scuba diving additional. Fitness center with Life Cycle equipment, treadmill, stair climber, weights, aerobics, and personalized
training. Horseback riding, golf, and fishing arranged.
Dress Code: Informal by day; casually elegant in the evening. For dining,
jeans, T-shirts, rubber shoes, and sneakers not accepted; no shorts in
the bar after 6 P.M. No swimwear at lunch or afternoon tea. Men requested to wear tie in Palm Terrace restaurant at dinner.
Children: Over 12 during winter season; all ages at other times; cribs,
baby-sitters
Meetings: Up to 50 people; equipment available
Day Visitors: With advance reservations
Handicapped: Facilities available
Packages: 7 and 14 nights; dive, honeymoon, wedding
Rates: Per person, daily, EP. *High Season* (mid-December–mid-April): $345-
$970. *Shoulder Season* (April 3–30; November 21–December 17):
$245–$310. *Low Season* (May 1–November 20): $180–$215.
Service Charge: 10 percent
Government Tax: 5 percent

Sandy Lane Hotel and Golf Club ◉ ◉ ◉ ◉ ◉

The imposing circular driveway and pillared entrance here remind me of a
grand hotel on the French Riviera with Roaring Twenties panache. I half expect to see Zelda and F. Scott Fitzgerald sitting on the terrace.

Built of native pale coral stone in classic Palladian style on 380 west-
coast acres, Sandy Lane Hotel and Golf Club was designed by renowned
Caribbean resort architect Robertson "Happy" Ward. It was built thirty years
ago by Sir Ronald Tree, M.P., whose famous aristocratic friends from both
sides of the Atlantic helped him establish its reputation quickly as the ultimate winter resort.

Some would say the legend lasted longer than the reality, but a $10 million face-lift in 1991 is part of a commitment by its current owners, Forte Hotels, to return Sandy Lane to its past glory—but updated in style and tenor. Gone is the staid, snobbish atmosphere but not the special touches.

All Sandy Lane guests are met at the airport by the hotel's representative and assisted to transportation. (For $100 you can ride in the same white Rolls-Royce the queen used during her visit.) Champagne and fruit await you in your room.

Among the major changes is the selection of a new, young staff who now account for more than two-thirds of the personnel. Many of them were trained at Forte hotels around the world, and it shows—the improvement in service is one of the most impressive features of the resort's renaissance.

The renovations were extensive inside and out. Eighty percent of the guest rooms were refurbished and given new bathrooms and floors of beautiful Zandobbio marble as well as elaborate new cabinet work done by Bajan artisans. All the public areas were redecorated and laid with new marble and terrazzo floors. Of particular pride are the carved coral-stone pillars and arches of the exterior.

The signature Palladian architecture was added to the north wing, where rooms were extended to create eighteen super-luxurious suites. These are among the finest for style and comfort in the Caribbean. They have huge balconies; oversized marble bathrooms, and amenities that include four telephones. Twelve rooms in the west wing were similarly upgraded.

The "tropical Palladian" decor is simple yet elegant. The soft beige and taupe tones of the handsome marble are repeated in the wood, furniture, and upholstery.

The resort has two oceanfront restaurants. The Seashell, an informal setting for lunch and dinner, features Italian specialties along with seafood, salads, and grills. The Sandy Bay serves a buffet and à la carte breakfast and becomes an elegant setting for gourmet cuisine in the evening. A third restaurant by the swimming pool, The Oasis, offers lunch and bar service. Sandy Lane, one of the seven Elegant Resorts of Barbados, also has a dinner exchange with any one of the other members.

The lobby and other public rooms form a crescent around a two-tiered beachside terrace shaded by huge mahogany and manchineel trees that lead down to the sea and add a distinctive character. In the evening, it becomes the Starlight Terrace, a romantic setting for dancing under the stars and enjoying a variety of musical entertainment from classical to calypso and a Saturday night cabaret.

The Terrace Bar and lounge, a popular gathering spot, has piano music at cocktail time. The manager's party, a well-attended festive occasion, is held here before the weekly West Indian buffet and Bajan folklore show.

Most guests come from Britain, Germany, and Italy; less than a quarter are from the United States.

Sandy Lane has the most extensive sports facilities—water sports, tennis, golf—on the island. Most are free to guests, including golf. The resort is set on one of Barbados's prettiest beaches, protected by a reef within swimming distance from shore and swept pristine every morning.

Sandy Lane's eighteen-hole golf course is the only international standard one in Barbados and has a local membership. Its clubhouse, with a pro shop, caddies, carts, and bar, was once the mill of the sugar plantation on which the resort is set. The course (6,600 yards; par 72) was designed by Robertson Ward in two stages. The lower nine holes feature tight fairways following the site's hilly contours and winding through an area with some of Barbados's most palatial homes. The upper nine are more undulating, less demanding, and provide golfers with panoramic views. A more challenging nine holes are being added. There is a driving range, putting green, and chipping green. The pro is available for lessons for a fee.

Sandy Lane has a magic and style all its own—tony, romantic, glamorous with a touch of the Old World, yet casual. It combines luxury and comfort in a genteel ambience that continues to reflect its founder's notion that a stay at Sandy Lane would be like "an elegant country house party in the English tradition." It attracts older, affluent couples in winter, many honeymooners in spring and summer, and golf and tennis enthusiasts any time of the year.

From your terrace in the cool of evening when the doves coo and dusk bathes the gardens, you can watch the light of the setting sun turn the sea and sky so red the old mahogany trees look as though they are in flames. It's pure magic.

Address/Phone: St. James, Barbados; (809) 432–1311; Fax: (809) 432–2954
Owner: Forte Hotels International
General Manager: Richard R. Williams
Open: Year-round
Credit Cards: All major
U.S. Reservations: Forte Hotels, (800) 225–5843, (212) 541–4400; 800-223-5672; or Leading Hotels of the World, (800) 223–6800, (212) 838–3110 (in New York)
Deposit: 14 days cancellation
Minimum Stay: 14 days at Christmas; 7 days in February
Arrival/Departure: Transfer service available for fee: Rolls-Royce, $100 or Mercedes, $60
Distance from Airport: 20 miles (30 minutes); taxi one-way, $20
Distance from Bridgetown: 9 miles (15 minutes) taxi one-way, $13

Accommodations: 121 units with terraces (91 doubles and 30 suites with twin, queen, or king beds) in 3, two- and four-story wings; all but 10 with ocean views

Amenities: Air-conditioning, ceiling fans, refrigerator, toaster, clock-radio, telephones, room safe, hairdryer, bath with tub and shower, bathrobes, basket of toiletries; television in suites, in other rooms on request for fee; 24-hour room service, daily newspaper, nightly turndown service, hair salon, boutiques, concierge

Electricity: 110 volts A.C., 50 cycles

Sports: Freshwater swimming pool; 5 Laykold tennis courts (2 lighted), golf, snorkeling, waterskiing, Hobies and Sunfish, and windsurfing in room rate. Scuba diving and deep-sea fishing arranged.

Dress Code: Casual by day; coverup over swimwear in restaurants. Elegantly casual in evening. In winter, Wednesday and Saturday evenings formal; gentlemen requested to wear jacket and tie in Sandy Bay Restaurant.

Children: All ages; children's dining hour; none allowed in bars after 7:00 P.M. nor in dining room or dance floor in evening if under 8; cribs, high chairs, baby-sitters

Meetings: Small groups, up to 35 people, in off season

Day Visitors: Welcome with reservations

Handicapped: No facilities

Packages: 3–14 nights, golf, honeymoon, wedding, anniversary

Rates: Two persons, daily, MAP. *High Season* (mid-December–mid-April): $795–$2,000. *Low Season:* $395–$950.

Service Charge: 10 percent

Government Tax: 5 percent

Bonaire

Harbour Village Beach Resort

The second largest island in the Netherlands Antilles, Bonaire is located 50 miles north of Venezuela and 86 miles east of Aruba. For three decades it has been a haven for divers coming to enjoy the island's remarkable marine life. The entire coastline from the high tide mark to a depth of 200 feet is a Marine Park with over 80 dive sites.

Most island hotels cater to divers and have excellent operations on their premises. In some places the reefs are so near you can wade to them; others are only a swim or short boat ride away. These assets enable divers to enjoy unlimited diving from the beach any time of the day or night—the kind of ease and convenience few places in the world can duplicate. Indeed, there's no better place in the Caribbean to learn scuba.

Even for travelers with no higher aspiration than snorkeling, this 24-mile crescent-shaped island has plenty to enjoy. Two of its attractions are certainly unusual, if not unique, and easily accessible. The hilly northern end is covered by the Washington/Slagbaai National Park, a 13,500-acre wildlife sanctuary, and includes the island's highest point, 784-foot Brandaris Hill. The park is a showcase of island flora and fauna with a variety of unusual formations and 130 species of birds.

The flat, dry southern part of the island has an equally interesting attraction. Salt pans, more than 150 years old and covered with white sparkling mountains of salt, are worked commercially, but amid the pans is a 135-acre flamingo sanctuary and breeding ground for about 10,000 birds. You can tour the perimeter of the pans to watch and photograph the birds.

A quiet island of 10,400 inhabitants, Bonaire's peaceful ambience belies its turbulent past. Discovered in 1499 by Amerigo Vespucci, for whom the Americas were named, it was colonized in the next century by the Spaniards, who carted off the entire Arawak population to Hispaniola. Later, the island was captured by the Dutch, fought over by the French and British, and leased to a New York merchant. Finally, in 1816, the Dutch took it over and kept it.

Kralendijk, the capital, is a colorful miniature city with distinctive Dutch colonial architecture. Among the oldest is historic Fort Oranje and the original administration building dating back to 1837. It has been restored as the Government Office. The island has a surprising variety of good restaurants and a neat little shopping area in the heart of town.

Information

Bonaire Government Tourist Office, Resorts Management, Inc., 201 1/2 East 29th Street, New York, NY 10016; (212) 779–0242.

Captain Don's Habitat ▣▣ ◈

A resort for divers, Captain Don's Habitat is owned by a diver who has become a legend in his own time.

I met Don Stewart, a salty California expatriate, on my first trip to Bonaire in the early 1970s, long before Habitat was born. He had wandered into Bonaire in 1962 on a 70-foot schooner called *Valerie Queen*, because, he said in his wry way, "I was thirsty and heard they had water." The good ship *Valerie* sank; Stewart stayed. He started Bonaire's first hotel and later opened his own very rustic inn for divers, one of the first of its kind.

Stewart, known to all as Captain Don, bent my ear most of the day and evening on the wonders of scuba diving, the unique qualities of Bonaire, the need to protect the marine environment, and just about anything else that came to his mind. He was not a man at a loss for words.

Since then not much has changed, except that this interesting character managed to get enough of the right people to listen. Today, after more than a decade of adhering to careful management of its reefs and sea life, Bonaire has one of the most magnificent marine parks in the world; diving is its number-one industry. On the twenty-fifth anniversary of his arrival on the island and for his contributions, the Bonaire government honored Stewart by naming a dive site for him. And along the way his once dinky little inn grew into quite a nice resort.

Perched on a coral bluff north of town overlooking a half-mile shoreline of great diving, Captain Don's Habitat is a very casual, relaxed resort. It is designed as clusters of white-stucco townhouses, some in attractive Dutch colonial architecture with high-pitched red roofs, others more modern with Spanish features such as courtyards and dark wood doors and windows.

In the past few years, the hotel has been substantially updated, upgraded, and expanded, now offering variety and flexibility to meet almost any need. There are two-bedroom garden-view cottages with kitchenettes set back from the water; deluxe junior suites with two queen-size beds, refrigerator, and furnished balcony overlooking the sea; and two- and three-bedroom villas.

The interiors are spacious, particularly in the newest units, with wood-beam ceilings and French doors leading to a patio overlooking the sea. Separated from their neighbors by greenery and walkways, the units convey a feeling of privacy and offer an unexpected level of luxury for their moderate rates. All the guest rooms are tastefully furnished, mostly with rattan.

Happy hours on the Kunuku Terrace, the oceanfront watering hole, attract divers from far and wide. Faucets, the open-air seaside restaurant, offers an eclectic menu of Italian, Cajun, and local dishes. A Texas barbecue one night and the Tex-Mex dinner another night are merry evenings that are usually well attended. Captain Don, although semiretired, usually appears for these special nights dressed in cowboy boots, Stetson, and fringe. You can't miss him.

The dive operation is one of the main PADI five-star training facilities in the Caribbean. You can dive here twenty-four hours a day, any day of the year. It has eight boats and a photo shop and offers every level of instruction, including underwater photography courses. Most guests come on packages that include tank, weights, and belt, unlimited free air, and at least one boat dive daily.

Although Habitat caters mainly to divers and would-be divers, it has other diversions such as Sunfish sailing and windsurfing. You can relax in the whirlpool, swim in the main pool set into a wooden deck by the sea, or soak up the sun on the resort's tiny strand of sand, appropriately named Seven Body Beach.

Habitat's exceptional staff is headed by Morey Ruza, a man of boundless energy, and his wife, Linda. They clearly want you to be comfortable and make every effort to help you enjoy your stay. Ruza has done an outstanding job in teaching the handicapped to dive. His young daughter conducts a snorkeling program for kids during the resort's two-week summer program in August. Children must be twelve years and older for scuba lessons. Captain Don, as loquacious as ever, is still a man with a mission. One of his recent projects enables individuals to sponsor and name their own site for donations of $150 or more. The program has added more than a hundred new sites to the marine park. Stewart also monitors popular sites, getting them closed temporarily when they show signs of distress.

Couples between the ages of thirty and fifty and families with kids old enough to dive make up the majority of guests. Most come on packages, which represent good value. You should, too.

Address/Phone: P.O. Box 88, Kralendijk, Bonaire, Netherlands Antilles; (599) 7–8290; Fax: (599) 7–8240
Owner: Don Stewart
Managing Director: Morey Ruza
Open: Year-round
Credit Cards: Major cards carry a 5 percent surcharge
U.S. Reservations: Captain Don's Habitat, (800) 327–6709, (305) 373–3341; Fax: (305) 371–2337
Deposit: $100 per person; full payment 30 days prior to arrival
Minimum Stay: None
Arrival/Departure: Transfer arranged on request
Distance from Airport: 6 miles; taxi one-way, $10
Distance from Kralendijk: 1 mile; taxi one-way, $3
Accommodations: 37 rooms and suites in cottages and villas (11 two-bedroom cottages, garden view); 16 deluxe, junior suites with kitchenette, furnished balcony; and 15 two- and three-bedroom villas with living room, kitchen on ground floor, and 2 superior bedrooms, private entrance on second floor, 1 bedroom has king-size bed and balcony, second bedroom has twin; the three-bedroom villas are similar with third bedroom on ground floor)
Amenities: Air-conditioning, ceiling fans; some bath with tub, most bath with shower, basket of toiletries; no room service
Electricity: 120 volts
Sports: Freshwater swimming pool. Full scuba program (see text). Boating, snorkeling, windsurfing, deep-sea fishing, hiking/trails arranged.
Dress Code: Bathing suits and shorts appropriate at all times
Children: Not suitable for children under 12, except during special family week, early August
Meetings: Up to 100 people

Day Visitors: Yes
Handicapped: Facilities
Packages: Dive, nondivers, family
Rates: Per person, weekly, with unlimited diving, CP. *High Season* (mid-December–mid-April): $928–$1,236. *Low Season:* Not available. Inquire for limited diving and non-diver rates.
Service Charge: 10 percent
Government Tax: 5 percent

Harbour Village Beach Resort ◓◓

Bonaire's first deluxe hotel, opened in 1990, is a real beauty. Harbour Village is set on a four-acre peninsula of a one-hundred-acre development on the leeward side of the island just north of town. It overlooks a quarter mile of palm-dotted white sand facing Bonaire's famous pristine reefs on one side and the resort's yacht-filled marina on the other.

A modern interpretation of Spanish colonial design, the resort is meant to resemble a small village by the sea, as the name implies—a very affluent small village, to be sure. It's complete with landscaped gardens, inner courtyards, arched doorways, terra-cotta patios, and cobblestone walkways. The two-story stucco "houses" painted ocher or salmon with white trim have balustraded balconies and red-tiled roofs. The setting is so picture-perfect that it looks like a movie set.

The spacious, stylish guest rooms and suites have white-tile floors and graceful French doors that open onto a patio or balcony. Most have views of the sea or the marina; some open onto a courtyard garden. They are smartly furnished in contemporary floral fabrics and quality wicker furniture. Each room has two double beds or a king-size one. If you stay in a beachfront room you can walk directly out through the French doors onto the beach. The complex also has villas, which are being sold as condominiums.

Kasa Coral, the dining terrace, is in the main building at the center of the resort and has an attractive setting overlooking the freshwater swimming pool. It serves breakfast, lunch, and dinner with a menu of island specialties and creative continental cuisine. A local combo entertains on weekends.

On a point at the end of the beach, La Balandra Bar and Grill serves lunch, happy-hour and after-dinner drinks, and special theme barbecues. This spot, while attractive, can be very windy at times. Lunch is also available poolside and on the beach.

Harbour Village's dive shop offers equipment rental, instruction, and certification and arranges snorkel and dive excursions to any of Bonaire's many renowned dive sites. The shop also offers fishing trips, boating, water-skiing, and more. Use of nonmotorized water-sports equipment—Sunfish, lasers, kayaks, windsurfers—is included in the room rate.

The resort has promotional packages with special low rates and free use of equipment for certified divers staying five nights or more. Check in advance from the hotel to learn what packages will be available during your visit. It could save you money.

Harbour Village's newest addition is a casino. For active travelers it has a fitness center, and it plans to add tennis and racquet courts and a spa. It is currently developing an ecotourism program with the assistance of experts from the University of Florida to stress Bonaire's other natural attractions, in addition to its coral gardens.

Harbour Village's marina, developed in conjunction with the government of Bonaire, has sixty slips accommodating boats up to 110 feet in length. The modern full-service facility is the only one of its kind on Bonaire and offers cable television, telephones, fax machines, rest rooms, showers, laundry machines, reception dock, trash removal, and VHF radio. A new marina fuel facility is opening soon; a 120-ton synchrolift and supply shop for on-site repair work are to be operational in early 1993.

The marina has sailing and fishing charters and can arrange for a captain. You can select anything from a day of pampering on a luxury yacht to a romantic sunset cruise on a 56-foot Siamese junk. A 30-foot fishing boat with gear and crew is available for half- or full-day deep-sea fishing.

In addition to being one of the prettiest resorts in the Caribbean, Harbour Village has the potential of becoming a truly outstanding one. It was plagued with growing pains for more than a year after it opened, but the arrivals in early 1992 of a new, well-qualified general manager and an equally experienced food and beverage manager have begun to make a difference.

Only a hop from the Venezuela coast, the resort has been discovered by Latin Americans as well as Europeans and North Americans. While any place on Bonaire would appeal to divers, Harbour Village is definitely a cut above the rest in style, ambience, and accommodations and has a broader appeal for anyone who wants a low-key beach holiday.

Address/Phone: Kaya Gobernador Debrot, Playa Lechi, Bonaire, N.A.; (599) 7-7500; Fax: (599) 7-7507
Owner: Coral Bay Resorts; Francisco Gonzalez, president of Tecnoconsult International
General Manager: John Lombardo
Open: Year-round

Credit Cards: All major

U.S. Reservations: First Class Resorts, (305) 669–0646; (800) 424–0004; Fax: (305) 669–0842

Deposit: One night, 3 nights during Christmas holidays

Minimum Stay: 7 nights during Christmas holidays

Arrival/Departure: Transfer service arranged for fee

Distance from Airport: 7 miles; taxi one-way, $8

Distance from Kralendijk: 2 miles; taxi one-way, $5

Accommodations: 64 guest rooms and 8 suites, all with terrace or balconies and 2 double beds or kings; 44 private villas

Amenities: Air-conditioning, ceiling fans, telephone, cable television, bath with tub and shower, basket of toiletries, bathrobe; ice service, nightly turndown service, room service 7:00 A.M. to 11:00 P.M., shop

Electricity: 120/220 volts

Sports: Private beach, freshwater swimming pool; marina, bicycle rentals. On-site water-sports operator with scuba diving, snorkeling, sailing, windsurfing, deep-sea fishing, and powerboat rides. Bike rental. Bird-watching excursions.

Dress Code: Casual by day; only slightly dressier in evening

Children: All ages; cribs, baby-sitters

Meetings: Up to 150 people

Day Visitors: Yes

Handicapped: Facilities

Packages: Dive, honeymoon

Rates: Per room, daily, EP. *High Season* (December 20–April 18): $235–$395. *Low Season*: $165–$195.

Service Charge: 10 percent on room rate; 15 percent on meal plans

Government Tax: 5 percent

British Virgin Islands

The Bitter End Yacht Club, Virgin Gorda

An archipelago of about fifty green, mountainous islands and cays scalloped with idyllic coves of white-sand beaches is spread over 59 square miles along Drake's Channel and the Anegada Passage between the Caribbean Sea and the Atlantic Ocean. Mostly volcanic in origin and uninhabited, the British Virgin Islands are almost as virgin as the day Christopher Columbus discovered them. Popular hiding places of pirates in olden days, these gems today are favorite hideaways of yachtsmen, for their good anchorage, and for vacationers fleeing the crowd.

The largest and most populated islands of this British Crown Colony are Tortola, the capital, and Virgin Gorda, to the east of Tortola. Several islands, such as Guana Island off Tortola's northeast coast and Peter Island to the southeast, have been developed as private resorts.

Tortola is best known as a yacht-chartering center. Its main town and port, Road Town, is the British Virgin Islands' commercial and residential hub. Other entry points are West End, where ferries from St. Thomas stop, and the airport on Beef Island, connected to Tortola's east end by a small bridge.

Virgin Gorda's largest settlement, Spanish Town, is located about mid-island. Little more than a hamlet a decade ago, the town has grown by leaps and bounds as the island has prospered from sheltering several of the Caribbean's most celebrated hideaways.

The B.V.I., as aficionados call them, do not appeal to everyone. They have no golf courses or casinos, and nighttime activity is very low-key. But they more than make up for the lack of razzle-dazzle with fabulous scenery and facilities, particularly for water sports.

Information

British Virgin Islands Tourist Board, 370 Lexington Avenue, New York, NY 10017; (212) 696–0400, (800) 835–8530.

Jost Van Dyke

Sandcastle ◙

Feel like dropping out? Want to hide out for a few days? Try Sandcastle. It's on tiny Jost Van Dyke, a remote island northeast of Tortola with only two hundred people.

That number is just fine for those who find their way to this heavenly haven. Here, there are no casinos, no native floor shows, no discos. There's no electricity either.

Sandcastle sits on a private half-mile stretch of powdery white sand with a lot of palm trees and tropical flowers, which seem to grow where they will. You stay in one of the four cottages, each housing two rooms. They are modestly but adequately furnished with most everything you'd need on a castaway island: twin beds that can be placed together, comfy chairs, coffee table, books, and an efficient toilet that is powered by dive tanks and works wonderfully well.

Light is supplied by propane lamps, and the water comes from heaven. Outdoor shower stalls are attached to each room; when you want a hot shower, you need to take it before the sun goes down, because the water is solar heated.

When you ask about the ceiling fans, an unusual part of the decor, considering the lack of electricity, owner Darrell Anderson, an expatriate from St. Petersburg, Florida, says he had installed them in anticipation several years ago when he was assured that electricity was due any day. The island road is progressing at about the same speed. But not to worry. No one seems to care. Life at Sandcastle is just too good the way it is.

The beachfront restaurant is the hotel's focal point and the food one of its highlights. Meals are included in the room rates, but dinner finds many other guests from yachts anchored offshore sitting down to savor dishes such as fresh grilled fish and key lime pie.

Sandcastle's reputation for superb food is well known in yachting circles; sailors simply pull their boats into the bay and transfer to shore via their dinghy. There is no dock; it's usually a step into the water before hitting dry land. Tables are lit by candlelight and adorned with soft pastel cloths and fresh flowers. It's all very romantic. Conversation can be lively or quiet, depending on the mix of guests.

You won't be at Sandcastle long before you'll be tempted to try a Painkiller. This yummy concoction (rum, coconut cream, fruit juice, and nutmeg), said to have originated here, comes in four versions from mild to lethal. Two at midday, and it's hammock time.

There's wonderful snorkeling on a reef within swimming distance from the beach. The first reef is in only 12 feet of water; the sea bottom then slopes to about 40 feet for a second reef, and about 400 yards from there is a wall with an 80-foot drop. It's great diving, if you come with dive gear. Windsurfing is good here, too, and when last we heard, Sandcastle was buying a new Sunfish.

For excitement it's a half-hour walk or a quick boat ride to Foxy's Tamarind Bar, the most famous watering hole in this part of the Caribbean. Foxy, the consummate Caribbean character, has a well-deserved reputation for his quick wit and talent on the guitar.

As you wander into his beachfront bar, Foxy is apt to pick out your red sun hat or spotted shirt and work it into the songs he composes as he goes along. Foxy doesn't miss much. Sailors make his bar a regular stop on their itinerary, as do some small cruise ships.

You could take an excursion or two to neighboring islands, but for most people the combination of sand, sea, and sun, along with the great cooking and a friendly staff, is enough.

Getting to Sandcastle requires a bit of scheduling and a lot of determination. You can fly to Tortola or St. Thomas. From Beef Island Airport on Tortola, it's a 45-minute taxi ride to the West End Ferry dock. From St. Thomas there's a ferry to West End several times daily, which takes one hour.

At West End Sandcastle's boat will meet you, and a half-hour or so later, you'll kick off your shoes and wade ashore while your boatman brings your luggage. Alternatively, from Red Hook on St. Thomas, the *Mona Queen* runs via St. John on Fridays and Sundays direct to Jost Van Dyke in forty-five minutes.

Pack light. You won't need much, just bathing suits and shorts. This is barefoot living at its best. Obviously, Sandcastle is not for everyone, but for some it's as near paradise as they need to be.

Address: Sandcastle, Ltd., Suite 237, Red Hook Plaza, St. Thomas, U.S.V.I. 00802. (809) 771–1611; Fax: (809) 775–3590
Owners: Kay and Darrell Anderson
Resident Manager: Robb Salvant
Open: Year-round
Credit Cards: Most major cards with 5 percent surcharge
U.S. Reservations: Direct to hotel
Deposit: $600 to confirm reservations; 60-day cancellation
Minimum Stay: 4 nights during winter season
Arrival/Departure: See text
Distance from West End (Tortola): 30 minutes by boat; from Red Hook (St. Thomas): 45 minutes
Accommodations: 8 rooms in 4 cottages, directly on beach, each room with twin beds and sitting area
Amenities: No appliances requiring electricity, outside shower stalls connected to each room, shop
Sports: Windsurfing and snorkeling equipment. Hammocks on beach.
Electricity: None
Dress Code: Very casual; bathing suits and bare feet
Children: None under 8 years of age
Meetings: None
Day Visitors: Welcome at restaurant and bar
Handicapped: No facilities
Packages: None
Rates: Two persons, daily, AP. *High Season* (mid-December–mid-April): $295. *Low Season:* $235.
Service Charge: $25 daily
Government Tax: 7 percent

Tortola

Guana Island ▣ ▣ ▣ ✿

A secluded rustic resort tucked into a far-from-it-all setting, Guana Island Club is one of the Caribbean's true hideaways. Low-key to a whisper, it is the sort of place that makes you happy to be alive to enjoy the simple beauty of nature.

Located off the northeast coast of Tortola, 850-acre Guana Island began as a private club in the 1930s. After purchasing it in 1974, its new owner modernized the facilities while retaining its rustic style and made it into a private nature sanctuary, leaving all but the small resort area crowning the topmost ridge undeveloped.

The resort, encased in gardens of hibiscus and oleander and shaded by flowering trees, accommodates a total of thirty guests in the main building and two clusters of whitewashed cottages, named for Caribbean islands. The cottages vary in size and layout, but each has its own special appeal. My favorite is Eleuthera, where you wake up to a fabulous view across the island and sea and in the evening take in 200 degrees of magnificent scenery bathed in sunset orange and red. Only the sounds of birds and crickets disturb the peace.

The guest rooms are actually junior suites with large verandas. The rooms are earthy, airy, comfortable, and cozy, furnished in rattan and local art against whitewashed stucco walls, set off by wood-beamed ceilings. All accommodations were recently upgraded and made very comfortable, particularly the bathrooms. Gone are the pull chains that used to be in the showers. Two new generators and a desalination plant have greatly increased the island's power and water supplies, so the electricity is no longer turned off at midnight as in the past.

Grenada, a modern villa with the resort's only pool, was added to the original six cottages. The villa rents as a three-bedroom unit with the pool or as three separate guest rooms without it. Another villa is being added next to it.

The main house, Dominica, is the social center. It includes a homey lounge with an honor bar, a library where winter evening chills are warmed by a fireplace, and a dining terrace where all meals and afternoon tea are served.

The lively atmosphere at cocktails in the lounge before dinner is more like a weekend house party than a hotel. Dinner is served family style, with seating arranged by the manager and rotated nightly. You dine by candlelight on a set menu that includes fresh seafood, home-baked breads, locally grown fruits and vegetables, and wine. There is a weekly beach barbecue.

After dinner you can join other guests in the lounge to listen to classical music over coffee, dance to recorded music, enjoy more conversation, or plan the next day's activities.

Guana Island boasts six untrampled porcelain beaches. Reef-protected White Bay, the "arrival" beach below the main house, is a powdery half-mile crest bathed by gin-clear waters ideal for swimming and snorkeling. A

Jeep will shuttle you to and fro, or you can walk on the island's only paved road. The more isolated beaches can be reached on hiking trails; two are accessible only by boat.

The owner's interest in conservation led him to make Guana a nature and wildlife preserve. He underwrites a summer program that due to the island's unusual nature—an ecosystem almost undisturbed for a century—brings a small army of scientists from Harvard University, The Nature Conservancy, and other institutions from afar to study and document its rich flora and fauna. They are also helping in a long-term program to restore the natural environment and reintroduce native species.

About fifty bird species can be seen regularly, and another fifty come at different times of the year. The pristine reefs near shore have 125 species of fish and dozens of species of coral. Maps of the island's two dozen trails are available. Be sure to bring comfortable walking shoes and binoculars.

While the personable managers are attentive and the friendly staff—most of whom have been at Guana for years—is helpful, no one pampers you. You set your own pace, do as little or as much as you want. There's lots of walking—hiking would be more accurate—to get to meals and the beach. But then, nature is what Guana is all about. If you need entertainment, or waiters at your beck and call, this is not the place for you.

Guana Island is limited to its guests; yachtees, cruise passengers, and day trippers are not welcomed. Although they have a legal right to come ashore, few do. The policy helps preserve Guana Island's ecology and the club's exclusivity.

Guana is designed for travelers who seek tranquillity, can operate on their own juices, and have a deep interest in nature. Your company will be mostly Americans from the East Coast, with a few British and other Europeans in the fifty-to-sixty age group. Guests at Christmas are younger, and honeymooners come in spring. If it's privacy you want, you can rent the entire island—as CEOs, wedding parties, and families on reunion sometimes do.

Address/Phone: Guana Island, B.V.I.; (809) 494–2354; Fax: (809) 494–2900
Owners: Henry and Gloria Jarecky
Resident Managers: Beverly and Walter Plachta
Open: Year-round except September and October
Credit Cards: None; personal and travelers checks accepted
U.S. Reservations: Guana Island, (800) 544–8262, (914) 967–6050; Fax: (914) 967–8048
Deposit: 3 nights per booking, 30 days cancellation; policy differs for Christmas/New Year's (inquire)
Minimum Stay: 3 nights
Arrival/Departure: Guests met at Beef Island Airport by Guana's boatman

and taken to nearby dock to board resort's motorboat for 10-minute ride to island; $25 per person is added to your bill for round-trip transfer.

Distance from Airport: 10 minutes by boat

Distance from Road Town: 30 minutes by boat and road; from launch dock to town, one-way, $12

Accommodations: 15 rooms and junior suites in 7 hillside cottages, all with twin or king beds and verandas

Amenities: Ceiling fans, flashlights, umbrellas, rack for wet bathing suits, baths with shower only; no air-conditioning, telephone, radio, or television

Electricity: 110 volts

Sports: 2 tennis courts (clay and all-weather Omni). Self-service beach bar with water-sports equipment, dressing and rest rooms, lounging chairs, and hammocks. Use of courts, racquets, fishing rods, snorkeling gear, sailboats, waterskis, and windsurfers free; deep-sea fishing charters arranged. Tennis balls and fishing tackle sold at tiny boutique.

Dress Code: Casual; coverup and shoes at breakfast and lunch. Dinner slightly dressier.

Children: None in high season; at other times inquire in advance.

Meetings: Groups up to 30 persons can rent the whole island.

Day Visitors: No

Handicapped: Very limited facilities

Packages: None

Rates: Two persons, daily, AP. *High Season* (December 15–March 31): $530. *Low Season:* $395.

Service Charge: 12 percent

Government Tax: 7 percent

Peter Island Resort & Yacht Harbour ◙◙◙◙

Set on some of the most beautiful beaches in the Caribbean and surrounded by forested hills with pretty vistas at every turn, posh Peter Island has evolved from a small exclusive yacht haven created in 1971 into a full-scale resort.

Covering 1,050 acres of the private island's 1,800 green, hilly acres, Peter Island is perennially named as one of the Caribbean's top resorts. It was all but blown away by Hurricane Hugo in 1989, and rebuilding took fifteen months.

The resort is laid out in two areas: the original A-frame cottages over-looking the yacht basin; and the newer, more deluxe, villas hidden beneath a forest of palm trees on Deadman Bay, the main beach. The latter have spacious beachfront junior suites, smartly dressed in bleached wood and rattan furniture.

A windowed section between the large bath and the bedroom looks onto a small garden, enhancing the tropical feeling. (You can actually see the sea while you are taking a shower.) A mini-bar and desk combination separates the bedroom from the sitting area; glass doors open onto open terraces with dreamy sea views. A bottle of wine and fruit will be waiting for you upon check-in.

The A-frames have been upgraded, but they're still less deluxe and thus less expensive than the beachfront rooms. Each cottage has four large bedrooms: two on the ground floor with patios and two above with high-beamed ceilings and decks overlooking the harbor on the south and Drake's Channel on the north.

The Crow's Nest is a fabulous villa with four bedrooms, each with a private balcony and bath, game room, entertainment system and library, wine cellar, and saltwater pool surrounded by flagstone terraces. It has a staff of two maids, gardener, and a cook; a Jeep for your exclusive use is provided. Situated on the highest point of the island, with spectacular views, its price is spectacular, too.

The main building, next to the pool, is convenient to the dock and A-frame cottages. It houses the lobby with television that carries CNN and other cable programs; dining room, where breakfast and dinner are served; a library with daily newspapers; and fitness room with an array of exercise equipment. First-run movies are shown nightly in the Meeting Room.

The Beach Bar and Grill on Deadman Bay Beach is the casual setting for lunch and the weekly evening barbecue with steel-band entertainment. Tea is served daily in the bar area near the pool. Dinner by candlelight is set in the main dining room, and al fresco by the pool, weather permiting. Menus are changed daily, and recently light fare was added to the classic repertoire. Hotel guests must reserve for dinner, as the dining terrace is a popular stop for yachts sailing the Virgin Islands. Drake's Channel, the main lounge, has a romantic terrace setting with music by a different combo nightly for dancing under the stars.

Each of Peter Island's five beaches is memorable. On Deadman Bay beach you will find thatched umbrellas and lounge chairs near the bar, the water-sports center, and hammocks hidden among the trees. Farther east, Little Deadman Bay is a mini-mirror image of the main beach, and secluded Honeymoon Beach has one thatched umbrella and two chairs. It's for all romantics, not just honeymooners, but only one couple at a time, please.

The grounds in the immediate vicinity of the resort are landscaped and manicured, but the remainder of the island has been left to nature. Peter Island's horticulturist conducts a walking tour weekly and the resort offers a free safari bus tour of the island with a guide. If you want to explore on your own, Peter Island has 10 miles of dirt roads and hiking paths to be taken on foot or by bike, conventional or mountain. There's a trail map to help you find your way home.

Peter Island has always enjoyed a glamorous image, and its location insures a certain privacy, but the increase in group and meeting business has lessened its exclusivity and added a commercial quality. It holds the most appeal for active couples, families with children, yachtsmen, and other outdoor enthusiasts.

Address/Phone: P.O. Box 211, Road Town, Tortola, B.V.I.; or P.O. Box 9409, St. Thomas, U.S.V.I. 00801; (809) 494–2561; Fax: (809) 494–2313

Owner: The Amway Corporation

General Manager: James Holmes

Open: Year-round

Credit Cards: All major

U.S. Reservations: Peter Island Resort and Yacht Harbour, (616) 776–6456, (800) 346–4451; Fax: (616) 776–6496. Preferred Hotels and Resorts Worldwide, (800) 323–7500

Deposit: 3 nights within 10 days of reservations

Minimum Stay: 7 nights during Christmas

Arrival/Departure: Guests arriving at Beef Island Airport transfer directly to resort's motorlaunch for 4-mile trip across Drake's Channel to Peter Island. Resort also operates up to 8 round trips of free ferry service to its dock at Baughers Bay in Tortola. Transfer by helicopter directly to resort's lighted helipad arranged from St. Thomas, San Juan, or neighboring islands as far south as Antigua. Guests also arrive by yacht.

Distance from Airport: (Tortola) Approximately 4 miles

Accommodations: 54 rooms (30 ocean/harbor view in A-frames with twin beds and kings, 20 junior suites in beachfront buildings with king beds; four-bedroom villa), all with verandas

Amenities: Air-conditioning, ceiling fans, mini-bar, coffee maker, telephone; bathrooms have double sinks, tub, shower, hairdryers, bathrobes, toiletries by Amway; room service for continental breakfast; no television

Electricity: 110 volts

Sports: 4 Tru-flex tennis courts (2 lighted); tennis pro; equipment. Small boats, windsurfers, and free introductory instructions; advanced lessons for fee. Yacht harbor with new dock and a fleet of Bertrams for fishing charters and custom-built motor launch for sight-seeing. Snorkeling gear free. Dive BVI, on-site operator.

Dress Code: Strict at dinner, men required to wear sport coats (no tie) in winter season

Children: All ages; cribs, high chairs, baby-sitters

Meetings: Up to 50 people; audiovisual equipment

Day Visitors: Welcome

Handicapped: Limited facilities

Packages: Learn-to-dive, ashore/afloat, honeymoon, Ultimate Fantasy week at hard-to-believe price of $35,000

Rates: Two persons, daily, FAP. *High Season* (mid-December–mid-April): $475–$595. *Low Season*: $375–$495.

Service Charge: 10 percent

Government Tax: 7 percent

Sugar Mill Hotel ◉◉

Set on a hillside overlooking Apple Bay on Tortola's quiet north coast, Sugar Mill is a cozy country inn as well known for its restaurant as for its hotel. Owned and operated by veteran travel and food writers Jinx and Jeff Morgan, Sugar Mill reflects their warm and engaging personalities in every way.

You will probably be invited to have drinks with the Morgans soon after you arrive, and they will certainly visit with you during dinner to make certain all is well. Minutes after your first meeting, you'll feel you have known them all your life.

A decade ago the Morgans gave up what many people might consider the ideal life to become Caribbean innkeepers. As successful California-based writers, they had traveled the globe on assignments for leading travel magazines and sampled food at world-renowned restaurants for their monthly column in *Bon Appétit*. Each had written books on food and wine, including such titles as *Saucepans and the Single Girl* and *Two Cooks in One Kitchen*.

Then in 1981 the Morgans saw a magazine ad for a manager for Sugar Mill; they replied with an offer to buy the hotel instead. With only forty-eight hours to spare between deadlines, they flew to Tortola for their first visit, and—well, you already know the result.

Sugar Mill is divided into two sections by the small road that skirts the north coast of Tortola. Instead of the usual lobby, at the hotel entrance you will find an outdoor gazebo-lounge, all but concealed in a riot of flowers and tropical greenery. It is adjacent to the bar, which doubles as the reception, library, and boutique, and leads to an open-air terrace where breakfast is served. Behind it is the restored remnant of a 350-year-old sugar mill for which the inn is named and which houses the main dining room.

Hugging the steep hillside above the mill are clusters of two-story buildings containing the hotel's rooms and suites—all with balconies overlooking the lovely gardens and a small terraced swimming pool. The rooms, furnished mainly in wicker, are comfortable but not fancy and, in fact, could benefit from some upgrading. They have small kitchen units that families with children particularly appreciate.

The lower section of the hotel sits at the edge of the sea where there are two waterside restaurants: the Sand Bar, a luncheon venue next to a small beach with lounging chairs; and the newest addition, Islands, with an informal, open-to-the breezes setting for lunch and dinner, where, as the name suggests, the specialties are Caribbean fare.

The old stone sugar mill, under a high, cedar-lined roof with ceiling fans, the warm glow of candlelight, fresh flowers, colorful Haitian paintings, and watercolors by Jinx on the walls—and classical music playing in the background—all make up the inviting setting in which you will enjoy the inn's celebrated cuisine. The Sugar Mill is usually filled with patrons from other hotels and residents of Tortola.

The Morgans have created their own California-cum-Caribbean treats, relying as much as possible on fresh local ingredients—often from their own garden—and working closely with their chefs to turn out interesting and imaginative dishes.

Menus are changed daily and rotated over several weeks. They feature such specialties as chilled mango or curried banana soup, poached scallops with roasted red pepper sauce, fresh fish with coral sunset sauce, grilled quail with mango-papaya sauce, and chicken breast with chutney cream sauce. Many of the recipes are included in the *Sugar Mill Hotel Cookbook*.

Given Jeff's expertise in California wines (he has written three books on the subject), it's no surprise that the extensive wine list highlights California vintages. He has written brief descriptions of each wine to help guests make their selections.

Sugar Mill gets a great variety of guests—celebrity friends, movie stars, artists, writers, and just plain folks. Many are repeaters—Americans, Canadians, and British—who appreciate the food and enjoy the inn's homey, informal atmosphere. Some come for the workshops conducted by established artists and sponsored by the Morgans from time to time.

Sugar Mill is a bit remote—for many that's part of its charm. Car rental can be arranged through the hotel; you'll need it if you want to explore the island.

Address/Phone: Box 425, Road Town, Apple Bay, Tortola, B.V.I.; (809)
495–4355, (800) 462–8834; Fax: (809) 495–4696

Owners: Jinx and Jeff Morgan

General Manager: Patrick Conway

Open: Year-round

Credit Cards: All major

U.S. Reservations: Caribbean Inns, (800) 633–7411, (803) 785–7411; Fax:
(803) 686-7411

Deposit: 3 days; 30 days cancellation

Minimum Stay: 7 nights for Christmas/New Year's; 3 nights high season

Arrival/Departure: Transfer arranged on request for fee

Distance from Airport: (Beef Island Airport) 18 miles (45 minutes); taxi
one-way, $24

Distance from Road Town: 10 miles; taxi one-way, $20, from West End
ferry dock, 3 miles; taxi one-way, $5.

Accommodations: 22 units (2 standard rooms; 18 double rooms with terrace and kitchen including 4 family suites; 1 two-bedroom villa; twin
and king-size beds)

Amenities: Ceiling fans, telephone, bath with shower only; no air-
conditioning (except villa) or room service

Electricity: 110 volts/60 cycles

Sports: Freshwater swimming pool, small beach and beautiful long strands
nearby. Free snorkeling gear. Free scuba resort course. Deep-sea fishing, hiking, and other sports arranged.

Dress Code: Casual

Children: Over 10 years in winter; baby-sitters

Meetings: No

Day Visitors: Welcome in small numbers

Handicapped: No facilities

Packages: Honeymoon

Rates: Two persons, daily, EP. *High Season* (mid-December–mid-April):
$150-$275. *Shoulder Season* (April 15–May 31; November 1–December
20): $125–$205. *Low Season* (June 1–October 31): $120–$180.

Service Charge: 10 percent

Government Tax: 7 percent

Virgin Gorda

Biras Creek ▣▣▣▣ 🍃

A masterpiece of British understatement far off the beaten path, Biras Creek is a hideaway in every sense. Small and secluded, the quietly posh resort is designed for relaxing and luxuriating in privacy in a casual, unpretentious, yet sophisticated, ambience.

Much of the resort's privacy is all but guaranteed by its location, accessible only by boat and reached by the resort's private launch—or by your own yacht. Set in 140 acres of nature preserve on an isthmus of green hills that brackets the northern end of Virgin Gorda, the resort overlooks North Sound, a huge deep-water bay that has long been a yachtsman's mecca. On the north and east is the Atlantic and to the west—the side on which you arrive—the Caribbean.

On approach from the water, all you see is a stone fortresslike structure with a steep carousel roof atop a small rise at the center of the property. Built in terraces and approached by several sets of interconnected stone steps, "the castle" serves as the reception, dining, and social center with an inside/outside terraced restaurant and bar commanding a lovely panoramic view.

The resort's size and layout also help to insure privacy. Hidden under enormous almond and seagrape trees that provide shade and maximize privacy are sixteen cottages, each with two suites. They skirt the crest of Bercher's Bay, where the Atlantic roars in—too rough for swimming but great for cooling breezes to lull you to sleep. Cottage 11A is so close to the sea, it's like being on a ship—in a storm.

Each suite has a large bedroom and sitting room with a comfortable chair, writing desk, and bed-cum-sofa with mountains of pillows. Sliding glass doors open onto an ocean-view terrace with lounging chairs—the perfect nook for afternoon reading or dozing. The bathroom features a delightful open-air shower with a tropical garden, enclosed by an 8-foot patio wall but open overhead to trees and blue skies.

Terra-cotta-tile floors and the ocean breezes sailing through the screen doors and louvered windows keep the tree-shaded rooms cool. A bottle of rum or wine and basket of fruit will be awaiting your arrival. Near your cottage door you'll find two bicycles for your exclusive use.

All but two suites are identical and were recently given a fresh new look by the talented artist/designer Jillian Dunlap, who has brightened the once-drab decor with color and touches of whimsy in unusual objets d'art.

They complement the cheerful, wispy designs on her hand-painted fabrics.

The two newest suites—16A and 16B—are super deluxe with luxuriously spacious sitting rooms, bedrooms, and baths and some of the most handsome, unusual decor of any hotel room in the Caribbean. Pelican Point, a hillside villa ideal for a family, has two bedrooms, two baths, a spacious living/dining area, a wraparound balcony, and a large patio—all with sweeping vistas.

Running from the castle to the hillsides are 25 landscaped acres watched over by Biras Creek's gardener, Alvin Harrigan, who has tended the gardens since the resort opened in 1974. Harrigan guides a weekly garden tour. The remaining 115 acres of the estate have been left to nature and have trails.

Biras Creek's freshwater pool at the foot of the castle has lounging chairs and thatched roof sun shelters. A secluded beach at tranquil Deep Bay is a ten-minute walk or a five-minute bike ride from your cottage. En route you pass the tennis courts and a small estuary, a favorite spot for bird-watchers. Next to the beach a large thatched-roof pavilion has a bar (open daily) and picnic tables where lunch barbecues are served twice weekly.

Biras Creek's open-air dining room in the hilltop castle is cheerful by day with sunlight flooding the open terraces and romantic by night with candlelit tables and soft background music. The restaurant serves three meals and afternoon tea. From its inception, Biras Creek established a reputation for fine cuisine and an impressive wine list, which it tries to maintain.

The bar adjoining the main dining room is a delightful open-air lounge and a popular gathering spot before dinner. The weekly manager's party here features a local combo. On Thursdays a ballad singer entertains at dinner, and on Saturday a combo plays for dancing under the stars; movie videos are shown nightly.

The service at Biras is as noteworthy in the restaurant, where a caring staff works quietly and efficiently, as in the rooms, where the housekeeping staff keeps your suite in top shape. They also change your towels twice daily, bring ice, take laundry, and turn down your bed at night.

Address/Phone: Box 54, Virgin Gorda, B.V.I.; (809) 494–3555/6; Fax: (809) 494–3557

Owner: Mowinekels Shipping Co.

Resident Managers: Nigel and Marion Adams

Open: Year-round

Credit Cards: All major

U.S. Reservations: Ralph Locke Islands, (800) 223–1108; Fax: (914) 763–5362

Deposit: 3 days

Minimum Stay: 7 days during Christmas

Arrival/Departure: Free transfer with 7-day stay. From Virgin Gorda Airport, you take a scenic, 25-minute jitney bus ride to dock at Gun Creek on north end (almost length of island). There resort's water taxi picks you up for a 10-minute ride across North Sound to Biras Creek. From Tortola, North Sound Express zips you from a dock near Beef Island Airport directly to Biras Creek. Ferries from Road Town go to Bitter End's dock, where Biras's boat picks you up.

Distance from Airport: (Spanish Town) 8 miles; taxi one-way, $10; ferry from Beef Island one-way, $15

Accommodations: 32 two-room suites in 16 cottages with twin, queen, or king beds (great mattress); 22 oceanview, 8 garden view, 2 grand suites, all with verandas; 1 two-bedroom villa

Amenities: Ceiling fans, coffee makers, small refrigerator; no air-conditioning, phones, television, locks on doors, or room service

Electricity: 110 volts/60 cycles

Sports: Freshwater pool, 2 lighted tennis courts; free use of courts, equipment, sailboats, snorkel, and windsurfing equipment and instruction, and frequent trips to nearby secluded sands. Waterskiing, fishing charters, day and sunset cruises, dive courses, and certification arranged for fee. Dive BVI dive masters conduct free introductory scuba lessons.

Dress code: Casual by day; cover-up and footwear required in dining room and bar. Informally elegant for evening. Men not required to wear tie and jacket, but many do.

Children: Over 6; baby-sitters

Meetings: Up to 20 people

Day Visitors: Welcome with 24-hour notice

Handicapped: No facilities

Packages: Off-season, honeymoon, Sailaway, family, wedding

Rates: Per person, double, daily, AP. *High Season* (mid-December–mid-April): $212.50–$237.50. *Low Season:* $175–$200. Weekly rates available.

Service Charge: 10 percent

Government Tax: 7 percent

The Bitter End Yacht Club ◙ ◙ ◙ ◙

Although The Bitter End Yacht Club and Resort shares the waters of North Sound, and partly the same owners, with Biras Creek, the two resorts are as different as you could imagine.

Bitter End, stretching almost a mile along the north shore of the sound, is as big and busy as Biras Creek is small and serene. The twenty-five-acre resort was begun in the 1960s as a watering hole for yachtsmen. When a Chicago businessman, Myron Hokin, sailed by on a fishing trip in 1972, he recognized the value of Bitter End's superb anchorage—the last outpost before the open waters of the Atlantic—and bought the property.

In 1988 Bitter End merged with neighboring Tradewinds, a more upscale resort, and doubled in size overnight. In addition to more facilities and rooms, Bitter End gained a wider range of style, broadening its appeal and transforming it from a boating haven to a full-scale resort.

Only steps from the beach, the original thatched cottages, upgraded in 1991, continue to be the most popular. They are nicely but simply furnished, most with twin beds.

Climbing the wooded hillsides above the Clubhouse to the east are the deluxe chalets in jungle gardens; they're connected to one another by wooden walkways and catwalks like tree houses. Each chalet has two units—one studio and one suite—and balconies with fabulous views of the sound. The two units can be combined into a two-bedroom cottage. The rooms have peaked, wooden ceilings and are tastefully decorated in wicker with rich fabrics and grass-cloth wallcovering. The Estate House is a posh, secluded two-bedroom villa above the clubhouse, with a large living room, separate dining area, screened porch, and wraparound veranda.

If you can't decide between a land or sea vacation, or simply want to sample life aboard a sailboat, you have an alternative. In combination with a hotel stay, you can rent a Freedom 20 complete with provisions—and never leave the marina. The live-aboard package includes meals at the resort's restaurants and unlimited free use of the resort's watercraft and other amenities.

Bitter End's facilities are in a medley of buildings by the water. Dining is set in two beachside pavilions, both with a comfortable ambience. The cuisine, created by European-trained chefs, is popular with the sailing community, which often ties up at the marina to enjoy the cocktail and dinner hour and entertainment.

The Clubhouse, an inside restaurant with a tree-shaded terrace, serves three meals daily. Continental breakfast and light lunches are available poolside; the English Pub at The Emporium serves pizza, Chicago hot dogs, nachos, and more.

The more sedate Pavilion Dining Room of the English Carvery, open four nights a week, has a traditional carving board along with other entrees. Candlelight dinners end with soft music and dancing.

Entertainment is one of the resort's big draws, attracting guests from neighboring hotels as well as boaters. You can enjoy music in the lobby on Monday and Wednesday, a piano bar, a jazz club, the mellow calypso melodies of guitarist Eldon John, beach barbecues with calypso, and sunset and moonlight cruises. Movies, major sporting events, and CNN's daily news program are shown at the Sand Palace, an open-air video and television theater. The Reflections, Bitter End's own steel band combo made up of eight employees, entertain several nights weekly at the Clubhouse.

Even with its expansion, Bitter End remains above all a yacht club. Nautical themes are everywhere, and the flags of yacht clubs from around the world hang in the Clubhouse. The resort's fleet of more than one hundred craft is available to guests for their unlimited use. It includes twenty-four Lasers and twelve Sunfish, among others. The resort offers day charters, deep-sea fishing boats, snorkeling, and sight-seeing boats, as well as a semisubmersible for underwater tours.

And if you don't know the difference between the jib and the spinnaker, Bitter End provides free sailing lessons, along with windsurfing and snorkeling instruction. Nick Trotter's Sailing School based here holds classes for all levels of skill. Fast Tack in November is an annual month-long, action-packed promotion of Bitter End's sailing facilities. Daily dive classes for beginners and trips for certified divers are also available.

Bitter End's easygoing atmosphere attracts sports enthusiasts of all ages—singles, couples, honeymooners, and families. Most are affluent, active, and somewhat preppie Americans, but there is a sprinkling of Europeans. Life here is so water-oriented that someone who has no interest in sailing or water sports should look elsewhere. But if you love the sea, this little corner of the Caribbean is paradise.

Address/Phone: North Sound, Virgin Gorda, B.V.I. (809) 494–2746; Fax: (809) 494–4756
Owner: Myron Hokin
General Manager: Bruce Hearn
Open: Year-round
Credit Cards: All major
U.S. Reservations: Bitter End Yacht Club and Resort, (312) 944–5855, (800) 872–2392; Fax: (312) 944–2860
Deposit: 3 nights
Minimum Stay: None

Arrival/Departure: Transfers included in 7-day packages; otherwise cost is $36 round-trip

Distance from Airport: (Virgin Island Airport, Spanish Town) 30-minute bus ride (one-way, $12), plus 10-minute boat ride

Accommodations: 83 rooms and suites with verandas (43 in rustic cottages; 38 in deluxe chalets with twin, queen, or king beds; two-bedroom villa) and 10 liveaboard boats

Amenities: Air-conditioning, ceiling fans, hairdryer, coffee makers, refrigerators; VCRs in suites; towels changed twice daily, turndown service nightly; no phones, television, or room service; bath with showers only; shops and mini-market

Electricity: 110 volts/60 cycles

Sports: Sailing/water sports (see text); 1 swimming pool, 3 beaches, jogging/exercise trail; marina with 30 slips.

Dress Code: Informal

Children: 7 and older; supervised activities; sailing lessons; baby-sitters

Meetings: Up to 100 persons; conference center, audiovisual equipment

Handicapped: Limited facilities

Day Visitors: Welcome

Packages: Honeymoon, family, Fast Tack, Liveaboard, weddings

Rates: Two persons, daily, FAP. *High Season* (mid-December–mid-April): $400-$475. *Shoulder Seasons* (September 6–October 22): $290–$320; (October 23–December 19): $320–$395. *Low Season* (April 19–September 5): $320-$395.

Service Charge: $12 per person per day

Government Tax: 7 percent

Little Dix Bay ▨▨▨▨

Opened in the early 1960s, Rockresorts—exclusive enclaves renowned for their spectacular natural settings, begun by conservationist pioneer Laurance Rockefeller (hence the name)—became the standard against which all other Caribbean resorts were measured.

Understated and environmentally sensitive long before conservation became a fashionable cause, they were a new kind of resort where less is more. The accommodations were almost spartan in their simplicity: no phones, air-conditioning, radios, television, or room keys. Peace, privacy, and natural beauty—no man-made trappings—were their special appeal.

The people who patronized them were not unlike Mr. Rockefeller— Eastern establishment, Wall Street bankers, old money, Ivy Leaguers, Junior

Leaguers, and their preppie offspring who could be themselves in a low-key, unpretentious atmosphere.

Despite changes in ownership over the years, the Rockresorts formula has remained intact, enabling Little Dix—one of the Caribbean's most expensive resorts—to boast a year-round occupancy of 90 percent, a repeat business of 70 percent, and a place on the coveted "Ten Best" list of *The Hideaway Report* year after year.

Little Dix is set in a five-hundred-acre garden paradise along a half-mile white sand beach on the northwest side of Virgin Gorda, with the green slopes of Gorda Peak as a backdrop. Still exclusive but not quite as snooty as in its formative years, Little Dix's service and country-club atmosphere begin as soon as you step off the plane at the tiny Virgin Gorda Airport (which Little Dix Bay owns). There you are met, registered (the hotel has no lobby or social desk), and driven directly to your beachside room, where you will find fresh flowers, a bottle of rum, and soft drinks.

Camouflaged under dense tropical foliage, Little Dix's spacious guest rooms, each with its own terrace overlooking the sea, are in clusters of cottages—some hexagonal and cone-topped, some conventional—with two to eight rooms. Those rooms behind the beachfront cottages are perched on stilts like tree houses to catch the trade winds; they have ground-level patios and hammocks.

The rooms make use of native stone and island hardwoods in their decor. Once dark and rather gloomy, the rooms have been redecorated in cheery pastels accented with bleached wicker and cane furniture and made more plush; there are good reading lamps. Walk-in closets contain umbrellas, walking sticks, and flashlights to help you find your way along the paths at night. Outside each cottage is a foot bath to rinse the sand from your feet; bicycles for guests' use are parked randomly throughout the hotel grounds.

Fifteen gardeners maintain the landscaped grounds. Walkways meander from one cottage cluster to another along softly sloping lawns under canopies of mahogany, samaan, and other tropical trees. A weekly garden tour conducted by the staff horticulturist is not to be missed.

Daytime activities—most included in the room rate—can be as strenuous as lazing on a bright yellow float on smooth azure water (a protective reef keeps it that way) or more demanding, with aerobics classes, tennis, Sunfish sailing, water-skiing, and scuba lessons. A water taxi will take you to one of eight pristine beaches to snorkel, sunbathe, and picnic.

Little Dix has a sloop-rigged trimaran for sailing, and a Bertram for fishing charters; Rockefeller's 49-foot Hinckley, *Evening Star,* is available for picnic day sails (for a fee). Near Little Dix, the Virgin Gorda Yacht Harbor, also owned by Rockresorts, is home to more than a hundred boats, many available for charter.

In the evening you can join other guests on the main terrace to listen to a local group play calypso, reggae, and easy-listening tunes; enjoy the guitarist after dinner; or take a sunset cruise. First-run movies are shown in an open-air living room.

The center of life at Little Dix Bay is The Pavilion, a terrace with four interconnected dining and lounge areas topped with a soaring, four-point shingled roof where lavish breakfasts and lunch buffets, afternoon tea, and candlelight dinners are served. The oceanfront Beach House offers light lunches and cocktails. For Thursday lunch guests are taken by Boston Whalers to Spring Bay for a beach party.

Cuisine in the Rockresort tradition is American and dependably good, if uninspired. Some updating has added nouvelle touches such as lightly sautéed seafood and chilled fruit soups. Menus change daily and feature grilled steak and local fish.

The informal Sugar Mill Restaurant and Bar, adjacent to the main terrace, is a dinner alternative with candlelit tables, dressed in fine linen, perched on the sand only a few feet from the lightly lapping waves. The service is first class all the way.

Indeed, service is one of Little Dix Bay's strengths. Most employees are Virgin Gorda natives who have been at Little Dix for more than a decade, giving the resort a sense of family.

Most of Little Dix's patrons are couples between the ages of fifty and sixty-five, but at the height of honeymoon season, Little Dix becomes a little love nest with many newlyweds following in the footsteps of their parents who honeymooned here.

Address/Phone: P.O. Box 70, Virgin Gorda, B.V.I.; (809) 495–5555, (800) 223–7637; Fax: (809) 495–5661

Owner: Rockresorts, Inc.

Vice President/Managing Director: David Brewer

Open: Year-round

Credit Cards: All major

U.S. Reservations: Rockresorts, Inc., (800) 223–7637, (212) 765–5950; Fax: (212) 956–6424

Deposit: 3 nights; 28-day cancellation, peak season; 7-day cancellation in low season

Minimum Stay: High season, inquire in advance

Arrival/Departure: Transfer service included

Distance from Airport: (Virgin Gorda Airport) About 1 mile

Distance from Spanish Town: 2 miles; taxi one-way, $5

Accommodations: 102 double rooms with twin or king-size beds in two-story villas and two-bedroom cottages, all with sitting area and terrace

Amenities: Ceiling fans, mini-bars, safes; bathrooms with double sinks and showers only, bathrobes, basket of toiletries; some have hairdryers; nightly turndown service, towels changed and ice service twice daily; room service for continental breakfast

Electricity: 110 volts/60 cycles

Sports: No swimming pool or windsurfing. Seven Decoralt tennis courts (none lit), clinics, free beginners' lesson; resident pro; hiking trails. Dive trips for fee.

Dress Code: Gracious informality. Trousers and long-sleeve shirts required after 6:30 P.M.; jackets and ties not required

Children: 8 or older; baby-sitters

Meetings: Up to 20 people

Handicapped: 4 rooms with facilities

Day Visitors: Individuals welcome with advance reservations

Packages: Honeymoon, family, tennis, Land-Sea, dive, wedding

Rates: Two persons, daily, EP. *High Season* (December 19–March 31): $390–$540. *Low Season* (April 1–December 18): $190–$270.

Service Charge: 5 percent of room rate; 15 percent of meals or meal plan

Government Tax: 7 percent hotel tax

Necker Island ⚙⚙⚙⚙⚙ 🌿

For the ultimate escape to the ultimate private island hideaway, there is only one choice: the island haven created by Richard Branson, Britain's boy-wonder entrepreneur (founder of Virgin Records and Virgin Airways), as a holiday retreat for his family and friends.

As laid-back as his resort, Branson is so low-key that it's hard to link the man with the success story—until you see how it all comes together in his Caribbean paradise.

Located at the northeastern end of the British Virgin Islands, Necker is a small, dry, rocky island encircled by coral reefs and lapped by the waters that run from cobalt and peacock blue to aquamarine. The island has dramatic scenery at every turn: jutting headlands interspersed with pristine beaches, panoramic hills, and cactus-studded ridges—and, always, that spectacular water.

By his telling, in the 1970s Branson (then still in his twenties), was in New York on business when he heard that some of the BVI were up for sale. He went to have a look, but it took two years before the price was right.

An environmental-impact study to help maintain the seventy-four-acre island's ecological balance was carried out, and construction atop "Devil's

Hill" began in 1982. Wherever possible, natural materials—including the stone removed from the hilltop—were used in construction.

"I wanted the house designed in an airy Balinese style . . . where the architecture blends so well with the country and culture," Branson says. "I also wanted the house to become the apex of Devil's Hill, as if it grew out of the rock."

He got his wish. On approach to Necker, you must look hard to see the Balinese-style villa, it harmonizes so well with the landscape.

The palatial mansion divides into two sections: an enormous living room and dining area in the front and ten bedrooms on two levels to the back. The huge, open living room with exposed beams of Brazilian hardwood overhead and Yorkshire granite floors underfoot is created around a tropical garden. Large sections of the roof left as natural skylights and a retractable roof allow sunlight to shower the garden, creating a magical effect during the day and a canopy of stars at night.

The enormous room is a combination living-dining-bar area and is furnished with elephant bamboo chairs and oversized cushions on natural stone banquettes. A giant oak refectory table seating twenty-two people occupies one corner, a snooker table occupies another, and a piano and television/video cabinet with a library of movie cassettes another. Steps in the center of the room lead up to a gallery lined with books, tapes, and games.

Surrounding the house on all sides are spacious terraces festooned with brilliant bougainvillea, allamanda, and other tropical flowers that overlook the sea and drop down to a lower level, where there is a swimming pool and Jacuzzi. There's a telescope for serious stargazers and hammocks for guests who simply want to dream.

A breezeway with tropical greenery leading to the bedroom wing ends in front of a ceiling-to-floor waterfall that catches the light as it tumbles through a chain sculpture. The bedrooms, all with terraces, have views that embrace the sea, the sky, sun, moon, and neighboring islands, too.

Named after Indonesian islands, the bedrooms combine vibrant Balinese fabrics—each with a different color scheme—and elephant bamboo furniture, accented by Haitian paintings. The master suite on the upper level is Branson's Bali—and it was Princess Diana's during her stay. It has a huge terrace and a large wooden deck with its own Jacuzzi. The villa has eight comfortable bathrooms with stone-grotto showers that actually cleverly conceal the drain pipes.

Dan and Barbara Reid, a charming English couple who manage the island, are in charge of menus and meals featuring sophisticated fare, as fresh as they can make it. You are summoned to dinner by a gong and will feel as royal as her highness when you dine at the regal dining table. There are outside dining areas, as well.

Both sides of the island are etched with dreamy white-sand beaches. Devil's Beach, on the west, has a fine coral reef only a short snorkel away. Well Beach, a long curve of sand on the southeast, has a raised Balinese pavilion with giant bamboo chairs and ottomans. It overlooks the tennis court.

Walks around the island are wonderful. A nature trail runs downhill to mangroves and ponds; other paths lead to lookouts. A part of Necker has been designated as a bird sanctuary, and whales are often sighted offshore in February and March. The Island has a full array of water sports for guests to use at will.

Necker is not rented in the conventional way of a hotel, and the price is prohibitive for most people unless they can round up nineteen friends— even ten affluent ones will do. The price includes the entire island and all its facilities; managers and staff (three maids, two gardeners, and a boatman); all meals for up to twenty persons; and open bar, wine, and champagne. When you stay for five nights or longer, a day yacht charter and a local calypso band for a party evening are added.

Necker is very romantic and very glamorous, and it probably would appeal to anyone who can afford it. But it helps if you relish unforgettable natural beauty and exquisite man-made comfort and don't need entertainment other than the company you bring with you.

Address/Phone: Box 1091, Virgin Gorda, Tortola, B.V.I.; (809) 494–2757; Fax: (809) 494–4396

Owner: Richard Branson

General Manager: Dan and Barbara Reid

Open: Year-round

Credit Cards: None

U.S. Reservations: Resorts Management, The Carriage House (800) 225–4255, (212) 696–4566; Fax: (212) 689–1598; Necker Island, BVI, Ltd., (800) 524–0004, (212) 691–3916; Fax: (212) 627–1494

Deposit: 10 percent of booking, 40 percent four months in advance; balance 2 months. Inquire regarding refund policy.

Minimum Stay: None

Arrival/Departure: Transfers included, for stays of five days or more, by helicopter from St. Thomas or Beef Island/Tortola; for less than 5 days, by boat from Gun Creek dock/Virgin Gorda (15 minutes) or Beef Island (40 minutes)

Distance from Other Islands: Virgin Gorda, 1 mile; Tortola, 8 miles

Accommodations: 1 master and 9 double bedrooms (4 convertible to 2 suites; all with terraces; twin beds or king; 8 bathrooms)

Amenities: Ceiling fans, satellite television, VCR; bath with shower only,

Peter Island Resort & Yacht Harbor

hairdryer, toiletry amenities, bathrobe; business facilities, helicopter
landing pad

Electricity: 110 volts

Sports: Swimming pool, 2 Jacuzzis; snorkeling, waterskiing, sailing, windsurfing. Lighted tennis court and equipment, exercise equipment,
Boston Whalers, Lasers, and fishing equipment.

Children: All ages

Dress Code: None

Meetings: Up to 20 people

Day Visitors: None

Handicapped: No facilities

Packages: All-inclusive

Rates: Daily, all inclusive. *High Season* (November 15–May 15): 1–10 persons, $8,250; 11–20 persons, $9,900. *Low Season* (May 16-November
14): 1–6 persons, $4,950; 7–12 persons, $6,950; 13–20 persons, $8,950.
The resort has several weeks in autumn when bookings on an individual basis are available. Inquire.

Service Charge: 2.5 percent

Government Tax: Included

Cayman Islands

Hyatt Regency Grand Cayman

Known as the Mount Everest of diving, the Cayman Islands are a British Crown Colony tucked under the western end of Cuba. They comprise three low-lying islands almost completely surrounded by reefs: Grand Cayman, the resort and commercial center; Cayman Brac, a stringbean of untamed wilderness, 89 miles to the northeast; and Little Cayman, the smallest, 5 miles west of Cayman Brac.

One of the most prosperous places in the Caribbean, the islands have excellent communications, their own airline and currency—and a population of only 25,000. Early in their history they were a favorite hiding place for pirates, and Pirates' Week is a frolicking annual commemoration of the island's history, held in October.

Grand Cayman, with the capital at George Town, is the largest of the trio. Seven Mile Beach, where the majority of the hotels are located, is a magnificent crest of powdery white sand just north of George Town. The 22-mile-long island rises only 60 feet above sea level and is made up largely of lagoons and mangroves rich in bird life.

Across one of these areas, North Sound, lies a barrier reef, and just inside the mouth is one of the Caribbean's most unusual sites. Dubbed Stingray City, it offers divers and snorkelers a thrilling opportunity to touch, feed, and photograph a dozen or so friendly stingray in only 12 feet of water.

Grand Cayman also has the world's only sea turtle farm where you can see turtles at various stages of development in their breeding pans; for a nominal fee you can sponsor a turtle for release to the ocean.

Under the sea the Caymans are surrounded by extensive cliffs, slopes, and valleys of submerged mountains, collectively known as the Cayman Wall, and densely encrusted with forests of corals, giant sponges, and other marine life. Nondivers can see the Caymans' underwater splendors thanks to recreational submarines.

Cayman Brac is 12 square miles of untamed tropics yet to be discovered by nature buffs for its hiking, fishing, birding, and caving. Little Cayman is even less developed. The 10-mile-long island has large expanses of mangroves and lagoons and is surrounded by long stretches of white-sand beaches, extensive reefs, and spectacular walls that some experts consider to make up the finest diving in the Western Hemisphere.

Information

Cayman Islands Department of Tourism, 250 Catalonia Avenue, #604, Coral Gables, FL 33134; (305) 444–6551

Hyatt Regency Grand Cayman ⊙ ⊙ ⊙ ⊙

Whether you are lounging around the elegant pool with its colonnaded gazebo and swim-up bar, sipping a cool drink on your private veranda by the golf course, or trying your hand at croquet, a glance at the Hyatt in any direction pleases the eye.

The overall impression is of harmony and beauty. Buildings, landscaping, lounges, guest rooms, and courtyards all point to the fact that the architects and interior designers really got this one right.

Another element that pleases is the pristine quality of the property. The resort's lawns, gardens, buildings, and facilities are all maintained to perfection. In 1988, only five days after Hurricane Gilbert hit the Caymans, I arrived to find that the water-damaged buildings had already been repainted, the walkways scrubbed, and the carpets replaced. I had to look hard to see any evidence that only a few days earlier an angry wind had swept through the property.

Located only a few miles outside George Town, the Hyatt Regency Grand Cayman is the centerpiece of the ninety-acre Britannia resort complex, which includes a golf course, a private marina, and a residential community of attractive villas. Its design is British colonial inspired, but don't look for any worn and faded chintz-covered chairs or sofas here. At the Hyatt all furnishings have a "spit and polish" look which speaks to travelers who seek a luxurious yet low-key ambience.

The architecture actually incorporates a variety of classic elements— French doors, colonnaded gazebos, Spanish courtyards, high beamed ceilings—that create a wonderful airy, sumptuous, tropical ambience on one of the Caribbean's driest islands.

The plush appointments use custom-designed bleached ash, rattan, wicker. teak, and Honduras mahogany furniture throughout, some accented with leather trim. The designer fabrics awash with the Caribbean colors— aqua, coral, pink, lilac, and earth tones—complement the flowers in the magnificently landscaped grounds.

Hyatt's sports facilities are a big attraction. Leading the list is the unusual golf course, designed by Jack Nicklaus. It's an eighteen-hole course built within the acres normally required for a regulation nine-hole one. Nicklaus had only forty acres, so he designed a special ball, known as the "short" ball, which goes only half the distance of a normal one. The game is now known as Cayman Golf.

The undulating greens are reminiscent of some famous Scottish layouts; to create a course in this dry environment that has the morning dew look of the highlands is an amazing achievement. The course can be played three ways: a nine-hole championship course, an eighteen-hole executive course, or an eighteen-hole Cayman Ball course. There are clinics and a pro shop. Hyatt guests may book tee time up to forty-eight hours in advance.

The Hyatt is not on the beach but directly across the road from Grand Cayman's famous Seven Mile Beach, where it has a private beach club with a swimming pool, restaurant, and bar. The resort's main free-form pool with swim-up bar and Jacuzzi covers one-third of an acre. There are tennis courts and an English Tea Garden with a croquet lawn.

Red Sail Sports, Hyatt's water-sports operator, offers a full range of water sports, a dive program, and deep-sea fishing for an extra charge. The hotel has its own 65-foot catamaran offering daily snorkeling, and sunset and evening cruises. From the marina, boats have direct access to Grand

Cayman's North Sound, the main area for diving, fishing, and snorkeling, and to an unusual site, Stingray City, where you can swim with a dozen friendly rays.

Guest rooms and suites, housed in clusters of low-rise buildings, are outstanding, with luxurious appointments in casual island style. All rooms have step-out French balconies, except Terrace rooms, which have large furnished patios. The suites are bilevel and have canopied king beds and stocked minibars. Some guest rooms look out at the tennis courts or croquet lawn, others at the golf course or the manicured gardens of the courtyard with waterfalls and reflecting pond. Two buildings house the Regency Club's one- and two-bedroom villas. The club has a concierge and lounge where continental breakfast and cocktails are served.

Along the edge of the golf course and by the marina are beautiful one- and two-bedroom villas, ideal for families. They have private patios or balconies that open onto the golf course through elegant French doors and come equipped with kitchens with microwave, dishwasher, washer, and dryer. Each has large walk-in closets and two bathrooms. Villa guests enjoy all the amenities and facilities offered at the Hyatt.

The main restaurant, the Garden Loggia, has a lovely indoor/outdoor setting in the interior courtyard gardens. Casual for breakfast and lunch, it is more elegant with candlelight dining in the evening. A seafood buffet is offered on Friday nights, and Sunday brunch is an elaborate affair.

Light lunches and sunset dining can be enjoyed at Hemingway's at the beach club. The Britannia Golf Club Bar and Grill also serves light meals, and there are grills by the pool and beach.

The Hyatt complex has several bars: the gazebo, which does double duty as a poolside bar and a swim-up bar; the outdoor bar at Hemingway's, popular for cocktails and after-dinner lingering; and the Golf Club Bar. Live entertainment usually can be enjoyed in the restaurants or bars daily except Sunday.

The Hyatt Regency Grand Cayman is geared to an upscale audience. It works very well for couples, singles, and families, as well as for business meeting participants and anyone who wants to play golf on one of the Caribbean's most unusual courses. And it would certainly make a fabulous prize for any incentive award winner.

Address/Phone: Seven Mile Beach, Grand Cayman, B.W.I.; (809) 949–1234; Fax: (809) 949–8528
Owner: Britannia/Ellesmere Development Ltd.
General Manager: Peter Iwanowski
Open: Year-round
Credit Cards: All major

U.S. Reservations: Hyatt Worldwide, (800) 233–1234
Deposit: None
Minimum Stay: None
Arrival/Departure: Transfer service arranged for fee
Distance from Airport: (Owen Roberts International Airport) 2.5 miles; taxi one-way, US $15.50 per person
Distance from George Town: 2 miles; taxi one-way, $8
Accommodations: 236 guest rooms and suites in two- to four-story buildings, including 44 Regency Club rooms; 35 one- to three-bedroom villas; guest rooms have 2 doubles or king. One-bedroom villas have king; two bedrooms have king, 2 doubles, and Roman tub in master bath.
Amenities: Air-conditioning, ceiling fans, international direct-dial telephone, radio-clock, stocked mini-bar, television, safe; bath with tub and shower, hairdryer, toiletries basket. kitchen, washer/dryer in villas; room service 24 hours daily; shops, concierge, beauty salon, massage
Electricity: 110 volts
Sports: Freshwater swimming pool, Jacuzzi, free use of 4 lighted tennis courts, croquet. Dive shop, water sports extra. Golf, see text.
Dress Code: Casual
Children: All ages; cribs, baby-sitters
Meetings: Up to 300 people
Day Visitors: Not encouraged
Handicapped: Facilities
Packages: Honeymoon, golf
Rates: Per room, single or double, daily, EP. *High Season* (mid-December–mid-April): $260–$465. *Shoulder Season* (April 15–May 31; October 1–December 19) $180–$360; *Low Season* (June 1–September 30): $170–$330.
Service Charge: 10 percent on room; 15 percent on food and beverage
Government Tax: 6 percent room only

Pirates Point Resort ▣

If not unique, certainly unusual, Pirates Point is a diver's resort owned and operated by Gladys Howard from Tyler, Texas.

What's unusual about that?

She also happens to be an award-winning cookbook author, a Cordon Bleu chef who has studied with Julia Child, James Beard, and Lucy Lo. And she operated an international cooking school and gourmet catering service in the East Texas area for twenty years.

When you arrive at the Edward Bodden International Airport, Gladys meets you in her Jeep or truck for the half-mile ride to the resort. Don't let the airport name fool you. It's a grass strip with a wooden shack; Little Cayman has a total population of twenty people.

Pirates Point consists of a central pavilion that includes the front desk, lounge and bar, dining room and outside barbecue, and four cottages constructed of cut stone and wood, They're only twenty steps from the beach. Three of the cottages have two units each, and one has four units. Two cottages, added in 1992, have large verandas.

The little inn is immaculate. Rooms are spacious and surprisingly pleasant and comfortable, given their rustic setting. They have white stucco and wood-paneled walls and high wood-beamed ceilings. Furnished in wicker, they have either two twin beds or one queen bed. In the bathroom you'll find fluffy towels and a shower with hot and cold water. Pirates Point has its own reverse-osmosis plant, which helps insure a freshwater supply. The resort has one telephone and a VCR and videocassettes in the lounge.

The complex is shaded by large almond, seagrape, and coconut palm trees. Along the path by the cactus garden leading to the reception, you will notice some sculptures made from coconuts, driftwood, and other natural material. What started as a past time has developed into a wacky tradition, and now these "works of art" by guests decorate the bar and add character to the inn. Since 1988 Gladys has run an annual contest for the most original creation; the prize is a week's vacation at the resort.

You can count on the food to be good. Gladys uses whatever she can get and works miracles in her small kitchen. It is difficult to get products locally, except fish. Her supplies come by boat from Grand Cayman, and she flies in fresh fruits and vegetables.

For this caterer-gourmet chef, dining is serious business. No roughing it here. You will dine with crystal stemware and linen napkins even on picnics. Lunch is an outdoor buffet under the seagrape trees in your swimsuit, and dinner offers a buffet and table service in the dining room. There is a beach barbecue on Thursdays and Saturdays, weather permitting, and sunset wine and cheese parties several times a week.

A coral atoll 10 miles long and a mile wide, Little Cayman is one of diving's last frontiers. Its Bloody Bay Wall is one of life's great diving experiences. Rising to within 20 feet of the surface and plunging in sheer cliffs more than a mile deep, these formations offer marine life found nowhere else. There are giant sponges, trees of black coral, elaborate sea fans, and eagle rays, to name a few. The late Philippe Cousteau called it one of the three finest dive areas in the world.

Pirates Point is located only 2 miles or a 5-minute fast boat ride from the wall. The resort has a full scuba operation with three instructors on staff who handle everything from a short resort course to PADI certification and advance training. The resort offers two dives daily.

Good snorkeling (gear costs extra) can be enjoyed directly in front of the resort about 100 feet from shore. There is diving nearby, and the resort has a fast boat to reach the more dramatic dive sites on the wall. You can have an underwater video of your dives for an additional charge.

The resort has a sandy beach, but the entrance into the water from shore is rocky and better made from its small pier, which puts you into about 3 feet of water. Pirates Point often takes all the guests for a picnic lunch on nearby cays and can arrange fishing and group-dive programs on request.

Gladys chairs the Little Cayman National Trust, which is creating trails for hiking and bird-watching. The Caymans are a flyover for North American birds, and Little Cayman is a sanctuary for the red-footed booby and frigate bird. It also has its own island lake for tarpon fishing, with an endemic subspecies.

Pirates Point, open in 1982, has been home for Gladys since 1986. From her travels and diving around the world, she has brought her experience to her tiny haven and given it a lot of personality. You will feel at home, too. You set your own schedule for diving and fishing, and the kitchen never closes.

Pirates Point is operated as an all-inclusive resort. The package includes accommodations with private bath, three meals daily with wine, an open bar with unlimited drinks, two boat dives daily, tanks, backpack, weights, belt, guide, transfer to and from the airport, the use of bicycles, and beach towels. Add the experience of diving at Little Cayman, and Gladys's food, and Pirates Point tallies up to be one of the best-quality buys in the Caribbean.

Address/Phone: Little Cayman, Cayman Islands, B.W.I.; (809) 948–4210; Fax: (809) 948–4210

Owner/Manager: Gladys B. Howard

Open: Year-round except mid-September to early October

Credit Cards: Visa, MasterCard

U.S. Reservations: Direct to hotel or Cayman Island Reservations, (800) 327–8777; Fax: (305) 441–0483

Deposit: Half total reservation within 10 days after booking; 30 days cancellation, refund half of deposit; after 30 days, deposit forfeited

Minimum Stay: 3 days

Arrival/Departure: Complimentary transfer service

Distance from Airport: (Boden Airport) $\frac{1}{2}$ mile; taxi: no taxi service (Little Cayman is 75 miles northeast of Grand Cayman; Cayman Airways provides daily service from George Town.)

Distance from South Town: ¾ mile

Accommodations: 10 rooms in bungalows; double with twins or king; maximum of 16 divers

Amenities: Ceiling fans, clock, bath with shower only; no room service

Electricity: 110 volts

Sports: See text

Dress Code: Very casual

Children: Over 5 years of age, but must be over 12 to dive

Meetings: Up to 16 people

Day Visitors: Welcome, with reservations

Handicapped: No facilities

Packages: All-inclusive/Dive

Rates: Two persons, daily, AP. *High Season* (mid-December–mid-April): $130–$240. *Low Season:* $115–$205.

Service Charge: 15 percent

Government Tax: 6 percent room only

Curaçao

Avila Beach Hotel

Only 39 miles off the coast of Venezuela, the cosmopolitan capital of the Netherlands Antilles is noted for its commerce, diversity of restaurants, and fashionable shops with goods from around the world. They are side by side with the colorful colonial harbor of Willemstad, making it easy and fun to explore on foot.

At the heart of the compact historic old city is Fort Amsterdam, the Governor's Palace, and the eighteenth-century Dutch Reform Church, and nearby, Mikve Israel-Emanuel Synagogue, the oldest synagogue in the Americas (founded in 1654).

Juxtaposed against the sophisticated city center is the little-known landscape of windswept shores, chalky mountains and rugged terrain, as well as two of the best nature parks in the Caribbean. In the 3,500-acre Christoffel National Park, the cactus grows as tall as trees. Dominated by the rocky peak of 1,238-foot Mt. Christoffel, the park has 20 miles of road with color-coded routes for self-guided tours and hiking trails.

Curaçao is completely surrounded by reefs with an extraordinary variety of coral and fish that are only now being discovered by divers. The

1,500-acre Curaçao Underwater Park, stretching for 12.5 miles from the Princess Beach Hotel to the eastern tip of the island, protects some of Curaçao's finest reefs. Many areas can be enjoyed by snorkelers as well as divers. East of the marine park is the Curaçao Aquarium, a private facility where four hundred species of marine life native to Curaçao waters are displayed.

Quiet seas wash Curaçao's western shores, but wild surf crashes against the windward north. The coast has many small coves with beaches and large bays or lagoons with very narrow entrances and wide basins. These waterways are among Curaçao's most distinctive features. Some lagoons are used for commerce, others for sport.

On the east, Spanish Water is one of the island's largest, prettiest lagoons with a long, narrow opening to the sea. It has hilly green fingers and coves, islands and beaches, and is the boating and fishing center with marinas and water-sports facilities. Santa Barbara, on its east side, is a popular public beach with changing facilities.

The constant northeast trade winds that cool the island have made windsurfing one of Curaçao's most popular sports, with international recognition and an Olympic champion. Annually in June the Curaçao Open International Pro-Am Windsurf Championship attracts world masters. The most popular windsurfing area is on the south coast between Willemstad and Spanish Water, also the site of the island's main hotels and water-sports centers.

Information

Curaçao Tourism Development Bureau, 400 Madison Avenue, New York, NY 10017; (212) 751–8266

Avila Beach Hotel ◙◙

Its very personal management, coupled with the ambience of a small European hotel in a historic building with charm and character, has long distinguished the Avila Beach Hotel from others in Curaçao, which tend to be large and fairly standard. As a result, the Avila has a loyal following, particularly among European visitors to the island.

Located by the sea about a fifteen-minute walk east of Willemstad, the Avila's centerpiece is a stately mansion of Dutch colonial architecture built in 1780 and restored to mint condition. Set in pretty, manicured gardens, the mustard yellow building is trimmed with small white balconies at each window. Historically known as the La Belle Alliance, it served as the residence of Curaçao's governors from 1812 to 1828 and, at a later date, was used as a medical clinic.

The Avila opened as a hotel in 1949, but it was not until 1977, with the advent of its present owner, Nic Moller, that the hotel began to acquire its special character. Moller, a Dane who has lived in the Netherlands Antilles since 1960, painstakingly rebuilt and renovated the hotel one room at a time. He added a beach, improved the restaurant, and trained his staff to give that extra measure of service that has become the hotel's hallmark.

The spacious lobby, with arched doorways and a high, dark wood beamed ceiling, has an eclectic decor that features rattan furniture, a piano, an Oriental rug on ceramic-tile floors, and overhead fans. Sometimes the venue for concerts, art exhibits, and other cultural events, the lobby opens onto a quiet patio that leads to the restaurant, bar, and beach area. Miniature turn-of-the-century lampposts decorate the gardens.

There are guest rooms in the main building and in the wings. Some have sea views, some garden. The rooms vary in size with different arrangements and are individually furnished. Some have Scandinavian modern decor with a sleek, neat look in contrast to the old architecture of the exterior; others have tropical rattan furniture. All guest rooms have private bathrooms; water is warmed by solar heat.

From 1991 to 1992, the Avila doubled in size and added a second beach. The extension, named La Belle Alliance after the historic name of the governor's mansion, is connected to the old part by gardens. While the new buildings retain the old Dutch colonial architecture of the exterior, inside they are completely modern, with deluxe oceanview guest rooms. Some have kitchenettes, while a group of one- and two-bedroom suites feature full kitchens.

The hotel's two restaurants serve Danish and Curaçao specialties prepared by Scandinavian chefs. The Avila Cafe, a covered patio restaurant, offers a breakfast buffet, lunch, and in-between snacks daily. Belle Terrace, an open-air restaurant under the spreading arms of an enormous old flamboyant tree, has a romantic setting overlooking the sea. Lunch and dinner offer full à la carte menus that are popular with local residents as well. Evening entertainment includes a special Antillean Night on Wednesday with local cuisine and live music and a Saturday night barbecue with steel band or mariachis.

The Schooner Bar, shaped like the bow of a ship with a tall white sail, has been given a facelift. It is situated between the two beaches, with a wooden boardwalk leading from the terrace to the new restaurant at the end of the pier. By day, lounge chairs with tables and thatched umbrellas provide a pleasant and comfortable spot for safe swimming and sunning.

The Avila Beach enjoys a high level of repeat visitors. Its location makes it popular with business travelers as much as with vacationers. Both groups appreciate its hospitality and friendly, hardworking staff. With expansion it will be quite an accomplishment if Moller, as much the hands-on manager as ever, can retain the intimate ambience that endeared the Avila to so many fans.

Address/Phone: Penstraat 130-134/P.O. Box 791, Curaçao, Netherlands Antilles; (599) 9–614–377; Fax: (599) 9–611–493

Owner/Managing Director: Nic Moller

General Manager: Tone Moller

Open: Year-round

Credit Cards: All major

U.S. Reservations: Utell International, (800) 448–8355; Fax: (402) 398–5484

Deposit: 3 nights

Minimum Stay: None

Arrival/Departure: No transfer service

Distance from Airport: 10 miles; taxi one-way, US $15

Distance from Willemstad: 1 mile; taxi one-way, US $5. Free minibus to/from city center in the morning

Accommodations: 90 units (30 double, 10 single in old building; 40 deluxe rooms, 10 suites with terraces in new addition) with queen, king, or twin beds in 10 one- to four-story buildings

Amenities: Telephone, cable television, mini-bar; some baths have tubs, others shower only, basket of toiletries; air-conditioning; no room service

Electricity: 220 and 110 volts

Sports: 1 tennis court; 2 beaches; water sports arranged

Dress Code: Casual

Children: All ages

Meetings: 3 rooms for 30, 40, and 100 persons

Day Visitors: No

Handicapped Facilities: Available

Packages: None

Rates: Per room, daily, EP. *High Season* (mid-December–mid-April): $80–$200. *Low Season:* $73–$180.

Service Charge: 10 percent

Government Tax: 7 percent

Lions Dive Hotel & Marina ▨▨

Curaçao's first and only hotel designed specifically for divers and water sports enthusiasts is located about fifteen minutes east of Willemstad in an area that has become the island's main dive and windsurfing location. You don't need to be a diver or windsurfer to enjoy a stay here, but those interested in either sport will benefit most from its facilities.

Opened in 1989, the Lions Dive Hotel & Marina is situated next to a stretch of manmade beach beside a marina and the popular Curaçao Aquarium complex, which has shops and restaurants in addition to displays of the marine life found in Curaçao's marine park.

Owned and financed by the Lions Club of Curaçao, Lions Dive was created to help develop and promote the splendid marine life surrounding the island, which heretofore had been overshadowed by neighboring Bonaire. The reefs that make up Curaçao's marine park begin directly in front of the hotel and stretch for 12 miles along the coast. Underwater Curaçao Nautico, an outstanding PADI five-star dive facility adjacent to the hotel, became part of Lions Dive in 1991.

Designed by Anko van der Woude, one of Curaçao's leading architects and an expert on historic architecture, the hotel is made up of clusters of two-, three- and four-story buildings with wooden balconies and gingerbread trim, inspired by West Indian style and a marked departure from the Dutch colonial architecture that typifies the island.

From the small, pleasant open-air lobby with a sitting area furnished in white wicker and pastel accents, landscaped walkways lead directly to the swimming pool, complete with a bar and terrace overlooking the sea. The guestroom buildings, set in flowering gardens, are grouped around a separate freshwater swimming pool and overlook the marina. The moderately sized guestrooms, each with two queen-size beds, have tile floors and are comfortably furnished in rattan with light floral decor. French doors open on to balconies or terraces with seaviews.

The dive facility offers introductory dives and resort courses, certification, and a variety of specialized advanced courses; there are dive packages of three to seven nights. It has a rental and retail shop, repair center, and private lockers and showers. Its two dive boats, each with a capacity for twenty-four divers, depart twice daily on scheduled excursions to selected sites in Curaçao's underwater park and to Klein Curaçao, an uninhabited island 8 miles east of Curaçao; night dives are offered as well.

The beachside water sports center (separate from the hotel) offers equipment and instruction for Sunfish and catamaran sailing, canoeing, and windsurfing, as well as glass-bottom boat trips and sunset sails, all at additional charge. Visits to the aquarium are free for Lions Dive guests. There is also a fitness center offering classes given by professional instructors and physical therapists.

Rumours, the resort's open-air restaurant and bar, serves three meals. In the past, when the hotel had not taken its restaurant operation as seriously as its dive facilities, it was criticized for its food. The hotel maintains it has addressed the problem, and recent visitors give the restaurant a passing grade. There are also two restaurants at the aquarium, one specializing in Italian dishes, the other serving Argentine steaks and Mexican specialties. Curaçao also has a wide variety of excellent restaurants in the vicinity of Willemstad.

The Dutch couple that manages the hotel has created a comfortable, casual environment for the largely young clientele who come mainly from the United States, Germany, and the Netherlands for the diving, the windsurfing, and the beach. The hotel offers a free daily shuttle bus to the downtown shopping area and discount coupons for several activities.

Address: Bapor Kibra, Curaçao, N.A.; Tel: 599–9–618–100; Fax: 599–9–ʻ618–200

Owner: The Lions Club of Curaçao

General Manager: J.C.M. Van Beurden

Open: Year-round

Credit Cards: All major

U.S. Reservations: International Travel & Resorts, (800) 223–9815; (212) 545–8469; Fax: (212) 545–8467

Deposit: 3 nights; 14 days cancellation

Minimum Stay: 3 nights in season

Arrival/Departure: Transfer service by taxi arranged for $17.50 round-trip per person.

Distance from Airport: 15 miles; taxi one-way, US $15

Distance from Willemstad: 3 miles; taxi one-way; US $8; daily free shuttle from resort

Accommodations: 72 rooms (2 queen-sized beds) with terrace or patio

Amenities: Air-conditioning, ceiling fans, cable television, radio, tiled bathroom with shower only, direct dial phones; hairdryers available; no room service

Electricity: 220 volts

Sports: Freshwater swimming pool; snorkeling, diving, and windsurfing equipment and instruction available for fee; bikes for rent.

Dress Code: Casual

Children: All ages; cribs, high-chairs, baby-sitters

Meetings: Up to 15 people; more on request

Day Visitors: Yes

Handicapped: Limited facilities
Packages: Dive
Rates: Per room for two, daily, AB. *High Season* (mid-December–mid-April): $126. *Low Season:* $124.
Service Charge: 12 percent, included
Government Hotel Tax: 7 percent, included

~~~~~ ON THE HORIZON ~~~~~

Sonesta Beach Hotel and Casino Curaçao

Located ten minutes from the airport and from Willemstad and next door to Curaçao's International Trade Center, the $41 million Sonesta Beach Hotel and Casino is the largest beachfront resort on the island.

Its architecture is a modern interpretation of the traditional Dutch colonial architecture that typifies Curaçao. It has an open-air lobby and lush landscaping, enhanced by numerous fountains, a free-form swimming pool, with swim-up bar, wading pool, and two large whirlpools. There are three restaurants and three lounges.

The sports and fitness facilities include two lighted tennis courts, a range of water sports, a health club with a gym, two saunas, two steam rooms, and massage room. There is a shopping arcade and meeting facilities for up to three hundred people.

Address/Phone: Piscadera Bay, Curaçao; (599) 936–8800
U.S. Reservations: (800) SONESTA
Accommodations: 248 ocean view rooms and suites
Rates: Per room, daily, EP. *High Season* (mid-December–mid-April): $225–$319. *Low Season:* $149–$209.

Dominican Republic

Ramada Renaissance Jaragua Resort, Casino & Spa

The Dominican Republic is the land of superlatives: the oldest country of the Caribbean, with the tallest mountains and the lowest lake. Historic Santo Domingo was the first Spanish settlement in the New World. Here the Spaniards built their first cathedral, first hospital, first university, and first fortress.

The Old City has been beautifully restored and is alive with restaurants, shops, art galleries, and museums. Columbus Square has the oldest cathedral in the Americas.

Modern Santo Domingo, the fun-loving sophisticated capital with Old World charm, has more than one million people and about the lowest prices in the Caribbean. The modern Plaza de la Cultura is the heart of the capital's cultural life. It includes the National Theatre, where plays, concerts by the National Symphony Orchestra, jazz ensembles, and performances by visiting artists are held.

But Santo Domingo is far more than history and culture. Dominicans are warm and friendly and love to have a good time, and their city bounces with every sort of entertainment from piano bars and smart supper clubs to brassy cabarets.

Shopping is best at the central market, Mercado Modelo. You'll know you're in the right place when you smell freshly roasted Dominican coffee. It's on sale at the entrance. The Mercado is stacked with fruits and vegetables and so many great buys that you could stock up on a year's worth of presents and pay for your trip with the savings!

One of the city's most unusual attractions, Los Tres Ojos (Three Eyes) Park, is a subterranean cave with three lagoons, each with different water: sweet, salt, and sulfur.

From the rolling terrain of the east and south, the land rises toward the center in two tree-covered spines where two national parks contain the country's highest peaks—three that are more than 10,000 feet high and several rising almost 9,000 feet—with trails.

In the northeastern corner, Samana Peninsula and Bay is one of the most beautiful and least-developed areas. From December to March whales play at the mouth of the bay. On the Rio Limon in the center of the peninsula, a footpath leads to a magnificent waterfall, all but hidden amid the savage beauty of the thickly forested mountains. On the south side of the bay, Los Haitises National Park is a 100-mile karst region with dense mangroves, estuaries, and tiny cays that are rookeries for seabirds.

Information

Dominican Republic Tourist Information, c/o Kahn Communications, 4 Park Avenue, New York, NY 10016; (212) 679–3200

Ramada Renaissance
Jaragua Resort, Casino & Spa ◙◙◙◙

Robert Redford spent weeks here while filming *Havana*. So, what else do you need to know? Yes, it's big, brassy, and painted in colors that will make you reach for your sunglasses. But it's also wonderfully Dominican.

Located on the Malecon, Santo Domingo's popular seashore boulevard overlooking the Caribbean, the Jaragua (pronounced Ha-*RAG*-wa) offers the best of two worlds: a resort set in fourteen acres of tropical gardens in the heart of the city and a city full of history, culture, and fun.

The Jaragua doesn't have a beach (there are no beaches in Santo Domingo), but it has lagoons spilling into a huge swimming pool, health club and spa, tennis complex, seven restaurants, four bars, nightclub, disco, casino, shops, and beautiful rooms. It's all within easy reach of any of Santo Domingo's many attractions.

Opened in 1987 on the site of the first Jaragua, a popular Havana-in-the-old-days hotel with outdoor gardens and a splashy nightclub, the new Jaragua is T-O-D-A-Y. A modern high-rise of ten floors combined with garden low-rise buildings, the design is sleek and the decor sophisticated, with stylish art deco details throughout. You might blink at the prevalence of pinks, mauves, and burgundies, but you will be impressed by the quality and high standards. Marble floors and satiny hard-finished fixtures are kept polished to such a shine you'll think they are mirrors.

And the luster on the floor isn't one bit more impressive than the polish of the service. The Jaragua puts the country's other hotels to shame and demonstrates what Dominicans can do when they set their mind to it. Ramada acquired The Jaragua in 1991 and has left well enough alone. It is, however, adding some enchancement such as a Renaissance floor.

You arrive at the hotel by way of a grand driveway graced with fountains and gardens and step from a large portico directly in to the lobby. Prepare yourself for the experience. On the left is the huge, wide-open casino, brimming with action and bouncing with salsa music most of the time. To the right is the quiet, elegant reception with soft indirect lighting that highlights the lobby's art deco features. The contrast of the two sides is staggering. But it works.

The guest rooms are in two areas: The majority are in the main ten-story tower, the others in two-story garden buildings on the west side of the main building. All are large, luxurious, and attractive, and the penthouse suites with their own Jacuzzis are small palazzos. The stylish appointments use wicker of contemporary design with plush upholstery, draperies, and bedspreads.

The rooms, designed with business travelers in mind as much as tourists, have a desk and three phones, including one in the marbled bathroom, where there is also a mini-television. You needn't miss a moment of what's playing on the big set in the room. The tower rooms, most with views of the sea, are for those who want to be at the center of the action. Being more removed, the garden rooms, which were refurbished in 1992, provide greater privacy and quiet, and are particularly popular with guests enrolled in the spa program.

Directly in front of the guest-room tower is the spa, with saunas, massage, herbal wraps, facials, aerobics classes, Nautilus equipment, and more. The hotel has packages for a full spa program. Beyond the lagoon and gardens is the swimming pool, which is likely to be crowded, particularly on the weekends, as it has a local membership. It can also be noisy with kids and music. To the rear is the tennis complex with four lighted clay courts, viewing stand, and a pro shop.

The Jaragua has seven dining outlets; each is a specialty restaurant with different chefs and menus. The Deli, open twenty-four hours a day, is more like a coffee shop than a deli. Located in a quiet corner on the main floor, it is the main venue for breakfast and lunch and offers American entrées along with their Spanish versions. Las Cascadas, overlooking the waterfalls and lagoon, serves snacks during the day and really comes to life on Sunday with a family buffet brunch. The grill and bar by the pool serves lunch and snacks.

Four other restaurants are grouped together next to the casino. The Lotus offers Chinese cuisine; Figaro serves Northern Italian fare, Latino has Dominican, other Caribbean, and Latin American selections; and the Manhattan Grill features steaks and American specialties. (If I had a complaint about the Jaragua, it would be the location of the dinner venues in a busy, noisy atmosphere. I would welcome one dinner restaurant in a quieter part of the hotel. But then, you don't go to the Jaragua for serenity.)

The Jaragua really jumps in the evening; and there's plenty of opportunity to be part of the action. In addition to the casino and the casino bar, the sixteen-hundred-seat La Fiesta Room has a Las Vegas–style show, often with headline entertainers. There are also Las Cascadas, where happy hour features guitars and different types of musical entertainment five times weekly; the Merengue Lounge for cocktails, live music, and dancing; and the disco.

The Jaragua indeed has glamor and style, not so much Caribbean as Latin, and is as popular with Italians and Latin Americans as it is with gringos. This hotel is not for the traveler who wants a laid-back Caribbean hideaway with a beach in front. If you prefer having the facilities and services of a large luxury hotel, thrive on a glittering, lively nightlife, and like to be in the center of the action, you'll love The Jaragua.

Address/Phone: 367 George Washington Avenue, Apartado Postal 769-2 Santo Domingo, Dominican Republic; (809) 221–2000; Fax: (809) 686–0528

Owner/Management Company: Ramada International Hotels and Resorts

General Manager: Alvaro Soto

Open: Year-round

Credit Cards: Most major

U.S. Reservations: Ramada International Hotels and Resorts, (305) 441–1255, (800) 228–9898; Fax: (305) 448–1656

Deposit: One night

Minimum Stay: None

Arrival/Departure: Transfer service arranged for charge

Distance from Airport: (Santo Domingo International Airport) 20 miles (40 minutes) taxi one-way, US $18

Distance from Old City: one mile; taxi one-way, $6

Accommodations: 300 rooms and suites with double or king-size beds (200 deluxe rooms with terraces, including 9 suites, in 10-story tower; 100 in two-story garden buildings)

Amenities: Air-conditioning, ceiling fans, cable television, radio, bathroom with tub and shower, hairdryer, makeup mirror, mini-TV, basket of toiletries, bathrobe, direct-dial telephone, mini-bar/refrigerator; ice service, nightly turndown service, 24-hour room service; Jacuzzis in penthouse suites

Electricity: 110 volts

Sports: Freshwater swimming pool; free use of tennis courts, rental equipment, lessons for fee. Golf, horseback riding, water sports, fishing arranged through concierge.

Dress Code: Casual

Children: All ages; cribs, high chairs; baby-sitters

Meetings: Up to 1,000 people

Day Visitors: Yes

Handicapped: Limited facilities

Packages: Spa, honeymoon, merengue, other Ramada standards

Rates: Per room, double, daily, EP. *High Season* (mid-December–mid-April): $170–$210. *Low Season*: $108–$135.

Service Charge: 10 percent

Government Tax: 11 percent on room rates; 6 percent on food and beverage

ON THE HORIZON

Hotel Gran Bahia

Located on beautiful Samana Bay in the northeast corner of the Dominican Republic, the stylish Hotel Gran Bahia is the first luxury resort in the Samana area. Its salmon facade and awnings, covered verandas, and gingerbread trim recall Victorian elegance. A twenty-minute drive from Samana town, the hotel is framed by forested mountains and overlooks a lovely panorama of small islands and two beaches. All rooms have verandas with water views.

Two restaurants—one with traditional mahogany furnishings and antiques; the other more informal with wicker and chintz—feature Caribbean and continental cuisine prepared by a Paris-trained chef. The resort has a large pool, lighted tennis courts, water sports, gym, and a riding stable. One of Samana's biggest attractions is the humpback whales, which come to the bay from December through March. The resort arranges whale-watch excursions.

Arriving guests are met at Santo Domingo Airport and transferred to Samana by private plane. The resort is under the watchful eye of general manager Paul Pedlow, who opened the well-known La Samana in St. Martin.

Address/Phone: Box 2024, Santo Domingo, D.R.; (809) 538–3111
U.S. Reservations: David Mitchell, (800) 372–1323; Fax: (800) 446–1323
Accommodations: 96 rooms and suites
Rates: Two persons, daily, EP: $225–$600; for MAP add $40 per person

Grenada

Grand Anse Beach at Spice Island Inn

Known as the Spice Island, Grenada is a tapestry of tropical splendor where banana trees by the side of the road grow as tall as the palm trees fringing the powdery beaches, and trade winds nourish the lush mountainous interior.

St. George's, the capital and one of the Caribbean's prettiest ports, is set on a deep horseshoe bay. Clinging to green hillsides behind it are yellow, blue, and pink houses topped with red roofs and historic buildings climbing to a series of colonial forts built to protect the strategic harbor.

Grand Anse Beach, south of St. George's, is a lovely 2-mile crescent of white sand bathed by calm Caribbean waters. It is the island's main resort and water-sports center, with snorkeling, sailing, diving, and windsurfing. Bay Gardens, a hillside botanic oasis, has trails covered with nutmeg shells that wind through woods of an estimated three thousand species of tropical flora.

The main cross-island highway from the capital winds up the mountains to the Grand Etang Forest Reserve, crossing it at 1,910 feet within a few hundred yards of Grand Etang, an extinct volcano whose crater is filled with a lake.

The Grand Etang National Park, part of Grenada's new national parks system protecting most of the interior mountains, has hiking trails around the lake, through surrounding rain forests, and to mountain peaks that showcase the island's exotic vegetation, birds, and wildlife.

North of St. George's, the road hugs the leeward coast, passing fishing villages and winding along the edge of magnificent tropical scenery on mountains that drop almost straight into the sea and hide little coves with black sand beaches.

Grenada is one of the world's largest producers of nutmeg and just about every fruit known in the tropics. In Gouyave you can visit the country's major nutmeg processing station. The staff at nearby Dougaldston Estates, a nutmeg plantation, is a wealth of information on the cultivation of spices and tropical fruits.

In the same vicinity, Concord Falls, a triple-stage cascade set deep in the central mountains, is about an hour's hike requiring some rock hopping, but the reward is a lovely waterfall that drops through jungle-thick vegetation to a pool where you can enjoy a refreshing swim.

Information

Grenada Tourist Board, 820 Second Avenue, #9D; New York, NY 10017; (212) 687–9554

The Calabash Hotel ◙◙◙

Having a private maid prepare your breakfast isn't a bad way to start a vacation—and she'll serve it to you in bed, if you like.

Since it opened in 1961, the Calabash has been the last word in British gentility, attracting lords and ladies and an occasional prince or princess who jet in on their private planes. Once they've checked in, though, no one (except the staff, of course) will know who they are or see them being treated differently from you or me. This is true even though the times and owners have changed.

In 1989 the new, young British owner, Leo Garbutt, updated, upgraded, and expanded the rather staid resort, making it much better (would you believe exciting?), but without diluting any of its grace. Among the improvements were more units with private pools and the addition of a swimming pool and pool bar. The tennis court was lighted, and the beach bar moved to a more convenient location at the center of the beach.

Now there is regular live entertainment and a full range of water sports from a beach concessionaire. Telephones have been installed in all rooms but—the management is quick to tell you—you may have yours removed if you consider it a nuisance. Now that's gentility.

The Calabash is spread over eight landscaped acres overlooking a quiet bay. Accommodations, each named for a tropical flower that grows in the gardens, are in one- and two-story cottages in a horseshoe around a broad, open green with the main building at the center. Each of the spacious, airy units has a bedroom and a bathroom, sitting area, and patio or balcony. Some of the rooms are furnished with canopied, four-poster beds. In the older, more cozy units, where the decor has a warm, Caribbean feeling, the bedrooms and sitting rooms are separate. In the new units they are combined in one spacious room and sport a contemporary look.

Adjacent to or, in some cases, within the unit, is a small pantry where the maid appointed to your room prepares your breakfast each morning, unless you prefer to take breakfast in the restaurant.

In the new two-story units, all those on the ground floor have private plunge pools; and those on the second floor have whirlpools. They also have pitched roofs, which make them seem all the larger and airier. Two units with pools were specially designed to accommodate handicapped or wheelchair-bound guests.

Each unit has a garden view leading down to the sandy beach, where you will find lounge chairs and lots of shade trees. Now that Grenada's famous Grand Anse beach is becoming crowded with resorts and vendors, Calabash's quiet shores are all the more desirable.

The keyhole shaped pool, in a quiet area near the main building, has men's and women's rest rooms and showers. The pool is next to the meeting room, which is also used for guests who want a late check-out. They may keep their luggage here and enjoy the pool and facilities while they wait.

The dining room of the main building and the beach bar both serve an à la carte lunch daily. On Sundays there is a buffet lunch with steel band. Afternoon tea is available in the main bar area. Dinner served family style features a set menu of four courses, each with choices of the daily specials made to order. The fare of continental standards and local specialties is dependably good.

The informal, breezy dining room, with natural stone walls and terracotta tile floors, steps down to a lower level under a trellis of thunbergia, a romantically decorative feature for which the hotel is known. The manager invites all the guests to cocktails at the pool bar on Mondays, and there is live entertainment on different nights.

Despite the assorted royalty that drops in, do not get the idea that the Calabash is a posh pleasure palace for jet-setters. Heaven forbid. It's anything but.

The Calabash is unpretentious and understated. It appeals to a wide range of visitors: couples, honeymooners, families with children, and nature lovers from age twenty-five to seventy-five. Most come from the United States and Britain, and there is a sprinkling of Germans and other Europeans. All appreciate the quality that has long made the Calabash the best resort in Grenada and one of the best in the Caribbean.

Address/Phone: P.O. Box 382, L'Anse Aux Epines Beach, St. George's, Grenada, W.I.; (809) 444–4334; Fax: (809) 444–4804
Owner: Leo Garbutt
General Manager: Clive Barnes
Open: Year-round
Credit Cards: All major
U.S. Reservations: Ralph Locke Islands, (800) 223–1108, (914) 763–5526; Fax: (914) 763–5362
Deposit: 3 nights; 21 days cancellation
Minimum Stay: 7 nights at Christmas and February
Arrival/Departure: Taxi Association rules do not permit hotels to send transportation to airport to pick up guests
Distance from Airport: (Point Salinas Airport) 2 miles; taxi one-way, EC $25 day; EC $35 night
Distance from St. George's: 5 miles; taxi one-way, US $15
Accommodations: 28 units in one- and two-story cottages with terrace/patio. 8 with pools, king beds; 6 with whirlpools and 2 double beds; 14 garden/beach view, queen or four-poster beds
Amenities: Air-conditioning, ceiling fans, telephone, safe, most baths with tub and shower—6 shower only, hairdryer, basket of toiletries; nightly turndown service, room service from 11:00 A.M. to 8:30 P.M., concierge, boutique, repeat guests greeted with fruit basket
Electricity: 220 volts
Sports: Freshwater swimming pool, free use of lighted tennis court, racquets, balls; snooker and billiards room; shuffleboard and beach boules. Hobiecat, snorkeling, windsurfing, and other water sports from beach concessionaire for charge. Golf, fishing, scuba, yacht charters, and hiking with guide in national park arranged.
Dress Code: Casual
Children: Over 12 in winter, all ages other times; cribs, high chairs, baby-sitters
Meetings: Up to 40 people; audiovisual equipment
Day Visitors: With reservations
Handicapped: Facilities
Packages: Honeymoon
Rates: Per person, daily, MAP. *High Season* (mid-December–mid-April): $147.50–$225. *Low Season:* $95–$140.
Service Charge: 10 percent
Government Tax: 8 percent

Ramada Renaissance Hotel ⊙⊙⊙

No hotel in the Ramada chain deserves to wear the "Renaissance" crown as much as this one in Grenada, having launched the island's renaissance in 1985.

Following the tumultuous events that led to U.S. intervention in Grenada in 1983, the hotel's opening was seen by travelers as a positive signal that Grenada was back in business and ready to welcome tourists.

Grenada's renaissance is still in full swing with the numbers of tourists growing annually and now the Ramada has launched a renaissance of its own. The hotel is being completely renovated, starting with the guest rooms, and it comes not a minute too soon. For the new winter season, all the rooms will have been refurbished and many renovated.

Located in twenty acres of landscaped tropical gardens on Grenada's famous 2-mile-long Grand Anse Beach, the Ramada Renaissance is the largest resort in Grenada. Built originally in the 1970s as a Holiday Inn, it has passed through several incarnations. The U.S. government once used it to billet troops—not exactly hardship duty.

A long circular driveway leads to an impressive portico where you enter the hotel, which is set back from the road, through an inviting, breezy lobby that looks through to a large expanse of gardens. On either side are the guest rooms, in long, low, two-story buildings facing the gardens, with a large swimming pool at the center of the complex. The buildings have little to redeem them architecturally, but their shingled roofs and wood-trimmed balconies lend a tropical look, and masses of palm trees and tropical foliage camouflage them so beautifully that the resort has a wonderfully sensual, romantic feeling.

The large guest rooms (typical Holiday Inn variety) are furnished with one king size or two double beds; they have a small sitting area with a table and chairs and sliding glass doors opening onto a balcony or patio. In the newly renovated rooms on the ground floor, carpets have been replaced with tile floors. Room carpeting has been retained upstairs, however, due to the noise factor. All the rooms are now dressed in new bedspreads and curtains of soft floral pastel fabric.

Some guest rooms overlook the beach, a pretty stretch of white sand and calm waters near the northern, slightly less trafficked end of Grand Anse, where vendors can be a nuisance. Indeed, the Ramada's gardens are separated from the beach by a low, hedge-covered fence that acts as a barrier to vendors or anyone else strolling in off the beach.

An open pavilion houses the restaurants, which include The Terrace, a bilevel, informal beachfront dining room offering a full American buffet breakfast and à la carte menus of international and local cuisine for breakfast, lunch, and dinner. Windwards is a bit fancier, an air-conditioned restaurant with à la carte menu; the poolside bar serves light meals and drinks during the day.

The Ramada has two tennis courts, volleyball, shuffleboard, and a full range of water sports, including an on-site dive operator who offers a resort course, PADI certification, and a variety of excursions for certified divers. Golf is nearby, and yacht charters and deep-sea fishing excursions can be arranged.

The pool and the shingled-roof poolside bar and terrace, two steps from the beach, are the hub of the resort's social life during the day. The cocktail lounge and bar in the pavilion become the gathering place after the sun goes down. Piano music is featured nightly, and there's a variety of local entertainment five nights a week. The manager hosts a weekly cocktail party and a beach barbecue on Mondays. Sunset cruises are available daily.

Americans make up the largest number of guests here, but the roster of Europeans is growing. The Ramada Renaissance is the type of resort that attracts people of all ages, and it is particularly suited to families with children. It should appeal to anyone who wants a low-key, very relaxing vacation by the beach in comfortable, unpretentious surroundings with a friendly, efficient staff.

Address/Phone: P.O. Box 441, St. George's, Grenada, W.I.; (809) 444–4371 to 4375; Fax: (809) 444–4800

Owner: Issa Nicholas

General Manager: Russel N. Mayer

Open: Year-round

Credit Cards: All major

U.S. Reservations: Ramada International Hotels & Resorts, (800) 228–9898

Deposit: None; 72 hours cancellation

Minimum Stay: None

Arrival/Departure: Taxi Association rules prohibit hotels from sending transportation to pick up guests

Distance from Airport: (Point Salines International Airport) 3 miles; taxi one-way, US $10

Distance from St. George's: 4 miles; taxi one-way, $5

Accommodations: 186 rooms, including 21 suites in two-story buildings, all with balcony or patio, with kings or 2 doubles

Amenities: Air-conditioning, direct-dial telephone, radio, cable television, in-house movies, clock, bath with tub and shower, hairdryer, basket of toiletries, mini-bar in suites; ice service, nightly turndown service, room service 7:00 A.M. to 10:30 P.M., hair salon

Electricity: 220 volts

Sports: Freshwater pool; free use of 2 tennis courts; lessons, equipment for fee; free snorkel gear. Dive shop; boating, windsurfing for fee; fishing, horseback riding, golf arranged.

Dress Code: Casual

Children: All ages; cribs, high chairs; baby-sitters

Meetings: Up to 300 people

Day Visitors: No

Handicapped: Facilities

Packages: Tennis, dive, honeymoon, Natural Fitness, VIP

Rates: Per room, double, daily, EP. *High Season* (mid-December–mid-April): $208–$300. *Low Season*: $125–$300.

Service Charge: 10 percent

Government Tax: 8 percent

Spice Island Inn ▨ ▨ ▨

Giant almond trees shade the entrance to your cottage, where there's a pan with water to rinse your feet of sand from the beach. This is one of the special touches you'll find at the Spice Island Inn.

Spice opened in 1961 as a rustic laid-back inn that defined the very notion of a Caribbean escape. In 1988 it was bought by some local businessmen headed by managing director Royston Hopkin, who was the 1991 Caribbean Hotelier of the Year. He has gradually updated, upgraded, and expanded Spice, now a Hopkin family enterprise, into a new hotel double in size.

The Spice welcome begins at the front door where you are greeted upon arrival with a cooling tropical fruit drink or a Grenada-style rum punch. It comes with a generous sprinkling of nutmeg—Spice's friendly reminder that Grenada, the Spice Island, is the world's second-largest producer of nutmeg.

The lobby and lounge, the most handsome part of the complex, have high beamed ceilings, terra-cotta floors and decorative tile trim, and quality furniture upholstered in attractive tropical fabrics. The lobby opens onto the beach. To one side is the bar and open-air dining room, directly on the beach; on the other side is a stylish boutique.

Spice has four types of guest rooms. Stretching along the beach on both sides of the main building are one-story cottages, each with two units. Behind them to the right are the honeymooners' favorite: suites with private pools a step away from a bedroom with a king-size bed. The 16-by-20-foot pools surrounded by high walls are large enough for laps—albeit, short laps—and secluded enough for skinny-dipping. Bathrooms here have just been completely renovated. To the left of the main building and also set back from the beach are newer, two-story bungalows where the ground-level suites have plunge pools.

The rooms, spacious and airy with tile floors and screened glass doors, are furnished with light rattan. With the latest renovations, all rooms now have whirlpools big enough for two: either in a tiny garden atrium open to the sky or in a corner of a large bathroom with a skylight.

Breakfast and lunch are à la carte in the dining room or delivered to your patio. Dinner is a set five-course menu with two or three choices of continental and local dishes. On Wednesday evenings a West Indian buffet highlights the most popular native dishes, and a barbecue with steel-band music livens up Friday nights. During the winter season there is music for dancing four nights of the week.

Spice's packages usually have the option of dining one night at its sister hotel La Belle Creole (the restaurant of Blue Horizon, a ten-minute walk from Spice, and one of the island's best), where breadfruit vichyssoise and callaloo quiche were first created.

Guests at Spice spend lazy days on the 1,200 feet of beach, occasionally cooling off in the languid waters or reading and dozing under leafy seagrape trees. To maintain the setting's serenity, motorized water sports are not available in this section of Grand Anse. The policy is laudable, but, unfortunately, it is undermined by hawkers of spice baskets or coral jewelry who shatter the tranquillity with annoying frequency.

If there is one consistent complaint about Spice—and, indeed, the other hotels on Grand Anse—this is it. While it's true that a polite "no, thank you" will usually send a vendor away, how many times should you have to say it? Many guests feel that, at Spice's prices, they should not be asked to deal with the matter at all. Overzealous vendors are not unique to Grenada, but some other islands have been more willing to deal with the problem, usually by creating an attractive area on the beach for them.

Alas, vendors are not the only source of complaints I receive about Spice. Of all the resorts in this book, none seems to have fans as ardent or critics as stern—to the extent that I hesitated about including it here. The fans say the service is wonderful, caring, and attentive; critics tell me it is either indifferent or oversolicitous. Fans rhapsodize over the food, critics claim it is barely edible.

So, I will tell you my experience. I have always enjoyed my stays at Spice and found the service and food good though not brilliant. I preferred the halcyon days of its unpretentious past to its more posh present. Some people can spend hours neck deep in hot, gurgling water looking up at the puffy white clouds rolling by and reveling in such bliss. Not I.

Address/Phone: Grand Anse, P.O. Box 6, St. George's, Grenada, W.I.; Tel: (800) 223–9815, (809) 444–4258; Fax: (809) 444–4807
Owners: The Hopkin family

General Manager: Augustus Cruichshank
Open: Year-round
Credit Cards: All major
U.S. Reservations: ITR; (800) 223–9815, (212) 545–8469; Fax: (212) 545–8467
Deposit: 3 nights; 30 days cancellation. December 16–January 1, cancellation by November 1
Minimum Stay: None
Arrival/Departure: Transfer service not available due to local Taxi Association regulations
Distance from Airport: (Pointe Salines Airport) 4 miles; taxi one-way, US $10 daytime; $14 after 6:00 P.M.
Distance from St. George's: 6 miles; taxi one-way, US $7
Accommodations: 56 rooms in two-unit bungalows with patio, most beachfront and ocean view, all with whirlpools; 10 private swimming pools, 7 plunge pools, twins, 2 doubles, or king beds
Amenities: Air-conditioning, ceiling fans, telephone, clock-radio; whirlpool tub, shower, hairdryer, basket of toiletries; stocked mini-bar, nightly turndown service, room service for meals and bar service, boutique
Electricity: 220 volts
Sports: Tennis court, balls, racquets; snorkel gear, Sunfish, windsurfers provided. Boating, diving, fishing, hiking arranged.
Dress Code: Casual by day; elegantly casual in evening
Children: None under 5 in high season; cribs, baby-sitters
Meetings: Up to 100 people
Day Visitors: Yes
Handicapped: Limited facilities
Packages: Honeymoon, all-inclusive
Rates: Two persons, daily, MAP. *High Season* (mid-December–mid-April): $320–$450. *Low Season*: $250–$320.
Service Charge: 10 percent
Government Tax: 8 percent

Twelve Degrees North 🔳🔳

If you were watching television when the United States landed troops in Grenada, you might recall a television interview with an American resident who watched the whole affair from his hillside home. That was Joe Gaylord, and he has lived here since 1969, when he gave up the real estate business in New York for his patch in paradise.

Joe created Twelve Degrees North, which takes its name from the latitude of Grenada, out of the frustration of not finding a resort like he wanted for his vacation. His nest is the most unhotel hotel you are ever likely to find. Joe believes it is unique in the Caribbean, and perhaps it is.

The small complex has only eight units of one and two bedrooms. They are situated in three two-story buildings that are interconnected by steps. The rooms have terra-cotta floors and are tastefully decorated with rattan furniture and colorful fabrics and local art on the walls.

The bedrooms have two twin beds joined by a king-size headboard. The two bedroom suites have two baths and large living rooms. The suites on the second floor have pitched ceilings, which make them seem more spacious; they also enjoy better views. All the units have kitchens and terraces with picture-postcard views of the Caribbean and the lush Grenada coast, and all face west, making your terrace the ideal perch at sunset for enjoying the full bottle of rum punch you will find in your refrigerator upon arrival. And that's not all you'll find in it.

Your refrigerator and pantry will be fully stocked with beverages and food—chicken, fish, fruits, vegetables, bread, and other staples—for your stay. The reason for this horn of plenty is one of the features that makes Twelve Degrees so unusual. Namely, for your entire stay, you will have a personal attendant (a combination maid, cook, and housekeeper) assigned exclusively to your suite.

Joe and his wife, Pat, have devised a system that seems to work like magic for them, the women attendants, and their guests. Each unit is assigned a maid whose sole job is to care for the occupants of her unit and her unit only, year in and year out. She is available from 8:00 A.M. to 2:30 P.M. daily and will keep your room immaculate, change the linens, do your personal laundry, and cook and serve your breakfast and lunch.

If you do not want her to come as early as 8:00 A.M., no problem; just say so. If you don't need her to hang around to serve you lunch, just tell her. She can make your lunch and leave. For the evening you are on your own, but if you would like her to prepare your dinner in advance she will do that, too. If you don't care to bother with dinner, there are restaurants nearby and some fine ones around the island.

You pay for the provisions that are stocked for you in advance of your arrival. If you do not intend to use certain items, you can tell Joe or your attendant, and they will be deducted from your bill.

You will find that these women are good cooks and are pleased to introduce you to Grenadian cuisine, but if you prefer your own style of cooking, they will prepare meals as you request.

Joe was as careful about selecting his location as he is about picking his staff or getting the right kind of guests—namely, ones who are suited to the quiet, intimate ambience of this resort. He does not welcome children, for example, simply because his guests do not want them around. Most people come for the tranquillity, and, anyone who needs activity or entertainment would definitely be in the wrong place.

Twelve Degrees North is about as low-key and laid-back as the Caribbean gets. It is set in a little cove on a hillside of tropical woods and gardens that fall to a small beach. A stone path leads from the cottages downhill to the beach. There you find an ample-size kidney-shaped freshwater pool, two hammocks, lounging chairs, and a thatched hut with a self-service bar and library of well-read books. Pick a spot, and spend the day.

You might converse with some of the other guests around the pool or by the beach. Most will be from the States—professionals, a university professor, a stockbroker, a television producer—and most are good company.

They usually are experienced travelers who have tried many of the better known, ritzier places in the Caribbean. They probably heard about Joe's place from a friend or from their own research. They are not likely to learn about it from their travel agent, unless they have a very knowledgeable one.

To the right of the beach is a 100-foot pier with a gazebo and benches. It juts out into the sea where the water is deep enough to swim (by the beach the water is very shallow), and there's a reef for snorkeling. The use of snorkel gear, Sunfish, and windsurfers, as well as the tennis court, is included in the rate. Joe has a Boston Whaler and his own fishing boat available for charter. Scuba diving and waterskiing can be arranged for a fee.

When you look up from the pier, you will see the Gaylords' home. If you think you have a wonderful view, wait until you see theirs. And you are likely to do so. The Gaylords often invite their guests to join them for cocktails. Most consider it the highlight of their visit. The house sits out on a point; the entire front is open to the view.

Oh, I forgot to mention, Twelve Degrees North has no office; it's in Joe's house. But if the Gaylords know you are coming, one of them will be standing by the driveway to greet you when you arrive. You can count on it.

Address/Phone: P.O. Box 241, St. George's, Grenada, W.I.; (809) 444–4580; Fax: Same as phone

Owner/Manager: Joe and Pat Gaylord

Open: Year-round

Credit Cards: None

U.S. Reservations: Direct to the hotel

Deposit: 3 nights

Minimum Stay: 7 to 10 nights at Christmas and in February

Arrival/Departure: No transfer service

Distance from Airport: (Pointe Salines International Airport) 5 miles; taxi one-way, US $10

Distance from St. George's: 7 miles; taxi one-way, US $15; to Grand Anse: 4 miles; taxi one-way, US $8

Accommodations: 8 suites (6 one-bedroom; 2 two-bedroom), all with terrace and kitchen, and twin beds
Amenities: Ceiling fans, telephone, television; kitchen, bath with shower, basket of toiletries, personal attendant
Electricity: 220 volts
Sports: Freshwater swimming pool. Use of tennis court, snorkel gear, Sunfish, windsurfing included. Scuba, fishing, waterskiing for fee. Trail hiking, birding arranged.
Dress Code: Casual
Children: None under 15, year-round
Meetings: None
Day Visitors: Not suitable
Handicapped: No facilities
Packages: None
Rates: Two persons, daily, FAP. *High Season* (mid-December–mid-April): $150. *Low Season*: $115.
Service Charge: 10 percent
Government Tax: 8 percent

~~~~ ON THE HORIZON ~~~~

La Source

Those who know Le Sport in St. Lucia will cheer at the news that this well-known health and fitness haven is soon to have a sibling in Grenada. It, too, will have an "Oasis" with similar spa features—loofah rubs, saunas, facials, Swiss needle shower, yoga, and stress management—and an array of sports facilities including water sports, tennis, and fencing.

Guest rooms are designed for the luxury-minded with such amenities as bathrobes, fresh fruit on arrival, special soaps and lotions, and hairdryers. The decor is fresh and tropical to complement the mood. Dining at either the Terrace Bar or the main restaurant will feature tasty but "good-for-you" cuisine.

La Source is an all-inclusive resort. Its opening is planned for mid-1993.

Address/Phone: Pointe Salines, St. George's, Grenada
U.S. Reservations: Tropical Holidays, (800) 544–2883
Accommodations: 100 ocean-view rooms and suites
Rates: Per person, daily, all-inclusive. *High Season* (December 18–April 15): $230–$290; (April 16–April 27): $205–$225. *Low Season*: Not available.

Guadeloupe

Les Petits Saints aux Anacardiers

A department of France, Guadeloupe is the center of the French West Indies, where the people, cuisine, and language are as French as the ambience. It is actually two islands in the shape of a butterfly, connected by a bridge. The two parts are so close it is difficult to see the separation, but they're so different it is easy to tell them apart.

Grande-Terre, the eastern wing, is a low, limestone island with rolling terrain and white sand beaches. Pointe-à-Pitre, in the southwest corner, is Guadeloupe's main city and the center of its commerce. A pretty central square is bordered by colonial townhouses, which recently have been renovated as restaurants, cafes, and boutiques.

The main resorts are located along the south coast between Pointe-à-Pitre and the eastern end, Pointe des Chateaux, a scenic headland where the Atlantic and Caribbean waves collide. Biking, as big a sport here as in France, is a popular way to tour. Windsurfing and yachting are also well established.

Basse-Terre, the western wing, is mostly covered by the National Park of Guadeloupe, with towering mountains and a smoking volcano, La Soufrière, at over 4,000 feet; steep gorges; and the highest waterfalls in the Caribbean. The Route de la Traversée, the cross-island highway, passes through the heart of the park and provides access to more than a dozen trails from a ten-minute stroll to a 10 mile trek in the forested mountains. On the west coast, the Underwater Park of Pigeon Island, also known as the Cousteau Underwater Reserve, is a popular spot for snorkeling and diving. Deep-sea fishing is also available.

The picturesque old town of Basse-Terre in the southwest corner is Guadeloupe's capital. From here a road leads up to the cone of the volcano, from which there are trails to the summit. Throughout the mountains behind the capital, magnificent rain forests have trails and spectacular scenery.

Directly south of Basse-Terre, Iles des Saintes is an archipelago of eight tiny islets scalloped with white-sand beaches. Of the group, only Terre-de-Haut has hotels and tourist facilities. The island is particularly popular for day excursions from Basse-Terre and Pointe-à-Pitre.

Information

French West Indies Tourist Board, 610 Fifth Avenue, New York, NY 10020; (212) 757–1125

Hamak ◙◙◙ ✿

Six weeks after Hurricane Hugo ripped through the Caribbean in 1989, I made an inspection trip to report on the damage. Guadeloupe, one of the most severely damaged islands, was busy at work rebuilding but the evidence of destruction was everywhere—everywhere except Hamak.

Although it's located in St. François, which was leveled by the storm, Hamak looked barely touched. I was astonished. The repairs had already been completed, including replacing five thousand plants in its beautiful gardens. Owner Jean François Rozan doesn't waste much time, anytime.

Located by the sea on a six-and-a-half-acre plot at the southeastern end of Grande-Terre, about as far as you can get and still be on the mainland, Hamak is a secluded tropical escape with an ambience of elegant informality, appreciated most by Francophiles. Step into the entrance and you really are in another world. Walk outside, and there's a Robert Trent Jones golf course at the front door, and less than a mile down the road a marina, water sports, shops, restaurants, bars, a disco, and a casino.

I have the feeling that Hamak's location was selected with the same efficiency with which the resort was designed, reflected in its practical guest rooms, man-made beach, and swift cleanup after Hugo.

From a small lobby garden walkways lead to the bungalows, which are barely visible in the jungle of tropical foliage around them. The bungalows are clustered in groups at various locations—beach, seafront, or garden view—and priced accordingly.

Each cottage has two parallel units with a connecting door, opened when both units are occupied by one family or friends. Otherwise each unit is totally private. It has a bedroom/living room with two patios: a covered one in front furnished with a table and chairs and a hammock (*le hamak* in French; the emblem is everywhere) and another in the rear, a walled garden patio with lounges where you can sunbathe au naturel and cool off in the large, tiled garden shower. Both ends of the interior room open onto the patios through glass doors, so that the gardens outside are always inside.

Hamak's rooms are small, simple, and functional. Within the unit the sitting room is separated from the bedroom by a wall unit. It has a drop-leaf desk and shelves on the living room side and a closet with sliding mirrored doors in the bedroom, furnished with side-by-side twins/king-size bed. The kitchenette in an alcove is for not-serious cooking, such as morning coffee and lunchtime sandwiches. The bathroom is large and well equipped.

Hamak has two dining rooms, one opening onto the beach, the other beside an enclosed garden. Both are intimate and romantic in the evening, with indirect lighting in the gardens and candlelight on the tables. At lunch, service is limited to the hotel guests, but in the evening dinner reservations in advance are taken for outside visitors. À la carte menus highlight seafood, creole, and French cuisine with daily specials. A buffet is served at breakfast along with hot dishes made to order.

A small plaque hangs in the open-air dining pavilion and bar called Kalumet (from the Amerindian word, *calumet*, the ceremonial peace pipe). It commemorates the summit meeting held here by presidents Jimmy Carter, Valéry Giscard d'Estaing, James Callaghan, and Helmut Schmidt in 1979, a year after the resort opened.

Hamak does not have a swimming pool, but it has a swimming lagoon, a Jacuzzi by the beach, and three man-made beaches. Two are tiny islands of sand above the sea wall at the water's edge; the third is a stretch of sand by the sea with lounge chairs and umbrellas, and topless sunbathers (you're in France, remember?).

The 18-hole Robert Trent Jones golf course, which has a clubhouse and snack bar in front of the hotel, provides guaranteed starting times for Hamak guests. The hotel shares lighted tennis courts with the Meridien, less than a quarter of a mile down the road.

The water-sports center rents snorkel gear, Sunfish and Hobiecats, jet skis, and water skis. The area is particularly popular for windsurfing. But guests at Hamak are not really here for a great deal of sports activity. They are more likely the type who want to relax, explore the island by car, and perhaps charter the resort's plane that leaves from its private airstrip on day trips to nearby islands.

Hamak's well-trained staff speak English, some more than others, but among the guests you will hear more French, German, and Italian than English. Anytime you want a change of pace or ambience, you need only take a five- or ten-minute walk down the road to find the action.

Address/Phone: St. François, 97118 Guadeloupe, F.W.I.; (590) 88–59–99; Fax: (590) 88–41–92

Owner/General Manager: Jean François Rozan

Open: Year-round except September to early October

Credit Cards: All major

U.S. Reservations: Caribbean Inns Ltd., (800) 633–7411, (803) 785–7411; Fax: (803) 686–7411

Deposit: 3 nights; 30 days cancellation

Minimum Stay: 13 nights during Christmas, 7 nights in February, 3 nights balance of year.

Arrival/Departure: Transfer arranged

Distance from Airport: (Pointe-à-Pitre Airport) 21 miles (45 minutes); taxi one-way, one to three passengers, FF 325 daytime; FF 350 night; private airport on premises; private charter from Antigua or St. Martin

Distance from Pointe-à-Pitre: 23 miles; taxi one-way, FF 250 daytime; FF 300 nighttime

Accommodations: 56 units in 28 bungalows (25 sea views; 31 garden view) all with terrace and patio; king beds

Amenities: Air-conditioning, direct-dial telephone, wall safe, kitchenette with refrigerator; bath with tub and shower, hairdryer, bidet; outdoor shower, room service, boutique; television and radios on request

Electricity: 220 volts; adapter necessary

Sports: Jacuzzi; no swimming pool. Tennis included. Special arrangements/ fees for golf. Boating, fishing, horseback riding, scuba (not good in this area), waterski arranged.

Dress Code: Casual but chic; no bathing attire in restaurants; men must wear shirt, but tie not required.

Children: All ages; cribs, baby-sitters

Meetings: Up to 30 people

Day Visitors: Welcome for dinner with reservations

Handicapped: Limited facilities

Packages: Honeymoon
Rates: Per room, double, daily, EP. *High Season* (mid-December–mid-April): $300–$350. *Low Season* (April 4–October 31): $200–$250.
Service Charge: Included
Government Tax: Included

Les Petits Saints aux Anacardiers ◉

Formerly the house of the mayor of Terre-de-Haut, who opened it to guests as the Auberge des Anacardiers in 1986, the small hilltop inn is named for the *anacardier* (cashew tree in French). In 1991 two Guadeloupeans who are no strangers to the hospitality business bought it.

Jean-Paul Colas and Didier Spindler are the proprietors of Chez Deux Gros ("The Two Fat Guys' Place"), a popular restaurant in Gosier, Guadeloupe's main resort center. Didier spent several years with Club Med, and is also a successful artist whose work hangs in the inn.

Their latest venture is a delightful hideaway set in exuberant tropical gardens—cashew trees are only one of the varieties—with a fabulous view of the pretty little town of Bourg and its yacht-filled harbor embraced by the steep green hills of Terre-de-Haut. The hotel will charm travelers who like unusual, very personal, offbeat places.

The cozy inn is furnished in antiques, country inn cupboards and sideboards, locally hand-carved rocking chairs, and lots of your aunt's collectibles and grandma's attic. The dining room opens onto a plant-filled terrace with several tables. Guests from town and other hotels come to dine here, too, on cuisine as inviting as the surroundings.

The inn was completely renovated and refurbished by the new owners. The guest rooms are small (some very small) but comfortable and to the scale of the island: simple, basic, nothing fancy. All guest rooms are air-conditioned and have private toilets, but only about half have private bath with shower; others share between two rooms.

The house and guest quarters are built around the swimming pool—one of the few on the island. It is surrounded by a small terrace where you are likely to find some of the inn's habitués sunning topless and taking an occasional dip. Two of the guest rooms open directly onto the pool terrace. Another guest room was added in a small separate building at the side of the house. Also new is a sauna; and next year the owners plan to add an outdoor Jacuzzi near the pool.

The hotel is in the center of the tiny island, just up from the lilliputian town. Although it is not on the beach, the island is so small that you don't have far to go to reach the water. There are no cars to rent, but there are bikes, scooters, and a few taxis, and the hotel will shuttle guests to town and the beach. Most people walk, however—amble would be more accurate.

Guests with lots of energy hike to Fort Napoleon to see the well-preserved eighteenth-century fortification surrounded by botanic gardens and commanding spectacular views of the harbor and neighboring islands. It houses an unusual museum of contemporary art. Who but the French would think to put an art gallery in a fort?

If you have even greater vigor, you can climb Le Chameau peak for heart-stopping views of Terre-de-Haut and the seven surrounding green dots known as Les Saintes, as well as brooding La Soufrière, Guadeloupe's volcano that dominates the south end of Basse Terre across the straits.

In the evening the main entertainment is dining, as is usually the case with the French, particularly in the Caribbean. The inn has a lounge, bar, and library, and there is a piano that guests are welcome to play. But this little jewel essentially is a quiet retreat for "simple, sympathique" people, as Jean-Paul describes their guests.

Bourg, an old fishing village settled by Normans and Bretons, has one street, running east-west from one end of the 3-mile-long island to the other (part of it is a quiet nudist beach). In the town center around the dock, there are boutiques of French fashions and perfumes, art galleries, and cafes catering mostly to day-trippers from Guadeloupe who fill the island until the last ferry departs in the afternoon.

Terre-de-Haut, like Les Petits Saints des Anacardiers, is a snapshot of the Caribbean past, still innocent and unspoiled. It is changing, however. Several new hotels have been added in the past two or three years. A few are near town; the larger ones are over the hill, out of sight in another cove. Many people call Terre-de-Haut the next St. Barts. I hope not and so will you.

Both Jean-Paul and Didier speak English, but most people you will meet here do not. So, if you want to enjoy the hotel and the island, you'll need to brush up on your French. If you are not totally comfortable in a French milieu, you might be wise to stick with St. Martin and St. Barts.

Address/Phone: La Savane 97137, Terre-de-Haut, Les Saintes, Guadeloupe; Phone (590) 99–50–99; Fax: (590) 99–54–51
Owners/Managers: Didier Spindler and Jean-Paul Colas
Open: Year-round
Credit Cards: Most major, except American Express
U.S. Reservations: Direct to hotel
Deposit: $100; 15 days cancellation
Minimum Stay: 1 day
Arrival/Departure: Complimentary transfer arranged

Distance from Airport: (Terre-de-Haut Airport) 1.5 miles; taxi one-way, US $4

Distance from Bourg: Resort is on a knoll just above the town and harbor.

Accommodations: 11 rooms; 3 with patio (4 single rooms; 5 double with queen bed and 2 with twin beds)

Amenities: Air-conditioning, telephone, cable television, and VCR; all with private toilet; 6 private bath with shower, 1 with adjacent shower, 4 sharing 2 showers; mini-bar; hairdryer, basket of toiletries; ice service; room service 7:30 A.M.–11:00 P.M.

Electricity: 220 volts

Sports: Freshwater swimming pool. Sauna. Snorkel gear for rent. Boating, scuba, windsurfing, deep-sea fishing arranged for charge.

Dress Code: Casual

Children: All ages, but not encouraged; crib, baby-sitter

Meetings: Up to 20 people

Day Visitors: Yes

Handicapped: No facilities

Packages: None

Rates: Two persons, daily, CP. *High Season* (mid-December–mid-April): $120. *Low Season*: $90. Single: $80 and $70, respectively.

Service Charge: Included in rate

Government Tax: Included in rate

Jamaica

Jamaica Inn, Ocho Rios

From the 7,400-foot peaks of the Blue Mountains, where the famous coffee is grown, Jamaica's terrain drops to foothills of banana groves and sugarcane fields and orchards of mango and limes. Brilliant flowers, vivid birds, exotic fruit, gentle people whose voices lilt as though they are singing—these are the charms with which this Caribbean beauty seduces her admirers.

Jamaica, the land of reggae, is the quintessence of the Caribbean and offers diversity—in landscape and life-style, culture and cuisine, sports and attractions—that few islands can match. There are waterfalls to climb, mountains to hike, trails to ride, golf, tennis, polo, diving, fishing, plus attractions that are unique to Jamaica, such as the Catadupa Choo Choo, a train that takes you into the mountainous Cockpit country that once sheltered the Maroons, runaway slaves who defied British rule.

A raft will take you down the Rio Grande near Port Antonio. A hot-air balloon can give you an unforgettable view of the countryside, or you can see its beauty up close in the Royal Gardens in Kingston. South Coast Safaris takes you to "undiscovered" Jamaica by boat on the Black River. Helitours flies you over the eastern end of the island.

Jamaica, 144 miles long and 49 miles wide, is located 90 miles south of Cuba. The third-largest Caribbean island, Jamaica was called Xaymaca, meaning land of wood and water, by the Arawaks who populated the island when Columbus arrived in 1494.

The British took Jamaica in 1655 and stayed for the next three hundred years. Although the colonial trappings disappeared on the road to nationhood since independence in 1962, some British vestiges like cricket and croquet, tea parties and polo, are very much a part of the Jamaican fabric, incongruous as they may seem.

If its British past was the stock for the Jamaican bouillabaisse, the traders, slaves, and settlers who came to the island were the ingredients that created a culture as diverse as its scenery. Jamaica's influence in art, dance, and music extends far beyond the Caribbean.

Jamaica's diversity enables every visitor to find a niche. From the laidback beaches of Negril on the west to the quiet coves and busy resorts along the 100-mile north coast to Port Antonio on the east, there are resorts to suit most travelers, regardless of interest and budget.

Information

Jamaica Tourist Board, 1320 South Dixie Highway, Coral Gables, FL 33146; (800) 327–9857, (305) 665–0557

Kingston

Ivor ◉

At night it's magic. In the early morning it's enchanting. And all the rest of the day, it is simply beautiful. The place is Ivor, and it's the best-kept secret in Jamaica.

Jamaica has beauty in every corner of the island, but for landscapes on a grand scale, for heart-stopping vistas, nothing can match the Blue Mountains. Yet you can count on one hand the number of places to stay in the mountains, and most of them are not places you would *want* to stay, unless you bring your own sleeping bag.

Imagine, you can leave steamy Kingston and in twenty minutes you can be at 2,000 feet on a mountainside in the Blue Mountains where you are likely to need a sweater. At Ivor, nestled in ten acres on Jack's Hill, you get a double treat: The peaks of the Blue Mountains, reaching more than

7,400 feet, form the background; and all of Kingston and the coast stretch to the sea at your feet.

But the spectacular location is not the only reason that Ivor is such a special place. Hellen Aitkens, the owner and manager, and her staff are as special as the view every minute. She greets her guests upon their arrival with warmth and charm and insures their comfort. The staff is gracious and refined. Immediately, you feel you are a guest in a friend's home.

And then there's the house, which dates from the 1870s, a structure that has held up through fire and several hurricanes. In 1988 Hurricane Gilbert gave it a whack when its tail peeled off the roof. But now, totally restored, the house has three spacious, comfortable guest rooms and lovely antique-filled dining rooms that have become one of Kingston's favorite restaurants since Ivor opened in 1985.

The guest rooms, too, are furnished in antiques as well as island-crafted period pieces. One has a four-poster bed; a second one, two double beds; and the third, twin beds—all with private bath. Each room has a porch.

The dining rooms are furnished with lovely old mahogany tables and Windsor chairs and a king's ransom of fine old silver on the sideboards and cabinets. A small sitting room/library has a good selection of books on the West Indies, birds, and nature.

The main dining room and two of the guest rooms step down to a covered terrace that runs the length of the house. Here in the early morning, under the cool of enormous trees, you can watch the mist lift its veil over the Blue Mountains while the birds hop about the hibiscus in the gardens that are terraced down the hill. Before you Kingston is a stage coming to life.

In the afternoon while you enjoy tea, you will see the landscape bathed in the soft light of the setting sun. Yet nothing quite compares to the magic of the evening when, from your perch, you see millions of flickering lights, stretching seemingly forever.

If you can tear yourself away, Ivor makes a splendid base for birding or hiking in the Blue Mountains. The nearest trails lead to tiny mountain settlements at 4,000 feet; if you're ambitious, you can hike to Newcastle, the main junction on the road through the Blue Mountains between Kingston and Buff Bay on the north coast.

Ivor will help you organize any type of excursion, including climbing to Blue Mountain Peak. Mrs. Aitkens is active in local birding and nature organizations and has a roster of knowledgeable guides that she can match to your particular needs.

A continental breakfast is included in the room rates as well as a free trip to and from New Kingston each day. Upon request the inn meets reserved guests at the international airport.

Ivor attracts a loyal following from Kingston for lunch, afternoon tea, and dinner; it does not offer entertainment. There is a television in the lounge, and there's always music—from classics to country—which you sometimes need to ask to be turned down (done obligingly).

Ivor's friendly atmosphere appeals to people traveling on their own and anyone who wants a quiet, restful vacation in gracious, simple surroundings. But it will be most attractive to nature lovers, birders, and hikers. On the other hand, who wouldn't enjoy waking up to a view of the Blue Mountains with Kingston sitting below on the plains stretching to the sea?

Address/Phone: Ivor, Jacks Hill, Kingston 6, Jamaica, W.I.; (809) 977–0033, (809) 927–1460; Fax: (809) 926–7061

Owner: Hilltop Services

General Manager: Hellen Aitken

Open: Year-round except 3 weeks in September

Credit Cards: All major

U.S. Reservations: Direct to hotel

Deposit: Amount of the cost of first night's stay

Minimum Stay: None

Arrival/Departure: Transfer arranged; pickup from airport, US $22.50; waiting time after the first hour, US $2.50 per half hour

Distance from Airport: (Kingston Airport) 20 miles (45 minutes); taxi one-way, $22

Distance from Kingston: 6 miles; taxi one-way, JD 150

Accommodations: 3 rooms in main building with patio (1 with twins, 1 double, 1 with 2 doubles)

Amenities: Ceiling or other fan, telephone, television on request, bath with shower, hairdryer available, ice service; no room service

Electricity: 110 volts

Sports: Croquet, hiking, birding. No pool. Tennis and squash arranged.

Dress Code: Informal, but please, no shorts, tams, hats, bare feet, or jeans while dining.

Children: All ages; cribs, baby-sitters

Meetings: Up to 25 people

Day Visitors: Welcome with reservations for lunch or dinner

Handicapped: Facilities

Packages: None

Rates: Per person, daily, EP. *High Season* (December 15–May 31): $80, single; $95, double. *Low Season:* $60 single; $80 double.

Service Charge: 12 percent

Government Tax: None

Montego Bay

Half Moon Golf, Tennis & Beach Club ◙◙◙◙

Perhaps Hurricane Gilbert wasn't all bad. At least not when you can turn such adversity into providence as Half Moon did, emerging in the aftermath better and more beautiful than ever.

The fierce storm that tore through Jamaica in 1988 left Half Moon in shambles, but Heinz Simonitsch, part-owner and hotelier par excellence, did not skip a beat. Austrian-born Simonitsch, who has been managing the resort since 1963, set about rebuilding by creating twenty-three royal suites to replace a group of devastated cottages. He also added a fabulous children's playground and beautified the gardens from end to end. Gradually, all guest rooms have been renovated, including those that were not damaged.

For Half Moon habitués, the most striking change is the entrance: a wedding cake of arches and filigree wrapped in bouquets of exuberant tropical flowers. The approach is so pretty that when you turn into the long flower-festooned driveway, you barely notice that you have passed security gates. Walls are camouflaged with flowered hedges to protect this fairyland of snow-white villas and gazebos.

Set in manicured lawns and gardens at the edge of a 2-mile stretch of white-sand beach, Half Moon is one of the most complete resorts in Jamaica and in the Caribbean. Since it opened in 1954, it has grown from a cluster of cottages around Half Moon Bay—truly a perfect crescent—to a vast resort spread over four-hundred acres. It boasts a wide range of accommodations and extensive sports facilities including a championship golf course, a tennis and squash complex, and fitness center, along with an array of activities, services, and award-winning cuisine.

Its plantation-style buildings house spacious guest rooms, most with sitting areas, large suites, and baronial one- and two-story villas with patios and balconies. The villas have kitchens and large tiled bath rooms and separate dressing areas; some have private or semiprivate pools. They offer privacy, but they are quite a distance from the main restaurant and bar. There is a grocery shop in the hotel's shopping arcade, and the resort can supply private cooks if you don't care to spend your vacation laboring over a hot stove.

Throughout, from the lobby to the guest rooms and air-conditioned meeting rooms, British colonial architecture harmonizes with English country-house interiors that use white wicker and Chippendale-style furniture made in Jamaica. Brightened with floral chintz and Jamaican art, some rooms have four-poster beds.

The lobby, sprightly yellow with white, is alongside a courtyard and shops; it opens onto a large, tree-shaded terrace with the resort's main restaurant, Seagrapes, directly next to the beach. The open-air terrace and its breezy bar are the center of activity throughout the day. In the evening the setting is especially pretty for candlelight dining under the stars. The restaurant offers a wide selection of continental and nouvelle Caribbean-Jamaican cuisine.

The Sugar Mill, on the hillside above Half Moon, has an enchanting garden setting by a two-hundred-year-old waterwheel. Under the watchful eye of master chef Hans Schenk, the gourmet restaurant offers its own original Caribbean haute cuisine, which includes such delights as smoked marlin fettuccine and Jamaican bouillabaisse.

Half Moon's beach is not deep but it is long. Swimmers also have the choice of two large freshwater pools: one near the main building and the other at the eastern end by the hotel block. Guests in some villas enjoy one of the seventeen private or semiprivate pools. The new royal suites have two pools specifically for their occupants. Snorkeling, scuba diving, sailing, windsurfing, and deep-sea fishing (all at additional charge) are available from the water-sports center.

Half Moon's beautiful eighteen-hole championship golf course, designed by Robert Trent Jones, is one of Jamaica's best. Built on undulating terrain in the foothills and by the sea, the 7,115-yard, 72-par course is considered difficult because of the tricky breezes that blow in off the ocean.

A championship tennis pavilion adjoins the tennis complex with squash and tennis courts and a fitness center. There are aerobics classes, saunas, and massages, as well as jogging and biking paths, and horseback-riding trails.

Live music—combo, calypso, or steel band—is available for dancing most evenings in the bar or Seagrape Terrace, and there is a folklore show at least one night a week. A lounge and meeting room above the shops has cable television.

Half Moon is one of the Elegant Resorts of Jamaica and one of its numerous packages includes a dine-around and a sleep-around plan with Jamaica's other Elegant Resorts: Round Hill, Trident, and Tryall.

Half Moon is the very definition of barefoot elegance, combining a certain glamor and style with a laid-back Caribbean ambience. Its clientele is the most international of Jamaica's resorts. It has long attracted a glittering array of British and European princes and princesses—not to mention Hollywood ones—captains of industry, and sportsmen as well as business-meeting participants and groups. The Japanese, particularly honeymooners and golfers, are the latest travelers to have discovered Half Moon. Somehow it all seems to fit together.

Address/Phone: P.O. Box 80, Montego Bay, Jamaica, W.I.; (809) 953–2211; Fax: (809) 953–2731

Owner/Managing Director: Heinz Simonitsch

General Manager: Joseph Berger

Open: Year-round

Credit Cards: All major

U.S. Reservations: Robert Reid Associates, (809) 953–2615, (800) 626–0592; Fax: (809) 953–2731; Elegant Resorts of Jamaica, (305) 666–3566, (800) 237–3237; Fax: (305) 665–3163; CHARMS, (800) 742–4276

Deposit: 3 nights

Minimum Stay: 14 nights during Christmas/New Year's

Arrival/Departure: Transfer service arranged for fee

Distance from Airport: (Montego Bay Airport) 7 miles ; taxi one-way, US $15

Distance from Montego Bay: 9 miles; taxi one-way, US $20

Accommodations: 220 units (89 rooms, 118 suites, 36 one- to three-bedroom villas) of which 90 units in hotel blocks, 12 in villas; some units with private and semiprivate pools; most with terrace; all doubles with twins or kings

Amenities: Air-conditioning, ceiling fans, direct-dial telephone, safe, television; bath with tub and shower, some with bidet, hairdryer, basket of toiletries, bathrobe (in royal suites); mini-bar or refrigerator, kitchen in villas; nightly turndown service, room service 7:00 A.M. to midnight

Electricity: 110/220 volts

Sports: 2 large freshwater swimming pools; 17 private or semiprivate pools; children's pool. Fitness center, sauna, Nautilus gym, bikes, 4 squash (lighted) and 13 Laykold tennis courts (7 lighted), free use; lessons, rental equipment. Windsurfing, Sunfish sailing, scuba, snorkeling, guided horseback riding for fee. Golf, 50 percent discount for hotel guests; pro, pro shop, equipment, caddies, carts for fee.

Dress Code: Casual by day, but long-sleeved shirts after 6:00 in winter; jacket and tie requested on Saturdays. Informal in summer, but shorts, T-shirts, and jeans are not allowed at dinner.

Children: All ages; cribs, high chairs, playground, supervised activities at Christmas, baby-sitters

Meetings: Up to 300 people

Day Visitors: Welcome

Handicapped: Facilities

Packages: Golf, Platinum/all-inclusive, honeymoon, wedding

Rates: Per person, daily, EP. *High Season* (mid-December–mid-April): $150–$400. *Low Season:* $95–$200.
Service Charge: 10 percent
Government Tax: $12 per day winter, $8 summer

Round Hill Hotel and Villas ◎◎◎◎

If you like the idea of sunset cocktails around the same piano Cole Porter played, or dining on the terrace next to Ralph Lauren or the queen of Norway, Round Hill may be just the place for you.

Nothing guaranteed, of course, but for more than three decades this hillside enclave has been one of the Caribbean's most cherished hideaways for the rich and famous. It's still not a bad place to hang out, if you think Audrey Hepburn, Bruce Willis, and Demi Moore—some recent guests—make good company.

You can't mistake the roadside entrance to Round Hill: white pillars with round (what else?) tops. The road along the ninety-eight-acre peninsula rounds the hill at the crest before descending quickly to the main building by the sea.

Round Hill was started in 1953 by John Pringle, a prominent Jamaican who purchased the property. After selling land to some titled Europeans and affluent Jamaicans, he created a deluxe resort by getting his celebrity friends to become shareholders and build houses. Noel Coward, Adele Astaire, the William Paleys, and the Oscar Hammersteins were among those who flocked here in the 1950s and came to regard Round Hill as their club.

Set amid acres of marvelous gardens, the villas cascade from the hilltop to the beach. Today they are more or less as they were originally built: light, airy, and unforgettably beautiful, combining easy Caribbean living with indulgent luxury.

Practical as well as pretty, they are made up of two to four separate suites. Each has a private entrance, but they share the kitchen and central living/dining room. You can rent the entire villa or a suite and still have your privacy along with the services of the villa staff: a cook, maid, and gardener. More than half of the villas have private swimming pools.

The exteriors are similar in design: one-story stone and white clapboard with shingled roofs and louvered shutters and doors opening onto terraces and seaward views. Inside, no two villas are alike, but most merit a spread in *House Beautiful.* Your maid prepares and serves breakfast on your private terrace, from which you can feast on Jamaica's beauty framed by the flowering gardens which surround you.

Pringle's original hotel, once known as the "Barracks," is now the lovely beachfront Pineapple House, a white two-story building at the water's edge. All rooms have wide picture windows with louvered shutters. Rooms are furnished comfortably in traditional colonial style, some with four-poster mahogany beds with carved pineapple bedposts.

Pineapple House takes its name from Round Hill's logo, a Caribbean sign of welcome and a reminder that this was once a pineapple plantation. The emblem seems to be everywhere: carved into headboards, shaped into lamps, and printed on all stationery.

Pineapple House guests can breakfast in their rooms or on the upper level of the Georgian Pavilion, an open-air dining terrace.

Lunch for all is served al fresco on the hotel's tree-shaded dining terrace overlooking the bay. The kitchen at Round Hill was never its strength, but recently there has been a major effort to improve the fare with a new chef and contemporary menus.

You will not have to wait for the manager's cocktail party on Tuesdays to meet Josef Forstmayr. He is a hands-on, ever-present manager and gracious host. Either he or Mary Phillips, the Jamacian executive assistant manager, will greet you on arrival or the first time you dine on the terrace. Mary, a former tennis pro, will help you improve your game during your stay if you ask.

Evenings at Round Hill begin with cocktails in the piano bar, which was recently given a new look by homeowner Ralph Lauren. Dinner settings change from Monday night's barefoot picnic on the beach to Saturday night's black-tie dinner dance in the Georgian Pavilion. On four nights dinner in the upper dining terrace is followed by entertainment featuring the resident band and local artists, with dancing under the stars. Friday is Jamaica Night, featuring a folklore group and reggae band, while a steel band livens up the Sunday scene.

The freshwater pool by Pineapple House compensates somewhat for Round Hill's small beach. A coral reef lies within swimming distance of shore, and use of snorkel gear is included in the rates (as is use of the tennis courts and the transfers to nearby golf at Tryall). And whatever you do, don't overlook the art gallery. It specializes in the fabulous whimsical animal sculpture from Liz DeLisser's Gallery of West Indian Art in Montego Bay.

Times have changed, and Jamaica is no longer the new "hot" island it was in the fifties. But Round Hill is still glamorous in a way hard to find these days. You can be as social or as private as you wish here.

Address/Phone: P.O. Box 64, Montego Bay, Jamaica, W.I.; (809) 952–5150/5; Fax: (809) 952–2505
Owner: Round Hill Developments Ltd.

General Manager: Josef F. Forstmayr
Open: Year-round
Credit Cards: All major
U.S. Reservations: Elegant Resorts of Jamaica, (800) 237–3237; Fax: (305) 666–8505 or Robert Reid Associates, (800) 223–6510
Deposit: 3 nights
Minimum Stay: 10 nights, December 27 to January 2
Arrival/Departure: Transfer service arranged for fee
Distance from Airport: (Montego Bay Airport) 10 miles; taxi one-way, $25
Distance from Montego Bay: 10 miles; taxi one-way, $20; daily free shuttle to town
Accommodations: 110 rooms (36 in Pineapple House, 16 with twin beds, 20 king; 74 rooms/suites in 27 private villas with twins and kings, all staffed); 18 of the villas have private pools
Amenities: Air-conditioning, ceiling fans, telephone; bath with tub and shower, basket of toiletries; kitchen in villas; ice service, nightly turndown service, room service from 7:30 A.M. to 10:00 P.M.; beauty salon; television, radio, and VCR for rent
Electricity: 110 volts
Sports: Hotel swimming pool, 18 private pools; aerobics, exercise classes, jogging trail; 5 Laykold tennis courts (2 lighted), equipment free; proper tennis attire required. Snorkel gear, transfers to Tryall for golf free. Water sports for fee. Deep-sea fishing, horseback riding arranged.
Dress Code: Casual; but shoes, shirts, coverup required in dining areas; no T-shirts, shorts, sneakers in evening, except Monday beach party. After 7 P.M., in winter, jacket requested.
Children: All ages; cribs, high chair, baby-sitters; children can be served dinner from 6:00 P.M.
Meetings: Up to 180 people
Day Visitors: Welcome
Handicapped: No facilities
Packages: Honeymoon, wedding, Platinum
Rates: Two persons, daily, EP. *High Season* (mid-December–mid-April): $300–$620. *Low Season*: $150–$300.
Service Charge: 12 percent
Government Tax: $8 per room per day

Tryall Golf, Tennis & Beach Resort ▣▣▣

To take afternoon tea on the terrace of the Great House at tradition-bound Tryall is to glimpse the grand style of colonial life in bygone days. (No wonder the British didn't want to give up the empire!)

To spend a week in a villa at Tryall is to peek at the life-style of the rich, more than the famous—and today more American than British.

To play golf on Tryall's famous eighteen-hole championship course, the best in Jamaica, is to experience the island's beauty while being humbled by the difficulty of these benign greens. And to travel the twenty-two-hundred acres of this former sugar and coconut plantation is to understand why its aficionados say, "There will never be another Tryall."

Located on the northern shores of Jamaica, Tryall is an exclusive luxury hotel and villa resort of great distinction. Its vast acres flow from forested mountainsides through manicured gardens to the sea. At the center the restored early nineteenth-century manor house sits high on the hillside with gardens sloping down to the beach. The site catches a constant breeze and commands breathtaking, wide-angle views. The waterwheel, installed in 1834 when the Great House was built, is the backdrop of the golf course's sixth hole.

The Great House and nearby cottages house the hotel guest rooms, which are among the finest in the Caribbean. Some of the region's most palatial vacation homes, belonging to Tryall's owners, are in the hills and by the sea.

The gracious Great House, with its antiques-filled parlors, dining room, and broad terraces, is the hub of the resort's social life. Its spacious, elegant guest rooms are situated in one- and two-story wings on both sides of a wide driveway leading to the manor house and in cottages near the tennis courts. There are three categories of rooms, based on their view. Some overlook the gardens and the fairways; the more costly ones enjoy magnificent, expansive views stretching to Montego Bay. Junior suites on the upper floors have small balconies; those below have terraces.

The guest rooms are individually furnished in British-colonial style, accented with a museum-quality collection of antiques. Recently all the rooms and suites were refurbished with handsome new fabrics and posh marble bathrooms.

You can take breakfast in your room or in the Great House and a casual lunch in the delightful setting of the Beach Cafe or by the pretty pool with a swim-up bar below the Great House terrace.

The villas are Tryall's crown jewels. All in harmonious, traditional design, the privately owned mansions, with names like Linger Longer, Tranquillity, and No Problem, are exquisitely furnished and fully staffed. They are set in spacious lawns and gardens, providing greater privacy than the Great House suites. Each villa has its own pool and staff: a cook, chambermaid, laundress, and gardener. Larger three- and four-bedroom villas have a bigger staff. You may choose to dine in your villa or at one of the hotel facilities. (A shuttle service for all guests circles the property throughout the day and evening until 11:00 P.M.)

On Fridays down by the beach, an afternoon barbecue features Jamaican dishes, entertainment by a Jamaican folklore group, and a crafts fair. The setting for dinner—in the Great House or, weather permitting, on its pleasant terrace—may be more grand than the food, although new menus, changed daily and relying more on fresh ingredients, had improved the fare noticeably on my last visit. The service is exemplary. Dinner is followed by light entertainment, usually a Jamaican ballad or cabaret singer or a guitarist, with music for listening and dancing provided by the resident band.

The golf course, familiar to television audiences as the site of the Johnnie Walker Championships, tops the list of Tryall's sports facilities, of course. The attractive course runs along Tryall's 1.5 miles of seafront and through palm groves and rolling terrain, with fairways bordered by fruit and flowering trees, and rises to forested hills before returning to the sea. A tennis complex and a jogging track are near the Great House and water sports are by the beach.

Tryall is tony, gracious living at its best with the facilities of a modern resort. Brides, honeymooners, and romantics of all ages will not find a more beautiful place. But Tryall is a club with a clubby ambience. If you are a part of the club, you will love it. If not, come with friends.

Address/Phone: P.O. Box 1206, Montego Bay, Jamaica, W.I.; (809) 956–5660; Fax: (809) 956–5673
Owner: Tryall Homeowners Association
General Manager: Reinhard Heermann
Open: Year-round
Credit Cards: All major
U.S. Reservations: Elegant Resorts of Jamaica, (305) 666–3566, (800) 336–4571; Fax: (305) 665–3163
Deposit: 3 nights; 90 days cancellation in winter, 30 days in summer; penalty of 1 night's rate otherwise
Minimum Stay: 14 nights at Christmas; 7 nights in villas
Arrival/Departure: Transfer service with packages
Distance from Airport: (Montego Bay Airport) 14 miles; taxi one-way, $30
Distance from Montego Bay: 12 miles; taxi one-way, $25
Accommodations: 52 rooms in main building (20 junior suites, 8 garden

terrace rooms, 24 Hibiscus rooms with twins and king); 45 villas with 1 to 5 bedrooms

Amenities: Air-conditioning, ceiling fans, telephone, kitchen in villas; bath with tub and shower, hairdryer, basket of toiletries, bathrobe; mini-bar on request, ice service, nightly turndown service, room service from 7:15 A.M. to 11:00 P.M., beauty salon

Electricity: 110 volts

Sports: Freshwater swimming pool; some Jacuzzis in villas; 9 Laykold tennis courts (5 lighted); one-day advance reservations required; fee for court, equipment; resident pro. Golf, green fees, caddies required, pro, pro shop. Jogging trail. Sunfish, windsurfing, paddle boats, snorkeling, scuba diving at beach. Fishing, waterskiing, sailing, and horseback riding arranged.

Dress Code: Casual by day; elegantly casual for evening. December to April, jackets required in Great House after 6:30 P.M. (ties optional); jackets not required in summer.

Children: All ages; cribs, baby-sitters

Meetings: Up to 100 people

Day Visitors: Welcome

Handicapped: Facilities

Packages: Platinum, golf, honeymoon, wedding

Rates: Greathouse, two persons, daily, EP. *High Season* (mid-December–April 11): $280–$460. *Low Season:* $165–$235. Inquire for villa prices.

Service Charge: Included

Government Tax: Included

Negril

Swept Away ▣ ▣ ▣

If eight tennis courts, a fully equipped gym, a squash court, an aerobics center, an Olympic swimming pool, and yoga sessions hit the right buttons, you'll think you are in heaven when you arrive at this spiffy resort, which sweeps around the white sands of Negril Beach. These marvels are part of an all-inclusive package: Nothing extra for meals, beverages, use of sports facilities, or even transfers and gratuities. But there is a hitch: Like the Sandals resorts, it's for couples only.

Swept Away has found a niche within the niche of Jamaica's all-inclusive resorts. Not as frenetic or glitzy as the rest, but more romantic than some of its neighbors down the beach, Swept Away enjoys a laid-back, serene ambience geared to people interested in keeping fit even when on vacation.

The twenty-acre resort is the brainchild of successful businessman Lee Issa, whose late father, Abe, is often called the father of Jamaican tourism. Lee shunned the travel business until he opened Swept Away in 1990, but since then he's been swept away more than anyone. This hands-on owner enjoys the resort so much, he spends more time there than at any of his other businesses.

You don't really have to be a health and fitness nut to enjoy Swept Away—mildly interested will do. No one will push you to rise at 7:00 A.M. and hit the courts before the sun gets too hot (besides, the courts are lit for night play). And no one threatens to cut off your goodies rations if you don't show up for aerobics. The marvelous sports facilities are right there, on the premises, when—or if—you want to work out and use them.

Here you vacation in sync with nature. Wind chimes fill the air; flowers and tropical foliage dress the grounds. The Veggie Bar serves up incredible fresh fruit and vegetable drinks that look more like works of art than something to drink.

The architecture and decor throughout show a sense of style. Low-key and in stellar good taste, the guest rooms as well as public areas make use of the best examples of Jamaica's superior quality furniture, crafts, and art. Earth-tone fabrics, natural woods and ceramics, and rattan pieces contrast well with the terra-cotta floors, which are practical as well as attractive.

The guest rooms, clustered tightly between the road and the beach, are in villa-style buildings of cream stucco trimmed in rich, dark hardwood and linked by a labyrinth of garden walkways. Floor-to-ceiling louvered doors and windows, helped by ceiling fans, encourage sea breezes to cool your suite. Spacious verandas with built-in divans and comfy rattan lounges lure you to laze away the hours gazing out to sea.

There are three categories of rooms. Garden view are the farthest from the beach. Atrium suites, closer to the beach, are in groups of four rooms with a central garden. These can be a bit noisy if your neighbors have loud voices. (Also, if you are a light sleeper, avoid the villas along the back of the layout, because they pick up the sound of traffic from the road.) Both the garden and atrium rooms have huge verandas.

The third type are the villas, directly on the beach. Each has two bedrooms upstairs with a shared veranda, and on the ground floor, a kitchenette, dining room, living room, and shared veranda. They are particularly suitable for couples traveling together.

Directly across the road from the resort's front entrance is the Sports and Fitness Complex, the most comprehensive facility of its kind in Jamaica, if not in the Caribbean. In addition to the air-conditioned racquetball and squash courts and the lighted tennis courts (hard and clay), the fully staffed facilities include an exercise lap pool, complete gym with Profi-Sport (European fitness equipment); an aerobics center with an EverFlex floor (it gives when you bounce), basketball, aquacize, sauna, steam room, whirlpool, bicycles, and pro shop.

Water sports include Sunfish sailing, windsurfing, waterskiing, snorkeling, and scuba diving—all with instruction. A dive resort course is included; PADI certification is extra, as is massage. And there is a free-form pool and a whirlpool alongside a great beach.

A commodious, two-level open pavilion next to the pool and beach houses the dining room and entertainment area. Regrettably, it is not in keeping with the sense of style that characterizes Swept Away and is a jarring note to an otherwise idyllic setting. Buffets feature international fare with a Jamaican flair, and table service is available. Pasta and pizza lovers might easily get swept away with the fresh renderings at Feathers, the specialty restaurant in the Sports Complex.

The piano bar is lively in the early evening, and a resident band plays nightly for dancing. Varied entertainment—a native floor show or a Jamaican band with cabaret singer—is scheduled throughout the week. You'll find a game room with billiards and cable television for people who need their periodic fix.

Most guests here come from the United States and Canada, but the number coming from Europe, other Caribbean islands, and Latin America is growing as word spreads about this unusual resort. In addition to its obvious appeal to fitness-oriented couples, Swept Away has great charm for honeymooners and romantics of all ages.

Address/Phone: Norman Manley Boulevard, Box 77, Negril, Jamaica, W.I.; (809) 947–4061, (809) 957–4040; Fax: (809) 957–4060

Owner: Lee Issa

General Manager: Freddie DePass

Open: Year-round

Credit Cards: All major

U.S. Reservations: Swept Away Reservations, (800) 545–7937

Deposit: 3 nights; 14 days cancellation

Minimum Stay: 3 nights

Arrival/Departure: Transfer included in all-inclusive package

Distance from Airport: (Montego Bay Airport) 60 miles; 1.5 hours by car

Distance from Negril: One mile; taxi one-way, about US $3

Accommodations: 134 suites in 26 two-story villas with verandas; 58 garden (24 with 2 doubles; 34 with king); 48 atrium (all kings); 28 beach-front rooms, all kings

Amenities: Air-conditioning, ceiling fans, telephone; bathrooms with shower only, hairdryer, basket of toiletries; television in lounge, room service for continental breakfast, ice service, nightly turndown service.

Electricity: 120 volts

Sports: See text

Dress Code: Casual

Children: None

Day Visitors: US $12 per day provides access to Sports Complex

Meetings: Up to 120 people

Handicapped: No facilities

Packages: All inclusive, honeymoon, wedding (no charge)

Rates: Per couple, per week, all inclusive. *High Season* (mid-December–mid-April): $2,700–$3,150. *Low Season:* $2,550–$3,000.

Service Charge: Included

Government Tax: Included

Ocho Rios

Boscobel Beach ▣▣▣

Freckled-face kids in snorkel masks, clowns entertaining little ones, and father-son tennis matches—you get the idea: round-the-clock activities, counselors, kid food. From beach towels to beach burgers, these tykes want for nothing. The price is even better than paradise; up to two children under fourteen can tag along for free.

Boscobel Beach is SuperClub's country club for kids. It was Jamaica's first all-inclusive property geared specifically toward families with children when it opened in 1987. (Others, since, have seen the light.)

Boscobel Beach, sprawled around an arc of white-sand beach, is absolutely beautiful, with green palms throughout and white tile underfoot. Its various levels are built into a gentle hill, so everything is open, sun-bleached, and lushly landscaped.

The kids are as pampered as their parents. A tangle of woods here, a little carp pond there, and a tropical zoo provide secret corners for kids to explore. Getting around with strollers is easy, as ramps serve some rooms, and an elevator provides access to the beach.

Junior suites, with thick carpet and floor-to-ceiling windows, are equipped with alarm clocks, makeup mirrors, and refrigerators. The sunken living room's plump couch opens into a second bed. In the cavernous bath-room, fresh towels miraculously appear when your wicker basket spills over. You could easily fit the whole car pool in the resort's larger-than-life showers.

Smaller, more private lanai rooms offer more seclusion for couples alone or those with infants. French doors, framed by cabana curtains and flowers, open onto a boardwalk. Here you get a glorious, unobstructed view of sunrises and sunsets over the rippling Caribbean Sea.

The array of activities (and inactivities!) available at Boscobel Beach would challenge even an Olympic contender. To sort it out, attend the daily orientation session with your children. Friendly, twenty-ish coordina-tors chase away timidness and assure parents of unfettered, sybaritic days. Left in charge of your offspring is the Mini Club's battalion of supernannies, whose infectious enthusiasm draws out even the most reticent children.

HQ for the Mini Club is a glass-walled pavilion shaded by palm trees and greenery. Inside, teeny ones are coddled with cribs, baby bottles, and all the diaper-bag necessities. Toddlers can get cozy on the carpet with big colorful cushions. Older children—somehow oblivious to the glorious weather outdoors—play Atari games and take computer workshops, and there's a large-screen TV for the addicted.

Activities are broken into half-hour segments, so you can drop off and pick up your child whenever you want. If you're out on the reefs, super-nannies supervise lunch on the Jippy Jappy Terrace, the casual outdoor dining area.

Little Sarah's day may be even more fun than yours. As you delve into your long-awaited paperback mystery, she'll be into morning Mousercise. Then comes a nature walk, where she may discover her first lizard or man-goes ripe for picking. Toddlers get a kick out of the petting zoo, where ex-otic creatures like mongoose, parrots, guinea hens, and pheasants strut their stuff. (Boscobel is creating a larger zoo and adding a kids campground with tree houses and other facilities to be opened in 1993.)

Small groups go on shell hunts along the beach and splash in the pool with swimming instructors. In reggae class a tumble of giggles and little bottoms helps kids make fast friends. And there's even an enclosed play area with swing sets, merry-go-round, and donkey rides.

Your teenagers need never experience even one hunger pang. They can belly up to the beach bar for a free burger at eleven in the morning or wash it down with a double dipper in any of a variety of flavors at almost any hour of the day. Outdoor table tennis, tennis classes, and pool volley-ball encourage socializing. They can also snorkel among "totally awesome" reefs or try windsurfing, always in the hands of an experienced team.

For the less adventurous, beachside craft classes show you how to weave straw hats or baskets, design a tie-dyed T-shirt, and make kites. At the edge of the beach, girls wait patiently as Jamaican women weave beads and braid corn rows into their hair.

If you haven't seen your kids since breakfast, it's possible to catch up with them at Coketails. Staggered mealtimes let you supervise their supper (in fact, it's encouraged, just to make sure they eat at least once a day!) and dine *à deux* later. Baby-sitters accompany children to the movies and tuck them in.

While teens expend their last bit of energy at the disco or No-Talent show, Boscobel Beach has provided grown-ups with a place to wind down, too.

Couples who come to Boscobel without kids can enjoy Chela Bay, with junior and one-bedroom suites; its own pool and pool bar; Jacuzzi; Allegro, a dinner restaurant; and a piano bar—all off-limits to children.

There is entertainment nightly; weekly highlights include a Jamaican buffet and native show on Wednesday, a staff and guest show on Thursday, and a poolside barbecue and food spectacular on Saturday and Sunday.

At Boscobel Beach you can have it all. Sign up for golf outings or scuba diving instruction, or go to patois class—it's good for laughs (at yourself, of course). For the singularly driven, there are aerobics sessions and a workout gym. Indulge in a massage and pedicure (along with some informative chat about Jamaican life). Who knows, after this you may find yourself mistakenly writing postcards to your kids!

Address/Phone: P.O. Box 63, Ocho Rios, St. Ann, Jamaica, W.I.; (809) 975–3330/6; Fax: (809) 975–3270

Owner: Jamaica Hotels Ltd.

General Manager: Jeff McKitty

Open: Year-round

Credit Cards: All major

U.S. Reservations: Superclubs, NY, (800) 858–8009; Fax: (516) 868–6957

Deposit: $200 per person within 7 days of reservation

Minimum Stay: 3 nights; 7 nights Easter, Presidents Week, and Christmas

Arrival/Departure: All arrivals are met by Superclub representative at airport; complimentary transfers included.

Distance from Airport: (Montego Bay Airport) 73 miles

Distance from Ocho Rios: 8 miles; taxi one-way, $30 (1–4 persons); daily free shuttle to town for shopping

Accommodations: 207 rooms; 156 with terraces

Amenities: Air-conditioning, ceiling fans, telephone, television, radio, bath with tub and shower, hairdryer, basket of toiletries, mini-refrigerator, room service for continental breakfast

Electricity: 110 volts

Sports: 2 freshwater swimming pools, 1 for adults only; children's wading
   pool, 2 Jacuzzis, hammocks; 4 tennis courts, lessons, equipment;
   kayaking, Hobie Cat and Sunfish sailing; snorkeling, windsurfing, instruction, equipment; Scuba for 12 years and older, resort course and
   certification for fee. Golf greens fees and transfers included.

Dress Code: Casual

Children: See text

Meetings: Up to 80 persons

Day Visitors: $45 pass provides access to all facilities from 10:00 A.M. to
   6:00 P.M.

Handicapped: Limited facilities

Packages: Summer, single parent

Rates: Per person, daily, all inclusive. *High Season* (mid-December–mid-
   April): $185–$245. *Low Season:* $145–$235. One child under 14 per
   adult, free, all inclusive; each additional child, 25 percent of adult rate.

Service Charge: Included

Government Tax: Included

Jamaica Inn ▣▣▣▣▣

Located by a pretty beach on Jamaica's north coast, Jamaica Inn is not fancy
or even up-to-date. Yet this unpretentious inn has an elegance and timeless
grace that can only be acquired through years of not trying to be anything
more than it is, just simply the best.

From the moment you arrive, you can sense that Jamaica Inn is a very
special place. Set on a six-acre rise, the inn overlooks a cove with a crest of
golden sand anchored by rocky fingers at each end. A reef, within swimming distance from shore, protects the waters and the beach, and a gentle
breeze cools the air.

Built originally in 1949 as a four-room inn, Jamaica Inn is run by the
second generation of Morrows from New England: Peter and Eric, who
grew up here and consider it their home. They have inherited a fine tradition along with a fine inn and their pride shows in every minute detail.

The staff, as polished as the silver with which you dine, is part of the
attraction. Most have been here at least ten years and underscore the inn's
continuity. When you have breakfast on your terrace—and don't think of
doing anything else—a courtly waiter will lay out a starched white damask
cloth, set the table, and provide fresh fruit and home-baked bread.

The inn's exterior is painted a distinctive blue—deeper than Wedgwood—mixed specially for the hotel and is trimmed with snow-white

balustrades and louvered windows. Guest rooms are located in wings that extend from each side of the house, embracing the lawn, pool, and beach.

The hotel's crowning glory is its accommodations. Your bedroom opens onto a large balustraded balcony with a beautiful view. No hotel in the Caribbean has balconies quite like these. Fully furnished like a living room, each has a sofa, wingback chair and ottoman, breakfast table, antique writing desk, rocking chair, window boxes with hanging vines, and a bathing suit–drying rack with large beach towels. It's like living in a villa.

The bedrooms are tastefully furnished with Jamaican antiques and period pieces. Twin beds joined by a pencil-post headboard can be converted to a king.

Room categories—premier, deluxe, superior—are determined by location: on the beach, on the water, or viewing the beach and sea. Each location has something going for it, but the rooms in the one-story West Wing (rooms 16 to 20) are very special. They are right at the edge of the sea, with the water lapping the rocks at the foot of your balcony. The water is so clear you can see to the bottom. Throw a bit of your morning bread into the water and watch the fish rush to nibble.

Adjacent to the reception is a homey lounge furnished in English-country style. Next door is a wood-paneled bar, reminiscent of an English club. The rooms open through louvered doors onto a large colonnaded terrace that runs the length of the main building and overlooks the gardens and beach. All meals and tea are served on the terrace, except in bad weather when the Pavilion is used. If you prefer, meals can be served in your room.

Jamaica Inn is definitely the place to wind down, not up. Everything is calculated to create a quiet, gracious ambience. If you can pull yourself away from your comfortable room, you will find the beach to be one of Jamaica's finest. You can take up residence under a thatched umbrella for an hour or a day; and the pretty oval pool and sea are both only a few steps away.

If you are more energetic, there's a croquet lawn, tennis next door, and terrific snorkeling off the beach. Arthur, the beachman, will take you sailing, or you can rent Sunfish and Windsurfers at Shaw Park next door.

Dining at Jamaica Inn is a special experience, whether in the romantic ambience of evening or at the famous Sunday brunch created by Chef Battista Greco, who has come from Europe every winter for three decades to take charge of the kitchen. New this season is a young food and beverage manager who has added lighter, contemporary fare to the traditional repertoire.

Guests gather for cocktails at 7:00 P.M. on the front terrace and dine at 8:00 P.M. on the lamp-lit lower terrace, where soft music of the resident band sets the mood. The palms sway gently overhead, and the band serenades with quiet tunes for dancing under the stars. It's straight out of a

Dick Powell or Myrna Loy late-night movie: the romance of the tropics to the point of pure schmaltz. And it's wonderful.

While some might find Jamaica Inn stuffy—a refined ambience with ladies in long dresses and men in black tie—most guests want it no other way. The Morrows frequently ask their guests, most of whom come from the United States, if they want less formality. The answer is always, "Don't change a thing." I agree.

Address/Phone: P.O. Box 1, Ocho Rios, Jamaica, W.I.; (809) 974–2514/6 Fax: (809) 974–2449

Owners: Eric and Peter Morrow

General Manager: Rudi Schoenbein

Open: Year-round

Credit Cards: All major

U.S. Reservations: Caribbean World Resorts, (800) 243–9420

Deposit: 3 nights, winter; 1 summer

Minimum Stay: None

Distance from Airport: (Montego Bay airport) 1.5-hour drive; taxi one-way, $80

Arrival/Departure: Transfer service arranged for charge

Distance from Ocho Rios: 2 miles; taxi one-way, $3

Accommodations: 45 rooms and suites in one- and two-story wings with terrace and twin beds convertible to kings

Amenities: Air-conditioning, ceiling fans, telephone, bath with tub and shower, hairdryer; nightly turndown service, ice service, room service from 8:00 A.M. to 10:00 P.M.

Electricity: 110 volts

Sports: Freshwater swimming pool; free tennis at Shaw Park, water sports for fee. Special rates for golf at Upton Country Club; horseback riding arranged.

Dress Code: Informal during the day. After 7 P.M. in summer, jacket required for men. December 16 to April 15, coat and tie required. Men often wear black tie for dinner; women prefer long dresses; neither is required.

Children: No children under 14 years of age

Meetings: Off season, may book entire hotel

Day Visitors: No

Handicapped: Facilities

Packages: Honeymoon, weddings; no packages in winter season

Rates: Two persons, daily, FAP. *High Season* (mid-December–mid-April): $370–$420. *Low Season,* MAP: $210–$235.

Service Charge: 10 percent

Government Tax: Included in rate

Sandals Dunn's River ▣▣▣▣

If you have never been to a Sandals resort, you need to understand what it is before you even think of spending a week at one. Essentially, Sandals is a well-orchestrated, twenty-four-hour beach party for couples only.

A decade ago Jamaican businessman Gordon "Butch" Stewart (Sandals's founder, owner, and number-one asset) took a dying hotel, applied the all-inclusive Club Med concept, but with a Jamaican spin, limited the resort to couples only, and launched one of the Caribbean's biggest success stories. The $30 million Sandals Dunn's River, which opened in 1991, became the chain's sixth and largest resort in Jamaica (in addition to ones in Antigua and the Bahamas). It's the best yet.

The beachfront hotel, only seven minutes from famous Ocho Rios's Dunn's River Falls, typifies the Sandals experience and reflects Stewart's bounce and boyish enthusiasm. Here, as in all Sandals Resorts, you have already paid for all your accommodations, meals, snacks, beverages (alcoholic included), sports (including equipment and instruction), entertainment, gratuities, taxes, and airport transfers in one package at one price. Now just dive in and enjoy it.

At Sandals Dunn's River there's such an array of attractions to enjoy, you would need a month to do them all, unless you can manage twenty-four hours of nonstop action without end. Should you tire of this Sandals, which is unlikely, you can take advantage of the Sandals special "stay at one, enjoy all six" feature. Couples at any Sandals resort have access to all other Sandals at no additional cost.

Set on twenty-five tropical acres, the multistory Sandals Dunn's River was formerly the Eden II and several other hotels. Before it opened as Sandals, the hotel underwent a complete transformation. Now the impressive structures are in Italian Mediterranean style with Jamaican touches and painted a pale ocher with red tile roofs and wood-trimmed balconies, reminiscent of villas on the Italian Riviera.

You enter from a long garden driveway into an open colonnaded lobby furnished with rather grand divans; a welcoming-arms staircase with iron-filigree banisters leads to a mezzanine. The lobby opens onto a large tree-shaded terrace and two free-form swimming pools. One has a waterfall cascading over rocks, meant to resemble the resort's namesake, and a swim-up bar. The second pool, more sedate, has a wooden deck and a sunken bar on one side. The whirlpool at the water's edge is big enough to accommodate the neighborhood; two smaller ones are located elsewhere.

Guest rooms, in two mid-rise buildings and low-rise lanais, offer a choice of five room categories based on location: standard, superior mountain view, superior ocean view, deluxe oceanfront, and one-bedroom oceanfront suites. The spacious rooms, predictably, have a bright, cheerful decor. An arched doorway bordered with pretty tiles leads into a dressing area and the tiled bathroom. French doors lead out to balconies with views of the sea and gardens or mountains.

The resort's main restaurant serves breakfast and lunch buffets but with an army of waiters on hand. A beach grill has quick snacks such as hamburgers, hot dogs, popcorn, and fresh fruit. In the evening, dinner at candlelit tables in the continental restaurant features an à la carte menu, which is changed daily.

You can also enjoy gourmet dining and white-glove service in three specialty restaurants: Windies, serving Jamaican cuisine; Teppanyaki, offering Oriental foods; and Ristorante d'Amore, featuring Italian fare. Reservations are required, but dining is at no extra cost. Alcoholic and nonalcoholic beverages are available anytime from any of the resort's seven bars and cocktail lounges.

Sandals's staff of young men and women, known as the Playmakers, schedule activities on the beach and in and around the pool, as well as entertainment and special events throughout the day and evening. It's their job to make sure you don't have an idle moment—unless you want to, of course (though, in this action-packed atmosphere, it may be a bit difficult to find many places to hide).

In addition to the white-sand beach and offshore reef, good for snorkeling, there are tennis courts (lit for night play), basketball, pitch-and-putt golf, billiards, shuffleboard, and complete water-sports facilities: diving, sailing, snorkeling, waterskiing, windsurfing, kayaking, and more.

If you're into fitness, you'll enjoy the bilevel health center with exercise and weight rooms, aerobics classes, two steam rooms, wet and dry heat saunas, and hot and cool Japanese tubs. Every guest may receive one free twenty-minute massage during his or her stay.

Other activities include croquet, pool tables, horseshoes, table tennis, and outdoor chess, as well as an indoor game room, movies, slot machines, a television room, and library. There is a weekly craft show; an excursion to Dunn's River Falls and round-trip transportation to Sandals Ocho Rios are also included.

Nightly entertainment features regular appearances by Jamaica's premier performers, theme parties, and staff-produced shows. There is dancing every evening and informal social gatherings at the poolside piano bar.

Most guests are from the United States. While Sandals is for couples, don't think that means only young couples. Every time I have been to a Sandals resort, I have seen couples of all ages, although each resort has its special ambience. For anyone who wants a fun-filled, active holiday in a casual, friendly atmosphere, Sandals is a great deal.

Address/Phone: Box 51, Ocho Rios, Jamaica, W.I.; (809) 974–2544, (800) SANDALS; Fax: (809) 972–2300

Owner: Gordon "Butch" Stewart

General Manager: Louis Grant

Open: Year-round

Credit Cards: All major

U.S. Reservations: Unique Vacations, (305) 284–1300; (800) SANDALS; Fax: (305) 284–1336

Deposit: $300 7 days after reservations; full payment 30 days prior to arrival; 21 days cancellation

Minimum Stay: 3 nights

Arrival/Departure: Transfer from Montego Bay included

Distance from Airport: (Montego Bay Airport) 56 miles (1.5-hour drive)

Distance from Ocho Rios: 5 miles; taxi one-way, US $15

Accommodations: 256 rooms, including 10 suites in five- and six-story buildings, two-story lanais; all with terrace and king beds

Amenities: Air-conditioning, television, clock radio, telephone, safe; bath with tub and shower, hairdryer, basket of toiletries; mini-bar in 5 suites; ice stations, nightly turndown service; no room service

Electricity: 110 volts

Sports: 2 freshwater swimming pools with swim-up bar, 3 Jacuzzi; hammocks; 4 lighted tennis courts and equipment; boating, snorkeling, scuba (two-day resort course), windsurfing. Horseback riding, deep-sea fishing and golf arranged.

Dress Code: Casual

Children: None

Meetings: Up to 60 people

Day Visitors: Day pass, JD 800; separate evening pass

Handicapped: Limited facilities

Packages: All inclusive, 3 to 7 nights; honeymoon, wedding ($250 additional charge)

Rates: Per couple, per week, all inclusive. *High Season* (December 18–April 1): $2,920–4,195. *Low Season* (April 2–December 17): $2,640–$3,395.

Service Charge: Included

Government Tax: Included

Sans Souci Hotel and Spa ◉◙◉

Romance, *toujours*. It's always in the air at Sans Souci. Is it the gorgeous setting or the mellow air of tradition? Or is it the ambience of Sans Souci?

In French *sans souci* means "without a care," and you will not have many either in this pink palazzo by the sea, one of Jamaica's oldest resorts. Sans Souci falls tight between the mountains and sea on a bluff in terraced gardens. Enormous African tulip trees form umbrellas beside a mineral spring that spills down the rockbound cove to the sea. The springs, the centerpiece of the resort's spa, were known for their curative powers as far back as the 1700s. Recent tests found the springs to be on a par with the most famous spa waters in Europe.

The present resort was born in the 1960s when a Jamaican company created a luxurious beachside residential complex to replace an earlier spa on the site. Stanhope Joel, one of Britain's wealthiest men, teamed up with well-known Caribbean architect Robertson "Happy" Ward. Under their watchful eye, Sans Souci was designed with a charming blend of Georgian colonial and Italian Renaissance styles. At Ward's request Berger Paints created an exclusive color—"Sans Souci Pink"—for the hotel, which is still used.

Ward's plans, advanced for the times, put electrical and phone wires underground; an outdoor elevator from the lobby level to the mineral pool below for easy access; and an oversized outdoor chessboard on the terrace with two-foot-high pieces (carved by a local Rastafarian who had never seen a chess set!). In all forty-three apartments were built and sold to wealthy and titled British travelers.

The complex changed ownership several times over the years, but the major transformation came in 1984, when a Jamaican businessman formed the Sans Souci Hotel and Club. His wife, an interior designer, renovated the entire complex, dividing the apartments into deluxe rooms and one-bedroom suites. Her signature is the charming Balloon Bar, with its tiny papier-mâché figures of famous balloonists. In 1988 Charlie's Spa, named for a giant green sea turtle that lives in the grotto of the mineral springs, was added.

Recently a new complex, divorced from the older hotel, was added on a 400-foot private white-sand beach at the west end of the property. It has similar architecture, but the setting and the style of the ultra-posh interiors leave you feeling you are in another hotel.

The new suites are a vision of pinks and corals with buff ceramic tiles and walls. They have folding French doors that separate the bedroom from the sitting room and other doors that open onto the terra-cotta-tiled terrace. The bathroom, marbled from top to bottom, has twin sinks, a Jacuzzi bathtub, and separate shower.

The units are convenient to the tennis courts and to Place Pagelle, a restaurant on the terrace of a new beachside building where lunch and dinner are served. The informal setting is convenient for sunbathers (often topless Europeans), who need only add a top for lunch. Unfortunately, Place Pagelle is so warm under its pretty, translucent awnings you will not care to linger.

Accommodations in the older wings include rooms and one- and two-bedroom suites with large bedrooms and living rooms, most in soft yellow decor with custom-designed fabrics. The largest have dining areas; all have verandas, and all the units are being renovated with a decor similar to the new suites.

In the modern, redesigned main lobby, which has elegant carved-wood furniture, about the only item familiar to previous guests is Sir Walter Raleigh, Sans Souci's famous parrot, who frequently makes his presence known. A game room by the lobby has a pool table, backgammon, chess, and television.

From the lobby, several terraces (one for dining, another with a fresh-water pool) shaded by Sans Souci pink–and–white striped umbrellas and huge tulip trees, step down to quiet lanes that wind through the gardens. They lead to the mineral pool, spa, and beachside pavilion with a gym and exercise room; the fully equipped health center offers a six-day "his and her" spa program. Guests can also take advantage of a free shuttle to Ocho Rios for shopping.

Piano music for cocktails in the Balloon Bar launches the evening, and the resident band and Jamaican entertainers perform on the terrace nightly. And with a restaurant named Casanova in a candlelight-and-wine setting for dinner and music for dancing under the stars, what else is there but romance in the air?

Except, perhaps, Sans Souci's plans to add a large complex of villas on the headland beyond the beach. Let's hope it floats away into the night's balmy breezes.

Address/Phone: P.O. Box 103, Ocho Rios, Jamaica, W.I.; (809) 974–2353; Fax: (809) 974–2544

Owner: Carreras Group of Companies

General Manager: Werner Dietl

Open: Year-round

Credit Cards: All major

U.S. Reservations: FDR Holidays, (800) 654–1337, (516) 223–1786; Fax: (516) 223–4815

Deposit: 3 nights in winter with 14 days to secure confirmation; and balance due 21 days prior to arrival; 1 night in summer and 14 days prior to arrival

Minimum Stay: 7 days at Christmas; 3 nights at other times

Arrival/Departure: Complimentary transfer with L'Espirit package

Distance from Airport: (Montego Bay Airport) 60 miles; taxi one-way, US $80; $30 round-trip in an air-conditioned mini-bus; from Boscobel Airport, 10 miles; taxi one-way, US $20

Distance from Ocho Rios: 1 mile; taxi one-way, US $2

Accommodations: 111 rooms and suites, most with terraces in 5 two- and three-story buildings (12 rooms with twins; 56 one-bedroom—29 twins, 27 kings; 1 two-bedroom, 6 penthouse—twins and kings; 36 beach-front suites, kings)

Amenities: Air-conditioning, ceiling fans, telephone, television; bath with tub and shower, hairdryer, basket of toiletries, bathrobe; mini-bar, tea/coffee makers; ice service, nightly turndown service; room service to 10:00 P.M. for meals, to midnight for beverages, hair salon, spa

Electricity: 110 volts

Sports: 2 swimming pools (freshwater, mineral water); 1 whirlpool; gym with Universal equipment; 3 Laykold tennis courts (2 lit), clinics, lessons free; Sunfloats, snorkel gear, windsurfing, glass- bottom-boat excursion free. Golf greens fees complimentary. Scuba for fee. Fishing, horseback riding, polo (clinics, instruction) arranged.

Dress Code: Casual by day, but no bathing suits in Casanova Restaurant and Balloon Bar. After 7 P.M. jackets required for men from December 15 to April 16

Children: All ages; cribs, high chairs, baby-sitters available

Meetings: Up to 80 persons

Day Visitors: Yes

Handicapped: No facilities

Packages: Spa, honeymoon, wedding, L'Espirit all inclusive

Rates: Per room, double, daily, EP. *High Season* (mid-December–mid-April): $362–$616. *Low Season:* $204–$440.

Service Charge: 10 percent on EP plans only

Government Tax: 10 percent on EP plans only

Port Antonio

Trident Villas & Hotel ▣▣▣ ✿

Trident must be unique. Where else could you find peacocks sleeping on your veranda or roaming the grounds, baronial bedrooms and English parlors opening onto huge chessboard verandas of black and white tile—all so close to the edge of the rockbound coast that you can feel the sea spray?

There is an air of make-believe about Trident. Perhaps it is the gazebos—most villas have one—where you can breakfast in your own private white-filigree perch watching the sea crash against the shore. Or maybe it's the mento band: a combo of spirited elderly Jamaicans who were playing the old native tunes on their homemade instruments long before anyone had heard of Bob Marley.

Opened in 1968, the exclusive retreat skirts the sea on fourteen mani-cured acres along Jamaica's northeast coast with the Blue Mountain peaks towering in the background.

Other resorts have more activity, more social life, and other attractions, but Trident is where the famous—even more than the rich—come when they truly want to relax in magnificently beautiful surroundings.

Approached from the road, Trident resembles an English country post house, its snow-white walls and peaked roofs topped with dark-wood trim and shingles. You fully expect a footman to come out to assist you in alighting from your carriage. The paneled reception room reassures and the clipped hedges and manicured lawn suggest rural England rather than lush Jamaica. Trident's turrets, towers, and gazebos—even a castle—give it a fairyland appearance.

Some guest rooms are in the main building, but most are in villas strung along the shore and connected by a stone walkway framed in well-behaved tropical foliage. The villas have a large living room with hip roofs, white-paneled ceilings, casement windows, louvered shutters that open onto the gardens, and louvered doors that let in the sea breezes (and the peacocks). All have a private veranda with fabulous sea views.

Furnishings and interior decor are created by the owner, Earl Levy, one of Jamaica's leading designers and a self-taught architect. Inside, each villa, in a different pastel color, is furnished in a gracious British-colonial style, combining mahogany antiques with handsome Victorian wicker. The villa on the south side holds the Imperial Suite, and the name is an understate-ment. On the ground floor, the beautifully furnished drawing room runs the length of the villa. The second-floor 30-foot bedroom is larger than most New York apartments. It has a large, four-poster bed (Tom Cruise slept here while he was filming *Cocktail*) and a large terrace. The adjacent small sitting room is where Whoopi Goldberg's bodyguard slept when she occu-pied the villa.

Your day at Trident begins with breakfast on your patio or the dining terrace overlooking the lovely freshwater swimming pool and its pretty gazebo, so popular with brides and photographers.

If it's May—mating season—your day will begin at daybreak, whether you want it to or not, with the raucous cackle and clamor of Oskar, Otto, Olga, and Ophelia, the resident peacocks (earplugs don't make a dent).

There is no menu for breakfast. You will automatically get a platter of fresh tropical fruits, juice, and hot freshly baked Jamaican breads; and you can order any egg dish, French toast, pancakes, or a daily Jamaican special.

If you can tear yourself away from your villa, Trident's two hard tennis courts are located directly across the main road away from the strong sea breezes and sun; racquets and balls are available at the reception area. A quiet beach in a small cove at the end of the villas has lounges and umbrellas.

Beach boys provide snorkel gear and will take you for a sail on a Sunfish, if you don't know how to sail yourself. Scuba and deep-sea fishing can be arranged at nearby San Beach. The most popular excursion is rafting on the Rio Grande, another Levy enterprise, begun long before he came to Port Antonio.

An informal lunch is served on the dining terrace, and there is usually a full English tea at 4:30 P.M. with sandwiches and freshly baked cakes. Dinner is at 8:00 P.M. in the rather grand dining room; a different set menu each evening features continental and Jamaican cuisine. But for all its style, food is not Trident's strong point. It's inconsistent: Dinner one night will be superb; the next evening you might wonder if the chef took a walk.

After dinner, guests gather for drinks and conversation at the piano bar; some will probably dance a while under the stars to the music of the hotel's band.

Visible from the pool, on the south, is an impressive white wedding-cake structure with domes and balconies. Its construction was started by a rather unusual German baroness who ran out of money and left Levy to finish the job. If you have always wanted to spend a night or two in a castle, you can rent Trident's, as did a famous British rock star who had his wedding there.

Trident has a style and glamour all its own. It is easy to understand why it's popular with honeymooners—I can't imagine a more romantic spot.

Address/Phone: P.O. Box 119, Port Antonio, Jamaica, W.I.; (809) 993–2602; Fax: (809) 993–2590

Owner: Earl A. Levy

General Manager: To be announced

Acting General Manager: Suzanne Levy

Open: Year-round

Credit Cards: All major

U.S. Reservations: Elegant Resorts of Jamaica, (800) 237–3237; Fax: (305) 666–7239

Deposit: 3 nights, winter; 1 night, summer

Minimum Stay: None

Arrival/Departure: Complimentary transfer arranged for 7 nights or longer and on Platinum Plan

Distance from Airport: (Kingston Airport) 60 miles; taxi one-way, $80; (Montego Bay Airport) 120 miles; US $120
Distance from Port Antonio: 2 miles; taxi one-way, US $2
Accommodations: 28 guest rooms and suites, all with terraces (12 in main building; 14 in villas), with twins and king beds.
Amenities: Ceiling fans, telephone, mini-bar; bath with tub and shower, hairdryer, basket of toiletries; ice service, nightly turndown service, room service for full breakfast
Electricity: 110 volts
Sports: Freshwater swimming pool, Jacuzzi; 2 tennis courts and equipment. Boating, snorkeling, scuba, deep-sea fishing, horseback riding, hiking and biking tours arranged.
Dress Code: Jacket and tie for men in evenings
Children: All ages; cribs, baby-sitters
Meetings: Up to 50 people
Day Visitors: Yes
Handicapped: Very limited facilities
Packages: Honeymoon, wedding, Platinum
Rates: Per person, daily, EP. *High Season* (mid-December–mid-April): $150–$375. *Low Season*: $95–$225.
Service Charge: 10 percent
Government Tax: $12 per room daily winter; $10 summer

Runaway Bay

Jamaica-Jamaica 🔲🔲

Two major attractions set Jamaica Jamaica apart from its SuperClubs cousins and its all-inclusive competitors: the Jamaica experience and an unusual golf program.

From the locally crafted furniture and art to the music and menus, the emphasis here is on celebrating Jamaica's culture. Unlike some resorts, which could be anywhere in the tropics, when you stay at Jamaica Jamaica you know exactly where you are. It is also in keeping with the SuperClubs policy of giving each of its resorts a strong, distinguishing feature.

Fabrics from the island's mills, lessons in patois, Jamaican food specialties, and a lethal drink called a "Mudslide" are all offered to help you experience what is unique about Jamaica. (The headboards in the shape of palm trees and a setting sun are more than is necessary to make the point, but they were carved by local craftsmen, and that's what matters.)

Next to the resort is its other distinguishing feature and an enormous asset: the eighteen-hole Runaway Bay Golf Course, which SuperClubs owns. Guests staying at Jamaica Jamaica enjoy *free, unlimited* golf. Better yet, Jamaica Jamaica offers the Golf Academy, which, when it was inaugurated in 1990, was the first year-round golf school in the Caribbean. It is available only to Jamaica Jamaica guests.

You can have up to twenty-eight hours of instruction weekly, and the school has a lecture room with video equipment and analysis facilities, ten practice bays, practice sand bunker, and chipping green. Golf clubs and carts are available for rent at the pro shop. On the west side of the resort's entrance is an eighteen-hole putting green; to the east is the Club House. Before SuperClubs acquired the course, it had been allowed to deteriorate. With the aid of a top Jamaican pro, SuperClubs shaped it into a first-rate course with immaculate greens and interesting and challenging fairways.

Travelers who don't know a wood from a five iron need not fear: Jamaica Jamaica has a lot more going for it than just golf. The resort is located on a wide 2-mile stretch of golden sand on Jamaica's north shore on Runaway Bay. It has two freshwater swimming pools and three Jacuzzis, and a secluded corner of the beach is set aside for sunning in the buff.

Other sports facilities include four lighted tennis courts with instruction; a full water-sports program including snorkeling, windsurfing, sailing, kayaking, and scuba for certified divers and a resort course for beginners. PADI certification is also available for a fee. The gym has Nautilus equipment and a daily aerobics and exercise program. There is a jogging track, cricket (and cricket and soccer instruction), volleyball, bicycles and bicycle tours, horseback riding instruction and trail rides, and a nature walk.

The resort has a game room, a croquet lawn, and table tennis, and there are enough scheduled activities daily to keep you busy into the night, even if you never get near a fairway. You might try your hand at arts and crafts, learning to carve wood or make batik. There are reggae and calypso classes, pool games, and glass-bottom boat rides. And when you want to take a break from all the activity, you'll find plenty of hammocks strung throughout the property.

The week starts with an orientation and the introduction of the young, cheerful staff, and the manager's cocktail party on Sunday. Buffet meals are served in the Beach Terrace, a large open-air pavilion conveniently located at the center of the resort by the beach. The Greathouse, which is open for dinner, has a more formal setting.

The piano bar opens for cocktails and different entertainment is presented every evening: beach barbecue on Mondays; nightclub or folklore

San Souci Hotel and Spa, Ocho Rios

show on Wednesdays; staff and guest night on Friday; and a cabaret featuring Jamaican performers on Tuesday, Thursday, and Saturday (no artists are duplicated in a two-week stretch). The Disco opens at 11:00 P.M. and goes until the wee hours. There is a television room, and as part of the current renovations, guest rooms are being wired for cable television.

Guest rooms are located in three two-story buildings on both sides of the main building and the expansive gardens. All the accommodations are being upgraded as part of a long-range program to bring all SuperClubs up to a higher standard of luxury set by its Grand Lido in Negril and Couples in Ocho Rios.

The guest rooms are comfortable, with private balconies overlooking gardens and beach. But the headboards aside, their decor is still not Jamaica Jamaica's strong point. The craftsmanship is to be admired, but the designs are, well, hokey. More attractive are the gardens, which have their own "rain forest," and the fitness center, which is in a lovely open-air pavilion.

Jamaica Jamaica is one all-inclusive resort that welcomes singles. The resort is popular with honeymooners (weddings are offered without additional charge) and it's a bargain for any sports enthusiast.

Address/Phone: P.O. Box 58, Runaway Bay, St. Ann, Jamaica, W.I.; (809) 973–2436; Fax: (809) 973–2352

Owner: SuperClubs
General Manager: Cargill Brown
Open: Year-round
Credit Cards: All major
U.S. Reservations: SuperClubs, (800) 858–8009; Fax: (516) 868–6957
Deposit: Payment in full
Minimum Stay: 3 nights
Arrival/Departure: Complimentary transfer service from Montego Bay Airport
Distance from Airport: (Montego Bay Airport) 42 miles (1 hour by car)
Distance from Ocho Rios: 17 miles; daily free shuttle to Ocho Rios daily except Sunday and to Dunn's River Falls daily
Accommodations: 238 guest rooms including 4 suites in 3 two-story wings, all with terraces; all with twin or king beds
Amenities: Air-conditioning, telephone, television in suites, radio; bath with tub and shower, hairdryer, basket of toiletries; room service for continental breakfast
Electricity: 110 volts, 50 cycles
Sports: See text
Dress Code: Casual; beachwear on Beach Terrace; no shorts or T-shirts in Greathouse dining room
Children: Only 16 years and over
Meetings: Up to 60 persons
Handicapped: Facilities
Day Visitors: Day and evening passes, US $30; disco pass, US $20
Packages: All inclusive, including greens fee
Rates: Per person, per week, all inclusive. *High Season* (December 18–April 29): $1,230-$1,330. *Low Season* (April 30–December 17): $969–$1,169.
Service Charge: Included
Government Tax: Included

Martinique

Hotel Bakoua Martinique

As French as France and equally stylish, Martinique, the island of flowers, is a seductive beauty of savage mountain scenery and sophisticated resorts. From the north the land drops from razorback peaks covered with rain forests and an active volcano to flowing meadows and pastureland to bone-dry desert. White-capped Atlantic waves crash against eastern shores; quiet, dreamy beaches hide in coves on the west. And it's all within a day's drive.

Fort-de-France, the pretty capital, is the shopper's favorite for French perfumes and designer fashions. La Savanne, the central square overlooking Fort-de-France Bay, is bordered by historic buildings and eighteenth-century townhouses; and it's graced with a statue of Napoleon's Empress Josephine, who was born in Martinique.

South of Fort-de-France, the Caribbean coast is scalloped with white-sand beaches. Pointe-du-Bout, a finger in Fort-de-France Bay, is the island's main tourist center, with hotels, marinas, a Robert Trent Jones golf course, restaurants, bistros, and a casino. The two sides of the bay are connected by frequent ferries.

On the south shore overlooking Diamond Rock, a 2-mile stretch of palm-shaded beach is popular for windsurfing. Sainte-Anne, an idyllic colonial village around a tree-shaded square, is known for its seafood restaurants. Grande Anse des Salines at the southern tip has the island's most idyllic beaches.

Dominating the northern profile of Martinique is 4,584-foot Mt. Pelée, usually crowned with swirling clouds. Its eruption in 1902 was one of the most devastating ever recorded. A north-country tour often returns via the extraordinary memorial of St. Pierre, the town buried in seconds under Mt. Pelée's ashes.

Route de la Trace, a central highland road between Fort-de-France and Mt. Pelée, winds north through rain forests; each hairpin turn looks across sweeping views of the capital and coast. On a hillside at 1,475 feet is Le Jardin de Balata, a private botanic garden with more than a thousand varieties of tropical plants.

On the north skirt of Mt. Pelée, Grand' Riviere, an old fishing village of spectacular scenery, is reminiscent of a Gauguin painting. Big volcanic rocks from Mt. Pelée rest at the edge of black-sand beaches where vertical cliffs carpeted with wind-sheared foliage drop to the sea and huge white-caps roll in from the Atlantic.

Information

French West Indies Tourist Board, 610 Fifth Avenue, Fifth Floor, New York, NY 10020; (212) 757–1125.

Hotel Bakoua Martinique ◉◉◉

The first time I visited Martinique two decades ago, the Bakoua was the only hotel of any size or merit in the area of Pointe-du-Bout—all thirty rooms of it. Today the Bakoua has more than quadrupled in size, and Pointe-du-Bout has mushroomed into the center of Martinique's tourism with many hotels, restaurants, cafes, discos, marinas, and water-sports centers.

Of course, the ambience of the hotel and its environs has changed completely. If you like to be at the heart of the action rather than sequestered in a quiet retreat, and if you prefer the conveniences of a large resort to the intimacy of a small inn, you will be happy at the Bakoua.

In January 1991 the Bakoua reopened after being closed for six months for a total renovation by its new owners, a large French chain, to upgrade it to the Sofitel four-star category. Surprisingly, the hotel now has more of the feeling of the earlier hotel than it did in the intermediate years when it had lost its personality.

The Bakoua's new lobby has been redesigned to capture a panoramic view of the Bay of Fort-de-France. The dining room, with its open-air creole architecture, embraces the tropical setting that faces the cove of Anse Mitan. You can watch the yachts at breakfast and have a romantic view of the distant lights of Fort-de-France in the evening.

The biggest change, however, is in the guest rooms and suites; which have been given a more classic look with rich mahogany colonial-style furniture—including some carved headboards on four-poster beds and cane-backed chairs—accented by pretty pastel designer fabrics and ceramic-tile floors. They have fashionable new marble and tile bathrooms.

Accommodations are located in four large, long white-stucco buildings topped by red roofs, all with balconies, overlooking either the gardens or the sea. Three of the buildings are built in the gardens on a rise above the bay; the third is a two-story block directly on the hotel's small beach, with the upper-story balconies shaded by coral-and-white-striped awnings.

In addition to its pretty, oval swimming pool perched on a terrace overlooking the beach and the bay, the Bakoua offers tennis, windsurfing, an introductory dive lesson, and a putting green for no additional charge. The fitness center with a gym, exercise equipment, and aerobic classes costs extra, and water sports such as sailing, diving, and waterskiing are available from a nearby dive shop for a fee.

The resort has twice-daily shuttle service to the island's only eighteen-hole course designed by Robert Trent Jones, which is nearby. Sailing excursions, deep-sea fishing, and horseback riding can be arranged. The Bakoua has its own dock where visiting yachts tie up and from which you can take an odyssey of a day or longer.

From the lobby and dining level at the top of the rise, steps lead down to the beach and water sports. Le Coco is the beach bar at the water's edge; and La Sirène, a casual but not inexpensive beachside restaurant, serves snacks and a light lunch of salads, fish, and grilled meats. Le Chateaubriand is the main restaurant. It has a buffet-style breakfast room and a gourmet dining room for evening, featuring French creole and international cuisine, as well as nightly musical entertainment.

Le Gommier, the open-air cocktail lounge off the lobby, has a ringside seat for sunset along with music for listening. The cozy lounge, with its circular sunken bar, is something of the hotel's social center. The balmy tropical air, the convivial ambience, and the wonderful views of the sailboats in the bay impart the warmth and friendliness of the old Bakoua.

Even with its new luxury, the Bakoua is essentially low-key. Its biggest attraction is its location at the center of Pointe-du-Bout resort life, yet quietly secluded in its own gardens. It's connected by frequent, inexpensive ferries to the heart of the capital directly across the bay and offers the services of a modern resort hotel in the French milieu of Martinique. You might want to brush up on your French.

Address/Phone: La Pointe-du-Bout, 97229 Les Trois Ilets, Martinique; (596) 66–02–02; Fax: (596) 66–00–41
Owner: Accor/Pullman Resort Hotels
General Manager: Claude Chevauche
Open: Year-round
Credit Cards: All major
U.S. Reservations: Resinter, (800) 221–4542, (212) 575–2228; Fax: (212) 719–5763
Deposit: 3 nights winter, 1 night summer; 30 days in advance; 21 days cancellation winter, 7 days summer
Minimum Stay: None
Arrival/Departure: Meeting service at the airport
Distance from Airport: (Lamentin Airport) 10 miles; taxi one-way, FF 100
Distance from Fort-de-France: 20 miles (45 minutes by road; 20 minutes by ferry); ferry one-way, FF 16
Accommodations: 138 rooms and suites (38 beachside, 53 ocean view, 39 garden view) in 3 four-story buildings and 1 two-story block, all with balconies or patios; king or twin beds
Amenities: Air-conditioning, direct-dial telephone, cable television, VCR, radio, safe; bath with tub, shower, and radio, hair dryer, makeup mirror, basket of toiletries; mini-bar; room service when restaurants operating; concierge; shop
Electricity: 220 volts
Sports: Freshwater swimming pool, 2 lit tennis courts (night-play charge), windsurfing, putting green, kayaks, table tennis. Scuba, waterskiing, sailing trips, deep-sea fishing, Sunfish, fishing dock, squash, aerobics, exercise center, and gym for fee. Golf, horseback riding, biking, hiking arranged.
Dress Code: Casual
Children: All ages; cribs, baby-sitters
Meetings: Up to 50 persons
Day Visitors: Yes
Handicapped: No facilities
Packages: Summer
Rates: Per room, single or double, daily, EP. *High Season* (mid-December–mid-April): $208–$300. *Low Season*: $138–$224.
Service Charge: Included in rate
Government Tax: Included in rate

~~~~~~~~~ ON THE HORIZON ~~~~~~~~~

Habitation Lagrange

Built into the ruins of a former sugar plantation, the Habitation Lagrange is a delight for travelers who prefer mountain vistas and tropical gardens to the beach. It's nestled in the hills above Marigot on the Atlantic coast. Your transportation around the environs is by horse-drawn carriage, recalling old plantation days. The staff is attired in costumes of eighteenth-century Martinique.

A manor house encompasses the drawing room, dining room, and library. Guest rooms furnished in creole style with four-poster beds, rocking chairs, and armoires are located in restored buildings nearby. The ambience is traditional, but the rooms have modern amenities: air-conditioning, television, video, radio, mini-bar, and direct-dial phones. Food stresses Martinique's creole fare as well as French cuisine. Facilities include a pool, tennis court, and a golf practice area (all lighted).

Address/Phone: 97225 Le Marigot, La Martinique, F.W.I.; (596) 53–60–60; Fax: (596) 53–50–58
U.S. Reservations: Caribbean Inns, (800) 633–7411
Accommodations: 16 rooms and 1 suite
Rates: Per room, daily, CP. *High Season* (mid-December–mid-April): $350–$375. *Low Season*: Not available.

Nevis

Nisbet Plantation and Mt. Nevis

The lovely island of Nevis still typifies the Caribbean as it used to be and as many would like it to remain: gracious, innocent, and charming. Separated from St. Kitts by a 2-mile channel, Nevis rises from the sea in almost perfect symmetry to a dark green cone more than 3,000 feet at its cloud-capped peak. Stretches of golden beach protected by coral reefs outline the coast.

Nevis was discovered by Christopher Columbus in 1493, and the first settlers came from St. Kitts in 1628. Tobacco was their first export. By the eighteenth century it had been replaced by sugar as the main crop, bringing with it large plantations and great wealth. Soon Nevis became the social hub of the Caribbean and developed an international reputation as the "Queen of the Caribbees."

Charlestown, on the west side of the island, is a West Indian colonial village lined with a medley of colorful old buildings so perfectly caught in time, it could almost be a movie set. The Hamilton Museum was the home of Nevis's most famous native son, Alexander Hamilton, the first United States Secretary of the Treasury, who was born in Nevis in 1755.

North of Charlestown, Pinney's Beach is a 4-mile stretch of palm-fringed sands, where the Four Seasons Resort—the island's first large modern hotel and golf course—opened in January 1991, bringing with it jobs and a tourist boomlet.

Nevis and its sister island of St. Kitts have something of a monopoly on charming historic inns set in old sugar plantations, much as the plantations themselves cornered the market on sugar in their heyday. Morning Star, known locally as Gingerland, has several plantation inns located at about 1,000-foot elevation on the southern slopes of Mount Nevis. Lanes and footpaths, ideal for hikers, run from one estate to the other. For the first time, organized tours of Nevis with particular emphasis on the historical and natural attractions are available through The Nevis Academy (Box 493, Nevis, W.I.; (809) 469–5346).

Information

St. Kitts and Nevis Tourist Board, 414 East 75th Street, New York, NY 10021; (212) 535–1234.

Four Seasons Resort Nevis ◎ ◎ ◎ ◎

Guidebook writers like me spend a lot of time thinking about "what might have been." We are inclined to redesign hotels, rearrange room furniture, add a touch here and there—all in our head, of course. My mind was working overtime when I visited the new Four Seasons in Nevis, the first Caribbean resort of the prestigious, luxury hotel group.

Located on Nevis' leeward coast, Four Seasons enjoys a glorious setting along a 2,000-foot stretch of golden sand on Pinney's Beach, where hundreds of stately palms grace the property from the beach to the foothills of lofty Mt. Nevis. Arriving by boat from St. Kitts, you see the resort in the distance after twenty minutes at sea.

The Four Seasons literature describes the architecture as "plantation-style cottages," so I had expected to see colonial-type villas on the hillside, taking advantage of the view and the breezes as smart plantation owners had done when they built their estate houses in colonial times. To my surprise I found twelve long, two-story buildings, devoid of any Caribbean character, strung out along the beach. They reminded me of army barracks. What might have been, I thought—Four Seasons missed a fantastic opportunity.

Why, if I was so disappointed, have I included it here? The answer is simple. The resort delivers the high standards for which Four Seasons is known, and its outstanding facilities go a long way to overcome the lousy architecture.

The resort's commitment to hire and train local people is another plus. The younger Nevisians are still learning the ways of a deluxe hotel, but they are unfailingly courteous and gracious.

The modern Great House with lounges, bars, and restaurants anchors the complex. Its rather opulent lobby rises high to a mahogany-beamed ceiling with ornate lights; a wall of French doors opens onto flower-filled terraces and the pool. To one side is a mahogany-paneled library/bar complete, surprisingly, with a fireplace and paintings of tall-masted sailing ships.

Two restaurants offer a choice of casual or elegant dining. Both highlight local fresh fruits, vegetables, and seafood, including lobster from the resort's grotto, which holds up to five hundred lobsters. The casual Grill Room is a large, open-air restaurant with colorful decor.

The more formal Dining Room, set with candlelit tables, flowers, and linens, is designed to evoke the grand life-style of colonial plantation owners. The room has a wide-plank hardwood floor, a high beamed ceiling with ornate chandeliers, cut-stone fireplace (another fireplace!) flanked by mahogany sideboards, and French doors on three sides. There is a small dance floor and music by a local combo. Wednesday evenings feature an outdoor buffet of West Indian food and dancing under the stars to a steeldrum band. The Tap Room, a bar and game room with darts and pool tables, has live entertainment at cocktails and in the evening.

The large, luxurious guest rooms are actually junior suites, furnished in mahogany Ethan Allen lookalikes and rattan, upholstered in textured pastel fabrics. But the huge bathrooms (with telephones) are the real showstoppers, marbled from top to bottom.

All rooms have large verandas where you can dine. They are furnished with a teak dining table and chairs and have a toaster so your waiter can make fresh toast. Other nice touches include genuine down pillows, individual reading lights that clip on books, and free laundry-room facilities in each building.

Four Seasons, with its spectacular eighteen-hole championship course designed by Robert Trent Jones II, has made Nevis the Caribbean's hottest new golf destination. The 6,725-yard course climbs from sea level up the volcanic slopes of Mount Nevis to almost 1,000-foot altitude to the signature fifteenth hole: an awesome 660-yard, Par 5 across a deep ravine with a breadth of 240 yards from the tee. From there the course descends quickly to the eighteenth hole, ending at the ocean's edge. Throughout golfers enjoy breathtaking vistas. Guest greens fees are $71, including carts.

The resort has a large tennis complex, extensive water sports, and a health club. Demonstration sessions are free, lessons are not. Check the daily schedule or inquire before signing up.

"Kids for All Seasons" is Four Seasons's program for children ages three to twelve and includes a playroom and supervised activities. The resort provides children's beach toys, bottle-/food-warming service, and supervised dining at 6:00 P.M.

Reminiscent of a Florida golf resort, the hotel is designed to attract groups: small meetings and golfers. Guests, mainly from North America, range from tots to seniors, but most are active couples eager to enjoy the resort's sporting facilities.

Address/Phone: Box 565, Charlestown, Nevis, W.I.; (809) 469–1111, (800) 332–3442; Fax: (809) 469–1112

Owner: Nevis Hotel Development, Ltd.

General Manager: John Stauss

Open: Year-round

Credit Cards: All major

U.S. Reservations: Four Seasons Resort Nevis, (800) 332–3442 (U.S.), (800) 268–6282 (Canada)

Deposit: 3 nights; 21 days cancellation

Minimum Stay: 10 nights at Christmas

Arrival/Departure: Transfers, $35 per person round trip by land and sea. Most guests arrive by air in St. Kitts, where Four Seasons representatives meet and drive them to dockside lounge in Basseterre to board deluxe launch for 30-minute zoom across channel to hotel. En route, staff completes check-in while you enjoy refreshments and scenic cruise.

Distance from Airport: 6 miles; taxi one-way, $12

Distance from Charlestown: 1 mile; taxi one-way, $6

Accommodations: 196 rooms and suites (43 with 2 double beds, 130 with king-size beds; 17 suites) all with verandas

Amenities: Air-conditioning, ceiling fan, telephone, clock-radio, remote control television (with CNN and 18 channels), VCR, hairdryer, bathrobes, lit makeup mirror, bathroom scale, lavish toiletries; stocked mini-bar; 24-hour room service, hair salon

Electricity: 110 volts

Sports: Golf (see text); ten lighted tennis courts (3 lighted), $15 per hour; clinics, $12. Proper attire requested. Health Club with lockers and saunas for men and women, air-conditioned exercise room with Nautilus equipment, massage rooms. Daily aerobics, stretch and tone classes, fitness walks, aqua-aerobics, jogging; volleyball, croquet, shuffleboard. Freshwater pool, children's pool, whirlpool. Snorkel gear and 2 hours free instruction, kayaks, pedal boats, sailboats; introductory scuba, windsurfing, sailing, waterskiing.

Dress Code: Casual by day; coverup and footwear in Great House. After sunset, collared shirts, trousers, closed footwear for men; jacket and tie not required.

Children: "Kids for All Seasons" program

Meetings: Up to 350 people

Day Visitors: Welcome with advance reservations

Handicapped: Facilities

Packages: Romance, golf, sports, tennis

Rates: Two persons, daily, EP. *High Season* (December 19–January 3) $500–$2,000. *Shoulder Seasons* (January 3–April 12 and November 15–December 18): $450–$2,000. *Low Season* (April 13–November 14): $250–$2,000

Service Charge: 10 percent

Government Tax: 7 percent

Golden Rock Hotel ▣▣ ❦

High on the side of Mount Nevis in an area known as Gingerland, is an unusual small inn at 1,000 feet above the sea. It's on the grounds of an eighteenth-century sugar plantation operated by a direct descendant of the plantation's original owner.

Pam Berry, a Philadelphia native, came to Nevis on a visit in 1965 and stayed. She eventually became owner/manager of Golden Rock and runs the inn as though she has invited you to her home. She sets the tone for Golden Rock in a chatty letter that guests find in their rooms.

The tireless innkeeper dines with her guests, organizes garden walks, hikes, and tours, shuttles them back and forth from town and the beach, and takes them to interesting folklore shows and other activities around the island. If you prefer to go off on your own, she can arrange car rentals at a very good rate.

Set in 25 acres of flower-filled gardens and surrounded by another 150 acres of tropical beauty, Golden Rock was built in the early 1800s by Edward Huggins, Pam's great-great-great-grandfather, a self-made man who was an estate overseer at only 19. Huggins built many other estates and is said to have owned seven.

As soon as you start up the narrow lane from the main road to the inn, you know you have arrived at a special place. Rooms with walls of century-old stone masonry, barely visible under curtains of brightly colored tropical flowers, have been converted into the living and dining spaces, with practical additions only where needed.

The Long House, formerly the estate's kitchen and storeroom, contains the dining room, bar, and library and is the center of social activity. The rustic bar has a vaulted ceiling exposing the building's old walls. From it hang two large wicker baskets—lobster traps used by local fishermen—woven in a typical West Indian design that originated with the Carib Indians, who once inhabited the island. The congenial atmosphere at cocktails and after dinner makes it easy to be part of the family of new friends. Recorded classical music can be heard almost anytime, and musical entertainment is often provided by a staff member—or a guest.

The Courtyard, a flower-graced terrace with the bougainvillea-laden stone walls of the Long House as its backdrop, is the setting for lunch, afternoon tea, and cocktails, served to the musical accompaniment of birds and crickets.

The Sugar Mill, the original stone windmill tower pictured in the hotel's literature, was built in 1815, to supply power to the plantation. Today it houses the honeymoon suite but is large enough for a family of four or five. It has two floors connected by a winding wooden stairway and is furnished with three antique four-poster mahogany beds.

Accommodations are in cottages on the mountainside above the Long House. Each has linoleum floors covered with rush throw rugs, a private bathroom, and a front porch with a grandstand view. The rooms are basic but comfortable, with island-made furnishings. The most noteworthy are the canopied, four-poster bamboo beds made by the multitalented bartender Ralston, who is also acclaimed for his rum punch and his guitar music. Ralston is typical of Golden Rock's gracious, friendly staff, most of whom come from the area and have been with the inn many years.

Dinner is served family style in the Long House. You will dine (tables for two are also avaiable) on homemade soups and other specialties prepared with herbs grown in the estate's own gardens, fresh produce from village farmers, and fresh seafood caught by local fishermen. For guests on the hotel's meal plan, wine is included with dinner.

In the gardens between the Long House and the cottages is a large spring-fed pool with a shaded terrace from which you'll find wonderful views across the southern part of the island and the sea. The estate has a strand of sand on 4-mile Pinney's Beach for its guests' exclusive use. The beach bar, open in the winter season, prepares a daily lunch of fresh seafood, with the weekly highlight being a lobster bake. Golden Rock owns another sandy surf-washed beach on the windward side, where the snorkeling (gear provided) is good and the beachcombing excellent. When you go off on your own, the hotel will pack you a picnic lunch.

Environmentalists will appreciate Pam's strong commitment to protecting the environment. Golden Rock is a natural for nature lovers, with trails and unpaved roads in the immediate area for hiking. The Rainforest Trail, beginning from Golden Rock, leads up the mountain past several hamlets to the rain forest on the side of Mount Nevis. Pam has drawn a map for her guests to use. The trail is an easy hike, but finding the trail on the return can be difficult. Keep a watchful eye and you are likely to see some wild monkeys watching you from behind a tree. In cooperation with The Nevis Academy, the inn offers excellent guided historic and nature walks around Nevis.

A stay at Golden Rock is an unusual experience. The inn has a loyal clientele: an intellectually curious, well-traveled, eclectic group as likely to come from the United States and Canada as from Europe. Its historic setting is relished by romantics and history buffs. Its cozy, homey atmosphere makes everyone feel welcome, particularly someone traveling alone.

Address/Phone: Box 493, St. Georges Parish, Nevis, W.I.; (809) 469–3346; Fax: (809) 469–2113
Owner/Manager: Pam Barry
Open: Year-round
Credit Cards: All major
U.S. Reservations: ITR (International Travel and Resorts, Inc.), (800) 223–9815, (212) 545–8469; Fax: (212) 545–8467
Deposit: 3 nights; 30 days cancellation
Minimum Stay: None
Arrival/Departure: Transfer can be arranged for fee
Distance from Airport: 7 miles; taxi one-way, $16
Distance from Charlestown: 7 miles; taxi one-way, $8
Accommodations: 14 hillside cottages with porches; all rooms with twin or king-size beds; 1 sugar mill tower for up to 4 persons
Amenities: Bath with shower; no air-conditioning; fans provided
Electricity: 110 volts
Sports: Freshwater pool, tennis, transport to 2 private beaches. Waterskiing, scuba diving, sailing, windsurfing, sportfishing, golf, and horseback riding arranged.
Dress Code: Informal
Children: All ages; baby-sitters available
Handicapped: No facilities
Meetings: Small groups and wedding parties
Day Visitors: Welcome
Packages: Honeymoon; wedding; Discover Nevis; art, nature; and photography study with The Nevis Academy
Rates: Per room, double, daily, EP. *High Season* (mid-December–mid-April): $175–$200. *Low Season*: $100–$125.
Service Charge: 10 percent
Government Tax: 7 percent

The Hermitage ▣▣ 🍃

Hugging the forested southern slopes of Nevis Peak, 800 feet above sea level, this one-of-a-kind resort resembles a Lilliputian village of dollhouses tucked into acres of tropical gardens. Its centerpiece is a small, 250-year-old greathouse, said to be the oldest all-wood house standing in Nevis. It is surrounded by traditional West Indian cottages with gingerbread trim, brought here from various locations around the island and reconstructed to serve as guest quarters.

The house was probably built about 1740—perhaps as early as 1680—by a family from Wales. Its longevity is attributed to the termite-resistant wood used for its heavy timbers, *lignum vitae,* which is highly prized for its strength and was perhaps taken from the original forest of Nevis.

The house remained in the same family until 1971 when it was bought by Maureen and Richard Lupinacci, then newly arrived from Quaker Town, Pennsylvania. The couple made extensive renovations and added the cottages before they opened the inn in 1985. Maureen runs the daily operation and overseas the kitchen (Richard, one of Nevis's most active hoteliers, is managing director of the Bank of Nevis.)

The greathouse is small (less than 2,000 square feet) even by Caribbean standards and built in the shape of a cross aligned to the points of the compass. The drawing room has a high beamed ceiling constructed in the old style with dovetailed corners to strengthen the frame.

The north and south extensions have two stories, each with lounges on the first level and bedrooms above. The greathouse has a formal dining room, a bar, and, to one side, a small music room/library walled with books and a VCR—all comfortably furnished in antiques and Victoriana like your grandmother's parlor. The music room opens onto a pretty veranda, and the drawing room steps down to a covered terrace with garden tables and chairs in a romantic setting with latticework and arches draped with flowering shrubs. The terrace is used for breakfast and lunch.

Guests stay in picturesque cottages—some old and some made to look old. The charming old ones have been carefully restored using original construction methods when possible. They are surrounded by tropical gardens brimming with flowers and exotic fruit trees. The guest rooms are furnished with romantic four-poster canopy beds with colonial-print coverlets; they have small bathrooms and private porches.

Another three cottages by the swimming pool are newer and more deluxe. They have self-catering units, one on each of their two floors, and a separate sitting room, kitchenette, and patio or balcony with a hammock for taking in distant views of the sea. A cottage may be rented as a duplex as well.

Mahogany Manor, a replica of a Nevis manor house, sits in private gardens at the top of the hill. It has two large master bedrooms with large baths and dressing rooms, living room, dining room, and full kitchen with laundry. Cook and daily maid service can be arranged.

Among The Hermitage's most unusual features are its two-horse carriages pulled by two-thousand-pound Belgian horses (originally used as Amish farm horses in Pennsylvania). They depart weekdays on trips through the countryside. The inn also has riding horses.

In the evening guests and island friends congregate in the parlor for cocktails and congenial conversation. Dinner, announced by ringing bells, is a family affair served in the dining room or on the cozy veranda, depending on the number of guests and the ambience they prefer. If you prefer, you can dine romantically on your private balcony.

The Lupinaccis, known for their warm hospitality, usually dine with guests at a communal table. The couple has a reputation for serving some of the finest cuisine and wines on the island.

A set menu, changed nightly, has four courses of French, Italian or Caribbean specialties stressing fresh local fish, vegetables, and fruits. On Wednesday evenings there is a West Indian buffet with a string or "scratch" band (local musicians playing homemade instruments). Your companions are as likely to be English or European as American, and most, will be in their midforties.

The Lupinaccis will drive guests the 4 miles to Pinney's Beach for swimming and water sports. They will also organize outings, prepare picnic baskets, and arrange car rentals. But The Hermitage is a homey, easygoing sort of place. You need not stir farther than the gracious gardens for afternoon tea or to a hammock strung between the breadfruit and mango trees where gentle breezes will rock you to sleep.

Families are still important in Nevis, the Lupinaccis say. "We invite you to join ours at The Hermitage, a place where the cool breeze off the mountains meets the warm breezes from the sea . . . a special place where you make friends forever."

Address/Phone: Figtree Parish, St. John, Nevis, W.I.; (809) 469–3477; Fax: (809) 469–2481
Owner/General Manager: Richard and Maureen Lupinacci
Open: Year-round
Credit Cards: All major
U.S. Reservations: International Travel and Resorts, (800) 223–9815, (212) 545–8469; Fax: (212) 545–8467
Deposit: 3 nights; 3 weeks cancellation in winter, 2 weeks in summer
Minimum Stay: 4 nights in winter

Arrival/Departure: Transfer service not provided
Distance from Airport: 12 miles; taxi one-way, $12
Distance from Charlestown: 3 miles; taxi one-way, $8
Accommodations: 14 units (10 rooms and suites in cottages with private
    bath, 7 with kitchenettes; 2 guest rooms in greathouse; 2 in manor
    house); rooms have king, twins, or queens that can be configured to
    suit need.
Amenities: Two rooms have bathtubs, others have showers. Ceiling fan,
    refrigerator, tea kettle, hairdryers; room service from 8:00 A.M. to 10:00
    P.M.; nightly turndown service
Electricity: 110 volts
Sports: Freshwater pool, tennis, horseback riding. Sailing, fishing, and hik-
    ing with a guide arranged.
Dress Code: Informal
Children: All ages; cribs, baby-sitters available
Meetings: None
Day Visitors: Lunch and dinner with advance reservations
Handicapped: No facilities
Packages: Honeymoon, weddings
Rates: Per room, double, daily, EP. *High Season* (mid-December–mid-
    April): $195–$295. *Low Season:* $100–$180.
Service Charge: 10 percent
Government Tax: 7 percent

Montpelier Plantation Inn ◙◙

Nestled in lovely gardens and surrounded by sixty acres of rolling terrain,
Montpelier Plantation Inn has an air of timeworn grandeur that gives the
impression it has been there for three centuries, rather than a mere three
decades.

Well, it has, and it hasn't.

The Montpelier Estate, in the interior hills at 650 feet above sea level on
the south side of Mt. Nevis, was a prominent sugar plantation in the eighteenth century, belonging to the governor of the Leeward Islands. Here in
1787 his niece, Frances Nisbet, wed Lord Nelson, the famous British admiral.

By the time James Gaskell acquired the property in 1964, the original
Great House was long gone, but remnants of the mill and other structures
were enough to provide foundations to build a small inn. By reusing the
original stones and retaining the traditional architecture, Gaskell achieved
the inn's authentic appearance—at least for the main buildings.

An imposing brimstone structure that appears to be a greathouse was actually the old sugar boiling room, which Gaskell rebuilt into a grand drawing room where dinner is served and other evening activities take place. The attractive room has a high, vaulted ceiling that adds to its grandeur, and its antique furnishings are reminiscent of an English country manor, with portraits and old paintings on the walls and a mahogany bar.

The drawing room opens onto a colonnaded stone terrace where breakfast and lunch are served. It overlooks pretty gardens heavily laced with tropical ferns around a huge eighteenth-century windmill that once powered the sugar factory. Birds are everywhere, and Gaskell has compiled Nevis's only bird list, full of entertaining notes to help birders unfamiliar with Caribbean species locate them.

Beyond the mill is a modern spring-fed swimming pool with bright blue tiles and bordered by a masonry wall painted with murals. The poolside terrace has a bar with tables and chairs under a canvas awning.

The inn's guest rooms are in modest cottages behind the main hall, all with patios overlooking Nevis's southern landscape and the sea. After Montpelier's grand centerpiece, the cottages are something of a letdown, although they are gradually being upgraded following the damage caused by Hurricane Hugo. High beamed ceilings and terra-cotta floors have been added, making the rooms more spacious and airy; the bathrooms have also been upgraded.

The hotel has a long-established reputation for good cuisine prepared by a staff of local chefs supervised by Ian Hart, the resident manager, and his wife, Pinky. Much of the food is grown at Montpelier's own farm and orchards.

Breakfast on the flower-filled terrace by the pool is a treat of local fruits and honey and homemade brown bread and johnnycakes. Lunch—à la carte or buffet—and tea are served outdoors as well. The inn's charming historic setting attracts guests from other hotels for lunch or dinner and is a popular stop on island tours.

In the evening guests gather in the bar or lounge for cocktails in an English weekend-in-the-country atmosphere where new and returning British guests greatly outnumber the Americans and Canadians. Dinner is a candlelight affair with a set three-course menu offering a choice of entrée. You can dine at tables for two, or you may join others. The dining terrace has views past the floodlit palm trees to the sea and the lights of St. Kitts. A dance with a local band is held between Montpelier and its neighboring hotels once or twice a week during the winter season.

Montpelier provides a free shuttle daily except Sunday to and from its beach club on the north end of Pinney's Beach, about twenty-five minutes away. The inn will prepare a picnic lunch for you, and there is a weekly beach barbecue lunch, followed by a seaside game of cricket (yes, it's terribly British!).

The informal retreat has a wonderful staff and a timeless, unspoiled quality, attracting nature lovers and couples of all ages as well as those traveling alone who appreciate its homey atmosphere. More English than other Nevis inns, Montpelier is like a gracious private house where the Gaskells are usually in residence.

Address/Phone: Box 474, Montpelier Estate, Nevis; (809) 469–3462, (800) 243–9420; Fax: (809) 469–2932

Owner/General Manager: James and Celia Gaskell

Resident Managers: Ian and Pinky Hart

Open: Year-round except August 21 to October 1

Credit Cards: Most major, except American Express

U.S. Reservations: Ray Morrow Associates, (804) 460–2343, (800) 243–9420.

Deposit: 3 nights; 42 days cancellation

Minimum Stay: 1 week at Christmas

Arrival/Departure: No transfer service.

Distance from Airport: 12 miles; taxi one-way, US $20

Distance from Charlestown: 4 miles; daily free transport to town and private beach

Accommodations: 17 rooms in cottages (12 with 2 queen beds, 5 with king), all with inside sitting area and outside patios

Amenities: Telephone with international direct dial, tea and coffee maker, hairdryer; bathrooms have showers, tubs being added; no radio, television, or air-conditioning, but fans available; room service for continental breakfast

Electricity: 220–240 volts

Sports: Tennis and equipment. Beach club has 17-foot Boston Whaler for waterskiing, snorkeling, and fishing trips. Golf, horseback riding, hiking arranged.

Dress Code: Informal but with style. Men wear long trousers in evening; jackets and ties not required.

Children: All ages—inform hotel in advance; special children's tea; baby-sitters evenings only

Meetings: Small executive groups

Day Visitors: Welcome with advance reservations

Handicapped: Limited facilities

Packages: None

Rates: Two persons, daily, CP. *High Season* (mid-December–mid-April): $240. *Low Season*: $140.

Service Charge: 10 percent

Government Tax: 7 percent

Nisbet Plantation ▢▢▢

The keystone of the old windmill indicates that William Nisbet began building the greathouse of his sugar plantation on the north shore of Nevis for his young bride, Frances, in 1778. Nisbet died a few years later, soon after the wealthy widow attracted the attention of the famous British admiral, Lord Nelson—and, as they say, the rest is history.

Today Nisbet Plantation, which has an idyllic location at the foot of Mt. Nevis on its own beach (most Nevis plantations were on the mountainside), is an antique-filled plantation inn with a magnificent lawn that flows to the water's edge between double rows of stately palms and flowering gardens. With a little imagination, you can easily picture the opulent life here in bygone days.

Nisbet continued as a sugar and coconut plantation until the 1960s, changing hands several times. In 1989 David Dodwell, a well-known Bermuda hotelier, acquired the inn and made extensive renovations as well as adding deluxe cottages and a handsome beach complex with a freshwater pool, a restaurant, and a bar.

An aura of the past continues to permeate the gracious inn, particularly its eighteenth-century greathouse in classic West Indian architecture of gray volcanic stone. The resort's centerpiece, it houses the main dining room furnished with attractive antiques, the lounge with television and VCR, a bar, and library. Recent renovations added walls of windows around a screened veranda, stylishly furnished with rattan sofas and chairs. It makes an inviting setting for afternoon tea and cocktails when guests gather to socialize before dinner and to hear Goldie, an English music hall–style singer with a wide repertoire, who entertains nightly during the winter season.

Next to the greathouse is an open pavilion with the reception desk and Gingerland, a small pink gingerbread-trimmed cottage housing a boutique.

Accommodations are in pretty, pale yellow Nevis-style cottages generously spaced in the quarter-mile palm grove between the greathouse and the beach, assuring ample privacy. The cottages, with louvered windows providing cross ventilation from the ever-present trade winds, are actually duplex suites with furnished screened patios serving as sitting rooms.

The newest accommodations—three two-story villas near the beach—have four premier units each, more spacious and luxurious than those in the duplexes. Each unit has a king-size bed separate from a step-down living room and an open patio with a wet bar and refrigerator. Bathrooms have tub as well as shower.

All new, as well as newly refurbished, guest rooms are furnished and painted in white, with stylish colorful fabrics accented with local paintings, terra-cotta pottery, and fresh flowers.

Nisbet's beautiful palm-studded beach is protected by reefs, but it can be windy, as it faces the Atlantic Ocean. It was the wind, however, that enabled Nisbet to put the plantation here in the first place. Now, as then, the wind keeps the air cool and relatively insect free—and gently rocks the hammocks strung between the palm trees. The resort has a tennis court; complimentary use is limited to one hour at a time, and proper tennis attire is required.

Breakfast is served on the outdoor terrace of the greathouse and in an informal setting at Coconuts, the restaurant in the attractive beach pavilion. The latter is also the venue for lunch, the manager's cocktail party, and the beach seafood barbecue.

Dinner at the greathouse, looking out across the avenue of royal palms to the sea, is the evening's highlight. The romantic candlelight setting in the antiques-filled room, with its original mahogany floors, is ideal for the leisurely five-course dinners of sophisticated European and Caribbean cuisine. At full moon when the light shines through the palm trees and reflects on the water, the scene is magical.

Nisbet is the Caribbean as it used to be, appealing to those who appreciate the island's serenity and want their space. In the relaxing setting you can chose privacy or the company of others, who are likely to be an even mix of Americans and British with a sprinkling of Europeans. Families with children are welcome and will appreciate the space. Brides will not find a lovelier wedding setting.

Some people say Nisbet's atmosphere is formal in an English manner, but I find the inn delightful. It's a bit tony, yes, but not stuffy. Tim Thuell, the omnipresent general manager, is on the job from early morning until the last guest retires. He and his wife are as friendly and caring as any hotel couple you could ever meet.

Address/Phone: St. James Parish, Nevis; (809) 469–9325; Fax: (809) 469–9864
Owner: David Dodwell
General Manager: Tim Thuell
Open: Year-round
Credit Cards: Most major
U.S. Reservations: Jenkins & Gibson Ltd., (800) 344–2049, (410) 321–1231; Fax: (410) 494–1910
Deposit: 3 nights; 28 days cancellation, high season; 14 days, low season
Minimum Stay: None
Arrival/Departure: Airport transfer, $7
Distance from Airport: 1 mile; taxi one-way, $7
Distance from Charlestown: 8 miles; taxi one-way, $16

Accommodations: 38 units (with twin or king-size beds in 26 duplex cottages with screened patios; deluxe units have separate living room; 12 suites with living room, terrace, king-size beds and couch that converts to queen; 1 unit with four-poster bed)

Amenities: Telephone, ceiling fan, mini-bar, tea/coffee maker, hairdryer, bathrobes, basket of toiletries; nightly turndown service; room service for continental breakfast; tubs in suites, shower only in cottages; no air-conditioning or television

Electricity: 110 volts

Sports: Freshwater pool; free snorkeling gear and tennis; croquet lawn. Golf, fishing, windsurfing, scuba, horseback riding, and hiking arranged.

Dress Code: Informal by day; in greathouse no beach attire and no jeans, shorts, or T-shirts after 6 P.M. Casually elegant for evening; jackets and ties not required.

Children: All ages; children under 12 served dinner at 6:00 P.M. or by special arrangement, cribs, high-chairs, baby-sitters

Meetings: None

Day Visitors: Welcome with advance reservations

Handicapped: No facilities

Packages: Honeymoon, anniversary, wedding

Rates: Per person, daily, MAP. *High Season* (mid-December–mid-April): $149–$199. *Low Season:* $95–$145.

Service Charge: $15 per day

Government Tax: 7 percent

Puerto Rico

El San Juan Hotel & Casino

American in tempo, Latin at heart, Puerto Rico is the gateway to the Caribbean. It has big-city action in San Juan and tranquillity in the country-side; glamourous resorts and friendly inns; plus golf, tennis, fishing, diving, horse racing, and baseball; and more history and scenic wonders than places many times its size.

In June 1992 Puerto Rico launched a two-year celebration of its five hundred years of history with the arrival of the Tall Ships in San Juan harbor, the first stop on their transatlantic tour. Central to the events has been the exquisite restoration of Old San Juan, the oldest city under the U.S. flag. Along cobblestone streets, magnificent old mansions are alive with the city's smartest restaurants, shops, art galleries, and museums.

Only thirty minutes from San Juan, the Caribbean National Forest, commonly known as El Yunque, is the only tropical rain forest in the U.S. Forestry Service. It has recreation areas and trails. And that's only the beginning. Across the center of Puerto Rico, a spine of tall green mountains divides the north and south coasts. The 165-mile Panoramic Route winds through the mountains and provides spectacular panoramas, hiking trails, swimming holes, and picnic areas.

Ponce, an architectural gem on the south coast, is Puerto Rico's second-largest town. It undertook a citywide restoration to mark the 300th anniversary of its founding in 1692. West of Ponce on the Caribbean coast, near La Parguera, is one of Puerto Rico's two bioluminescent bays where microorganisms in the water light up like shooting stars with any movement.

Rio Camuy Caves Park near Hatillo is part of the Camuy River, the world's third largest underground river; you can see caverns as high as a 20-story building. These are but a few of the attractions that enable Puerto Rico to claim it is the "Complete Island."

Information

Puerto Rico Tourism Company, 575 Fifth Avenue, New York, NY 10017; (212) 599–6262

Dorado

Hyatt Dorado Beach ◙◙◙◙

The elegant Hyatt Dorado Beach has matured well. Built on a former coconut-and-grapefruit plantation in 1958 by Laurance Rockefeller, it was part of his ecologically oriented Rockresort group. The resort has retained its quality and distinction despite changing times and owners and new competitors.

Set on Puerto Rico's north shore near the town of Dorado, the resort is hidden under acres of palms and flowering gardens. In its front yard are four of the best golf courses in the Caribbean, and in the back two miles of beach.

After thriving for years as a Rockresort, the resort passed through several owners before being purchased by Hyatt in 1985. Since its acquisition, Hyatt has put millions into renovations to make it one of the chain's showplaces.

The Hyatt Dorado and its next-door sibling—the larger, more convention-oriented Hyatt Regency Cerromar—sprawl over a thousand seaside acres. Together they offer so many options for recreation, dining, and nighttime activities that you don't need to leave the property or rent a car during your stay; shuttle buses make it easy to get from place to place.

Indeed, one of the beauties of the Hyatt Dorado is that it gives you the best of both worlds: the ambience of a small hotel with a main reception building that's a former plantation house, and the hustle-bustle and nightlife of Cerromar, only a short shuttle ride away: 1 mile, to be exact.

Certainly, the quartet of Robert Trent Jones championship golf courses is one of the major draws. Not only are they among the top courses in the Caribbean but they have world ranking. An entire wing of guest rooms has verandas overlooking the beautiful fairways, for travelers who are passionate about the game.

You can hone your skills with practice at Dorado's driving range or putting greens, or take lessons and clinics from one of Hyatt's pros. There is a well-stocked pro shop, and the restaurant adjacent to the course offers light meals and beverages.

Tennis is just as much of an attraction as golf. Together the sister resorts have twenty-one courts (four lighted for night play) of which seven courts are on the Dorado's grounds. More extensive clinics and lessons are available at Cerromar's large complex.

The 2-mile long white-sand beach is sometimes better for sunbathing and viewing from your balcony than it is for swimming—the surf can be rough. But not to worry. Dorado has two swimming pools, one Olympic-size; and Hyatt's famous signature lagoon connects six free-form swimming pools at the Cerromar, winding through almost five acres between the two hotels.

Dorado has its own placid lagoon where gentle breezes offer a good place for fledgling windsurfers to try their boards. A team of instructors led by Lisa Penfield, former world freestyle champ, teaches first-timers the sport. They also give an eight-hour certification course in three sessions.

Since it was first built, the Hyatt Dorado has more than doubled in size, yet it has never seemed like a big hotel. Its rooms have such variety, due to their style and location, that it avoids the cookie-cutter look of a large chain hotel. In addition to the guest rooms by the golf course, you have a choice of casita suites, poolside and beachfront rooms, and ocean-view ones in three locations: all in low-rise buildings extending from the large, graceful open-air lobby.

The spacious rooms have terra-cotta floors, marble baths with separate dressing room, and terraces; some have private lawns, sitting areas, and showers with skylights. They are decorated with rattan furniture in delightful island decor of soft Caribbean colors.

You can choose to breakfast on the terrace of your room or at the Ocean Terrace Cafe overlooking the magnificent turquoise sea. The cafe serves lunch and dinner, too. Beach and golf bars also serve light meals. The Surf Room offers music with dinner, specializing in Caribbean dishes along with continental cuisine; it features a champagne brunch on Sundays.

The real treat at the Hyatt Dorado is *Su Casa*, an intimate, romantic restaurant housed in an authentic hacienda built in 1905. The elegant stucco house with terra-cotta tiles and iron-filigree trim is barely visible behind a jungle of tropical foliage. The gourmet menu features Spanish and Mediterranean selections, and there is live entertainment. It is one of Puerto Rico's priciest restaurants.

The Hyatt Dorado has a quiet casino, but if you want action, you will find plenty next door at the more glitzy casino of the Hyatt Regency Cerromar—not to mention its nightclub, bars, and disco. Dorado guests can also enjoy Cerromar's four specialty restaurants as well as its spa and health club, shops, barber and beauty salons, and a private airstrip. Costa del Mar is the Hyatt Dorado's sumptuous new conference center.

The Hyatt Dorado is designed for experienced, affluent travelers who like large resort facilities with small-hotel charm. The beauty of the Hyatt Dorado's setting; a well-trained, friendly staff; consistency; and an elegant yet unpretentious ambience have kept loyal fans returning year after year.

Address/Phone: Dorado, Puerto Rico 00646; (809) 796–1234; Fax: (809) 796–2022

Owner: Hyatt Hotels

General Manager: Hendrick Santos

Open: Year-round

Credit Cards: All major

U.S. Reservations: Hyatt Hotels, (800) 233–1234

Deposit: 3 nights; 14 days cancellation

Minimum Stay: 10 nights at Christmas; cancellation by Oct. 31

Arrival/Departure: Transfers arranged for fee

Distance from Airport: (San Juan International Airport) 32 miles; taxi one-way, $40 to $60; from Hyatt's private airfield: 2 miles

Distance from San Juan: 22 miles; taxi one-way, $40–$50

Accommodations: 298 units with terrace or balcony: 48 golf view (18 king/18 double); 28 pool view (26 king/2 double); 36 ocean view in Su Casa building (27 king/9 double); 168 beachfront (84 king/84 double); 18 casitas/suites (all king)

Amenities: Air-conditioning, ceiling fans, telephone, television, radio, clock; bath with tub and shower, basket of toiletries; ice service, stocked mini-bar, nightly turndown service, 24-hour room service, concierge

Electricity: 110 volts

Sports: 2 swimming pools, 4 golf courses, 21 tennis courts, water-sports center, jogging and biking trails, windsurfing instruction, and certification course, spa

Dress Code: Casual by day; casually elegant in evening; jacket for men required in winter

Children: All ages; cribs
Meetings: Up to 800 people; additional facilities at Hyatt Regency Cerromar
Day Visitors: Yes
Handicapped: Facilities
Packages: Honeymoon, family, golf, tennis
Rates: Per room, single or double, daily, EP. *High Season* (mid-December–mid-April): $325–$605. *Low Season* (June 1–September 30): $150–$245.
Service Charge: 15 percent on food and beverage
Government Tax: 9 percent

Jayuya

Parador Hacienda Gripinas ◉

A restored nineteenth-century coffee plantation in the central mountains near the town of Jayuya, Parador Hacienda Gripinas is a working plantation that evokes the atmosphere of bygone days more than any other of the island's paradores, or country inns.

Named for the tangy sweet flavor of its coffee, Gripinas is perched at 3,000 feet on twenty-three acres where the coffee aroma lingers in the air. A narrow, country road (Route 527) overhung with mango trees winds up to the parador through pastoral settings that are light-years from the glitter of San Juan.

The two-hundred-year-old hacienda, which opened to guests in 1975, is a traditional, gracefully simple island home built of wood, with a wide veranda and shuttered windows. Painted white with green trim, it is surrounded by gardens of tropical flowers and shaded by large fruit and flowering trees. Inside, the parlors, newly spruced up, are furnished with some quality carved-wood pieces.

Most of the accommodations are set in a separate wing and furnished simply with bare wood floors. Arrangements differ, but all rooms have modern baths. They also have lovely views of the countryside. If you are a light sleeper or not accustomed to the sounds of the Caribbean countryside, you will need to use a pair of earplugs. A chorus of coqui, the minuscule Puerto Rican tree frog, sings nonstop through the night, and at 4:00 A.M. a neighborhood rooster begins trumpeting loud enough to wake the dead.

The dining room is made up of three rooms, one of which has a small interior patio with pretty greenery. Gripinas is counted among Puerto Rico's gastronomic inns. All meals are served at set hours and feature Puerto Rican cuisine and regional specialties. The Sunday buffets are popular with local people; the seafood and lobster are especially good. You will have fresh local fruits and juices and sample the rich Tres Picachos coffee grown here.

Guests, mostly from the United States mainland and Puerto Rico and occasionally some Europeans, pass the time reading to the accompaniment of the frequent rain, lazing in the hammocks and rockers on the veranda looking over the countryside, and conversing with other guests. There is a tiny room with a television set that receives CNN and other cable services in addition to local broadcasting.

Footpaths along a riverbed bordered by stands of bamboo and tree ferns lead to a large swimming pool fed by a pretty waterfall and an outdoor bar in a beautiful setting. The inn has a basketball court, and if you are really energetic, you can take hikes in the woods and perhaps pick your fruit for breakfast along the way.

The homey, unpretentious parador, with its quiet, rural setting, typifies "the other Puerto Rico" and appeals mainly to outdoor enthusiasts, nature lovers, birders, history and culture buffs, and people who simply want to escape from the city.

Address/Phone: Road 527, Km. 215, Barrio Vegita, Jayuya, Puerto Rico; (809) 721–2884, 828–1717; Fax: (809) 828–1719
Owner/Manager: Edgardo Dedos
Open: Year-round
Credit Cards: MasterCard; Visa
U.S. Reservations: Paradores Puertorriquenos, (800) 443–0266 (8:00 A.M.–noon; 1:00–4:30 P.M.); (809) 721–4698
Deposit: None
Minimum Stay: None
Arrival/Departure: No transfer service; must have a car
Distance from Ponce: 2-hour drive on winding road; no taxi; local bus only
Distance from Airport: (San Juan) 2.5-hour drive
Distance from San Juan: 2.5-hour drive; local bus only
Accommodations: 19 rooms in separate wing
Amenities: No air-conditioning; ceiling fans, bath with shower only; no phones, television, or room service
Electricity: 110 volts
Sports: Freshwater swimming pool; basketball court; walking and hiking trails, birding.
Children: Yes; baby-sitters
Meetings: Up to 40 people

Day Visitors: Welcome
Handicapped: No facilities
Packages: Honeymoon, weddings
Rates: Per person, daily, EP. *Year-round:* $50 single; $60 double.
Service Charge: Room 10 percent; food 15 percent
Government Tax: 7 percent

Rincon

The Horned Dorset Primavera Hotel ▣ ▣ ▣ ▣

With its atriumlike lobby, sculpted archways, and stunning views of the Mayaguez coast and the sea, the Horned Dorset Primavera has what the Spanish would term *tremendo cache,* that indefinable blend of grace and good taste seen only in the best of Caribbean hostelries.

Ever since former academicians Harold Davies and Kingsley Wratten opened it in May 1988, an elite list of islanders and a growing number of mainland Americans and Europeans have been discovering the special charms of this unique hideaway on Puerto Rico's undeveloped west end, mostly by word of mouth and favorable reviews.

The intimate European-style inn with first-rate service was a welcome addition to Puerto Rican shores, heretofore known primarily for the miles of high-rise hotel-casinos on metropolitan beaches.

As longtime proprietors of the small, highly acclaimed Horned Dorset Inn in upstate New York (named for a breed of sheep the men once raised there), Davies and Wratten were no strangers to the hotel business when they began scouting the Caribbean for a second property in the early eighties. They settled on a hilly four-acre site at the foot of the Cordillera Central in the "middle of nowhere," as they describe it.

Working closely within the context of its luxuriant garden setting, leading Puerto Rican architect and naturalist Otto Octavio Reyes Casanova created a graciously proportioned Spanish-colonial manor house complete with classic arches, black-and-white marble floors, and a fountain-splashed lobby. Nearby a cluster of five whitewashed, red-tile-roofed buildings house the villa suites, all with private balconies.

Throughout the public rooms massive carved mahogany pieces, terra-cotta floors, and Portuguese decorative tiles add richness and depth to the airy, tropical decor along with abundant arrangements of exotics plucked from the surrounding botanical gardens. From the English floral prints covering commodious rattan sofas and chairs to the Chinese porcelain lamps, everywhere the profusion of shapes, colors, and designs blends harmoniously.

The suites, varying somewhat in individual character, are given equal thought and attention with an eye toward total comfort. Handsome armoires and mahogany-pillared queen beds, made by well-known woodworkers from Ponce, are equipped with firm mattresses and soft down pillows. Italian marble lines floors and walls in the generous bathrooms fitted with brass fixtures and old-fashioned footed tubs, bidets, and toilets from Lille, France. Louvered doors open onto a balcony with a view of the small beach; a wicker settee and tables complete the adjoining sitting room.

True to the culinary precedent established by its North American sibling, the Horned Dorset Primavera serves a classical French menu but showcases a wealth of regional flavors and products as well. Wratten's Cordon Bleu–trained son, Aaron Wratten, is part of a three-chef team that rotates between the kitchens of the two hotels.

Shopping outings are the ongoing occupation of both proprietors, who hit the streets of the neighboring Rincón, Mayagüez, and Aguadilla for the freshest goods. Breakfast includes such delights as hearty Yauco coffee from the island's mountain slopes, crusty French bread, delicious finger bananas, papaya, and pineapple from the fertile fields of nearby Lajas. Luncheon selections feature fresh grilled fish along with a variety of salads and sandwiches.

Dinner is in the air-conditioned, formal waterfront dining room draped with Spanish linens over lacy table covers and lighted by turn-of-the-century wrought-iron chandeliers. A graciously served multicourse set menu of haute cuisine might begin with a rich vichyssoise followed by poached salmon in fragrant watercress sauce, tangy tamarind sorbet, and grilled tenderloin of lamb with cassis sauce, along with salad and luscious desserts. There is a well-selected wine list and a good reasonably priced house wine.

The Horned Dorset Primavera promotes itself as "a place without activities" as the owners' way of saying their hotel is not for everyone. It's geared for travelers who want a quiet vacation away from crowds, and most guests seem to welcome this respite, spending entire days about the pool, in the lounge filled with classical music, or the library brimming with books, breaking the pace with an occasional walk on the beach. The sea can be rough here, and the narrow beach is not the hotel's strong suit. Arrangements can be made for golf, diving, deep-sea fishing, or whale watching.

Whatever the daytime activities, come early evening the expansive front terrace beckons guests for drinks, *tapas* tasting, and a last tantalizing view of the molten tropic sun dissolving by inches into the Mona Straits beyond. As the horizon dims and waves lap at sea walls just below, far off to the south the lights of Mayaguez begin to twinkle.

Address/Phone: Rincón, Puerto Rico, 00677; (809) 823–4030; Fax: (809) 823–5580

Owners/Managers: Harold Davies and Kingsley Wratten

Open: Year-round

Credit Cards: All major

U.S. Reservations: Direct to hotel

Deposit: Reservation secured with credit card

Minimum Stay: 4 to 7 nights in winter

Arrival/Departure: Transfer arranged by hotel for fee

Distance from Airport: (Mayaguez Airport) 3 miles (10 minutes); taxi one-way, $20; from San Juan, 2.5-hour drive

Distance from Rincón: 5 miles; taxi one-way, $20

Accommodations: 24 ocean-view villa suites with terrace in 5 buildings; all with queen beds

Amenities: Air-conditioning, ceiling fans; bath with tub and shower, basket of toiletries; ice service, hairdryers available, room service for breakfast; no phone, television, radio

Electricity: 110 volts

Sports: Freshwater swimming pool. Golf, snorkeling, diving, deep-sea fishing, hiking, birding nearby.

Dress Code: Casual

Children: None under 12

Meetings: None

Day Visitors: Yes

Handicapped: Limited facilities

Packages: Honeymoon

Rates: Per person, daily, EP. *High Season* (December 1–April 30): $162.50. *Low Season:* $95.

Service Charge: 15 percent on dining room and bar bills

Government Tax: 7 percent

San Juan

Caribe Hilton and Casino ▣▣▣

Ideally located between historic Old San Juan and bustling new San Juan and between the ocean and the lagoon, the Caribe Hilton International is one of Puerto Rico's most complete resorts within easy reach of the city's shopping, business, and entertainment areas. A self-contained world set amid seventeen tropical acres of fountains and lush gardens, it provides views of the ocean on one side, a secluded beach and swimming cove on another, and an array of entertainment and recreational facilities.

Host to countless dignitaries and celebrities, the landmark property has been the city's pacesetter since it opened with a splash in 1949. Thirty planeloads of furniture were airlifted to the island by Eastern Airlines and Pan Am; it was described then as the "largest single commercial air movement of freight" in history. Newspapers of the time noted "private baths" and the extra touches such as "running ice water."

In 1991, the Caribe completed a $50-million renovation. The entire hotel was refurbished from top to bottom. The casino was moved to a new location and nearly doubled in size; the terrace bar was expanded; the gym got a new spa; and the Patisserie, Player's Bar, and eight lanai suites in the garden wing were added.

The hotel is set back from the main road and reached by a long circular driveway that leads to a spacious open-air lobby with gardens and a waterfall. It rises in two towers—the older ten-story building and the newer twenty-story tower connected by walkways—and provides grand views of the ocean and lagoon from all rooms except those on the lower floors.

The Caribe's restaurants and bars, located on the main floor between the lobby, the terrace bar, and the pool, offer choices from casual to gourmet. Indeed, one of the most pleasant aspects of the Caribe is that despite its size, you enjoy both choice and convenience. It might not be an intimate ambience, but the various restaurants and bars do flow from one to the other in an informal, yet orderly way.

El Cafe, the coffee shop overlooking the gardens, is a casual setting for meals throughout the day. El Batey del Pescador, overlooking the sea and the beach, specializes in seafood. The informal Caribe Terrace serves deli sandwiches and salad buffets for lunch and features outstanding stone-cooking for dinner. La Islita, by the beach and surrounded by water, is open during the day, as are the poolside deli bar and La Rotisserie, a gourmet grill.

The Caribe Terrace Bar, adjoining the lobby and overlooking the large free-form pool, is active day and night. It has nightly entertainment and claims to be the birthplace of the piña colada. Peacock Paradise specializes in Chinese cuisine, and The Patisserie is there to satisfy your sweet tooth or take care of that coffee craving with a large selection of coffees.

For entertainment there is the casino and its adjacent Players Bar. The Caribar lounge is one of San Juan's leading night spots, with live music nightly, and the Juliana's nightclub counts many of the city's movers and shakers among its regulars.

Guest rooms and suites throughout the hotel are spacious and feature contemporary decor combined with a tropical flavor. Each has a private terrace or balcony, most with an extraordinary view. Garden-wing guest rooms, designed for business travelers (the hotel's mainstay), have king beds, picture windows (but no balconies), extra phones, mini-bars, large desks, and roomy baths.

The tower guest rooms are plusher but slightly smaller. There are three Vista Executive Floors and a concierge-staffed lounge with separate check-in/out and business services. In Vista's clublike lounge, guests receive complimentary continental breakfast, morning newspapers, and refreshments throughout the day are available.

The Caribe's sports facilities turn this city hotel into a resort in the city. There are two swimming pools, a secluded white-sand beach with snorkeling, a putting green, six lighted tennis courts, air-conditioned squash and racquetball courts, and water sports. The health club has sauna and an air-conditioned gym with Nautilus equipment and offers a schedule of daily activities. The Spa Caribe, open seven days a week, features Swedish and sports massages, herbal wraps, and facials.

At the Caribe children are not forgotten either. The resort has a youth program with regularly scheduled activities, a playground, access to the Disney channel in all rooms, and a video arcade. Camp Caribe, which operates during major holidays and throughout July and August, offers arts and crafts, swimming, tennis, tours, Spanish lessons, and more. The Caribe Hilton even has its own historic site: Fort San Jeronimo, on a point of land separating the ocean from the lagoon that lies between the commercial center and the Condado strip.

The Caribe Hilton is one of the best known hotels in the Americas and draws affluent travelers from around the globe.

Address/Phone: Rosales Street, Box 1872, Fort Jeronimo, San Juan, Puerto Rico 00902-1872; (809) 721-0303; Fax: (809) 721-0303 or (800) HILTONS; Fax: (809) 722-2910

Owner: Hilton International

General Manager: Raul Bustamante

Open: Year-round
Credit Cards: All major
U.S. Reservations: Hilton Reservations Service, (800) 445–8667; (800) HILTONS in U.S., (800) 268–9275 in Canada
Deposit: 1 day
Minimum Stay: None
Arrival/Departure: No transfer service
Distance from Airport: (Muñoz International Airport) 7 miles (25 minutes); taxi one-way, $12
Distance from San Juan: ½ mile from Condado; 2 miles from Old San Juan or Santurce; taxi one-way, $5
Accommodations: 668 rooms and suites, all with terrace (except garden wing), most with water views
Amenities: Air-conditioning, direct-dial telephone, cable television, radio, bath with tub and shower, basket of toiletries, mini-bar; nightly turn-down service, 24-hour room service. 2 floors of nonsmokers' rooms; quick check-in/out available; shopping gallery, game room, beauty salon
Electricity: 110 volt
Sports: 2 freshwater pools; 6 lighted tennis courts, practice court, air-conditioned racquetball and squash courts; pro shop. Snorkel gear, windsurfing. Scuba diving, waterskiing, deep-sea fishing, horseback riding, hiking on rain-forest trails arranged.
Dress Code: Casual by day; casual to city elegant in evening, depending on venue.
Children: All ages; cribs, high chairs; playground, supervised activities, baby-sitters
Meetings: Up to 2,000 people; Audiovisual equipment
Day Visitors: Yes
Handicapped: 6 rooms
Packages: Caribe Countdown
Rates: Per room, double, daily, EP. *High Season* (mid-December–mid-April): $295–$715; *Low Season:* $170–$715.
Service Charge: None
Government Tax: 9 percent

Casa San José (N)

Historic Old San Juan has many new attractions but none more delightful than Casa San José, an exquisitely restored three-story mansion–turned–boutique hotel.

Located at the heart of the 7-square-block Old City, the spacious nineteenth-century townhouse is only steps from Plaza de Armas, one of the main squares; the Church of San José, second oldest in the Western Hemisphere; the Pablo Casals and other museums; and the trendy shops, restaurants, and art galleries of Cristo and Fortaleza streets.

Opened in late 1991 following a $1.5 million restoration, this antiques-filled gem scored a hit with locals as well as visitors right from the start. In the best of Spanish architectural tradition, the Casa's prim lemon-ice facade offers nary a hint of the treasures within. Tiers of balconies rise from the interior patio, a small oasis of tropical foliage cooled by a fountain. From the foyer to the skylight at the top, your eyes lift from light-gray-and-white-marble floors to high beam and brick ceilings and graceful arches.

The parlors and bedrooms are filled throughout with an eclectic mix of European and local antique furnishings against a backdrop of soothing cream and white walls and fabrics. Turkish kilim rugs in soft salmon and beige hues, gilt-frame mirrors, and European prints and drawings complete the setting.

The grace, refinement, and, above all, exquisite taste, that mark Casa San José's interiors are the trademark of English-born interior designer Simone Mehta. She holds the distinction of being the youngest decorator ever requested at the time to design the suites for Queen Elizabeth for her visit to Vancouver, Canada, in the 1960s.

She and her husband, Jag Mehta, one of the Caribbean's best known and most respected hoteliers (his career spans thirty years as general manager of the Caribe Hilton and leading hotels in Jamaica and the Bahamas), teamed up to plan and develop the historic inn.

In her work designer Mehta has knowingly capitalized on the building's magnificent lines and graceful proportions, maintaining its original spatial distribution. For example, the sunny Salon Grande—1,000 square feet of marble-covered expanse spanning the width of the house on the second floor with 18-foot ceilings—is a large living room, indeed; it brings to mind the grace of an earlier era.

With its grand piano, traditional sofas, overstuffed couches and chairs, and bric-a-brac–filled armoire, the drawing room makes a serene retreat for reading and relaxing, as well as an inviting setting for afternoon tea and evening cocktails. Breakfast and light lunches are served in the small dining room, also on the second floor.

Each guest room is different in size and layout, and, as in an elegant private home, each is decorated individually and filled with antiques and objets d'art. A commodious double bed with a cane headboard is the highlight of one deluxe room overlooking the Casa's interior patio. Its other furnishings include an antique cane wingback chair and a mirrored Puerto Rican armoire. The two-bedroom suite has a sun deck.

All guest quarters have phone and private, marble-lined bathrooms—some even have marble tubs; none have television. Marble stairs connect the four floors, and Casa San José is one of the few historic buildings in Old San Juan that has an elevator.

Casa San José is intended for sophisticated travelers who relish the intimate atmosphere of a small, elegant hotel. If you have a keen interest in the beauty and history of Old San Juan, you'll appreciate it all the more for its setting and location within easy walking distance of the Old City's great treasures. Many have recently been restored and refurbished in commemoration of Puerto Rico's Quincentennial. The new Plaza of the Five Centuries, for example, is only 2 blocks away.

Singles or couples who prefer sightseeing, shopping, and gourmet dining to the beach (although beaches are only about ten minutes away by car or bus) and families with older children who would appreciate a painless history lesson or two will enjoy this friendly, comfortable inn in the oldest city under the American flag.

Address/Phone: 159 San José Street, Old San Juan, Puerto Rico 00901; (809) 723–1212; Fax: (809) 723–7620

Owner: Jag Mehta

General Manager: Maruja Herniz

Open: Year-round

Credit Cards: All major

U.S. Reservations: Direct to the hotel

Deposit: 1 night; 3 days cancellation

Minimum Stay: None

Arrival/Departure: Transfer service on request for a fee

Distance from Airport: (Muñoz International Airport) 10 miles; taxi one-way, $12

Distance from San Juan/Condado: 5 miles; taxi one-way, $7

Accommodations: 10 rooms (4 double rooms, 4 one-bedroom suites, 1 two-bedroom suite with sun deck) 2 with queen beds, 7 with double beds, 1 king

Amenities: Air-conditioning, 4 rooms with ceiling fans; telephone, bathroom with tub, 2 with shower only; hairdryer on request, basket of toiletries; ice service on request, room service for breakfast

Electricity: 110 volts

Sports: No facilities on premises. Swimming, tennis, boating, snorkeling, scuba, windsurfing, deep-sea fishing, horseback riding arranged.

Dress Code: City casual

Children: 12 years and older

Meetings: Up to 20 people

Day Visitors: No facilities
Handicapped: No facilities
Packages: Honeymoon
Rates: Per person, daily, FAB & cocktails. *High Season* (December 1–April 15): $160–$500. *Low Season* (April 16–November 30): $130–$425.
Service Charge: None
Government Tax: 7 percent

El San Juan Hotel & Casino ◎ ◎ ◎ ◎ ◎

Stylish, luxurious, and fun, the El San Juan lets you have your cake and eat it, too. It's a complete beachside resort only a few miles from the airport but within easy reach of the city center. It's large enough to offer all the facilities you could want but not so large that it loses its personality.

Indeed, the El San Juan is so distinctive you could never confuse it with another hotel. Walk through the hotel's lavish lobby, brimming with art and activity. Or stroll over to the poolside veranda, with its 1930s decor and gardens, and you'll know immediately it's like no other place.

The El San Juan does have its quiet corners, but this hotel is really for people who want to be in the center of the action, day or night. It has five restaurants, eight bars, a casino, a nightclub, a disco, two swimming pools, three tennis courts, water sports, a health club, and an arcade of chic boutiques, and a staff of more than a thousand making sure it hums around the clock.

Set in fifteen acres of tropical gardens on the Atlantic north coast, the El San Juan is located on the eastern edge of San Juan. The landmark hotel reigned as the grande dame of Caribbean hotels in the 1960s with jet-setters flocking to see Liza Minnelli and other headliners in the Club Tropicoro. But by the decade's end, when Puerto Rico's fortunes had tumbled, the El San Juan closed, and the Isla Verde area deteriorated. Williams Hospitality bought the hotel in 1984 and reopened it one year and fifty million dollars later, launching Puerto Rico's tourism renaissance.

The El San Juan actually has undergone two transformations by two interior designers, with completely different ideas, working more than a decade apart but resulting in a remarkable duet.

In the sixties, New York designer Alan Lanigan traveled through Africa, Asia, and Europe collecting artwork, relics, balustrades, and other decorative and architectural elements to embellish the hotel. He acquired storefronts to design a shopping arcade; shipped heavy wooden doors, many more than a century old, from North Africa; oil paintings and art deco lamps from Europe; statues and jardinières from the Orient; as well as mahogany from the Dominican Republic.

In the eighties Puerto Rican interior designer Jorge Rosello recognized the uniqueness of Lanigan's work and built on it, essentially keeping the old intact. He added his imprint, enlivening the interior with a more cheerful environment, extending it to the outdoors to create a more tropical feeling and sparking the night life.

The lobby is the hub of the hotel and the best people-watching spot in San Juan. To one side is the Wine Bar, upbeat yet restrained, surrounded by black-lacquered, Japanese-style tables and chairs around a small, stylish service bar where caviar, foie gras, sushi, and cheese are served. It's the only Cruvinet wine bar in the Caribbean and offers twenty-two champagnes and wines by the glass. To the other side is the casino, where Rosello added the Winners Circle, a plush lounge that serves as both a piano bar and a sports bar.

Today live entertainment in the lobby is featured from 5:30 P.M. until the wee hours: at El Chico, a hacienda-style saloon with balconies, gilded mirrors, and western street scenes (framed by real cacti), where you can hear Latin music; the main nightclub, Club Tropicoro, fashioned to convey the feel of El Yunque, Puerto Rico's tropical rain forest, presenting international revues and headliners; and Amadeus, one of San Juan's "hot" discos.

Back Street Hong Kong, an Oriental restaurant, is approached through a replica of a Hong Kong street (created for the 1964 New York World's Fair). Other dining choices include La Veranda Cafe, a casual outdoor terrace overlooking the pool and gardens; Dar Tiffany for aged beef and fresh seafood; Don Juan, a gourmet restaurant for innovative, contemporary cuisine; and La Piccola Fontana, which serves northern Italian dishes.

Guest rooms are posh and contemporary, offering great variety: casitas with Roman baths; poolside, ocean, and garden lanais, some with private terrace or outdoor spa; and moderate, standard, and superior rooms and suites in the tower. Some one- and two-bedroom suites have kitchenettes.

The hotel has a rooftop health club and solarium, tennis, and a comprehensive water sports program. In 1991 it added a new complimentary service: a computer-customized vacation. It can work in conjunction with the "Kids' Klub," a daily supervised program for children ages five to twelve. You select your preferences from a menu of activities as varied as merengue classes, botanical garden tours, and deep-sea fishing. Afterward a counselor provides you with a computerized printout and personalized schedule. The Kids' Klub costs ten dollars per day per child, including lunch.

Address/Phone: Avenida Isla Verde #187; P.O. Box 2872, San Juan, Puerto Rico 00902; (809) 791–1000, (800) 468–2818; Fax: (809) 791–2856, (809) 791–6985

Owner: Posadas de San Juan Assoc.

Management: Williams Hospitality Management Corp.

Managing Director: Andreas T. Meinhold, vice president

Open: Year-round

Credit Cards: All major

U.S. Reservations: El San Juan Hotel & Casino, (800) 468–2818, (212) 755–9030; Fax: (212) 980–3766

Deposit: 1 night; 3 days cancellation

Minimum Stay: None

Arrival/Departure: No transfer service

Distance from Airport: (Luis Marin Muñoz International Airport) 5 miles; taxi one-way, about $5 (metered)

Distance from Old San Juan: 10 miles; taxi one-way, about $15

Accommodations: 389 rooms and suites, most with verandas (261 in main building, 128 in lanais and casitas); 174 with 2 double beds, 195 with kings; 57 suites

Amenities: Air-conditioning, ceiling fan, cable television, VCR, 3 telephones, safe, clock radio/cassette player; 5-inch TV in bathroom, hairdryer; bath with tub, shower, vanity, bathrobe, toiletry basket; nightly turndown service, ice service, stocked mini-bar, safe. 24-hour concierge, room service, business services

Electricity: 110 volts

Sports: Beach, 2 freshwater swimming pools, children's pool; 3 Jacuzzis, health club; 3 lighted tennis courts, equipment, daily clinics free. Snorkeling, scuba, windsurfing for fee. Golf, boating, fishing, horseback riding, and hiking arranged.

Dress Code: Casual by day; elegantly casual in evening

Children: All ages; Kids' Klub, supervised activities, game room, cribs, high chairs; baby-sitters

Meetings: Up to 1,500 people

Day Visitors: Welcome

Handicapped: Limited facilities; wheelchairs

Packages: Honeymoon, Caribbean Magic

Rates: Two persons, daily, EP. *High Season* (December 1–April 30): $295–$415, rooms; $450–$1,510, suites. *Low Season* (May 1–November 30): $215–$335, rooms; $380–$975, suites.

Service Charge: None

Government Tax: 9 percent

The Gallery Inn/Galería San Juan (S)

Artists don't usually have the temperament for managing a hotel, but for Jan D'Esopo, it's only one of several things on her plate—or palette, in this case. This is an art gallery-cum-inn, as the name implies, and there is nothing quite like it in the Caribbean. But what really sets the Gallery Inn apart is that it occupies one of the oldest buildings in Old San Juan.

La Cueva del Indio, as the rambling old building was known, faces north to the Atlantic Ocean from the topmost crest of the old city. Strategically located between the two large forts, the structure is the oldest military residence (built about 1750) on the north side of the old walled city. Historians believe it served as the captain's quarters for the Spanish Artillery.

New York–born Jan and her husband Manuco Gandía, a native of Puerto Rico, acquired the building in 1961, and the restoration took two years. Today the complex is made up of two buildings with more than fifty spaces: a maze of rooms, passageways, courtyards, balconies, and gardens. You need a map to find your way around.

The art gallery and its exhibit rooms occupy most of the ground floor and double as the inn's lobby. The entrance is marked only by a street-number sign, but you will know you are in the right place when you see a row of sculpted heads on the window sill of the silk-screening studio at the front of the house. The gate leads into a small bricked courtyard filled with plants and more sculpture. You may need to step over a sleeping dog to get into the gallery.

The guest rooms are situated in every nook of the three-story white-stucco building, and you make your way along narrow steps, around tight corners, and under broad arches. You will discover that the old stone, brick, and wood floors are seldom even, and steps go up and back down to reach some rooms. The handsome, beamed ceilings of ausubo wood (a termite-resistent native tree) are high in most places, but occasionally you might need to bend slightly to make your way. And everywhere plants and flowers overflow their bases, some hanging from upper balconies of the inner courtyard to the ground.

Every wall and surface, bookshelf and ledge, is enlivened with sculpture and paintings, either by Jan or a young artist she is helping to get established, or by acclaimed artists who come to give seminars or simply to visit. Special rates are extended to artists, who are often seen painting in a courtyard, depending on season and availability (inquire in advance if you qualify).

No two guest rooms are alike in size, decor, or amenities. Some have terraces; all have their own bath with shower except two adjacent rooms that share a private bath. A third-floor suite has a living room and an extra

Parador Hacienda Gripinas

bed for a third person and two terraces with views over Old San Juan and the sea.

Basically, the rooms are furnished in Spanish-colonial decor, but the artist in Jan has enabled her to mix contemporary pieces, art, and antiques in an eclectic way without being funky. Well, maybe, not too funky. To be honest, the entire house, from workshops to the new sundeck on top, has a chaotic order to it—and that, of course, defines a great deal of its charm.

The Gallery offers a continental breakfast, and occasionally Jan creates one of her famous dinners. (In addition to being an artist and innkeeper, she is an accomplished chef and caters elegant dinner parties for local businesses and visiting VIPs. She says she can seat as many as ninety people for dinner, but I haven't figured out where.) Old San Juan now has many super restaurants, all within walking distance; they are among the pleasures of visiting the Old City. The Gallery has a refreshment bar in the main gallery that works on the honor system. You keep tabs and pay upon check-out.

Jan made her name in Puerto Rico painting scenes of Old San Juan. Recently, however, she has returned to her first love, sculpture. The Gallery offers an unusual—perhaps unique—package. For one price of $2,500 for two people, guests can have a five-night stay in the gallery suite and their portrait bust in clay and cast in Jesmonite by the artist. You pose twice daily in about six 20-minute sessions over morning coffee or afternoon refreshments. The finished art will be shipped to you. The package also includes a welcome drink, continental breakfast daily, and dinner for two one evening with your hosts.

The guests who come here—as many from Europe as from the United States—are a group as eclectic as the house. If you are exacting or need orderly surroundings to feel comfortable, pass up this one. On the other hand, if being amid art and artists is stimulating for you and you are flexible, undemanding, and willing to forgo some of the usual amenities of a hotel, you could enjoy a stay here immensely.

The inn is homey as well as historic, but there's no one to pamper you. The owners and their staff will try to accommodate you but essentially, you fend for yourself. You are welcome as part of the family, encouraged to explore the house, enjoy the paintings and sculpture, ask questions, and even pick up a paint brush if you feel so inspired.

Address/Phone: Boulevard del Valle #204-206, Old San Juan, Puerto Rico 00901; (809) 722–1808, 723–6515; Fax: (809) 724–7360

Owner/Manager: Jan D'Esopo

Open: Year-round

Credit Cards: All major

U.S. Reservations: Direct to hotel

Deposit: 1 night, payable by credit card

Minimum Stay: 1 night

Arrival/Departure: No transfer service

Distance from Airport: 12 miles; taxi one-way, $12

Distance from Condado Beach area: 3 miles ; taxi one-way, $7

Accommodations: 8 rooms and suites, some with terrace or balcony; all with double or twins; 2 with sofa, suitable for child

Amenities: 6 rooms with air-conditioning, 2 with ceiling fans, one with phone; television in lounge, 1 bath with tub, others with shower only; honor bar, room service on request

Electricity: 110 volts

Sports: None. Horseback riding, tennis, boating, snorkeling, scuba, windsurfing, deep-sea fishing, hiking arranged.

Dress Code: Informal

Children: 9 years old minimum age

Meetings: Up to 40 for meeting, 90 for dinner

Day Visitors: Yes

Handicapped: No facilities

Packages: Portrait

Rates: Two persons, daily, CP. *Year-round:* $95, room; $150–$175, suite.

Service Charge: Included

Government Tax: Included

St. Barts

View of Gustavia from Hotel Carl Gustaf

Tiny St. Barts is an Eden of 8 square miles with green hills and rolling terrain edged with pretty white-sand beaches and ringed by shallow reefs ideal for snorkeling. The darling of jet-setters and others who can afford it, this hideaway was found three decades ago by the Rockefellers and the Rothschilds, who wisely kept it a secret as long as they could.

A ten-minute flight from St. Martin, St. Barthélemy, as it is properly named, is one of the French West Indies. The language is French, the currency is the franc, and the boutiques are stocked with famous French designer perfumes and accessories. It is also the gastronomic capital of the Caribbean, with sixty gourmet restaurants at last count.

Arawak Indians, Columbus (who named the island for his brother's patron saint), French settlers from St. Kitts, the Knights of Malta, Carib Indians, Frenchmen from Normandy and Brittany, the British, and the Swedes all were here. Those who left a permanent mark were the Swedes, who named the tiny harbor Gustavia, and the Frenchmen from Normandy, from whom most of the population is descended.

At Corossol, the most traditional of the tiny fishing villages, shy elderly women still don the *calèche,* a stiff-brimmed bonnet derived from a seventeenth-century Breton style, and make handwoven straw hats and other products from the supple straw of latania palms' fan-shaped fronds.

The tiny island is a beguiling beauty on which every turn in the road—and there are many—reveals striking panoramas. It is easy to tour by car on its roller-coaster roads.

Gustavia, the miniature port on the west coast, is a yachting mecca. On the north, St. Jean Bay is the center of resort and water-sports activity. Grand Cul-de-Sac, a large reef-protected bay on the northeast, is another resort center. Colombier on the northwest end is a pretty cove accessible by foot or boat.

Anse des Flamands to the north is one of the most beautiful beaches; Governor's Cove and Anse de Grande Saline, on the south, are the most secluded ones. Signs banning nude bathing abound but are not always obeyed. Teeny monokinis, however, are the fashion.

Information

French West Indies Tourist Board, 610 Fifth Avenue, Fifth Floor, New York, NY 10020; (212) 757–1125

Filao Beach Hotel ◙◙

Location, location, location. What's true for real estate is just as true for hotels, and the Filao has *the* location at the heart of St. Jean beach in the elbow of Eden Rock, the resort that launched St. Barts's tourism less than two decades ago. You can not get closer to the action.

Opened originally in 1981, the Filao Beach makes the most of its location, offering a convivial, laid-back atmosphere that attracts the neighbors, and almost everyone else on St. Barts, to its bar and pleasant open-air beachfront restaurant.

Set in a jungle of tropical flowers and flowering trees, the hotel comprises one-story white-stucco, red-roofed bungalows, each with two units. They are arranged close to the sea in more or less a tight U around the central beachfront pavilion with the restaurant, bar and swimming pool where the faithful, the onlookers, and the newcomers come throughout the day (it's the best people-watching spot in town).

The rooms, each named after a French château, are identical in size and layout but may vary in furnishings. You don't come to Filao for stylish accommodations. The rooms are comfortable but rather ordinary; given the resort's reputation, they may in fact disappoint. They have white wood-beamed ceilings and rather old-fashioned rattan or new white bamboo furnishings. The floors are carpeted—that dates them—and the baths have dark brown tiles—that *really* dates them.

All the rooms are being renovated and more than half have been completed at this writing. The newly renovated rooms have king beds; the others queen-size beds and sleeping sofas, which are particularly suited for a family with a child. Sliding glass doors open onto a front porch, but the dense vegetation that gives you privacy all but blocks any view of the sea.

One of Filao's most convenient features is its entrance. By being set back from the main road, it can provide a parking area for guests' cars: a blessing in the most heavily traveled part of the beach. You don't actually need a car for immediate transportation, but you may want to rent one for part of your stay to explore the island.

From the small lobby you pass directly into the gardens to the open-air dining pavilion and bar, directly on the beach. Swimming, snorkeling, and windsurfing are good here. The hotel has its own windsurfers for rent, and scuba diving and other water sports are available from nearby concessionnaires on the beach.

The Filao is the place to be, particularly at lunch. Along with sunbathers from the beach, the town's business people who close shop for lunch are found here, socializing at the bar and enjoying salads, grilled fish, and the specialties of the day. The restaurant serves breakfast and lunch, but not dinner, having the good sense not to compete with the many excellent restaurants nearby and around the island.

That also makes the evenings here quiet and private, a welcome change from the busy daytime activity. And when you want to stay in for the evening, you will find two films—one in English, another in French—shown nightly on your closed-circuit television.

A member of France's prestigious Relais et Chateaux group, the Filao Beach is relaxing, sociable, and fun. Its friendly staff, unpretentious environment, and lack of the self-conscious chic that afflicts some other St. Barts resorts, enables everyone to feel welcome and comfortable here. If any one person is responsible for this invitation to enjoyment, it is Pierre Verdier, one of the most hospitable hoteliers in the islands.

Filao Beach is the laid-back Caribbean at its easiest. It appeals to travelers who care less for what their digs look like and more for where they are: directly on the beach and at the heart of the action. The hotel enjoys a long-established reputation as the best on the beach, with loyal fans—as many American as French—who return in large numbers year after year. It's not spectacular, just dependable.

Address/Phone: P.O. Box 667, 97099 St. Barthélemy, Cedex F.W.I.; (590) 27–64–84; Fax: (590) 27–62–24

Owner: S.A.I.T., S.A.

General Manager: Pierre Verdier

Open: Year-round except September to mid-October

Credit Cards: All major

U.S. Reservations: Direct to hotel

Deposit: 3 nights winter, 1 summer

Minimum Stay: 10 days at Christmas, 7 days in February

Arrival/Departure: Complimentary transfers included in the rate

Distance from Airport: 1 mile; taxi one-way, $5

Distance from Gustavia: 4 miles; taxi one-way, $7

Accommodations: 30 rooms in 15 bungalows, all with terraces; all with twins or king

Amenities: Air-conditioning, ceiling fans, telephone, cable television with English and French films; bath with tub and shower, bidet, hairdryer, basket of toiletries, makeup mirrors, bathrobe in deluxe units; small refrigerators, safes; nightly turndown service; room service for breakfast only (in summer, continental breakfast; in winter, full American breakfast)

Electricity: 220 volts

Sports: Freshwater swimming pool. Tennis, boating, snorkeling, scuba, windsurfing, deep-sea fishing, and other water sports arranged.

Dress Code: Casual

Children: All ages; cribs, baby-sitters

Meetings: None

Day Visitors: Yes

Handicapped: No facilities

Packages: None

Rates: Per room, daily, AB. *High Season* (December 21–January 3 and February 1–28): $420–$580. *Shoulder Season* (January 4–31 and March 1–April 20): $320–$480. *Low Season,* CP (April 21–May 31 and October 10–December 18): $180–$300; (June 1–August 31): $160–260.

Service Charge: Included

Government Tax: None

Guanahani ◙◙◙◙◙

Gingerbread-trimmed creole cottages in Easter egg colors sit in baskets of flowering gardens on fifty hillside acres sloping down to inviting beaches. Overlooking Grand Cul de Sac to the east and Marigot Bay to the west, Guanahani is an exclusive luxury oasis of refined simplicity.

But this stylish haven has more to it than simply a touch of class. It's *très sympathique.* Friendly, not intimidating, this charmer manages to be classy and cozy at the same time. Since it opened in 1986, Guanahani has been a hit with an international array of celebrities and well-heeled sophisticates in search of privacy and comfort in a quiet setting of tropical luxury.

Guest rooms and suites are situated in colorful one-story cottages, each with one and two units, at various levels of the hillside. Due to their location, some afford a greater sense of privacy and better views than others. They also differ in size, layout, and decor.

For all the exuberant colors of the exterior, Guanahani's guest rooms are marked by the elegance of simplicity: a soft, light, fresh decor in white with pastel accents rendered in the finest of fabrics and linens. All rooms face the sea and have their own covered wooden veranda secluded in a garden.

Most have the high beamed ceilings typical of creole architecture, which make them seem spacious, and are furnished with a four-poster king bed or twins, a sitting area with a desk, stocked mini-bar, and a large tiled bath. Some suites have kitchenettes; some have whirlpools, others splash pools. The landscaping is impeccable and the housekeeping immaculate.

Already the largest resort on St. Barts, Guanahani was recently expanded, adding eighteen deluxe villa suites, a second swimming pool, and a new reception cottage whose interior resembles the large parlor of a private home, furnished in handsome wicker with stylish fabrics of tropical colors.

Early on Guanahani established a reputation for fine, albeit expensive, cuisine in both of its restaurants. L'Indigo, the informal open-air restaurant, has a delightful setting beside one of the Caribbean's prettiest swimming pools, with a wide wooden deck overlooking the grove of palm trees that lines the beach. Like all else about Guanahani, it has style. Breakfast is served here, or you can breakfast on tropical fruit and freshly baked croissants on your terrace. L'Indigo serves lunch until late afternoon. It is also the venue for a beach barbecue with a Carib and French show on Wednesdays and a Saturday evening lobster barbecue.

Bartolomeo is the more formal (but only slightly) restaurant serving gourmet French cuisine at dinner. The only "formal" elements are the crystal and china glowing in the candlelight and the five-star service, not always matched, alas, by the cuisine, despite its reputation. But there can hardly be a more pleasant setting for dining al fresco than the restaurant's new outdoor terrace bordered with hedges of exotic flowers and cooled by the gentle trade winds that rustle the palm trees overhead.

Guanahani has two beaches (neither as inviting as the pretty freshwater swimming pool or Jacuzzi), and tennis, as well as a tennis pro for private instruction. A wide range of water sports are available. Horseback riding and trips by private planes, yachts, or helicopters can be arranged.

You can get your exercise walking between the upper sections and the beach pavilion, reception, tennis courts, restaurants, boutique, and a Jacques Dessange beauty salon; a road barely wide enough for a car winds through the property, connecting the facilities. There is also a fitness center at St. Barts Gym, about a five-minute walk from the main road.

Consider the setting, the style, the panache, and add to these excellent service and a superb staff, and you have what Guanahani is truly about. Directed by Bruno Hill who, despite his non-Gallic-sounding name, is a seasoned French hotelier, the Guanahani staff, from the front desk to the young women who take care of your room and bring breakfast to your cottage, is cheerful, yet refined and efficient. They pamper without pandering in quietly attentive ways.

Although it is the island's largest hotel, Guanahani does not seem large, but that's the secret of St. Barts. Its hotels are on the scale of the island, the ambience low-key. Gracious and romantic, Guanahani is glamorous in a quiet understated way.

Address/Phone: Grand Cul de Sac, P.O. Box 609, 97098 St. Barthélemy, F.W.I.; Phone: 011–590–27.66.60; Fax: 011–590–27.70.70

Owner: Societé Hoteliére des Antiles Francaises

General Manager: Bruno Hill

Open: November to August

Credit Cards: All major

U.S. Reservations: Leading Hotels of the World, (800) 223–6800, (212) 838–3110; Fax: (212) 758–7367

Deposit: 3 nights

Minimum Stay: 10 nights, Christmas; 5 nights, February; 3 nights balance of year

Arrival/Departure: Airport transfers included in rate

Distance from Airport: 3 miles; taxi one-way, $15

Distance from Gustavia: 5 miles; taxi one-way, $15

Accommodations: 80 units in villas with terrace/patio; 68 bungalows with 1 or 2 units; 14 with pools; 23 with twins convertible to king, 57 with king

Amenities: Air-conditioning, ceiling fans, telephone, cable television; VCR and radio on request; bath with tub and/or shower, hairdryer, Hermès toiletries, bathrobe; stocked mini-bar; nightly turndown service, 18-hour room service

Electricity: 220 volts

Sports: Two freshwater swimming pools; private plunge pools and Jacuzzis; 2 lighted tennis courts and equipment, snorkel gear free use. Scuba, windsurfing for fee. Boating, fishing, horseback riding arranged. Fitness center nearby.

Dress Code: Casual but chic at all times; no shorts, tank tops, swimsuits, T-shirts, or similar attire in dining room after dark
Children: All ages; cribs, high chairs, baby-sitters
Meetings: Up to 30 people
Day Visitors: Welcome
Handicapped: No facilities
Packages: Dive, honeymoon, weekend
Rates: Per person, daily, CP. *High Season* (mid-December–mid-April): $213–$375. *Low Season:* $130–$245.
Service Charge: Included
Government Tax: None

L'Hibiscus ◉

A small collection of red-roofed, white dollhouse cottages climbs the steep hill that frames the pretty little port of Gustavia. From your perch you can enjoy wonderful views of the yacht-filled harbor and surrounding hills and watch the town come to life in the soft early-morning light, as the sun comes up over the mountains behind the town.

From the street entrance at about the center of the small complex, you step into a large open lounge that accommodates a cozy bar and piano in one corner and extends to the homey dining room on one side and a swimming pool with a wooden deck on the other. Each "room" is slightly separated from the other by latticework and potted palms, and all look out on Gustavia and the harbor—and the setting sun.

Indeed, cocktails at its lively sunset bar is a favorite rendezvous for islanders and visitors alike. You can watch sailboats return to the harbor bathed in sunset pinks, oranges, and reds—like the hibiscus of the gardens around your terrace—until dusk, when the twinkling lights of the tiny port begin to compete with the stars overhead.

Then it's time for dinner in the inn's candlelit restaurant, known for its fine French cuisine, or at one in town only a short walk down the hill. L'Hibiscus has piano music nightly and entertainment—jazz or a small combo—on another evening or two.

A labyrinth of brick walkways and steps branches off from the main building to the cottages on the flowering hillside. The cottages are typical of St. Barts's creole architecture, with pitched, beamed ceilings and terra-cotta floors. They match their surroundings so well that when you look up the hill from the port, you cannot distinguish them except for the landmark at their side, the 200-year-old clock tower of the town hall. The clock, which chimes every hour on the hour, day and night, can be something of a problem for light sleepers.

Guest rooms, redecorated recently with a pleasant fresh look, are tasteful and comfortable but furnished basically; they have twin beds or a king. The room extends to a wood deck, where you can enjoy your private view on a lounging chair, in a hammock, or at a small table over breakfast. Not all units have good harbor views, however.

Tucked in a corner of the veranda of your inside/outside room is an outdoor pullman-style kitchenette equipped with table service and a small two-burner stove, sink, and refrigerator. It is convenient for making breakfast or a light lunch, although the hotel has room service, and its restaurant serves three meals daily.

Opened originally in the late 1970s, the tidy hotel is under the watchful eye of David Henderson, who will likely meet you at the airport or at the front door on your arrival. This friendly Scotsman, who says that 95 percent of his guests are from the United States, will make sure you have what you need from soup to soap.

L'Hibiscus is for people who care less about beaches and more about being within easy reach of town, but even here the shops, restaurants, water sports, and a beach suitable for swimming are less than a ten-minute walk away. The inn will help you arrange sports and excursions, but you will probably want to rent a car for at least part of your stay, for the fun of St. Barts is discovery.

Casual and unpretentious, L'Hibiscus offers good value—and that's surely nothing to ignore on an island whose reputation for being very expensive is well earned. The cozy inn attracts singles and couples, most in their forties. The accommodations are suited for families but might be somewhat confining for kids—unless, of course, you take them to the beach and wear them out every day.

Address/Phone: Rue Thiers, Gustavia, 97133 St. Barthélemy, F.W.I.; (590) 27–64–82; Fax: (590) 27–73–04
Owner: Gerard Basset
General Manager: David Henderson
Open: Year-round (restaurant closed in October)
Credit Cards: All major
U.S. Reservations: WIMCO, (800) 932–3222, (401) 849–8012; Fax: (401) 847–6290
Deposit: 3 nights
Minimum Stay: Inquire for Christmas/New Year's
Arrival/Departure: Complimentary transfer
Distance from Airport: (St. Barts Airport) 2 miles; taxi one-way, US $5.

Distance from Gustavia: Located in town
Accommodations: 11 units in cottages, all with kitchenettes and terraces; with twins or king
Amenities: air-conditioning, ceiling fans, telephone, kitchenette, cable television with videos; bath with shower only, hairdryer available, basket of toiletries; nightly turndown service in season, room service from 8:00 A.M. to midnight
Electricity: 220 volts
Sports: Freshwater swimming pool. Tennis, boating, snorkeling, scuba, windsurfing, deep-sea fishing, horseback riding arranged for charge.
Dress Code: Casual
Children: All ages; cribs, baby-sitters
Meetings: Up to 40 people
Day Visitors: Yes
Handicapped: No facilities
Packages: Inquire
Rates: Two persons, daily, EP. *High Season:* $260. *Low Season:* $150.
Service Charge: 15 percent included
Government Tax: None

Sapore di Mare (T)

When the Italians arrived last year on this very French island, it was unquestionably an island-shaking event. High at the top of Morne Lurin sits the dramatically dignified inn, known to all as Les Castelets, that originally put St. Barts on the map nearly two decades ago.

Behind the unflagging success of this sophisticated and gastronomically superb gem was one of the island's most respected, beloved innkeepers: a slight, unassuming, gracious *française* named Geneviève Jouany. Was it possible that she had sold out to, *ooh la la,* Italians, who dared change the name to Sapore di Mare ("Taste of the Sea")? Mon Dieu!

St. Barts felt betrayed. Castelets was something of a landmark, the island's Rock of Gibraltar. This tiny inn had become a refuge for the world's most distinguished luminaries, from the occasional president of France to such international artists as Baryshnikov and David Bowie, Beverly Sills and Leon Uris. Rumbles shook the island, visions of pasta replacing pâté.

In her inimitable good taste and sensible style, Mme. Jouany published a brief "Epilogue" in the Christmas 1991 issue of the widely read *St. Barth Magazine,* in which she warmly welcomed the newcomers, whom she had chosen with great care and conviction. She conceded that "I never would have imagined that my fading out of Castelets after seventen years would have affected the local and the outside communities so much."

The newcomers—Pino Luongo and Cesare and Kristen Dell'Aguzzo—in the past five years or so have become something of a tradition themselves in the restaurant business. Florentine restaurateur Luongo teamed up on St. Barts with Rome-born Cesare, his partner at the original Sapore di Mare in East Hampton. Luongo's other credits include the wildly successful Le Madri and Coco Pazzo in New York, as well as a handful of renowned eateries from Chicago to California. Both men are former stage actors, and the key to their success is in providing the sort of star quality that makes theater out of restaurants.

The formal French ambience of Castelets has been replaced by a more relaxed, fun-filled ambience that the Italians do so well. Gallic gastronomes and traditionalists may miss the refined atmosphere and classic haute cuisine of the mountaintop auberge, with its antiques-filled salon and whisper of classical music, but others are bound to delight in the island's first authentic Italian ristorante, with its earthy Tuscan fare and a jovial staff that exudes Mediterranean warmth and cheer.

For now the hotel rooms remain as they are, pleasantly furnished in French country style, with rustic antiques and the feeling of a private home. Stephan of the former Castelets staff (he's one of the world's great waiters) stayed on. The spectacular view toward St. Jean beach remains, too.

Habitués may be taken aback by the *buon giorno* greeting at check-in and at the "gutsy" Tuscan cuisine, as Pino describes it. A few more tables were added to the dining room in the former salon, and an open-air cafe with grill is being readied for the new season. In the future the pool may be enlarged and some spa facilities added, but no major changes are contemplated for now. Perhaps the biggest change has been the inn's remaining open in summer.

Sapore di Mare is actually a cluster of four villas with broad terraces that offer heart-stopping views over the St. Barts countryside and coast. In addition, the main building with the reception and restaurant has two small upstairs guest rooms. There is a minuscule swimming pool with a small terrace for sunning and contemplating the charms of St. Barts and the choices for dinner.

Address/Phone: Morne Lurin, St. Barthélemy, F.W.I.; Phone: (590) 27–61–73; Fax: (590) 27–85–27

Owner: Geneviève Jouany/Pino Luongo, Cesare Dell'Aguzzo

General Manager: Lorenzo T. Baldocchi

Open: Early October to early August

Credit Cards: None for reservations or settlement of hotel account; all major cards for restaurant meals

U.S. Reservations: Jane Martin, (212) 319–7488; Fax: (212) 879–1276

Deposit: 4 days or less, prepaid in full; longer stays, half of reserved days plus last 2 days; 21 days cancellation

Minimum Stay: None

Arrival/Departure: No transfer service

Distance from Airport: 1.7 miles; taxi one-way, US $8

Distance from Gustavia: 0.7 miles; taxi one-way, US $5

Accommodations: 10 rooms, most with terraces (2 in main building with double bed; 8 in villas, including 2 duplexes with lofts and queens; twins or twin beds converted to kings)

Amenities: air-conditioning in bedrooms; some with refrigerator; bath with tub and shower; 2 shower only, basket of toiletries; some with refrigerator; room service for meals

Electricity: 220 volts

Sports: Freshwater swimming pool. Tennis, water sports and horseback riding arranged.

Dress Code: Casual

Children: All ages; cribs, baby-sitters

Meetings: None

Day Visitors: Yes

Handicapped: No facilities

Packages: Summer

Rates: Per room, double, daily, CP. *High Season* (mid-December–mid-April): $100–$225; duplex suite, $400. *Low Season* (April 12–December 19) $70–$190; duplex suite, $250.

Service Charge: 10 percent

Government Tax: None

Village St. Jean Hotel ▣▣ ✿

This cluster of hillside cottages is the best kept secret on St. Barts. Set high on the side of a steep hill overlooking St. Jean Bay at the heart of St. Barts, Village Saint Jean combines quiet villa living with hotel facilities and amenities. It's all within walking distance of popular restaurants, shops, and the island's liveliest beach.

For years the unpretentious resort has attracted an impressive list of distinguished guests, including the Zabars of New York deli fame; well-known food critic Craig Claiborne, who comes annually at Christmas, sometimes bringing his pots and pans; an occasional French or American movie star, and an array of smart people from eighteen to eighty who know a good value when they see it.

But even with its great location, grand views, sensible accommodations, and moderate prices, its biggest assets, many habitués will tell you, are the friendliness and care that its savvy family owners convey.

Created in 1970 by André and Gaby Charneau, who came to St. Barts from Guadeloupe, the Village is now operated by their daughter Catherine and son Bertrand and his wife, New York-born "I.B.". Their youthful energy and commitment add that extra sparkle to this hilltop gem. One or all will greet you on arrival with a welcome drink.

The white-stucco cottages trimmed with wood and native stone are designed to resemble a hillside village with a variety of styles and accommodations: hotel rooms, studios, one- and two-bedroom suites with covered sun decks in two-story cottages. The units are large for this island, and all are comfortably furnished with twin or king-size beds and have tile floors and tiled baths, some with bidets. Some rooms have sea views; others look over the gardens.

The four hotel rooms are spacious, high-ceilinged bedrooms with a balcony overlooking the sea and furnished with twin beds and mini-fridge; continental breakfast is included in the rate. The villa rooms have kitchens screened behind louvered doors on terraces. Those in the deluxe cottages—Claiborne's digs, for example—are larger than the regular ones and have the best views. Two units have second bedrooms suitable for children.

One suite with a Jacuzzi and kitchenette is actually a tiny villa with a wraparound terrace in a secluded garden with an outdoor shower. The small bedroom has a queen-size bed, the living room a convertible sofa.

Le Patio, true to its name, is a casual indoor/outdoor terrace restaurant and bar. The tables are attractively dressed with madras tablecloths in the Guadeloupe tradition. Its moderately priced Italian menu is a welcome alternative to the island's norm of expensive French cuisine. The kitchen makes its own pizzas and pasta, which are available also as take-out, if you want to enjoy lunch or dinner on your terrace. Le Patio is open daily during the winter season and closed in June and October.

Behind it, one level up from the restaurant, is the attractive freshwater swimming pool with cascading waters on one side and a terrace and Jacuzzi overlooking the bay on the other side. Other diversions include a lounge and game room with cable television, a video library, and a Ping-Pong table. Annually, in April, the Village hosts a two-week jazz festival.

It's about a three-minute spill down the hill to the beach (though a ten-minute climb on the return) to restaurants, shops, other hotels, and water-sport centers along St. Jean Bay. You don't need a car, but you might want one for exploring the island, checking out the other beaches, and sampling some of the expensive temples of haute cuisine (with the money you save staying at the Village).

Address/Phone: P.O. Box 23, 97133 St. Barthélemy, F.W.I.; Phone: (590) 27–61–39, (800) 633–7411; Fax: (590) 27–77–96
Owners: Charneau family
General Managers: Catherine, Bertrand, and I.B. Charneau
Open: Year-round
Credit Cards: All major
U.S. Reservations: Caribbean Inns, Ltd., (800) 633–7411, (803) 785–7411; Fax: (803) 686–7411
Deposit: 3 nights; 45 days cancellation in winter, 30 in summer. $25 penalty for cancellation year-round
Minimum Stay: 7 days at Christmas
Arrival/Departure: Complimentary airport transfer
Distance from Airport: 1.5 miles; taxi one-way, $7
Distance from Gustavia: 3 miles; taxi one-way, $10.
Accommodations: 25 units in 12 cottages and 1 villa-suite (4 hotel rooms, 18 one-bedroom units, 1 Jacuzzi suite, 2 two-bedroom); with twins, queen, or king beds
Amenities: Air-conditioning, ceiling fans, direct-dial telephone, cable television and VCR in lounge; bath with shower only, hairdryer available; ice machine, refrigerator; room service for breakfast
Electricity: 220 volts
Sports: Freshwater swimming pool; Jacuzzi. Tennis, boating, snorkeling, scuba, windsurfing, deep-sea fishing, horseback riding arranged for charge.
Dress Code: Casual
Children: All ages; cribs, high chair, baby-sitters
Meetings: Up to 50 people
Day Visitors: Yes
Handicapped: No facilities
Packages: Summer, honeymoon
Rates: Per room CP, cottage EP, daily. *High Season* (mid-December–mid-April): $120–$280. *Low Season:* $68–$170.
Service Charge: 10 percent
Government Tax: None

ON THE HORIZON

Hotel Carl Gustaf

Pink one- and two-bedroom villas climb the steep hill above Gustavia to a small reception area and a poolside restaurant and bar perched at the top. There you'll find incomparable views spanning the postage-stamp-size harbor in an amphitheater of green hills below.

Absolutely no expense was spared by long-time resident Lucien Couic in creating this super-posh haven, which opened in late 1991. The furnishings are exquisite throughout. Each unit has a small pool and deck with a fabulous view, along with a small kitchen equipped with a halogen stove, fridge, and Limoges china. Some guests (not workaholics) may question the need for such amenities as a fax machine, *two* direct-dial phones, *two* televisions, and *two* video/stereo systems in every suite—but not the twenty-four-hour room service, excellent restaurant, or private yacht to take you fishing or cruising to other islands.

Address/Phone: Rue des Normands, Gustavia 97113, St. Barthélemy, F.W.I.; Phone: (590) 27–82–83; Fax: (590) 27–82–37
U.S. Reservations: St. Barts Holidays, (800) 645–6030, (516) 466–4670
Accommodations: 12 one- and two-bedroom villa suites with pools
Rates: Per room, daily, EP. *High Season* (December 16–April 24): $840. *Shoulder Season* (October 15–December 15): $620. *Low Season* (April 25–August 31): $560.

Hotel St. Barth Isle de France

The new deluxe Hotel St. Barth Isle de France, opened in early 1992, is set in a grove of tatania palms on Anse des Flamands, described by *Paris Match* as *la plus belle* of St. Barts's beaches. The hotel has spacious rooms and suites, some in an elegant two-story plantation-style estate house, others across the road in woodsy cottages tucked among the palms in a secluded retreat quite unlike any other on the island. There are two swimming pools, an open-air bar and restaurant, a lighted tennis court, an air-conditioned squash court, exercise room, boutique, and reception area.

Most guest rooms are unusually roomy by St. Barts standards. The main house has twelve units, all with terraces overlooking the sea, which are beautifully furnished with obvious French flair. There are antique pieces, some splendid hand-carved four-poster creole beds, marble baths with Jacuzzi tubs, separate showers, double vanities, and bidets. All units are air-conditioned and have safes, mini-fridges, and coffee/tea makers.

Address/Phone: Baie des Flamands, 97133 St. Barthélemy; (590) 27–61–81; Fax: (590) 27–86–83

U.S. Reservations: Crown International, (800) 628–8929

Accommodations: 20 rooms and 5 suites

Rates: Per room, double, daily, CP. *High Season* (December 20–January 5): $365–$670. *Shoulder Season* (January 6–April 3): $320–630. *Low Season* (May 1–December 19): $225–$440.

Le Toiny

St. Barts's newest upscale resort is a hillside cottage complex on the southeast corner where, heretofore, tourism development had not been seen. Designed in plantation-house style, each cottage has two deluxe suites with a connecting living room, private pool, and covered terrace overlooking the sea.

Although the decor evokes the colonial era with mahogany furniture, including four-poster beds crafted in Martinique, kitchens have the latest high-tech equipment; bathrooms, the largest in the French West Indies, are ultra-posh; and each air-conditioned suite has two-line phones, two cable televisions, VCR, safe, and hairdryer. A main building contains an elegantly decorated reception room, bar, restaurant, and open-air terrace, which embraces a large swimming pool and overlooks extensive sea views. Water sports can be arranged. A footpath leads down to the shore, but the sea here is generally too rough for swimming.

Address/Phone: Anse de Toiny, 97133 St. Barthélemy, F.W.I.; Phone: (590) 27–88–88; Fax: (590) 27–89–30

U.S. Reservations: WIMCO, (800) 932–3222

Accommodations: 12 cottages with 2 suites and private pool

Rates: Per room, double, daily, CP. *High Season* (December 18–April 3): $420–$800. *Low Season* (April 27–December 17): $270–$540.

St. Eustatius

The Old Gin House

South of St. Maarten, the Dutch Windward island of St. Eustatius beckons visitors with fascinating historic ruins on land and under the sea and an extinct volcano with trails through a rain forest to the crater floor.

Statia, as the 8-square-mile island is known, was once the richest entrepôt in the Caribbean, trading everything from cotton to contraband from around the world. In the first two hundred years after Columbus discovered it, the island changed hands twenty-two times.

During the American Revolution St. Eustatius was used as a transit point for arms to the rebels. According to local lore, on November 16, 1776, after the island's garrison at Fort Oranje saluted the *Andrew Doria* flying the American flag—the first foreign port to do so after the United States declared its independence—the gesture so enraged the British that they sacked the town and destroyed the harbor. The island never recovered.

As a belated show of gratitude, the United States under President Franklin D. Roosevelt helped to restore the fort and other eighteenth-century buildings. In a colonial house near the fort is the town's museum.

Although you may ask why, Statia-America Day (November 16) is one of the island's main celebrations.

The island's only town, Oranjestad, is divided into two parts. Upper Town, a pretty little community of cobblestone streets lined with West Indian gingerbread-trimmed houses and flowering gardens, grew up around the old fort atop a 150-foot cliff overlooking the sea.

Lower Town, the site of the famous old harbor, is the docking area today, and to the north is the island's main beach. Only a few feet beneath the sea rests centuries-old debris that has led researchers to call Statia "an archaeologist's nightmare and a scuba diver's dream." Divers have a heyday exploring the ruins of the old houses and warehouses that have lain undisturbed for two hundred years. Farther out the sea bottom is littered with hundreds of shipwrecks, some dating back three hundred years.

The Quill, the crater of an extinct volcano, dominates the southern end of the island. Eight signposted trails designed as a series of contiguous paths enable hikers to walk up to and around the crater's rim, down into the cone.

Information

St. Eustatius Tourist Information Office, Medhurst & Associates, 271 Main Street, Northport, NY 11768; (800) 344–4606, (212) 936–0050

The Old Gin House ◉

On my first trip to St. Eustatius in the early 1970s, I discovered The Old Gin House: a dream-come-true for two New Yorkers who had given up the hectic pace of the city for the quietest, quaintest island in the Caribbean.

John May, a former advertising executive, and his late partner, Martin Scofield, an art teacher, had just finished transforming the ruins of an eighteenth-century cotton gin into a charming inn, after months of painstaking restoration. Their efforts helped to spark the restoration of other historic sites on the island, an endeavor that has continued for two decades.

The Old Gin House is located on the waterfront in Lower Town, a short stroll from a quiet beach and within walking distance of the historic center of Oranjestad. The hotel, reminiscent of a New England country inn, is beautifully appointed with antiques and period furniture, conveying an elegant setting in colonial times.

The hotel consists of three parts: The oldest part is the Gin House, the reconstructed eighteenth-century brick building, which contains a formal dining room, a comfortable lounge, and a bar named The Mooshay Bay

Publick House, where guests gather in the evening before dinner. The Publick House is meant to be a re-creation of an eighteenth-century tavern with walls of old ballast bricks, wooden rafters, and a gallery with a large brass chandelier hanging from the ceiling.

Immediately behind it and up the hill is a three-story annex with guest rooms facing a courtyard with a freshwater pool in tropical gardens filled with exotic flowers and singing birds. It also contains a library and game room for cards and backgammon and a boutique with locally made products.

Across the lane—Lower Town's only road—on the sea side is an outdoor patio and bar with a covered area for informal dining. It is adjacent to another section of The Old Gin House, a two-story structure with spacious guest rooms perched over the sea.

The airy and cheerful guest rooms all have private bath. Each room is individually and tastefully decorated with antiques and island-made fabrics designed by Scofield. Don't look for locks on the doors—on this tranquil island none are needed. The honeymoon suite has a bell hidden in the canopy of the four-poster bed, which rings at . . . well, you get the idea.

You breakfast and lunch outdoors at the grill by the sea and dine in the elegant, candlelit dining room. The inn was one of the first in the Caribbean to feature sophisticated, imaginative cuisine using fresh, local products and quickly became known for fine dining. Menus are changed daily. May, who gives his personal attention to every last detail, escorts guests to their tables to enjoy the carefully prepared dinner.

Two doors away from The Old Gin House is Dive Statia, the island's only dive shop, which offers dive excursions and packages. Swimming and snorkeling are available at the nearby beach. Walking around historic Oranjestad and hiking on the "Quill" are popular pastimes.

Over the years The Old Gin House has attracted an eclectic group of travelers—writers, artists, Dutch royalty, film executives—and true escapists who come year after year. It appeals particularly to people who are happy to spend time in quiet relaxation, reading, taking an occasional walk or hike, and dining leisurely on good food in good company. The island also has great charm for history buffs and nature lovers.

Address/Phone: Box 172, Oranjestad, St. Eustatius, Netherlands Antilles; (599) 38–2319; Fax: (599) 38–2555
Owner/Manager: John May
Open: October 16–August 31
Credit Cards: All major
U.S. Reservations: E & M Associates, (212) 599–8280, (800) 223–9832; Fax: (212) 599–1755
Deposit: 2 nights in summer; 3 in winter; 4 weeks cancellation

Minimum Stay: None; reservations required 30 days prior to arrival
Arrival/Departure: No transfer service
Distance from Airport: 2 miles; taxi one-way, $3.50
Distance from Oranjestad: .5-mile; taxi one-way, $2
Accommodations: 20 rooms (14 in three-story garden annex; 6 in two-story seaside building) with singles, doubles, twins, triples
Amenities: Ceiling fans, bath with shower only
Electricity: 110 volts
Sports: Freshwater swimming pool. Snorkeling, diving, hiking nearby.
Dress Code: Casual but stylish
Children: None under 10 years of age
Meetings: None
Day Visitors: Yes, with reservations
Handicapped: No facilities
Packages: Dive
Rates: Per person, daily, EP. *High Season* (mid-December–mid-April): $75. *Low Season:* $50.
Service Charge: 15 percent
Government Tax: 7 percent

St. Kitts

Ottley's Plantation Inn

Located in the heart of the Leeward Islands, St. Kitts has a beauty and grace that enchants visitors, taking them back to another era when life was more genteel. From all the islands he saw, Christopher Columbus selected St. Kitts to name for his patron saint, St. Christopher.

It's something of a newcomer to Caribbean tourism, but St. Kitts was the first island settled by the English in 1623, giving England great wealth from the land that produced the highest- yielding sugar crop in the world. From their base in St. Kitts, the English settled Nevis, Antigua, and Montserrat, but not before battling the French, who arrived in 1624 to stake out their claim. St. Kitts remained a British possession until 1983 when full independence was established.

Shaped like a paddle with an area of 65 square miles, St. Kitts rises from intensively cultivated lowland and foothills to a central spine of mountains covered with rain forests. The northern part of the island is dominated by Mount Liamuiga, known in colonial times as Mt. Misery, a dormant volcano that rises to almost 4,000 feet. A coastal road makes it easy to drive—or bike—around the island and provides access to the splendid hiking of the mountainous interior. There are no cross-island roads through the central mountains, but there are footpaths.

The Southeastern Peninsula, a hilly tongue of land different in climate and terrain from the main body of St. Kitts, is covered with dry woodland and salt ponds and scalloped with the island's best white-sand beaches. It has a new magnificently engineered highway of about 7 miles that has made this part of the island accessible by land for the first time.

St. Kitts and its sister island of Nevis are separated on the surface of the sea by a 2-mile-wide strait known as the Narrows but connected below the surface by a subterranean rock base on which their volcanic mountains were formed eons ago. Daily ferry service connects the two islands.

Information

St. Kitts and Nevis Tourist Board, 414 East 75th Street, New York, NY 10021; (212) 535–1234.

The Golden Lemon Inn and Villas ◙◙◙

If you are looking for a definition of "style," you will find it at The Golden Lemon, one of the most fashionable small inns in the Caribbean. To be sure, this is style as defined by the resort's owner, Arthur Leaman, but a more practiced arbiter you could not find. One look at this "country inn in the Caribbean," and you might say he invented the word.

On the north coast of St. Kitts at Dieppe Bay, The Golden Lemon is set in a seventeenth-century stone- and-wooden structure draped in tropical splendor and shaded by a grove of coconut palms. Leaman bought the historic building in 1962 and renovated it to resemble an island plantation house with a second-story balcony where you can enjoy breakfast along with sea views. The ground floor of the gracious old manor—dressed in bright lemon (what else?) with white trim—contains a cozy lounge and bar and the dining room which has an outside flagstone terrace, where lunch is served. To one side is a greenery-cloaked patio and swimming pool.

As he tells the story, Leaman came to St. Kitts by accident on a freighter headed for South America. The ship developed mechanical trouble, and since this was 1961, long before St. Kitts had an international airport, they waited a week or more while repairs were completed. Young and handsome, he soon caught the eye of the island's leading social maven, who took him under her wing.

Leaman had been scouting the Caribbean for a hideaway for himself. Smitten with the island, he decided there was no need to look further. He bought the remote building—with a damaged roof and no water or electricity—and combed the island for antiques and objets d'art to furnish his seven-room inn.

Leaman's friends told him he had bought a lemon, so he made it The Golden Lemon. For three decades it has garnered praise for its stylish accommodations, good food, and fine service, attracting an international set of urbane and sophisticated devotees.

The Golden Lemon now has rooms in the historic building and rooms and suites in modern buildings that blend with the old remarkably well. The Lemon Court, a small complex, with spacious super-deluxe studios and one- and two-bedroom suites, has a pool and private terrace at the water's edge. The Lemon Grove, a cluster of condominiums by the sea, adds ten one- and two-bedroom villas set in walled gardens, giving them a great deal of privacy. Each villa has steps leading from one of the rooms directly into a private swimming pool, a feature first used in the Lemon Court.

The decor throughout the Golden Lemon has the mark of "style by Leaman," a former decorating editor at *House & Garden* magazine. The spacious rooms, always with fresh flowers, are extremely comfortable and more like those in a private home than a hotel.

Each room is different but all are decorated in fresh, clean lines—no fuss, no frills—and furnished with Leaman's eclectic collection of antiques, objets d'art, island crafts, original art, wicker and wrought-iron furniture. Some have high four-poster or canopied beds; others are highlighted with antique chests, armoires or an unusual piece of furniture or interesting fabrics.

The quiet inn fronts a palm-shaded black-sand beach which might have been a drawback for some; for Leaman, it was just another element to make his resort unique. Good snorkeling can be enjoyed on a reef fronting the beach, and the resort has a tennis court.

Part of the "program" calls for guests to gather at the Brimstone Bar at 7:00 P.M. for a congenial cocktail hour and to dine at 8:00 P.M. Dinner by candlelight in the antiques-filled dining room is the real treat at The Golden Lemon. Leaman seats his guests, hosting one of the tables, and rotating them so they meet one another, unless they prefer a private table. The fixed dinner menu—soup, fresh fish or a classic European dish, local vegetables that you might not recognize, and dessert—is served with quiet attention and grace.

Rarely is it possible to say that a place is unique, but The Golden Lemon truly is. Leaman's personal management is omnipresent, down to the last flower and tea biscuit. That The Golden Lemon is not everyone's cup of tea would be good news to Arthur Leaman, since he's worked hard to insure it.

The Golden Lemon's distinctive flavor generally appeals to writers, actors, and artists, along with a group of sophisticated travelers—some famous, many just with style. Leaman says he designed The Golden Lemon for people who "enjoy being pampered in an ambience of informal elegance . . . people who enjoy doing nothing in grand style."

Address/Phone: Dieppe Bay, St. Kitts, W.I.; (809) 465–7260, (800) 633–7411; Fax: (809) 465–4019

Owner/Manager: Arthur Leaman

Open: Year-round

Credit Cards: Most major

U.S. Reservations: Caribbean Inns, Ltd., (800) 633–7411; Fax: (803) 686–7411

Deposit: 3 nights; 21 days cancellation, high season; 14 days, low season

Minimum Stay: 4 nights in high season; villa policy differs

Arrival/Departure: Transfer can be arranged; taxi one-way, $20 per couple

Distance from Airport: 14 miles (30-minute drive)

Distance from Basseterre: 16 miles; taxi one-way, $25

Accommodations: 32 units with double, twin, and king-size beds (8 rooms in main building with balcony; 6 suites in Lemon Court with pool; 10 in villa condos with private pools and terraces)

Amenities: Ceiling fans, telephones; bathrooms with shower, hairdryers, and basket of toiletries; room service available for all meals; no radios, television or air-conditioning; boutique

Sports: Freshwater pool, tennis, snorkeling on premise. Deep-sea fishing, scuba diving, hiking with guide on nearby Mt. Liamuiga arranged.

Dress Code: Casual but chic

Electricity: 110 volts

Children: 18 years and older

Meetings: None

Day Visitors: Welcome for lunch and swim; reserve in advance

Handicapped: No facilities

Packages: Honeymoon; wedding

Rates: Two persons, daily, MAP. *High Season* (mid-December–mid-April): $325–$475. *Low Season:* $260–$400.

Service Charge: 10 percent

Government Tax: 7 percent

Ottley's Plantation Inn ◉◉◉

You can expect to see Ottley's Plantation Inn in fashion magazines from California to the Champs Elysées. A steady stream of models and photographers has been using this gorgeous Caribbean "Tara" as a backdrop almost from the day it opened.

Perched on a hillside overlooking St. Kitt's east coast, the elegant inn is built into the historic ruins of a sugar plantation. It is set in ten magnificent acres of manicured lawns, with another twenty-five acres of rolling sugarcane fields edged by palm trees in the front and rain forested mountains in the rear.

Begun about 1703 when the Ottley family came to the island, it continued to operate as a plantation—under different owners—until the 1960s. In 1988 Americans Art and Ruth Keusch bought the Ottley's Plantation with their daughter and son-in-law, Martin and Nancy Lowell. After making extensive renovations and adding a second floor to the great house, they opened the inn in 1990.

The drive from the main east-coast road climbs through canefields and along columns of royal palms to lawns so well tended you'll think they are the fairways of a swank golf course. Upon arrival you will be greeted by the Lowells, the hands-on managers. Marty, a congenial host whose horticulturist training is evident everywhere, will offer you a welcome drink and show you to your room.

The great house, dating from 1832, is a majestic brimstone structure with two tiers of wraparound balconies trimmed with white railings, yellow shutters, and Brazilian hardwood doors. On the ground floor is a formal living room, beautifully appointed with antiques and period furniture, and a mahogany bar. It provides an elegant setting for afternoon tea, cocktails, and evening socializing. A small side room has the library, with a television set and VCR.

The first floor has three guest rooms, and upstairs are six wonderfully spacious ones with high beamed ceilings—Scarlet would have loved them. Each room is different, but all are delightfully furnished with antiques and white wicker. The look is more the Hamptons than the English country usually found at other plantation inns in St. Kitts and Nevis. Plush bedspreads and chair covers of handsome floral prints are set against white walls with island prints and white wooden floors with Portuguese scatter rugs. The spacious bathrooms have separate dressing areas, well-lit vanities, tubs, and showers.

Large bedroom windows with dark wood louvers let in the breezes and open onto grandstand views of the exquisite gardens and surrounding countryside flowing to the sea. In front of the window are a table and chairs where you can enjoy breakfast and take in the view. And everywhere there are enormous bouquets of fresh tropical flowers.

Another six rooms and suites are in stone cottages near the entrance. The English Cottage, once a cotton storehouse, provides the most privacy. It has a large bedroom, a separate sitting room, which can be converted into a bedroom, and a patio looking out to sea.

On the south side of the great house, steps lead down to garden terraces and the beautiful stone ruins of the boiling house, now converted into a spring-fed swimming pool with a bar and stone terrace at the far end. One wall of the boiling house, with arched windows opening onto the swimming pool, forms a backdrop for the Royal Palm, the inn's open-air restaurant.

The sophisticated cuisine blends New American and New Caribbean trends with oriental influences. Pam Yahn, who trained at the Culinary Institute of America, changes her menus daily. She is clearly an imaginative, innovative chef—perhaps too much so. If I have a complaint, it is that she combines too many flavors; my tastebuds don't know which to savor first. The restaurant is popular with Kittians and guests from other hotels as well.

Next to the great house is the remnant base of the windmill. Now encircled by allamanda bushes, it is a popular setting for outdoor weddings— a more romantic spot would be hard to imagine. Behind the great house is a mango orchard with wonderful old trees. All of Ottley's fruit- and flower-filled gardens attract birds by the dozens.

Farther on, a bridge leads to footpaths along a gully and stone walls to trails through the rain forest that borders the property. The vegetation is fabulous with enormous mahogany trees, gigantic elephant ears and other rain-forest species. Self-guided tours are available, but Marty is a wonderful guide, too.

Ottley's historic, romantic setting, coupled with its informal, friendly atmosphere, will appeal both to singles and couples who seek a quiet vacation in gracious surroundings. The numbers—fifteen rooms for thirty guests, on thirty-five acres, attended by a staff of forty—all but guarantee space, grace, and peace.

Address/Phone: Box 345, Basseterre, St. Kitts, W.I.; (800) 772–3039, (809) 465–7234, (609) 921–1259; Fax: (809) 465–4760

Owner/Managers: Martin and Nancy Lowell; Art and Ruth Keusch

Open: Year-round except September

Credit Cards: All major

U.S. Reservations: International Travel and Resorts (ITR), (800) 223–9815, (212) 251–1800; Fax: (212) 545–8467; or direct to hotel

Deposit: 3 nights with 50 percent deposit within 14 days of reservations; 30 days cancellation; 45 days for Christmas/New Year's

Minimum Stay: One week during Christmas/New Year's
Arrival/Departure: Airport transfer included in package
Distance from Airport: 6 miles (15 minutes); taxi one-way, $12
Distance from Basseterre: 10 miles; taxi one-way, $15
Accommodations: 15 rooms (9 in greathouse; 6 one- and two-bedroom suites in stone cottages) all with verandas; king-sized or queen-sized beds; one with twin beds; one with two queen beds.
Amenities: Telephone, air-conditioning, ceiling fans, baskets of toiletries, umbrellas; bathrooms have tubs, except English cottage has shower only; hairdryers available; one cottage with kitchen; room service on request; no mini-bar or television in rooms
Electricity: 110 volts
Sports: Hiking on trails adjacent to property. Daily free shuttle to beach with tennis and water sports at Frigate Bay. Golf, fishing, boating, snorkeling, scuba, windsurfing, horseback riding arranged.
Dress Code: Informal
Children: Year-round in Gatekeeper's Cottage
Meetings: Up to 30 people
Day Visitors: Limited basis with reservations for lunch and hike
Handicapped: No facilities
Packages: Honeymoon, wedding
Rates: Per room, double, daily, EP. *High Season* (mid-December–mid-April): $160–$275. *Low Season:* $110–$180.
Service Charge: 10 percent
Government Tax: 7 percent

Rawlins Plantation ▣▣

Near Dieppe Bay on the northwest coast of St. Kitts, at 350 feet above sea level, is one of the Caribbean's most delightful small inns, Rawlins Plantation. With cloud-capped Mount Liamuiga rising 4,000 feet to form the backdrop, this quiet country inn is located on twelve acres in a pastoral setting that looks across acres of gently sloping cane fields to panoramic views of the Caribbean and neighboring St. Eustatius.

The former sugar plantation began about 1690 and operated for almost three-hundred years. In 1968 Phillip Walwyn, a descendent of the family that took possession in 1790, returned to St. Kitts to live on the estate. He cleared the overgrown ruins of the sugar factory, removing tons of rock and rubble; rebuilt the main building, which had been destroyed by fire; restored others; and landscaped the surrounding land. He opened the inn in 1974.

In 1989 Walwyn's friends Paul Rawson, an English hotelier, and his Kittitian-born wife, Claire, who shared an unusual appreciation of the plantation, purchased the inn. Two months later Hurricane Hugo hit the island; undeterred, the Rawsons repaired the damage and took the opportunity to upgrade the inn.

From the main road a bumpy (much maligned) country road, improved by the new owners, trails up along royal palms to the main buildings, which are set in open lawns and flowering gardens.

The main house, built into the former boiling house—still with its 40-foot tall rock chimney—has a living room and library, a formal dining room, and some guest quarters, all with attractive mahogany antique furniture. The dining room extends onto a veranda that overlooks the swimming pool, fed by Rawlins' own mountain stream, and a latticework gazebo.

Pieces of the old machinery such as the coppers—round-bottomed vats used for boiling cane—are placed here and there around the grounds. Historic notes that interest guests, they also make decorative props for the flower-festooned gardens. Pretty fresh flowers grace the rooms and dining tables as well.

Most accommodations are in cottages built on the ruins using the salvaged rock and designed to blend with the plantation setting. Homey and personal, the rooms have pitched roofs and are individually decorated in light, fresh English country prints and furnished with four-poster beds and other antiques. All have modern bathrooms. The old windmill, dating from 1690, was made into a charming split-level unit of yellow-and-white decor, which is often used as the honeymoon suite.

Rawlins's outstanding cuisine, featuring produce grown in the inn's own gardens, is created with great care by Cordon Bleu–trained Claire Rawson, who combines French discipline and her West Indian heritage. Lunch, a buffet of West Indian specialties, draws guests from throughout the island. Paul, a wine connoisseur, stocks fine wines that are stored in an old, naturally cool cellar.

While lunch is casual, dinner is a more stylish, candlelit affair, with four courses served on fine English china and crystal surrounded by old family silver and antiques, evoking the life of a planter in bygone days. You may choose to dine alone or with other guests. Service by the attentive staff is laudable.

Life at Rawlins is very low-key and easy paced, intended for people who can get along on their own. Days are spent sunning by the pool, lazing in a hammock, playing tennis or croquet, reading in the library, and enjoying afternoon tea or one of the inn's famous rum punches on the veranda at sunset.

Those with more energy can hike up the rain-forested slopes of Mount

Liamuiga. The inn will pack you a picnic lunch and take you part of the way. (Bring good walking shoes). Nature lovers, particularly bird-watchers, will enjoy the gardens and nearby woods. The inn provides transportation to the closest beach, a palm-shaded stretch of black sand at Dieppe Bay that's fringed by a reef good for snorkeling.

A stay at Rawlins is like being a guest in someone's country home—which, of course, it is. Rawlins's guests, many of whom are annual visitors, are more often English than American.

Address/Phone: Box 340, Mount Pleasant, St. Kitts, W.I.; (809) 465–6221; Fax: (809) 465–4954

Owners/General Manager: Paul and Claire Rawson

Open: Year-round except September

Credit Cards: None

U.S. Reservations: Direct or JDB Associates, (800) 346–5358; Fax: (703) 548–5825

Deposit: 3 nights; 3 weeks cancellation

Minimum Stay: 4 days in season

Arrival/Departure: Transfer can be arranged for fee

Distance from Airport: 16 miles; taxi one-way, $25

Distance from Basseterre: 16 miles; taxi one-way, $25

Accommodations: 10 double rooms in cottages with verandas (5 with twin beds; 1 with double bed; 3 queens; 1 king)

Amenities: Ceiling fans, bathrooms with tubs, hairdryers, basket of toiletries, and nightly turndown service; laundry service included in rates; room service available on request; no air-conditioning, television, radio, or telephone

Electricity: 220 volts (110 for shavers); transformers available

Sports: Croquet court, grass tennis court, freshwater swimming pool. Hiking with guide, golf, deep-sea fishing, boating, diving, biking can be arranged.

Dress Code: Informal by day; casually elegant for evening.

Children: Over 12 years of age accepted, but not encouraged

Meetings: None

Day Visitors: Welcome for lunch with reservations

Handicapped: No facilities

Packages: None

Rates: Per person, daily, MAP. *High Season* (mid-December–mid-April): $187.50. *Low Season*: $117.50.

Service Charge: 10 percent

Government Tax: 7 percent

St. Lucia

Anse Chastanet Beach Hotel

Lush, mountainous St. Lucia, the second-largest island in the Windwards, is a nature lover's dream with scenic wonders on a grand scale. Every turn in the road—and there are many—reveals spectacular landscapes of rain-forested mountains and valleys covered with fruit and flowering trees. Mostly volcanic in origin and slightly pear-shaped, St. Lucia is only 27 miles in length, but its mountainous terrain rising to more than 3,000 feet makes it seem much larger.

Castries, the capital, on the northwest coast overlooks a deep natural harbor sheltered by an amphitheater of green hills. On the northern tip, Pigeon Point, an island connected to the mainland by a causeway, has been made into a national park. It has a historic fort and museum and was newly inaugurated as the venue for St. Lucia's first international jazz festival.

Soufrière, south of the capital, is the oldest settlement on St. Lucia. At its prime in the late eighteenth century, there were as many as one hundred sugar and coffee plantations in the vicinity. The quaint little port has a striking setting at the foot of the magnificent Pitons, sugarloaf twins that rise dramatically at the island's edge.

Soufrière lies amid a wonderland of steep mountain ridges and lush valleys, and it is the gateway to some of St. Lucia's most celebrated natural attractions: a drive-in volcano with gurgling mud and hot springs, pretty waterfalls, sulphur baths with curative powers that were tested by the soldiers of Louis XVI, and a rain forest with a trail across the heart of the island.

St. Lucia has some of the best and worst roads in the Caribbean. None encircles the island completely, but you can make a loop around the southern half, which has the main sight-seeing attractions. A new road is under construction along the west coast from Castries to Soufrière. An alternative is a 45-minute motorboat trip available daily between Castries and Soufriere. South of Soufriere the west coast road to Vieux Fort and the international airport is good and takes about 45 minutes.

Information

St. Lucia Tourist Board, 820 Second Avenue, New York, NY 10017; (212) 867–2950

Anse Chastanet Beach Hotel ▣ ▣ ▣ ▣

On the north side of Soufrière, facing the twin peaks of the Pitons is one of the Caribbean's most enchanting resorts. Anse Chastanet, built along a steep hillside of tropical splendor overlooking a secluded cove, has a setting so idyllic, you will forgive, if not forget, the atrocious road leading there. If you prefer, you can also reach this hideaway by boat, arriving directly on Anse Chastanet's golden beach.

In addition to hillside cottages, there are ten rooms in octagonal, gazebo-type cottages, all with grandstand views of the Pitons or the sea and the unforgettable St. Lucian sunsets.

The rooms are comfortable but not fancy—why compete with nature? They have wood-beam ceilings and walls of louvered windows and doors leading to wraparound verandas draped in brilliant bougainvillea and hiding under some of the flowering trees for which the cottages are named. Near the beach are three, two-story villas, which harmonize so well with their natural setting that they can hardly be seen. They have twelve spacious, deluxe suites.

All Anse Chastanet's rooms have rattan furnishings and other pieces in local woods—mahogany, wild breadfruit, and purple heart—designed by owner Nick Troubetzkoy, an architect, and crafted by local wood carvers. Woven grass rugs (a Dominica specialty) are on the earthen-tile floors; batik prints of tropical motifs decorate the walls; and bright plaid Madras cotton is used for the bed and cushion covers. (Madras is used by St. Lucian women for their traditional dress.)

Troubetzkoy's latest additions—eleven huge suites of bold, sensational design—have put Anse Chastanet in a new league. These handsome architectural wonders, perched high above the first cottages, offer luxury and space. Some rooms have atrium gardens, others are built around trees like a tree house. Each suite has a different arrangement and all have breathtaking views.

The best are four premium suites in Cottage 7 where the Pitons are the centerpiece. The enormous bedroom/sitting room extends to a terrace with no windows or walls; in the upper story suites, ceilings soar to 20 feet.

Anse Chastanet requires you to be something of a mountain goat. Nothing but your legs gets you up and down the one hundred or more stone steps that climb from the beach to the topmost rooms. But it's worth every heartpounding breath for the magnificent scenery. There is also an easier way, at least for part of the climb: If you rent a car as most guests do, you can drive on the service road from the reception pavilion midway on the hillside to the beach.

The reception pavilion contains an open-air bar, game room, library, the Pitons Restaurant where breakfast and dinner are served, and the Treehouse terrace, another dining area. All look down through jungle foliage to the beach.

Trou-au-Diable, the beach restaurant, features creole specialties at lunch; an ice-cream cart patrols the beach in the afternoon; and the beach bar is open all day. There are two boutiques, a tennis court, and a watersports center.

Anse Chastanet fronts some of St. Lucia's best reefs, which are protected as a marine park. They are close enough for snorkelers to reach directly from the beach. Some divers call the stretch between Anse Chastanet and the Pitons the best diving in the Caribbean.

Scuba St. Lucia, the resort's five-star PADI training facility, is directed by PADI master trainer Michael Allard, along with his wife, Karen, and a ten-member professional team. Also open to nonhotel guests, it offers beach and boat dives four times daily, night dives, and courses for beginners, certification, and underwater photography.

A more secluded strand of sand is a ten-minute walk (or a few minutes' motorboat ride) north of Anse Chastanet at Anse Mamin. Here you can also explore the extensive eighteenth-century ruins of Anse Mamin, one of the earliest sugar plantations on St. Lucia.

Anse Chastanet is close to some of St. Lucia's main natural attractions and offers guided hikes at no charge to guests. In connection with the St. Lucia National Trust, it has developed nature, bird-watching, and botanical tours.

You'll dine in the magical, romantic setting of the Piton Restaurant on cuisine created by New Zealander John DeJong, a chef who makes generous use of fresh seafood, vegetables, and other local ingredients.

The manager's wine party on Mondays starts the week's evening activities. There is live music nightly except Wednesday and a beach barbecue with a reggae band on Tuesday and Friday. But Anse Chastanet is not a place for nightlife; most guests are in their "tree houses" by 10:00 P.M.

Anse Chastanet isn't for everyone, but if you are something of an escapist and a romantic, yearn for tranquility, relish beauty, and are refreshed by remarkable tropical landscapes, you will love every minute at this friendly, unpretentious resort.

Address/Phone: Box 7000, Soufrière, St. Lucia, W.I.; (809) 454–7000; Fax: (809) 454–7700

Owner/Managing Director: Nick and Karolin Troubetzkoy

Open: Year-round

Credit Cards: All major

U.S. Reservations: Ralph Locke Islands, Inc., (800) 223–1108, (914) 763–5526; Fax: (914) 763–5362

Deposit: 3 nights in winter, 2 nights in low season; 30-day cancellation

Minimum Stay: 3 nights in winter, 5 nights Christmas/New Year's

Arrival/Departure: Airport transfer arranged for above prices; hotel runs a scheduled boat to Castries.

Distance from Airport: (Hewanorra International Airport) 18 miles (45 minutes); taxi one-way, $35; (Vigie Airport) (2 hours), $50

Distance from Castries: 20 miles; taxi one-way, $50; by sea, $50; from Soufrière, 1.5 miles; taxi one-way, $8

Accommodations: 48 units with twin or king beds (3 standard; 4 premium, 12 deluxe beachside, and 29 hillside gazebo-cottages; one- and two-bedroom suites), all with verandas

Amenities: Ceiling fans, hairdryers, basket of toiletries, tea/coffee makers, mini-bars with optional provisioning plans; no radios, telephones, televisions, or air-conditioning; bathrooms have showers only; room service for breakfast

Electricity: 220 volts/50 cycles

Sports: Tennis court (no lights); free snorkeling, Sunfish, windsurfing. No pool. Superior dive facilities with full range of equipment; 3 dive boats and 36-foot tri-hull flattop for up to 24 divers; film lab for underwater photography; changing rooms and freshwater showers.

Dress Code: Casual; men wear slacks or long cut Bermuda shorts and shirts in the evening.

Children: All ages; cribs, high chairs; baby-sitters
Meetings: Up to 75 people
Handicapped: No facilities
Day Visitors: Individuals with advance notice
Packages: Honeymoon, scuba diving, wedding
Rates: Per person, daily. *High Season* (mid-December–mid-April): $280–$450, MAP. *Shoulder Season* (April 16–May 16 and November 1–December 19): $150–$300, EP. *Low Season* (May 16–October 31): $125–$270, EP.
Service Charge: 10 percent
Government Tax: 8 percent

Le Sport ▨▨▨

Le Sport, a sports and spa resort offering an organized but unregimented vacation, is unique in the Caribbean (although a near copy, La Source, is opening in Grenada). Designed for today's professionals, Le Sport strikes the middle ground between the rigorous regime of a health spa and a sports-intensive vacation. For active and fitness-minded people, it's the best buy in the Caribbean—you will run out of time before you run out of things to do.

Le Sport is the ultimate all-inclusive resort. For one price, you get all meals, tea, and snacks; full use of the extensive spa and sports facilities with instruction; all drinks and beverages; nightly music and entertainment; all gratuities, taxes, round-trip airport transfers; and a special airfare credit that can be as high as $300 per person in summer and $350 per couple in winter.

Set on a secluded beach on the northwestern tip of St. Lucia, Le Sport climbs through fifteen hillside acres of tropical gardens. Opened in 1989 after extensive remodeling of a previous hotel, it has guestrooms in three two-, three-, and four-story buildings. Except for six with garden views, all have terraces or patios looking west to the sea—and what a treat. Sunsets are magnificent.

The guest rooms, with white rattan furnishings and bathrooms faced with white Italian and salmon Portuguese marble, were created by Lane Pettigrew Jones of St. Lucia and Miami.

In a spectacular hillside setting high above the resort is the Estate House, Le Sport's fabulous Victorian fantasy with West Indian gingerbread and New Orleans filigree, offering privacy in luxurious accommodations. The house has a large living room and dining room which open onto a wraparound balcony; three bedrooms, some with four-poster and some with canopied beds; and a wood-paneled library. All the rooms are attractively decorated with antiques and period furniture. On the terrace of the garden swimming pool, you can enjoy breakfast along with a grandstand view of St. Lucia. A housekeeper, butler, vehicle, and all Le Sport facilities are included in the price.

Le Sport's spa facilities are in the Oasis. The name is exactly right. Perched seventy-eight steps up from the main resort, the heavenly two-story haven with graceful colonnaded courtyards, keyhole arches, reflecting pools, and fountains is designed in the Moorish style of Alhambra Palace in Spain. It even has a serene marble relaxation temple.

In a series of exercise and treatment rooms, you are pampered and rejuvenated from head to toe in a program of thalassotherapy, which, for the uninitiated, is a string of baths and treatments using seaweed, seaweed products, and seawater. These include hydro massage, jet hose shower, Swiss needle shower, jet-stream pool, seaweed wraps, algae baths, loofah rubs, massage, facial, and hair care, as well as sauna, hot and cold plunge pools, and juice bar—all for no additional charge.

You begin with a health questionnaire and visit to the resident medical staff. Treatments are individually tailored, and you'll receive a printout of your schedule. The young staff, trained for ten months prior to the spa's opening, is versed in all the treatments. Like the entire Le Sport team, they are eager to please and have a pleasant, gentle manner.

To complement the spa, Le Sport features *cuisine légerè,* a style of light cooking developed by French chef Michel Guerard and imaginatively implemented by the resort's chef Xavier Ribot from Brittany. All meals, which include a wide choice of dishes in addition to *cuisine légerè* daily specials, are served in the Terrace, an open-air, beachside restaurant encased in tropical gardens. Breakfast and lunch are lavish buffets, along with à la carte menus.

Dinners are à la carte, except for a Caribbean buffet on Mondays and a barbecue dinner and beach party on Thursdays. Wines at lunch and dinner and all other beverages (except for French champagne) are included. At the beach beverages are served by an attendant who can be summoned by placing a red flag in the sand.

The air-conditioned piano bar, the gathering spot for cocktails and after-dinner socializing, has music by the resort's own pianist nightly from 7:00 P.M. until the last guest retires. On the Terrace, music by a live band is heard nightly except Friday, jazz by a terrific local combo is featured weekly, and local dance troupes perform several times a week. A West Indian show is staged in the Terrace Bar and Theatre once a week. After the live entertainment, the disco goes into action.

Each morning a schedule of the day's activities is posted. There's something for everyone, from stress management to calypso dance lessons.

Sports facilities are fabulous. Topping the list of water sports is full PADI certification for no additional charge. There are trips for certified divers and you can snorkel directly off the beach. Windsurfing and Sunfish sailing instruction is offered daily. The resort has three pools—for water volleyball; for swimming; and the spa lap and exercise pool; a tennis court (lighted), bicycles, aerobics, yoga, fencing, archery, volleyball, and weight training—all with instruction.

Walking and hiking excursions are scheduled daily; golf including greens fees is available at a nearby nine-hole course; and horseback riding can be arranged for a fee.

Le Sport, with its lush, secluded setting and body pampering (lots of pampering), has a sensual, romantic quality. In winter Americans and Europeans come in equal numbers, but in summer there are more Europeans. Although most guests are couples, this is one of the few Caribbean resorts where singles feel comfortable and find it easy to make friends.

Address/Phone: P.O. Box 437, Cariblue Beach, St. Lucia, W.I.; (809) 452–8551; Fax: (809) 452–0368

Owner: The Barnard Group, St. Lucia

General Manager: Mike Matthews

Open: Year-round

Credit Cards: All major

U.S. Reservations: Direct to Le Sport, St. Lucia, (800) 544–2883; Fax: (809) 452–0368

Deposit: $300 per person within 10 days of booking

Minimum Stay: none

Arrival/Departure: Transfer included for week stay

Distance from Airport: (Vigie Airport) 7 miles (20 minutes); (Hewanorra International Airport) 28 miles (90 minutes)

Distance from Castries: 8 miles; taxi one-way, EC $35

Accommodations: 102 rooms (90 doubles with twin beds; 10 with king-size beds; 2 oceanfront two-bedroom suites) all with terraces (76 ocean view, 16 oceanfront; 6 gardenview).

Amenities: Telephones, air-conditioning, bathroom with tub and shower, hairdryer, bathrobe, basket of toiletries; room service for continental breakfast; boutique, hair salon.

Electricity: 220/110 volts

Sports: See text

Dress Code: Sports and beachwear during day; only slightly dressier in the evening.

Children: Accepted but not encouraged; cribs, baby-sitters
Packages: Honeymoon; wedding; special airfare credit
Meetings: Up to 35 people
Day Visitors: Welcome with advance reservations
Handicapped: Limited facilities
Rates: Per person, daily, all inclusive. *High Season* (December 18–January 4; January 19–April 5): $260–$400. *Shoulder Season* (January 5–January 18): $220–$360; (April 6–30): $195–$280 *Low Season* (May 1–December 17): $190–$250.
Service Charge: Included in rate
Government Tax: Included in rate

The Royal St. Lucian (N)

The brisk and efficient check-in in the fountain-spouting atrium lobby, the personalized suite tour by a member of the management, and the phone and piped-in Muzak—in the bathroom—are typical accoutrements you would find in a plush New York or Tokyo hotel. But in laid-back St. Lucia? Hardly. Unless, of course, you've been to the new Royal St. Lucian.

Opened in late 1990 on Reduit Beach on St. Lucia's leeward shores, the Royal St. Lucian was the island's first all-suite luxury hotel and much more deluxe than its neighboring sister hotel, The St. Lucian. The three-story structure, designed in rather grand Georgian Palladian style, hugs a lavish pool and bar area; all suites face the sea.

The Royal St. Lucian is meant for the discriminating few (read rich, fast-track, Type As) who expect a full spectrum of services—from room service to turndown service—all delivered at lightning speed, even in the Caribbean where a slow pace, many would argue, is meant not only to be accepted but savored.

What's amazing is that at the Royal St. Lucian, it works. After registering in the open-air lobby, cool with marble and tropical greenery, the royal treatment at the Royal St. Lucian begins when guests are whisked off to their suites by a member of the Royal St. Lucian's management staff. What they find is pure luxury.

All suites boast tile floors and plush carpeting in the bedroom and separate sitting area (some with sleep sofas) and a full lineup of luxury amenities—air-conditioning, room safe, phones, fully stocked mini-bar, cable and local television, ceiling fans, bathrobes, and radio that run local stations in addition to the hotel's background music channel. The spacious, marbled bathrooms have separate shower and tub, phone, radio, scales, and hairdryer. Ceramics from Santo Domingo and original works by internationally acclaimed artists are showcased throughout the property.

All suites have private patios or balconies overlooking the gardens, pool, and beach. Eight beachfront suites feature larger sun decks and loggias with terrace bars; five deluxe suites boast extra-spacious interior rooms and lounge and dining terraces. And the Royal suite even has its own private garden and plunge pool—perfect for honeymooners.

You may be tempted to loll in the luxury of your suite 'til late morn, but there is plenty to do when you venture out. The resort's centerpiece, La Mirage, an expansive pool with a waterfall and bridge, invites you to sunbathe at its shallow end or have a drink at the swim-up bar.

On mile-long Reduit Beach, you can windsurf, sail a Sunfish, and snorkel (equipment included in the rate). Waterskiing and windsurfing lessons cost extra. You might also want to take advantage of the complimentary tennis facilities at the St. Lucian Hotel next door and golf at a nine-hole layout nearby.

Scuba diving and deep-sea fishing can be arranged for an extra fee. Reduit Beach's white sands are also a perfect spot to soak up the rays or to take a stroll, perhaps to nearby Rodney Bay Marina, the departure point for day sails and yacht charters.

By the pool the breezy La Nautique restaurant, offering all-day dining, specializes in Caribbean fare and seafood. For more elegant dining in the evening, the airy, beachfront L'Epicure offers an à la carte menu masterminded by 1989 Caribbean Chef of the Year Julian Waterer, who came to the Royal St. Lucian from the former Halcyon Cove's Clouds restaurant in Antigua. Its menu features a combination of nouvelle Caribbean and continental fare.

A "wall" of rainbow-colored sails joins L'Epicure to the Mistral Lounge, where soft piano music is followed by light jazz nightly. You can sip rum-and-coconut-laden concoctions like the Lucian Lush and the Smooth Talker with views of the moonlit sea providing a romantic backdrop.

The atmosphere at the Royal St. Lucian is sedate but if you want to step up the pace, limbo, lambada, and crab racing are daily occurrences at the neighboring St. Lucian Hotel. For a slice of night action, its Splash discotheque, open to Royal guests, draws a lively crowd of locals and visitors who come for the sound system/light show and dance hall lineup that rival any club in Manhattan.

The Royal St. Lucian is the sophisticated sister on Reduit Beach, for travelers who appreciate efficiency, luxury, and serenity—and don't mind some hints of pretension.

Address/Phone: Reduit Beach, Box 977, Castries, St. Lucia; (809) 452–9999; Fax: (809) 452–9639

Owner: Royal St. Lucian Hotel Ltd.

General Manager: David M. Hill

Open: Year-round

Credit Cards: All major

U.S. Reservations: MRI, (800) 255–5859, (305) 225–1740; Fax: (305) 225–1647

Deposit: 2 nights

Minimum Stay: None

Arrival/Departure: Transfer arranged for prices above

Distance from Airport: (Vigie Airport) 6 miles; taxi one-way, US $12; (Hewanorra Airport) 39 miles, taxi one-way, US $55

Distance from Castries: 6 miles; taxi one-way, US $12. Shuttle to town: US $5

Accommodations: 98 suites, all with terraces, and all with 2 twins or king; some with sofa beds

Amenities: air-conditioning, ceiling fans, telephones (including sitting room and bath), cable television, safe, radio; bath with tub and shower, hairdryer, basket of toiletries, scales, bathrobe; stocked mini-bar; ice service, nightly turndown service; room service daily until 10 P.M.

Electricity: 220 volts

Sports: Freshwater swimming pool, Children's pool; free use 2 tennis courts at St. Lucian; pro, lessons, equipment for fee. Complimentary snorkel gear, Sunfish, windsurfers. Scuba, deep-sea fishing, horseback riding, waterskiing arranged for fee.

Dress Code: Casual

Children: All ages; cribs, high chairs, baby-sitters

Meetings: No

Day Visitors: Welcome with dinner reservations and to bar

Handicapped: Yes; two suites fully equipped

Packages: Honeymoon

Rates: Two persons, daily, EP. *High Season* (December 19–January 5): $350–$436; (January 6–April 15): $260–$346. *Low Season* (April 16–December 18): $194–$280.

Service Charge: 10 percent

Government Tax: 8 percent

ON THE HORIZON

Jalousie Plantation

Situated on 320 tropical acres of the former Jalousie plantation, the long-awaited resort, Jalousie Plantation, opened in summer of 1992. It was embroiled in controversy before the first stone was set because of its location in the shadow of the towering Pitons, St. Lucia's most spectacular natural attraction. The owners, a consortium of Iranian backers who purchased the land from Lord Glenconner (the developer of Mustique) are developing 90 acres with the resort and private homes. The balance of the site will be left in its natural state.

The handsome luxury resort fits quietly into the setting with a greathouse housing the restaurants, lounges, and other facilities. Accommodations are in one- and two-bedroom cottages and suites, all designed in traditional colonial architecture. Jalousie is operating as an all-inclusive resort offering tennis, scuba diving, and other water sports, four restaurants, nightly entertainment, and a spa for one price.

Address/Phone: Soufrière, St. Lucia, W.I.; (809) 459–7666; Fax: (809) 459–7667

U.S. Reservations: Premier Resorts and Hotels; (800) 877–3643, (305) 856–5405

Accommodations: 115 one- and two-bedroom cottages and suites

Rates: Per person, double, daily, all-inclusive. *High Season* (mid-December–mid-April): $240–$460. *Low Season:* $215–$375.

St. Maarten/St. Martin

La Samanna

A small island in the heart of the Caribbean is Dutch on one side and French on the other. How this island of only 37 square miles became divided hardly seems to matter anymore except to history buffs and tax collectors.

Columbus discovered the island in 1493 and claimed it for Spain; several centuries later a young Dutchman, Peter Stuyvesant, lost a limb wresting the island from Spain. Still later the French got into the fray, and, somewhere along the way, the Dutch and the French agreed to stop fighting and to divide the island instead.

Today there are no border formalities as there are no real boundaries.

The only way you can tell you are crossing from one country to the other is by a welcome sign at the side of the road. Philipsburg, the capital of Dutch Sint Maarten; and Marigot, the capital of French St. Martin; are a twenty-minute drive apart. The two flags nonetheless give the island an unusual international flair.

Philipsburg is the main port for cruise ships and the commercial center. The international airport is also on the Dutch side. Until recently Marigot was a village, but with new development it has become as busy as its Dutch counterpart. Yet it is unmistakably Gallic.

Sint Maarten/St. Martin is intensively developed—overdeveloped is more accurate—for tourists. Still, it remains one of the Caribbean's most popular islands: It has something for everyone, whatever the style, and offers as much to do as places ten times its size.

The island has excellent sports facilities for tennis, golf, horseback riding, sailing, diving, windsurfing, and sport fishing. There's nightlife at discos and casinos. You can shop in trendy boutiques or air-conditioned malls for goods from around the world.

Sint Maarten/St. Martin has a well-deserved reputation as a gourmet's haven; and you can find restaurants serving Italian, Mexican, Vietnamese, Indonesian, Chinese, French, Dutch, and West Indian cuisine. The truly gourmet ones are in the village of Grand Case, near Marigot, but be prepared when the bill comes: Some of the French restaurants are very expensive.

St. Maarten is a transportation hub for the northeast Caribbean. Its location makes it an ideal base for exploring nearby Anguilla, Saba, Statia, St. Barts, St. Kitts/Nevis.

Information

St. Maarten Tourist Information Office, The Mallory Factor, 275 Seventh Avenue, New York, NY 10001; (212) 989–0000; French West Indies Tourist Board, 610 Fifth Avenue, New York, NY 10020; (212) 757–1125.

La Belle Creole ◨◧◧◧

This is probably the only resort in the world to become a legend—before it opened its doors. The intrigue surrounding the development of the fabled resort is the stuff from which television soap operas are spun.

Created by the famous hotelier Claude Philippe of the Waldorf-Astoria in the mid-1960s, the resort was designed to resemble a quaint Mediterranean village. La Belle Creole was almost ready to open when the owner had a series of financial reversals and died soon after. For years the resort sat empty like a ghost town or an abandoned Hollywood movie set slowly decaying, while one attempt after another was made to rescue it.

Finally in 1985, the property was taken over by a consortium of French investors and Conrad International Hotels, a subsidiary of Hilton Hotels, which spent millions renovating and rebuilding it. In 1988 the lady made her belated debut.

Situated on a twenty-five-acre peninsula, Pointe des Pierres à Chaux, La Belle Creole overlooks the ocean on the west and Marigot Bay, Nettle Bay, and the green mountains of St. Martin on the north and east. It is comprised of twenty-seven one-, two- and three-story buildings constructed in chaux, an ocher-colored local limestone, which enhances the resort's appearance as a real village.

The "villas" are finished in white and pastel stucco and trimmed with balconies and doorways of dark wood. A labyrinth of stone walkways and stairs and interconnecting courtyards links the various buildings, reinforcing the Mediterranean village look. The central plaza of the village, complete with a bell tower and cobblestone street, serves as the reception area. The handsome buildings bordering the plaza house some of the restaurants, bar, and guest rooms.

The majority of the guest rooms have shaded balconies or patios overlooking Marigot Bay or the hotel's lagoon. Spacious and airy, the accommodations are beautifully decorated in French Provincial style, many with French antiques. No two rooms are exactly alike but most have high beamed ceilings, stonework, hand-carved wood and oak furnishings including large armoires, Belgian carpets over terra-cotta tile floors, and handsome French provincial fabrics by leading European designers. Five rooms and seventeen suites are specially equipped for handicapped people.

For an informal lunch you can choose between the al fresco poolside snack bar, the beach kiosk, or La Provence, the main indoor/outdoor restaurant in the central plaza. The latter serves island fare and continental cuisine for all three meals. Its terrace cafe overlooks the pool; the adjoining cocktail lounge and piano bar offers entertainment nightly.

Three nights of the week the resort features specialty dinners—barbecue, creole buffet, and seafood—with live entertainment of a steel band and show; a West Indian combo, known locally as a "scratch" band; or an evening of jazz.

The central plaza is also the setting for craft fairs and concerts. Well-known artists such as Dave Brubeck, who played here last year, attract townfolks as well as hotel guests. The manager's cocktail party is held on Monday evenings.

The spacious resort has a freshwater pool, four lighted tennis courts, and extensive water-sports facilities. Neither of its two beaches measures up to St. Martin's gorgeous sands like, for example, those around the corner at Long Bay. Small, individual canvas cabanas by the beach provide privacy and a convenient escape from the afternoon sun. You can read, snooze, or bone up for the French lessons the resort offers.

The fitness center schedules regular aerobics classes; there's a jogging trail and a croquet lawn; and golf can be arranged at the Mullet Bay Beach Resort. The resort runs a water-taxi shuttle to Marigot where the boutiques are filled with French and other European fashions, and in the evening you can take in the casino and other night action at Port de Plaisance via the hotel's van or by private limousine.

La Belle Creole attracts a wide range of guests—families with children, honeymooners, and romantics of all ages—who want the services of an international hotel but who, at the same time, appreciate a resort with unique qualities. The luxury resort is favored by companies for executive meetings, and incentive winners, no doubt consider a vacation here an award indeed.

Although understated and low-key, La Belle Creole is still romantic with a certain glamorous, tony quality. Perhaps it comes from the combination of a sense of history and Old World atmosphere, which the design conveys, and the feeling of grace that its extensive, beautifully landscaped gardens and grounds add to the setting. It may also be that this resort is an oasis of refinement in St. Maarten/St. Martin's ocean of glitz.

Address/Phone: Pointe du Bluff, P.O. Box 578, Marigot 97150, St. Martin, F.W.I.; (590) 87–58–66; Fax: (590) 87–56–66

Owner: Conrad International/La Belle Creole, S.A.

General Manager: Frank Rodriguez

Open: Year-round

Credit Cards: All major

U.S. Reservations: Hilton Reservation Service, (800) HILTONS, (800) 445–8667 or (212) 355–1997

Deposit: 3 nights; 21 days cancellation

Minimum Stay: None

Arrival/Departure: Transfer service arranged with packages

Distance from Airport: (Philipsburg Airport) 4 miles; taxi one-way, $12

Distance from Marigot: 2 miles; taxi one-way, $5. Resort operates water taxi to Marigot. From Philipsburg: 8 miles; taxi one-way, $15.

Accommodations: 156 rooms and suites in 27 one- to three-story buildings with two doubles or king-size bed

Amenities: Air-conditioning, ceiling fans, telephone, television, mini-bar; VCR on request, radio; bath with tub, shower, bidet, hairdryer, basket of toiletries, bathrobe; nightly turndown service, room service for breakfast and snacks, ice machines

Electricity: 220 volts; converters available

Sports: Freshwater swimming pool; hammocks, individual beach tents; 4 lighted tennis courts, clinics, snorkeling, windsurfing and other nonmotorized water sports included. Dive shop. Equestrian center. Boating, deep-sea fishing, golf arranged.

Dress Code: Casual

Children: All ages; cribs; high chairs; supervised activities; baby-sitters

Meetings: Up to 150 people

Day Visitors: Welcome

Handicapped: Fully ramped property

Packages: Honeymoon, tennis, golf, dive, Great Escape

Rates: Per person, daily, CP. *High Season* (December 19–January 2): $305–$385; (January 3–mid-April): $285–365. *Low Season* (mid-April–December 18): $165–$225.

Service Charge: Included in price

Government Tax: $3.50 per person per night

La Samanna ◙◙◙◙

Snow-white villas draped in brilliant magenta bougainvillea sit between sea and sky on fifty-five tropical hillsides stretching along one of the Caribbean's most gorgeous beaches.

Small and ultra-exclusive, La Samanna was designed with the international jet-setter in mind, to provide unpretentious luxury far from the real world. Set on the crest of a hill overlooking a 3,500-foot arc of deep white sand on Long Bay, the resort combines striking Mediterranean-Moorish architecture and colorful decor with a sophisticated Riviera ambience. When it opened in 1974, it set a new style in casual elegance in the Caribbean.

La Samanna was conceived by the late James Frankel, a New York businessman who became enchanted with the Greek Islands and was inspired to bring the flavor of the Mediterranean to the Caribbean. He equated luxury with privacy and asked noted Caribbean architect Robertson "Happy" Ward to design a private oasis that would be more like a collection of villas on a secluded estate than a hotel. Organized activities and manager's cocktail parties were *verboten*. No bands, discos, or in-room television would intrude on the resort's peace.

Today, in contrast to St. Martin's unbridled growth, La Samanna is an oasis of untrammeled beauty, appreciated even more now than when it first burst on the scene. Upon entering the gardens, walled from the outside world, you find classic white stucco structures recalling a Greek Island village like Mykonos. Steps hewn from coral wind down a multilevel sweep of balconies, arches, terraced gardens, and shaded walkways to the beach below.

La Samanna is named for Frankel's three daughters—*Sam*antha (who's married to tennis great Ivan Lendl), *An*ouk, and *Na*thalie—who now direct the hotel. The resort has just completed a multimillion dollar renovation, which has not come a minute too soon and should put La Samanna back in the running as one of the Caribbean's crème de la crème. Some plans, however, like a more posh look, video players in rooms, a manager's cocktail party—could lessen the hotel's mystique and slightly alter the ambience. The introduction of a land and sea program with the cruise ship *Sea Goddess* (although it is every bit as posh as La Samanna) might raise a few eyebrows, too. Amenities such as being met at the airport and preregistration so you can go directly to your room will surely be appreciated.

Those familiar with La Samanna will notice renovations throughout the property. In the main building a concierge and an elegant reception desk have replaced the front-desk counter. The lobby still opens onto the terrace, smothered in tropical gardens, but the pretty tiled pool is bedecked with plush new teak lounging chairs. No doubt they will be occupied frequently by topless sunbathers. A poolside grill to prepare lunch has been added for guests who do not want to leave the informal comfort of the pool for the dining room.

La Samanna's signature cozy Indian Bar with its colorful Indian wedding-tent canopy, remains, only the furniture has been changed. Albert, the hotel's famed bartender, is presiding and remains on duty as long as guests linger.

Accommodations vary. Standard guest rooms are located in the three-story main building arranged off a winding, open-air staircase. Rooms open onto balconies that capture the fabulous view of curving Long Bay. The top floor has been made into the Terrace Suite, which boasts a grandstand view.

One- to three-bedroom suites in two-story units (some with rooftop terraces) and villas dot the hillsides that spill down to the beach. Most guest rooms and villas have individual entrances and private balconies, and are separated by a jungle of flowering hedges and trees that provide maximum privacy. Suites and villas have full kitchens, dining areas, large living rooms, and patios. Maid service includes food shopping upon request.

All guest rooms have been renovated and now have air-conditioned bedrooms. Among the new appointments are custom-designed, hand-carved furniture, colorful fabrics, and bed linens. The bathrooms have new fittings and amenities but the pretty hand-painted Mexican tiles were retained. Another new accommodation, the Private Estate Residence, is a two-bedroom villa with a private pool, staff, and car.

All meals are served in The Restaurant, an open-air terrace with an eagle's nest view of Long Bay. The dining room's new look includes high-back "zambale-peel" wicker chairs, blue and white table linens, and custom-designed tableware. Although the chef has changed, the kitchen is expected to continue as one of the Caribbean's best, most original—and most expensive. It offers French and creole dishes with ingredients selected by the resort's food buyer in Paris, flown in fresh from France. The restaurant has an extensive wine list.

The Pavilion, a multi-use building added in 1990, houses a lounge with the resort's only television and a small open-air fitness center with exercise equipment. Morning aerobics classes are held here; the building can be converted to meeting space.

La Samanna caters to a sophisticated, affluent clientele. Through the years the privacy and elegant informality have pleased a roster of stars and celebrities—including Robert Redford and Jackie O—captains of industry, and famous politicos, most from North America, some from Europe. The romantic resort is an ideal honeymoon spot, but its seclusion and villa facilities also make it desirable for couples and families with young children. Clearly, the tony resort is not for everyone (not many can afford it) but as one guest put it, "It is for everyone who knows what it is."

Address/Phone: P.O. Box 4077, Marigot 97064, St. Martin, F.W.I.; phone: (590) 87–51–22; Fax: (590) 87–87–86

Owner: Frankel Family

Manager Director: Ulrich Krauer

Open: Year-round, except September–October

Credit Cards: All major

U.S. Reservations: Rosewood Management/La Samanna, (800) 854–2252 (212) 319–5191; Fax: (212) 832–5390

Deposit: 3 nights; 21 days cancellation and 90 days for Christmas/New Year's

Minimum Stay: 5 nights during Christmas holidays

Arrival/Departure: Airport meet-and-assist service

Distance from Airport: 1.5 miles, taxi one-way, $8

Distance from Philipsburg: 2.5 miles; taxi one-way, $14

Distance from Marigot: 5 miles; taxi one-way, $15

Accommodations: 80 rooms (8 twins, two suites in main building; 24 one-bedroom, 16 two-bedroom apartments; 6 three-bedroom villas; 1 private estate

Amenities: Air-conditioning, ceiling fan, telephone, bath with tub and shower, bathrobe, hairdryer, deluxe toiletries; nightly turndown service, mini-bar or refrigerator with beverages; 24-hour room service, food order service, boutique.

Electricity: 220 volts

Sports: Freshwater swimming pool, 3 tennis courts, waterskiing, windsurf-
ing, Sunfish, snorkel gear free. Tennis pro, waterski lessons available.
Golf, horseback riding, fishing, sailing charters arranged. Fitness center.
Dress Code: Casual; no jacket or tie required at dinner
Children: Yes; cribs, baby-sitters
Meetings: Up to 60 people
Day Visitors: With reservations for lunch or dinner.
Handicapped: No facilities
Packages: Honeymoon, 3 or 7 days
Rates: Per room, daily, CP. *High Season* (December 18–April 18):
$440–$820. *Shoulder Season* (November 1–December 17 and April
19–May 31): $350–$655. *Low Season* (June 1–August 31): $275–$575.
Service Charge: Included in room rate
Government Tax: $4 per day per person (subject to change)

Pasanggrahan Royal Guest House ◙

With its back on Front Street and its front on the bay, Pasanggrahan Royal
Inn combines a bit of island beauty and city bustle with a touch of history
and a lot of charm—and all at budget prices.

The word *Pasanggrahan* (Indonesian for guesthouse) and royal in the
name reflect this landmark's history as the former government guesthouse,
after being the governor's mansion in the late 1800s. Its distinguished guests
included the Dutch queen Juliana (she was Princess Juliana at the time),
who stayed here for a time during World War II. (Indonesia, as well as St.
Maarten, were then Dutch colonies.)

Now hidden under tall palms in a tropical garden in the heart of
Philipsburg between the main street and the beach, the Pasanggrahan is a
casual and friendly hotel, which many would rank as the best bargain in
the Caribbean. A wood-frame building painted white with green trim, it has
an antiques-filled reception area and lounge presided over by a portrait of
Queen Wilhelmina. A long white veranda extends the length of the front,
overlooking the beach and the activity in the harbor.

It's the perfect setting for a Sidney Greenstreet movie. No doubt that's
why the bar was given his name. It is located in an area that was once part
of the room occupied by the royals. Happy hour here is especially popular
with local dignitaries and the business community—and everyone who
knows about the great strawberry daiquiris.

There is one guest room on the second floor of the main building; the
rest are in two, two-story beachfront buildings adjacent to the main build-

ing and in one cottage. The most spacious and appealing, the Queen-Room—what else?—is directly above the Greenstreet Bar and terrace. It is reached by a private spiral staircase. Pleasantly furnished, the room is cozy rather than queenly. It was once occupied by Juliana, and it does have a queen bed, although not the same one her highness used.

There are two types of rooms in the annex: standard which are rather small; superior, which are larger and deluxe. All superior and deluxe room have small refrigerators.

All rooms are furnished with either twins or king-size beds and have white tile and wood bathrooms. All beachfront rooms have balconies; shared in some cases. The furnishings are simple—basic wood furniture and some wicker. Colorful prints by local artists and Indonesian batik hangings decorate the walls but they must compete with the colors of the Caribbean and the sailboats in the harbor outside your window.

Meals are served at the Oceanview Restaurant with seating either on the beachside veranda or garden dining area, particularly enjoyable at sunset. The garden area is also a popular venue for cocktail parties and special events held by the business community, as well as the manager's cocktail party on Tuesdays.

Opened originally in 1904 as the government guesthouse, in 1983 the Pasanggrahan was acquired by Oli de Zela, a native of American Samoa, and her late husband.

The inn was never known in the past for its cuisine, and given the great restaurants in St. Maarten, it's hard to compete. Since 1989, however, restaurant manager Tini has featured the family tradition of Basque and Polynesian cuisine, helping increase the inn's popularity as a local eatery. A folklore show is performed four nights weekly from Thursday to Saturday.

The beach in front of the Pasanggrahan stretches the length of Front Street. The inn doesn't have a water-sports center, but at either end of the beach you'll find diving, sailing, and water-sports shops where almost anything can be arranged; they have scheduled activities daily.

Address/Phone: Front Street, P.O. Box 151, Philipsburg, St. Maarten, N.A.; (599) 5–23588; Fax: (599) 5–22885
Owner/General Manager: Oli de Zela
Open: Year-round except September
Credit Cards: MasterCard and Visa
U.S. Reservations: International Travel and Resorts , Inc. (ITR), (212) 840–6636, (800) 223–9815, (800) 468–0023 Canada; (212) 545–8647
Deposit: 3 nights winter; 1 night summer
Minimum Stay: None
Arrival/Departure: No transfer service

Distance from Airport: 5 miles; taxi one-way, $8

Accommodations: 26 rooms including Queen's room and cottage; 20 with terrace/patio; 12 standard rooms in west wing; 12 superior and deluxe in east wing (6 are garden, 20 beachfront. 8 with twins; 18 with kings).

Amenities: Air-conditioning in most bedrooms for extra $10 per day; ceiling fans; most bath with tub and shower; some with refrigerators; ice service, nightly turndown service; no telephone, television, radio, clock, or room service; 24-hour security.

Electricity: 110 volts

Sports: None on the premises; tennis, golf, boating, snorkeling, scuba, windsurfing, deep-sea fishing, horseback riding arranged.

Dress Code: Casual

Children: Off season only, all ages. Cribs, high chair

Meetings: Up to 200 people in garden

Day Visitors: Welcome

Handicapped: Facilities

Packages: None

Rates: Per room, daily, EP. *High Season* (mid-December–mid-April): $114–$148. *Low Season*: $68–$88.

Service Charge: 10 percent services

Government Tax: 5 percent tax, 5 percent energy surcharge

St. Vincent and The Grenadines

Young Island, St. Vincent

Nature's awesome power and exquisite beauty live side by side in this chain of idyllic islands. Mountainous and magnificent, St. Vincent is the largest island of the multi-island group. Its lush terrain, thick with tropical forests and banana plantations, rises quickly from the sea to more than 4,000 feet in the smoldering volcanic peaks of La Soufrière in the north.

The Botanic Gardens in Kingstown, the capital, are the oldest in the Western Hemisphere. Among its prized species is a breadfruit tree from the original plant brought from Tahiti by Captain Bligh of the *Bounty.*

St. Vincent has a series of mountain ranges up the center of the island. The Buccament Forest Nature Trail is a signposted loop through the fabulous rain forest where gigantic gommier and other hardwoods make up the thick canopy towering more than 100 feet.

La Soufrière has erupted five times since 1718, most recently in 1979. The crater, about a mile across, smolders and emits clouds of steam and sulfur fumes. The Falls of Baleine tumble 70 feet in one dramatic stage through a steep-sided gorge of volcanic rock at the foot of the Soufrière Mountains.

From Kingstown the falls are accessible only by sea; excursions depart almost daily.

The Grenadines, stretching south from St. Vincent over 65 miles to Grenada, are a chain of three dozen islands and cays often called by yachtsmen the most beautiful sailing waters in the world. Only eight are populated.

Bequia, the largest and most developed of the Grenadines, is known for its skilled sailors and boat builders. The island's laid-back life-style has made it a favorite of artists, writers, and old salts who never found their way back home.

Young, Palm and Petit St. Vincent are private island resorts; Mustique is a jet-setter's mecca made famous by Princess Margaret, Mick Jagger, and other celebrities. Other islands with resorts are Mayreau, Canouan, and Union, all with remarkable beaches and small resorts with facilities for sailing, diving, fishing, and other water sports. Tobago Cays are four uninhabited islets scalloped with seemingly untouched white-sand beaches and beckoning aquamarine waters.

Dive aficionados call St. Vincent the sleeper of Caribbean diving; reef life normally found at 80 feet in other locations grows here at depths of only 25 feet and has an extraordinary abundance and variety of tropical reef fish.

Information

St. Vincent and the Grenadines Tourist Office, 801 Second Avenue, New York, NY 10017; (212) 687–4981

St. Vincent

Young Island ▣▣▣▣ ✿

If painter Paul Gauguin had stopped here after leaving Martinique, he might not have pressed on to the South Seas in his search for the totally exotic. The lush, volcanic terrain of undeveloped St. Vincent is a dead ringer for Tahiti thirty years ago and it's still teeming with mystery.

But there's no mystery about Young Island. A thirty-five-acre private-island resort only 200 yards off St. Vincent's southern shore: it is luxury amid tropical profusion, a fantasy version of Polynesia in miniature. Your adventure begins when you board a Grenadine version of the *African Queen* for the 5-minute ride across the narrow channel to Young Island.

Lord of the isle Vidal Browne meets his guests at the dock usually preceded by a waiter carrying a tray of hibiscus-decorated rum punch. You'll need a drink after the day-long journey (two plane rides, taxi, and boat) it takes to reach Young's tropical shores. Vidal or one of his staff will lead you along stone paths through a maze of greenery to your island quarters—one of two dozen or so thatched bungalows of Brazilian hardwood and volcanic stone tucked on the beach or hidden on a hillside.

Vidal used to greet guests with a rare St. Vincent parrot perched on his shoulder. Misty, a pet left behind years ago by actress Vivien Leigh, has since retired to a spacious cage near the pool but still musters a perky hello to passersby.

Guests partial to bird's-eye views and aerobic hikes always choose the hillside aeries. These feel like tree houses but offer great comfort and enchanting island decor as well as unexpected amenities: a huge bowl of local fruits with cheese, fabulous homemade breads, and for guests on a return visit (often couples who honeymooned here) a bottle of Roederer champagne. Indeed, in recent years the only guest who could ask for more was the late Leonard Bernstein. A grand piano was hauled across the channel and up to the maestro's lofty retreat.

Inside the bungalow you feel as if you are outside. Vertical wooden louvers let in the outdoors, and sliding glass doors open onto a huge balcony suspended above the bush. A seductive hammock for two awaits, along with a splendid view of the mountainous mainland or the Grenadines, dribbling south toward Grenada. Even the shower, cleverly appended to the dressing quarter with its jungle canopy and shoulder-high bamboo "curtain" is al fresco.

Somewhere down below a free-form pool and tennis court hide amid the breadfruit and banana trees. Water spirits head for the dock to go snorkeling, windsurfing or sailing. Young has arrangements with Dive St. Vincent, headquartered directly across Young Cut. It offers resort and certification courses as well as excursions for certified divers. Young also keeps a couple of yachts at the ready, along with a captain and chef, for day or overnight sailing trips; it has a year-round package that combines a stay at Young with a three-day cruise of the Grenadines.

But most guests tend to plop on the beach under one of the *bohios,* the thatched-roof gazebos that enhance Young's South Pacific appearance. Occasional thirst may propel some to swim a few laps from shore to the Coconut Bar, a swim-up bar in a thachted hut that seems to float atop the Caribbean waters. Breakfast and lunch are taken in shaded garden nooks, some bounded by a moat, overlooking the beach.

By night guests gather in the wood-beamed bar and enjoy a variety of local entertainment several nights a week. The highlight is Thursday, when

guests are ferried the few hundred yards to Rock Fort, a neighboring uninhabited islet, for a sunset cocktail fête hosted by Vidal and Marlon, his better half.

Fort Duvernette, as the islet is known in history, was fortified in the
eighteenth century by the British. It was restored somewhat by John
Houser, who originally built Young Island in the early 1960s, and transferred to the St. Vincent National Trust in 1969. A steep, torch-lit path of
250 steps winds up to the top of the rock. There you'll find cocktails and
smoking grills on the rocks, along with the "Bamboo Melodians" band.

Then it's back to Young to dine on West Indian fare with a continental
dash. It's served with aplomb in a candle-lit grotto carved out of the hillside. Young offers a proper wine list, and the menu changes daily according to the whim of the Argentine chef (and what's available). The results
might be such tempting choices as papaya soup laced with garlic or an
island-grown avocado brimming with caviar, perhaps followed by just-
caught lobster or a fillet of red snapper in cream-and-pepper sauce.

What really catches guests off guard is the selection of French cheeses
that make their way to Young via Martinique. But just to remind you where
you are, try the bananas flambé or the coconut *gateau* for dessert—the fruit
could well have been picked from Young's own trees.

It's only when you hike back into the bush and up the hill that you
might regret the many-course dinner, nurtured with spirits of cane and
grape. But at least there's no need to worry about leaving behind the key to
your bungalow. They don't even give you one.

Address/Phone: Young Island Crossing, P.O. Box 211, St. Vincent, W.I.;
    (809) 458–4826; Fax: (809) 457–4567
Owner/General Manager: Vidal S. Browne
Open: Year-round
Credit Cards: All major
U.S. Reservations: Ralph Locke Islands, Inc., (914) 763–5526, (800)
    223–1108; Fax: (914) 763–5362
Deposit: 3 nights in winter, 2 nights summer; $1,000 on packages
Minimum Stay: 10 days during Christmas
Arrival/Departure: Transfer service arranged for fee
Distance from Airport: (St. Vincent Airport) 1.5 miles; taxi one-way, US $5
Distance from Kingstown: 3 miles; taxi one-way, US $10
Accommodations: 29 in bungalows, all with patio (26 with king beds, 3
    one-bedroom suites)
Amenities: Ceiling fans; bath with garden shower, hairdryer, basket of toi-
    letries, bathrobe, ice machine, small refrigerator, safe; nightly turndown
    service, room service for breakfast.

Electricity: 120 volts/240 volts

Sports: Saltwater swimming pool; 1 lighted Laykold tennis court; snorkel gear, windsurfing equipment and instruction free; sailing, deep-sea fishing, diving arranged.

Dress Code: Casual

Children: All ages except January 15 to March 15, none under 5 years of age. Cribs, high chairs, baby-sitters

Meetings: Up to 75 people

Day Visitors: None

Handicapped: Limited facilities

Packages: Honeymoon, dive, Sail-a-way-Getaway

Rates: Per person, daily, MAP. *High Season* (December 17–February 28): $205–$275. *Shoulder Season* (March 1–April 30): $160–$230. *Low Season* (May 1–December 18): $122.50–$192.50.

Service Charge: 10 percent

Government Tax: 5 percent

The Grenadines

Bequia

The Frangipani Hotel ◉

You've heard it said that if you stand long enough in Times Square or on Hollywood and Vine, sooner or later you will see the whole world go by. In its own (decidedly more laid-back) way, the beach bar at the Frangipani Hotel can make a similar claim. Okay, maybe not the whole world—but surely a good slice of its more interesting and eccentric citizens.

Bequia's Admiralty Bay is one of the finest deep-water harbors in the Caribbean, and often the first landfall for yachts cruising from the Mediterranean to these warm waters. The Frangi, as it is known to habitués, is smack in the heart of the waterfront, surrounded by flowering bushes and trees.

Once the family home of the present prime minister of St. Vincent and the Grenadines, James "Son" Mitchell, it has been welcoming yachties and tourists for so many years that it has achieved venerable-institution (if not legend) status throughout the Caribbean.

The Frangi has never tried to be anything other than what it is—a simple guesthouse—and there, in its utter lack of pretension, lies its charm. Mere steps from the yacht-filled bay, the hotel has been described in a novel this way: "like the white hunter bars in Kenya, it's a pickup place, social headquarters, news central, information booth, post office and telegraph (and now phone and fax) office, in short, the nerve center of the permanently-in-transit charter-boat trade."

Here you can gossip or flirt with serious salts who have circumnavigated the globe often, with boat bums and beach bunnies, Republican lawyers on bare-boat charters, college professors and freelance backpackers, couples with unpublishable biographies, locals and winter residents, dreadlocked Rastafarians in Batman T-shirts, some expatriate Inuit Eskimos, billionaire Arabs on zillion-dollar yachts, minor celebrities, bigamists, smugglers (of electronics, not drugs; the latter carry severe penalties here), older men with younger women, younger men with older women, and trios and combos of every age, nationality, and color imaginable.

On Thursday nights the Frangi holds its weekly jump-up (barbecue and steel band), so called because the music does in fact make it difficult not to jump up and dance. Around the bar, people are generally so chatty (and, as sundown turns the sky mauve, so full of rum) that Attila the Hun could make friends here. Needless to say, solo travelers love it, though most guests are couples.

Breakfast, lunch, and dinner are served in an open-air dining room by the lobby. The food is simple and very good, mostly West Indian fare cooked in mass quantities by local women who obviously enjoy their work. The drinks are good, too, once you've caught Harold's eye. Harold, you will quickly learn, has been tending bar here for two decades or so, and has no plans to adjust his inner clock to anything but Caribbean time.

Rooms at the Frangipani are simple, period. People stay here for what can honestly be called one of the last few "true Caribbean experiences" still available. If you're looking for professionally decorated, five-star polish don't give this one even a thought.

Not the Frangi's big attraction, the rooms are airy and adequate; some are even pleasant, but none remarkable. There are no amenities such as phone or television, and you will need to bring your own shampoo, but you are not likely to be spending much time indoors anyway, except to shower and sleep.

Rooms in the old house that face the water are simple to the point of bare—bed, table-top or ceiling fan, sink, mosquito netting. Most have no private bath, and some have no hot water (but how cold does water get in 82-degree weather?). The view—and the people-watching—make up for it. The nicer stone units with terraces are in the back of the main house, and therefore have no view of the bay.

Be aware, too, that you'll be living in close proximity to island critters as well as lush foliage. Geckos and creepy-crawlies on walls and ceilings, flies, mosquitoes and grasshoppers (all harmless) are common.

The tile-floor lobby is small but has maps and a take-one-leave-one paperback library. Anything you need, if it's humanly possible to obtain will be provided cheerfully by Marie Kingston and Lou Keane, two Canadian women who have been running the Frangi for decades. (In return, satisfied repeat guests happily run a supply train of everything from New York bagels to hard-to-find plumbing supplies.)

Noise isn't much of a problem; little happens past 9:00 P.M. on the island, and dinner is nearly impossible to find after 7:00. But on Thursdays, the barbecue, jump-up revelry and the band (playing the same five amplified songs, nearly every night at a different hotel) assault the eardrums till midnight or later.

Pack light; a T-shirt thrown over your swimsuit borders on "formal" attire. Serious resort wear and high heels will cause muffled giggles (if not a sprained ankle). There's some nice shopping, but the island offers no glitz, gambling, or Gucci. And with any luck, locals and longtime visitors pray, it never will.

The Frangi has a tennis court, and full water sports (diving, snorkeling, windsurfing) are available at The Clubhouse next door; two gorgeous beaches are a half-hour stroll or a short land- or water-taxi ride away.

Address/Phone: Box 1, Bequia, St. Vincent, W.I.; (809) 458–3255; Fax: (809) 458–3824

Owner: James "Son" Mitchell

General Manager: Marie Kingston

Open: Year-round except September–mid-October

Credit Cards: Most major (no American Express)

U.S. Reservations: Direct to hotel

Deposit: 3 days; 3 weeks cancellation less 10 percent

Minimum Stay: None

Arrival/Departure: No transfer service. If arriving by yacht, tie your dinghy to Frangi dock. By air at new airstrip; however, landing could be chancy due to winds on east side of island. Beautiful 20-minute roller-coaster drive across southern half of Bequia to hotel. Ferry daily between St. Vincent's Kingstown and Bequia, one-way, US $4

Distance from Airport: 3 miles; taxi one-way, US $10

Distance from Admiralty Bay: Resort is in town center

Accommodations: 13 rooms (5 in main building, 8 in garden units); 8 with terrace/patio

Amenities: Ceiling fans, bath with shower only; breakfast service in garden units

Electricity: 220 volts
Sports: Tennis free. Boating, snorkeling, diving, windsurfing instruction for
   fee. Hiking, birding. Sunset cruises. No pool.
Dress Code: Very casual
Children: Yes; cribs, baby-sitters
Meetings: No
Day Visitors: Welcome
Handicapped: No facilities
Packages: Dive
Rates: Per room double, daily, EP. *High Season* (mid-December–mid-April):
   $50–$120. *Low Season:* $40–$80.
Service Charge: 10 percent
Government Tax: 5 percent

Spring on Bequia ◙◙

Seekers of quiet and trance-inducing beauty may have found their nirvana
at this small country inn on Bequia, situated on thirty-five acres about
halfway up a gentle mountain overlooking Spring Bay on the windward
side of the island.

You reach it by a narrow winding road with flowering trees looking
out on sloping green fields and a wide grove of coconut palms curved
around a white-sand beach. Beyond, where the deep blue waters of the
Caribbean meet the horizon, other Grenadine islets are barely visible.

Spring on Bequia is a true hideaway with attentive and unobtrusive
service. But if you tire quickly of nothing more than fabulous scenery, it
may not be for you.

The inn is located on a working plantation that has been farmed for
more than two hundred years; the ruins of the old sugar mill are still visible. Nowadays it's sheep, poultry and pigs, though none so close you'll be
forced to notice, except perhaps a few black-and-white cows that graze
among the palm trees near the tennis court. But more important, much of
the food you are served comes fresh from the gardens and orchards—
mango, guava, grapefruit, to name a few.

The food is West Indian and good. Indeed, American manager Candy
Leslie's curry buffet is *the* place on the island for Sunday brunch, attracting
a weekly crowd of locals, tourists and other hotel guests who are usually
from the United States, Canada and Britain.

The main house is an airy structure of hand-cut stone and wood, built
on the foundations of the old Spring Plantation dating from 1767. It houses

an informal reception area, the spacious, open-air dining room and bar with beamed ceilings and stone floors.

Accommodations are in the main house and in hillside cottages of natural stone and wood that all but disappear into the trees. They are simple, even austere—a sort of meeting of Scandinavian modern and Japanese inn—with stone walls and floors and high wooden ceilings. They are tastefully furnished in contemporary style with dark wood furniture of straight, clean lines and platform twin beds with mosquito netting. Bathrooms have rock-lined showers with solar-heated water.

The rooms in the main house share a common veranda overlooking the bay, but each room has its own terrace at the rear. The hillside rooms, smothered in tropical foliage, are more spacious, with huge private stone decks and, sometimes, breezy enough for a sweater in the evening. Some have louvered windows and doors, others have sliding-glass doors. They are something of a hike up stone steps, but the rewards are spectacular views. Flashlights are provided to make your way in the evening.

Spring is the only resort on Bequia that is not situated directly on the water, but a large, hibiscus-trimmed swimming pool with a stone deck lies just below the dining area. The picture-postcard beach on Spring Bay in front of the hotel is fine for walking and exploring but too rocky for serious swimming, although there is snorkeling on the reef that protects the bay. A better beach, inaptly named Industry Bay, is about a fifteen-minute stroll away.

Children, especially teenagers, would find Spring a crashing bore. So, too, would travelers of any age who require a social life, planned activities, or luxurious accommodations. There's a tennis court, and Ms. Leslie and her Bequian husband will arrange island tours, yacht charters, water sports, or day sails to Mustique.

Hikers and other nature lovers have any number of trails, along with the pretty vistas, to enjoy. Birders can watch the hummingbirds drink nectar from the pink hibiscus by their room, spot any of the several dozen species that frequent the orchards, or look for birds on hillside trails or the road that leads into town.

Spring on Bequia, is, in short, for independent, island purists who value privacy, utter peace, and the simple pleasures of West Indian life. On these tranquil hillsides, there is nothing but the birds and the wind in the trees to interrupt the quiet.

Address/Phone: Spring, Bequia, St. Vincent, W.I.; (809) 458–3414
Owner/Manager: Candace Leslie
Open: November through June
Credit Cards: All major
U.S. Reservations: Spring on Bequia, (612) 823–1202, (612) 823–9225

Deposit: 3 days; 3 weeks cancellation
Minimum Stay: None
Arrival/Departure: No transfer service
Distance from Airport: 20 minutes; taxi one-way, about US $12
Distance from Port Elizabeth: 1 mile; taxi one-way, US $5
Accommodations: 10 rooms (4 with twin beds; 4 with two double, 2 with king) all with terraces; 3 in main building; others in 2 hillside cottages.
Amenities: Bath with shower
Electricity: 220 volts
Sports: Freshwater swimming pool, 1 tennis court. Boating, snorkeling, scuba, windsurfing can be arranged.
Dress Code: Very casual
Children: Yes
Meetings: No
Day Visitors: Welcome
Handicapped: No facilities
Packages: None
Rates: Per person, daily, EP. *High Season* (mid-December–mid-April): $65–$87.50. *Low Season:* $45–$65.
Service Charge: 10 percent
Government Tax: 5 percent

Mayreau

Saltwhistle Bay Club ▨▨

Sail into Mayreau's Saltwhistle Bay, and, like countless other first-time visitors, you will stare in disbelief: Lush foliage and a perfect beach greet you, but there's no resort to be seen. Even with the help of binoculars, the Saltwhistle Bay Club seems simply not to exist.

Even as your dinghy slips up to the dock (a boat is the only means of arrival), it is hard to pick out the stone cottages of this unusual resort. Then they appear, set far back from the water and spaced widely apart amid the refreshingly cool tropical jungle, sunlight dappling the sand; a sense of languor pervades the breeze.

You step from your boat onto a beautiful beach—perhaps the most perfect in the Caribbean: soft and wide and deep, sunny yet just shady enough, thanks to well-placed seagrape trees and flowering bushes and the coconut palms that rustle gently overhead.

Mayreau (pronounced MY-ro) has about 172 people, 223 goats, and one resort (with one telephone, installed in 1990). It is not precisely a private island, therefore, but it might as well be, since it alone occupies Saltwhistle Bay's seemingly endless half-moon beach.

The Club on its mirror-calm bay is located only yards from the rolling Atlantic surf on the other side of the island. A tiny spit of land separates the two bodies of water; owner/managers Tom and Undine Potter knew a perfect location when they saw one. They also tolerated living in tents for two years while they built the bar, restaurant, and bungalows, all constructed of native stone and local timbers, with hardwood louvers and hand-crafted furniture.

The unusually large, sparsely furnished rooms are pleasant but not fancy though they do have king-size beds (unusual in the Grenadines). The large baths come with stone showers; the precious water supply comes only from the sky.

Guests in each two-unit bungalow share an upstairs veranda; there are a table and chairs for private meals and hammocks for relaxing. Hammocks are also strung here and there along the beach and outside each unit.

Like the bungalows, the outdoor tables and bar were fashioned from stone, with cushions added for comfort where needed. Large circular dining tables spaced around the bar area are covered by thatched umbrellas. One can easily while away the afternoon by the bar enjoying the breeze, sipping cool drinks, and commenting on the navigational abilities of the few sailboats that weave in and out of the bay. There is snorkeling here as well as in the uninhabited Tobago Cays National Marine Park nearby.

Neither cruise passengers nor loud reggae music will intrude on your peace and quiet. But should you want a pinch of local color—pure West Indian—to salt your whistle during this do-nothing fantasy vacation, you can have a glimpse of genuine island life as it's been lived for nearly a century.

Just lace up your sneakers (wearing sandals to hike this cactus-lined path is a big mistake). A walk twenty minutes over the biggish hill will bring you to a tiny stone chapel atop the island's heights with sweeping views of the cays.

You could meander on down to Dennis Hideaway, Mayreau's one bar/restaurant, for a real slice of Caribbeana. Peopled with international yachties, wandering backpackers, and a few local folk, it alone is worth the hike. Dinners are generous. Be sure to bring a flashlight or two for the walk back over the hill at night.

It will come as no surprise that Saltwhistle Bay Club has no planned activities or night life, unless you count some audiocassettes, Scrabble, and conversation. It says everything about the ambience here that there used to be a jump-up (live band and barbecue) once a week, but the guests complained that there was too much noise.

Undine now manages the Club with unobtrusive Teutonic efficiency, while Tom handles the business end in Canada. Management here isn't as informal and chatty as you often find at other Grenadines resorts, but the service is as good. The laid-back, you're-part-of-the-family feeling comes from the other guests. Most of them are well-traveled, international couples, a few families, and yachtsmen in their mid-thirties and older.

There is no reason to wear anything more than a swimsuit and/or a sarong during your entire stay. The Saltwhistle Bay Club is the very definition of a barefoot hideaway.

Address/Phone: Saltwhistle Bay Club, Mayreau, St. Vincent, W.I.; Boat phone 493–9609; VHF channel 16
Owner: Tom Potter
General Manager: Undine Potter
Open: Year-round, except September and October
Credit Cards: None
U.S. Reservations: Saltwhistle Bay Club, (800) 263–2780, (613) 634–1963; Fax: (613) 384–6300
Deposit: 3 days, balance in 30 days before arrival; cancellation receives up to 18 months credit against future booking for themselves or others on their behalf.
Minimum Stay: None
Arrival/Departure: Transfer arranged by air from Barbados $125 including boat pickup; from Union $25, per person one-way.
Distance from Union Airport: 1.5 miles (45 minutes by yacht; 10 minutes by motorboat)
Accommodations: 14 rooms (10 in 5 duplex bungalows with covered, roof-top terraces; 4 junior suites in 1 building with patio), all with king-size beds; twins on request.
Amenities: Ceiling fans, bathroom with shower; solar- and electrical-heated water.
Electricity: 110 volts
Sports: Snorkeling gear and windsurfing free. Scuba, boating, deep-sea fishing arranged.
Dress Code: Very casual
Children: All ages
Meetings: Up to 24 people
Day Visitors: Yes
Handicapped: Facilities, but must consult in advance
Packages: None
Rates: Two persons, daily, MAP. *High Season* (December 16–March 31): $450. *Low Season* (April 1–December 15): $280.
Service Charge: 10 percent
Government Tax: 5 percent

Mustique

The Cotton House ▣▣

More charming than grand, the Cotton House is neither intimidating nor formal, despite its role as snooty Mustique's only hotel. Rather, it has the appeal of an English country inn set on manicured shores, where everything is *veddy* nice.

Opened in 1977, almost two decades after Colin Tennant bought Mustique and began developing it as a private tropical paradise for his royal and ritzy pals, the Cotton House was created out of the ruins of the stone and coral buildings of an eighteenth-century sugar and cotton plantation. The lovely two-story stone main house, originally the warehouse, was designed by the famous British theater designer Oliver Messel, whose genius created many of the posh homes on Mustique, including Princess Margaret's home, Les Jolies Eaux.

The main house, with its refined proportions, is highlighted by cedar shutters and arched louvered doors. It's ringed with wide, breezy verandas where afternoon tea and candlelit dinners are served. A handsome horseshoe-shaped wooden bar is at the entrance to the huge salon with high peaked, wood-beamed ceilings; the salon is lavished with antiques and amusing accoutrements and a piano for occasional entertainment and guests' enjoyment.

A small reception area at the back of the house is flanked by a bulletin board bearing various announcements and ads for charter boats offering day (and longer) sails. Just above and behind the main complex is the bizarre Messel-designed swimming pool area, nestled in what appear to be romanesque ruins or perhaps a theater backdrop (actually the former site of nothing grander than a chicken coop).

Here, breakfast and lunch are served al fresco under a covered colonnade, that's only somewhat protected from the bold blackbirds (West Indian grackles) by a nearly invisible net, which they negotiate easily. Entire slice of toast are spirited away while guests gaze over the pool or more distant countryside. A breezy bar in the corner, separating the lounge from eating area, serves fresh and surprisingly powerful papaya and mango punches until late afternoon when the main house bar opens.

Accommodations are in two Georgian-style houses framed in hibiscus and bougainvillea; in much newer cottages climbing up the steps to the pool; in a formerly private villa just below, overlooking the water-sports center at Honor Beach. Suites 23, 24, and 25 in the villa are the largest and most luxurious of the lot, with marble baths and full air-conditioning making them the most desirable during the warmer and more humid summer and fall months.

During the season from December to April, ceiling fans and cross ventilation provided by the louvered windows suffice. All rooms are attractively, but not elaborately, furnished and decorated in Messel style with whimsical touches, mosquito nets, and books in several languages. Some rooms have fridge; some have baths with showers, others with tubs; and all have terrace or patio.

All the deluxe rooms (numbers 1 to 8) in the stone houses have two terraces or wraparound patios with better cross ventilation and marvelous views. Number 6, a honeymoon favorite, overlooks Mick Jagger's house and the offshore cays in one direction; in another, you have a view of the old sugar mill, now a boutique, and Harding Lawrence's house high on a hill in the distance. Number 8 is fragrant with a huge frangipani on its patio.

The Cotton House restaurant, never one of the inn's strengths, has improved enormously under the hotel's newest management. Raymond and Liliane Polynice, Haitians with a flair for fine creole cuisine, have subtly enhanced the kitchen's international offerings with local flavors, bringing in the best meats and freshest produce available, and have trained the Vincentian chef not to overcook everything, as is the islanders' wont.

The Cotton House has two tennis courts and is set between two of the white-sand beaches which scallop the island. It has Sunfish, windsurfers, and other water-sports equipment, and the dive shop offers a resort course and PADI certification. Snorkeling within swimming distance from shore at Honor Beach is terrific. Deep-sea fishing and sailing excursions to nearby islands can be arranged. Only a short walk from the main house is a bird sanctuary and hiking almost anywhere on Mustique rewards with outstanding views.

The Mustique Company, the island's development company, which also handles the rental and sales of homes, usually hosts a party on Tuesday evenings for homeowners—often prospective ones— and guests to meet. Some of the other guests will be honeymooners; others globetrotters, as likely from Europe and South America as from the United States.

Address/Phone: Box 349, Mustique Island, St. Vincent, W.I.; (809) 456–4777; Fax: (809) 456–4777
Owner: Guy de La Houssaye
General Manager: Raymond Polynice
Open: Year-round
Credit Cards: All major
U.S. Reservations: Ralph Locke Islands, (800) 223–1108; (914) 763–5526; Fax: (914) 763–5362

Deposit: 3 days; 30 days cancellation
Minimum Stay: 10 nights at Christmas with full payment by November 1
Arrival/Departure: Complimentary transfer arranged.
Distance from Airport: 1 mile
Accommodations: 24 rooms in villas/bungalows (21 double and 3 suites); 18 with twins: 3 with kings.
Amenities: Telephone; hairdryer, basket of toiletries; mini-bar; 3 units with air-conditioning, 21 with ceiling fans; 16 bath with tub and shower; 8 shower only; ice service, nightly turndown service, room service from 7:00 A.M. to 10:00 P.M.
Electricity: 220 volts
Sports: Freshwater swimming pool; hammocks on beach. Free use of two tennis courts, Aquafinns, snorkel gear, windsurfing, Deep-sea fishing and horseback riding arranged.
Dress Code: Casual by day; casually elegant in the evening
Children: 6 years of age and older; baby-sitters
Meetings: No
Day Visitors: No
Handicapped: No facilities
Packages: Dive, honeymoon
Rates: Two persons, daily, EP. *High Season* (mid-December–mid-April): $575–$730. *Low Season:* $325–$550. Weekly rates available.
Service Charge: 10 percent
Government Tax: 5 percent

Palm Island

Palm Island Resort ▣▣▣ ✇

When poet John Donne wrote "no man is an island," he had not had the pleasure of meeting John Caldwell, the Johnny Appleseed of the Caribbean. He's the founder, manager, and, in a real sense, creator of the 110-acre Palm Island—an uninhabited, mosquito-infested swamp which Caldwell turned into his own private paradise.

But then probably anything seems easy after you have sailed 8,500 miles alone in a small boat from Panama to Australia, as Caldwell did, to find and marry his Mary, separated from him by World War II. If you want to read about the trip, his book *Desperate Voyage* is on sale in the island's shop.

Caldwell obtained the island from the government of St. Vincent for a one-dollar annual fee and a ninety-nine year lease and promptly changed the name from Prune (who would believe an island called Prune was Paradise?). Over the course of several decades, he planted thousands of coconuts all over the island (and neighboring islands), earning himself the title of Coconut Johnny. The palms grew into the magnificent specimens that sway in everyone's daydreams and dot the resort's pure-white beaches and undulating interior.

Small enough to be entirely private, big enough to offer secluded beaches as well as a congenial social scene, the barefoot Palm Island Beach Club (it's not really a club) might be called the ultimate summer camp for adults—but with the amenities adults have come to desire.

Palm's two-unit stone and wood bungalows are comfortable, unpretentious, and among the most appealing in the Grenadines. Each has solar-heated water, a ceiling fan over pastel-flowered linens, rattan furniture, a mini-fridge for cold drinks, louvered walls to catch the breezes, and sliding doors that open onto your private patio that's right on the pretty beach. You will find a footbath and a separate entrance with outdoor shower to keep the sand out of your room.

Tea and sugar cookies are served each afternoon in the open-air, covered dining pavilion, but they could just as easily appear on your veranda at 4:00 P.M.

All the units face one of the clearest, purest pale aqua stretches of Caribbean water ever to lap a beach. Mountain-peaked Union Island floats on the horizon.

Caldwell and his sons, John and Roger, who are now the hands-on managers, provide lots of activities for their guests. Topping the list is the superb snorkeling for which the island is known. It is surrounded by reefs, most within wading distance or a short swim from shore. Gear is provided free of charge, as is most equipment for water sports. Scuba is extra.

There is a parcourse/fitness walk (called "Highway 90" because Caldwell, a robust man in his seventies, has decided to live at least to that age), game room with table tennis and video library, library, boutique, and grocery store for yacht provisioning.

A day trip to the nearby Tobago Cays National Marine Park on the resort's 40-foot sailboat "*Illusion*" is an absolute must. Under these uninhabited islets, surrounded by water so brightly turquoise it almost hurts your eyes, lies some of the best snorkeling in the hemisphere. The water is shallow and so clear that scuba gear isn't necessary to see most of it.

Cruise ships call at Palm Island once a week, but their passengers seem not to bother the guests; the beach is large enough for everyone. Many guests seem to enjoy the chance to mingle with them at the separate "yacht club" restaurant. Yachts sailing the Grenadines pay a call at Palm Island as a matter of course. Indeed that's how many of them discover Palm for the first time and come back as long-staying guests year after year. Some have built small homes here, too. You will meet both types in Palm's friendly atmosphere, which is much more sociable and spirited than at most of the other exclusive hideaways in this part of the world. That's one of its most distinguishing features.

Most guests are young families and middle-aged couples, but there's enough activity to keep over-30 solo travelers happy, too. There are a few private homes on the island and villas for family or friends traveling together. If you prefer your privacy, it will be respected, but most guests seem to enjoy the low-key social scene around the very pleasant dining pavilion. It has a high-pitched wood ceiling, a large deck and wooden lounge chairs, and is surrounded by thick tropical foliage.

Caldwell is not only a friend of the coconut palm but of flora and fauna in general. Palm Island is a veritable, if not an official, nature preserve and wildlife refuge. He has planted every species of Caribbean tree that blossoms or bears fruit, and all attract an enormous variety of birds. Caldwell will give you a bird list and one of his favorite excursions is a sunset sail to a nearby island to watch the large flocks of tern return to their roost for the night.

Address/Phone: Palm Island, St. Vincent, W.I.; (809) 458–4824; Fax: (809) 458–8804
Owner: John Caldwell
General Manager: John Caldwell Jr.; Roger Caldwell
Open: Year-round
Credit Cards: All major
U.S. Reservations: Paradise Found; (800) 776-PALM
Deposit: 3 nights; 3 weeks cancellation
Minimum Stay: None
Arrival/Departure: Transfer service is included. The only way there is by boat, via small plane from Barbados or St. Lucia to Union Island, where Palm Island's boat picks you up; or by private charter boat from another of the Grenadines.
Distance from Airport: (Union Airport) 1 mile.
Distance from Main Town: Not applicable
Accommodations: 24 with patio in villas/bungalows with screened windows; all beachside doubles with twins
Amenities: Ceiling fans, mini-fridge, bath with shower only, basket of toiletries; room service during meals; no television, radio, air-conditioning, or swimming pool.
Electricity: 110 volts

Sports: Tennis, free snorkeling and most water sports included. Scuba extra.
Dress Code: Very casual
Children: All ages
Meetings: Small groups
Day Visitors: Welcome
Handicapped: Limited facilities
Packages: Honeymoon
Rates: Per room double, daily, AP. *High Season* (December 15–March 31):
$320. *Shoulder Season* (April 1–14): $265. *Low Season* (April 15–December
14): $210.
Service Charge: 10 percent
Government Tax: 5 percent

Petit St. Vincent

Petit St. Vincent Resort ◙◙◙

If you've ever fantasized about owning your own private tropical island—
complete with invisible elves to cook, clean, and bring you drinks in your
ultra-comfy abode—start packing.

Haze Richardson is one of those rare individuals who did more than
fantasize: He reclaimed what was basically a 113-acre, uninhabited speck of
land in the middle of nowhere, and over twenty years turned it into one of
the premier private-isle resorts in the Caribbean.

Other resorts may be more stylish and manicured, prettier and more
lush, but only on Petit St. Vincent (pronounced PET-ty St. Vincent, or just
PSV to the *cognoscenti*) can you live out your dream of being all alone, in
casual luxury, beyond the reach of time and care in the middle of an aqua
sea. You and your significant other can easily spend a week on PSV without ever having to see another human being. You can even miss the manager's cocktail party or the weekly jump-up and no one would bat an eye.

Then, too, what is paradise to some could drive others to the brink
within twenty-four hours. PSV has no town, no local bar to repair to, and
your fellow guests—while nothing if not well-bred and polite—wouldn't be
around to socialize. You'll spot other houses, but only in the distance. So
be sure you know you can handle it. PSV is a haven for honeymooners and
harried tycoons (few others can afford it) who expect superior service, security, peace, and privacy—and private beaches outside their widely spaced
stone houses.

Yes, houses: The accommodations on PSV aren't suites or even bungalows, they are full-size houses with one or two bedrooms.

Built of bluebitch stone with wood-beamed roofs and large windows, they have spacious living rooms; oversized bathrooms with large vanities, dressing room, and rock showers; big bedrooms with two queen beds; ceramic-tiled floors and patios. Large windows and sliding doors look out on foliage and sea views. They are furnished with tasteful, very comfortable couches and chairs, upholstered in neutral tones. No interior decorator was hired to jazz up PSV's accommodations, but the houses are a superior example of local materials that blend with their surroundings.

Small, secluded beaches are only steps from the door of most houses, but be warned, Windy Point is aptly named; the wind gusts can be enough to awaken even heavy sleepers.

Though room rates do not vary by type, there are definite variations in rooms. Those on hills and promontories are more secluded and offer the grandest views while those on the beach are closer together. Six cottages are especially suited to families or groups of friends as they offer larger living rooms separated from bedrooms by patios, with baths off both living rooms and bedrooms.

Meals are served in The Pavilion, the open-air dining and bar area near the dock, but many guests prefer room service—and it is room service like no other. You signal your needs by raising the yellow flag outside your door; the staff, who putt-putt continuously around the island in mini-mokes, take your written or spoken order for food, drink, or whatever else you fancy.

Guests are the only ones on Caribbean time; service is swift (there is a ratio of two staff per guest), assuming you haven't raised your red flag mistakenly in the interim. Red flags mean leave-me-alone, and the PSV staff has strict orders not to bother you for any reason when they see it.

Should you care to venture beyond your own patch of paradise, there is a lighted tennis court and a jogging/fitness trail that winds around the island. When that becomes too tiring, you'll find hammocks under thatched canopies, thoughtfully placed every 100 yards or so along the beach.

Water sports? Most are included in the rates. Scuba diving and water-skiing are extra. If island living has gotten into your blood, and even a house seems too civilized, you can live out your shipwreck fantasies in style. PSV will arrange a boat to drop you on a tiny island of blinding white sand, in turquoise water even more blinding. It looks unreal, with nothing on it but a thatched umbrella for shade. The islet's official name is Mopion; guests prefer to call it Petit St. Richardson.

PSV serves some of the best food in the Caribbean; some with a West Indian flavor. Richardson imports supplies almost daily from the States (filets, duck, wines, fresh produce) and the chef does wonderful things with them. After dinner a moke will drive you home after brandy, Scrabble, conversation, or a bit of music on the resident piano. Or, you can stroll your way home, flashlight in hand, perhaps accompanied by one of Haze's many yellow Labrador retrievers. A moonlight swim—and don't forget to hoist the red flag, darling, while I open the champagne.

Address/Phone: Petit St. Vincent, St. Vincent, W.I.; (809) 458–8801
Owner/Manager: Haze Richardson
Open: Year-round, except September and October
Credit Cards: None; checks and cash only
U.S. Reservations: Petit St. Vincent, P.O. Box 12506, Cincinnati, OH 45212; (513) 242–1333, (800) 654–9326; Fax: (513) 242–6951
Deposit: 3 nights; 30 days cancellation
Minimum Stay: 7 days at Christmas
Arrival/Departure: Complimentary transfer arranged by boat only; PSV picks up guests on Union Island who arrive by small plane from Barbados or St. Vincent or private charter.
Distance from Airport: (Union Airport) 4 miles;
Accommodations: 22 in villas with patios; doubles with 2 queen beds
Amenities: Ceiling fans; bath with shower, hairdryer, basket of toiletries, bathrobe; mini-bar; ice service, nightly turndown service: room service: 7:30 A.M.–7:30 P.M.; no air-conditioning, telephone, or television
Electricity: 110 volts
Sports: 1 tennis court; Sunfish sailing, snorkel gear, and windsurfing free. Scuba for charge.
Dress Code: Casual by day; elegantly casual in the evening
Children: All ages
Meetings: No
Day Visitors: No
Handicapped: Limited facilities
Packages: Honeymoon, summer
Rates: Per person, double, daily, FAP. *High Season* (December 20–March 14): $340. *Shoulder Season* (March 15–April 14) $277.50. *Low Season* (April 15–August 19; November 1–December 19): $215.
Service Charge: 10 percent
Government Tax: 5 percent

Trinidad and Tobago

Hilton International Trinidad

Different yet similar, this island duet is the ultimate Caribbean kaleidoscope: A melange of Europeans, Africans, and Asians has woven intricate cultural patterns into a tapestry of fabulous flora and fauna.

The birthplace of calypso and steel bands, Trinidad is the country's banking and trading center; its visitors are more interested in business than beaches. Twenty-two miles to the northeast lies tiny Tobago, an island so lavishly beautiful and serene that it makes even the worst Caribbean cynic smile.

The mating of Trinidad and Tobago is a bit of a historical irony. Columbus discovered Trinidad on his third voyage and named it for three southern mountain peaks symbolizing to him the Holy Trinity. The Spaniards held the island for three centuries until they were unseated by the British in 1797. But Tobago, because of its strategic location, was so prized by Europeans that it changed hands fourteen times. Finally, in 1889, Tobago asked to become a part of Trinidad; they became independent in 1962.

Trinidad has gone through the oil boom and bust. At the heart of Port-of-Spain, the capital, Victorian architectural relics give it a distinctive character. It has an interesting zoo, botanic gardens, and restaurants for local cuisine that reflect the country's West Indian, East Indian, and Chinese components.

Trinidad explodes once a year in Carnival, the granddaddy of all Caribbean Carnivals. The balance of the year, it offers tennis, golf, art galleries and museums in historic buildings, antiques in offbeat shops, and a music- and dance-filled nightlife.

The most southerly of the Caribbean island states, Trinidad is only 7 miles off the coast of Venezuela and originally was part of the South American mainland. As a result, its flora and fauna include many South American species not seen elsewhere in the Caribbean. It also has such strange natural features as mud volcanoes and an asphalt lake.

But of all its natural wonders, the most spectacular is the bird life. More than 425 species from North and South America and the Caribbean meet here in the forested mountains and mangroves. The most spectacular is the nightly sunset arrival of hundreds of scarlet ibis, the national bird, to roost in a sanctuary of the Caroni Swamp, only 7 miles south of the capital. Guided boat trips through the Caroni swamp end where the birds return daily.

Information

Trinidad & Tobago Tourism Development Authority, 25 West 43rd Street, #1508; New York, NY 10036; (212) 719–0540

Asa Wright Nature Centre ◉

Deep in a rain forest on the slopes of the Northern Range at 1,200 feet overlooking the Arima Valley is the Asa Wright Nature Centre, a bird sanctuary and wildlife reserve with an inn. Built in about 1906, the inn is in the Victorian estate house of the former coffee, citrus, and cocoa plantation, now mostly returned to the wild. It is surrounded by dense tropical vegetation; sitting on its veranda is like being in an aviary, except that the birds come and go freely from the surrounding rain forest.

The Centre, a private institution unique in the Caribbean, was established in 1967 on the Spring Hill Estate by its owner, Asa Wright, an Icelandic-born Englishwoman whose rugged manner may have helped give rise to many tall tales about her. She acquired the 197-acre property upon the death of her husband and was persuaded by naturalist friends to create a nonprofit trust to preserve the area and make it a study and recreation center.

The inn is rustic but comfortable; services are minimal. Most of the rooms are in bungalows, furnished with a bureau, desk, chair, and reading lamp; all have private bath. All the accommodations have been renovated and upgraded in the past two years. They now have attractive bedcovers and curtains and look much prettier than previous guests might remember. The rooms now also have screened porches or outside areas where you can enjoy the birds and the great outdoors in privacy.

At the entrance to the manor house, beyond the office where useful nature books can be purchased, are the main house's two bedrooms. Directly on, a hallway leads into the parlor and to one side, the dining room. Both rooms are comfortably furnished in a traditional, homey manner as they might have been in their plantation days. On the veranda outside the parlor, guests gather for afternoon tea and at other times to watch birds, as well as nightly before dinner for the inn's complimentary rum punch.

All meals, fresh and hearty, are served in the dining room family style. The tables even have lazy Susans in the center for diners to help themselves. The kitchen will prepare picnic baskets if you want to spend the day hiking and birding or drive to the beach on Trinidad's Caribbean north coast.

Natural history programs with slides, lectures, and videos are usually scheduled in the evening. But by evening, after an active and exhilarating day with nature, you will probably be happy to go quietly off to bed.

The Centre has its own guides and five hiking trails, which day visitors may also use for a small fee. The trails, ranging from half-hour strolls to difficult three-hour hikes, are designed to maximize viewing of particular species. Maps are available for self-guided forays into the rain forest.

With ease you will see tanagers, thrushes, trogons, blue-crowned motmots, many species of hummingbirds, the beautiful crested oropendola, and dozens of other bird species. The trails pass through magnificent rain forest where the upper-story canopy is often more than 100 feet. North of the Centre are other trails at 1,800 feet, where you can spot species that prefer high elevations. Generally, the best time to see the greatest variety of birds is from December to March.

The most celebrated species at Asa Wright is a nesting colony of oilbirds, which make their home in a cave located on the property. The rare bird is found only here and in northern South America. The site can be visited only with a guide.

The William Beebe Tropical Research Station, begun in 1950 near the Centre by Dr. William Beebe of the New York Zoological Society, has been part of the Centre since 1970 when the Society donated 230 acres and several small buildings as a gift. It accommodates scientists and other researchers.

While the inn takes guests on an individual basis, most people staying here are likely to be part of a natural-history or birding group from the United States, Canada, Britain, and Germany. For bird-watchers, naturalists, and hikers, the Asa Wright Centre, but I believe the quiet, friendly inn would appeal to anyone who is a true nature lover.

Address/Phone: P.O. Box 10, Port-of-Spain, Trinidad, W.I.; (809) 622–7480 (for messages only); Fax: (809) 667–0493
Owner: Asa Wright Nature Center
General Manager: Kingsley James
Open: Year-round
Credit Cards: None
U.S. Reservations: Caligo Ventures, 156 Bedford Road, Armonk, NY 10504; (800) 426–7781, (914) 273–6333; Fax: (914) 273–6370
Deposit: $100 per person
Minimum Stay: None
Arrival/Departure: Transfer service arranged for fee
Distance from Airport: 1.5-hour drive; taxi one-way, $20
Distance from Port-of-Spain: 2-hour drive; from Arima, 7.5 miles (30 minutes); taxi one-way, approximately US $10
Accommodations: 25 rooms, most with terraces (2 in main building, 23 in bungalows; 20 with twins; 2 with kings; 3 singles)
Amenities: ceiling fans, bath with shower only; no room service; no phones, television, radios, or air-conditioning
Electricity: 110 volts
Sports: No facilities. Natural pool for wading. Caribbean coastal beaches less than an hour's drive.
Dress Code: Very casual
Children: Over 14 years of age
Meetings: Up to 50 people
Day Visitors: Yes
Handicapped: Very limited facilities
Packages: Natural history and birding tours
Rates: Per person, daily, AP. *High Season* (mid-December–mid-April): $72, double; $98, single. *Low Season:* $56, double; $72, single.
Service Charge: 10 percent
Government Tax: 15 percent VAT

Hilton International Trinidad ⬡⬡

A Port-of-Spain landmark since it opened in the 1960s, the upside-down Hilton has the best views in town and ringside seats for Trinidad's famous Carnival staged at the Queen's Park Savannah, which stretches at the hotel's feet.

Built into a hillside, the dramatic design climbs the hill to the top where you will find the lobby after you, too, have climbed the circular driveway that leads to the entrance. From the lobby at the top, the rooms stretch down the hillside. It may be a bit confusing when you get into the elevator and push the down button to go to your room on the eighth floor, or push the up button to return to the lobby. But it doesn't take long to get adjusted, particularly when you discover the rewards of the innovative architecture. From the terrace of the lobby, en route to the guest-room wings, you get a spectacular view over Port-of-Spain and the Gulf of Paria.

Business travelers make up the majority of guests at the Trinidad Hilton, as in the case of most city-center Hiltons, and the hotel is geared to them. But this hotel is also the preferred place for tourists who can afford it. In addition to its hillside perch, the Trinidad Hilton has a wonderful central location within walking distance of many of the capital's main attractions. Steps through the gardens on the park side put you directly on the Savannah, from where you can walk to a museum and art gallery, botanic gardens, and a zoo, among other attractions. The staff throughout the hotel is pleasant and helpful, and the convenient hotel shops include branches of the main duty-free stores at the port and airport.

The Trinidad Hilton may have the best seats in town for Carnival, but it's really not the most ideal time to be a guest in the hotel and certainly not the time to judge it. During Carnival week the hotel is bursting at the seams with revelers and unless you are as revved up as they are, you may not think it's much fun at all.

At other times, however, the Trinidad Hilton is truly an oasis in the city, with 25 acres of beautiful gardens under the spreading arms of huge flamboyants, poui, jacaranda, and other flowering tropical trees. It has a large swimming pool in a garden setting, tennis courts, and a small health club. Yes, the rooms need to be updated and the furniture changed, but every time I have stayed here, I have always enjoyed it immensely.

The rooms are dependable Hilton rooms with the comforts people have come to expect from the international chain. All rooms have balconies and most with good views either on the Savannah, the gardens and pool, the Northern Mountain range, or the Gulf of Paria. Some on the lower floors (lower to the ground, that is) are up against the hill and heavy foliage and don't look out at much of anything. Rates do vary with the view.

Three executive floors with a lounge cater to business travelers with extra amenities, including airport meeting service, pre-registration, rapid check-in/check-out, and complimentary continental breakfast. A transportation desk in the lobby is available for concierge services. The hotel has the best meeting facilities in the city.

A staircase in the lobby winds down into the main, informal restaurant, a high-ceiling, airy, and air-conditioned room where breakfast buffets and à la carte menus are available for the meals. La Boucan, a more formal dining room, serves local and international fare. Be sure to try callaloo soup, a Trinidad favorite. Several nights weekly poolside buffets feature local cuisine along with local entertainment.

The poolside bar at the Gazebo and the Aviary Bar are popular rendezvous spots for Trinidadians as much as visitors. The Aviary features live bands and dancing on the weekends. If you miss Carnival, you can catch something of its flavor and of Trinidad's multi-cultural society at the Canboulay Fiesta, which is staged poolside on Monday nights. Trinidad, should you forget, was the birthplace of calypso and the steel drum.

Address/Phone: P.O. Box 442, Port-of-Spain, Trinidad, W.I.; (809) 624–3211; Fax: (809) 624–3211, ext. 6133

General Manager: William Aguiton

Open: Year-round

Credit Cards: All major

U.S. Reservations: Hilton Reservation Service, (800) HILTONS

Deposit: None; inquire for Carnival

Minimum Stay: None; inquire for Carnival

Arrival/Departure: Airport meeting service available on request.

Distance from Airport: 17 miles; taxi one-way, US $20 (day), $30 (night)

Distance from Port-of-Spain: 1 mile to port; taxi one-way, US $5

Accommodations: 394 rooms and suites with balconies (23 king, 236 twins, 135 queen; 54 executive-floor rooms.

Amenities: Air-conditioning, direct-dial telephone, radio, bath with tub and shower, mini-bar in 214 rooms, cable television; executive floor and lounge, business services; room service from 6 A.M. to 11:30 P.M.

Electricity: 110 volts

Sports: Freshwater swimming pool; 2 lighted Chevron Cushion tennis courts, free to hotel guests during day, nominal charge for evening; proper tennis attire required; racquets for rental, instruction available. Golf, boating, snorkeling, scuba, deep-sea fishing, hiking, birding arranged. Botanic gardens nearby.

Dress Code: City casual

Children: All ages. Cribs, high chair, baby-sitters

Meetings: Up to 800 people

Day Visitors: Yes

Handicapped: Facilities

Packages: Golf, Carnival

Rates: Per room, double, daily, EP. *Year-round:* $142–$179 (except Carnival, $219)

Service Charge: 10 percent

Government Tax: 15 percent

Turks and Caicos Islands

The Windmills Plantation at Salt Cay

A diver's paradise lying at the end of the Bahamas chain, the Turks and Caicos Islands have been dubbed the Caribbean's Last Frontier. A British Crown Colony made up of eight islands and several dozen cays, the islands stretch across 90 miles in two groups separated by the Turks Island Passage, a deep-water channel of 22 miles.

To the east is the Turks group, which has Grand Turk, the capital with about half of the colony's population of eight thousand; and neighboring Salt Cay, an old settlement with windmills and salt ponds, declared a Heritage site under UNESCO's World Heritage program.

To the west are the Caicos Islands—South, Middle, North—which form an arch on the north side of Caicos Bank. The small archipelago is surrounded by virgin reefs, most uncharted. Provo, as Providenciales is known, is the commercial center and the site of most of the resort and commercial development. North of Provo are Pine Cay, home of the Meridian Club, and Parrot Cay, which has a new resort development.

The islands are not richly blessed with tropical vegetation, but they do have a surprising variety of flora. Coconut palms, casuarinas, seagrapes and palmettos give them a rugged, windswept beauty. Middle Caicos and North Caicos have fertile soil with lush patches of citrus and fruit trees.

The islands have some exceptional natural attractions: almost 200 miles of untouched beaches, acres of tropical wilderness and wetlands, and magnificent seas with some of the most spectacular marine life in the world. Several locations recently were declared national parks and bird sanctuaries (two islets in the Turks and eight locations in the Caicos) as a first step in promoting the archipelago as a nature-lover's paradise. Of course, almost every cay in the colony could be a wildlife sanctuary.

Grand Turk is a long skinny island of 9 square miles along the Turks Island Passage. Here and Salt Cay are great places for whale watching in the spring and autumn when the passage becomes a thoroughfare for migratory humpback whales and giant manta rays.

Information

Turks and Caicos Tourist Information Office, c/o The Keating Group, 425 Madison Avenue, New York, NY 10017; (212) 888–4110

The Meridian Club on Pine Cay ▣▣▣ ✿

Since it does not have a telephone, and the only way to reach it is by boat or private plane, you could say the Meridian Club is remote and exclusive. But what really sets the resort apart and makes it one of the truly great hideaways is its refreshing simplicity and its wild natural setting along one of the world's most gorgeous beaches.

The small, unpretentious resort belongs to the homeowners of an exclusive residential development on Pine Cay, a privately owned eight-hundred-acre island—about the size of New York's Central Park—floating on spectacularly beautiful aquamarine water between Provo and North Caicos.

Set on two uninterrupted miles of pristine white sand washed by clear, languid water, the club is comprised of a clubhouse and clusters of cottages less than a stone's throw from the beach. Some of the private homes also are available for rent. No cars are allowed on the island; you get around on leg power by walking or biking or, when available, by golf cart.

The clubhouse is the reception and social center, with an inside-outside dining room on the first floor and an attractive upstairs lounge with a bar, corner library, and a veranda. Guests and homeowners—a well-traveled, well-heeled, and somewhat intellectual group—mingle here nightly for cocktails hosted by the manager and for after-dinner socializing.

The clubhouse opens onto the pool, which has a wide terrace used for breakfast, lunch, and tea, and for barbecues on Wednesday and Saturday nights. Dinner, served family-style, is an informal affair in the dining room. The food is good, not gourmet. On some Saturday nights a local band enlivens the evening with music for dancing, West Indian–style.

The beachfront cottages, powered by solar energy, are connected by a trellised walkway draped in bougainvillea. Most guest rooms are large junior suites, tastefully furnished with off-white rattan and colorful prints. They have twin or a king-size or twin beds, a separate sitting area, and screened porches facing the beach.

At the end, a bit separate from the group, is a hexagonal cottage that honeymooners like for its privacy. The rustic cottage has stone floors and a tiled bath with an enclosed outdoor shower. It has its own barbecue area and a thatched beach hut just large enough to shade two.

Use of water-sports equipment and daily excursions to nearby cays for snorkeling are included in the room rate. The snorkeling, with the reefs rich in marine life, is some of the best you will ever find.

Several features set the Meridian Club apart from other retreats. The very nature of Pine Cay, with its untamed appearance, is the most apparent and the one the homeowners are determined to maintain. Strong-willed environmentalists, they have resisted the temptation to expand and, instead, have converted about two-thirds of the island into a national park. They are equally vigilant about the coral reefs protecting the island.

Covered mostly with dry scrub, Pine Cay has freshwater lakes and gets its name from a type of tree that covers vast areas of the Caicos. It has a nature trail, and any dirt road can be used by birders to spot some of the 120 bird species here.

The camaraderie between owners and guests is unusual, too. (In most resort developments, the residents and resort guests seldom see one another.) The congeniality and high number of repeat visitors are also reflected in the warm relationship between guest and staff, who, if not polished to Savoy shine, are attentive and caring.

Although the Meridian Club is barefoot living most of the time, it has a certain gracious style and civility. Its small size makes it easy for guests to feel at home quickly. In addition to homeowners and their affluent friends, your companions are likely to be professionals, business executives, Eastern establishment types, and a titled European or two.

Address/Phone: Pine Cay, Turks and Caicos Islands, B.W.I.; (800) 331–9154, (212) 696–4566; Fax: (809) 946–5128
Owner: The Meridian Club
General Managers: Gene and Linda Spinner
Open: November 1–July 4

Credit Cards: None; personal checks accepted

U.S. Reservations: RMI Marketing, (800) 331–9154; (212) 696–4566; Fax: (212) 689–1598

Deposit: 3 nights; 30 days cancellation

Minimum Stay: None

Arrival/Departure: The club provides boat transfer between Provo and Pine Cay.

Distance from Airport: (Provo Airport) 10 miles; taxi to boat dock one-way, $15 (included in room rate); resort has 2,900-foot airstrip used by private planes, small charters, and interisland carriers

Distance from Provo Town Center: 15 miles

Accommodations: 12 suites in beachfront bungalows; 15 two- to four-bedroom cottages; all with terrace or patio

Amenities: Ceiling fans, bath with shower, basket of toiletries; ice service, nightly turndown service, room service for breakfast; no telephone, television, VCR, radio, or clock

Electricity: 110 volts/60 cycles

Sports: Freshwater pool, tennis and equipment, bikes, boating, snorkeling and equipment, sailboats, windsurfing included. Wilderness trails and birding. Deep-sea, bonefishing, tarpon, reef fishing, and scuba arranged.

Dress Code: Always casual

Children: All ages, but children under 6 not allowed in club rooms or in dining room during dinner hours; those under 18 not allowed in bar after 6:00 P.M. unless accompanied by an adult family member

Meetings: Up to 26 people

Day Visitors: No facilities

Handicapped: No facilities

Packages: Hideaway, Shell Seeker

Rates: Two persons double, daily, AP. *High Season* (December 19–January 3; January 23–March 13): $545. *Mid-season* (January 4–22 and March 14–April 11) $435. *Low Season* (April 12–December 18): $380.

Service Charge: 10 percent

Government Tax: 7 percent

The Windmills Plantation at Salt Cay ▣ ▣ ❦

Escapists, stressed-out executives, and anyone else with an urgent need to run away to the most remote spot in the tropics that has a delightful—if a bit eccentric—resort, listen up.

Salt Cay, a postage stamp of an island only a hop from Grand Turk, has a minuscule resort, The Windmills Plantation, that took a decade to build. The story of its construction is only slightly more fantasy-filled than the results.

In 1980 architect (and former actor) Guy Lovelace and his wife, Pat, an interior designer, discovered Salt Cay, a place untouched by time. They acquired 3 miles of untouched, blinding white sands on the island's north coast and began building their resort.

They wanted to replicate a colonial plantation and decided to use the same tools and technology available two hundred years ago. During his twenty-five years of designing resorts throughout the Caribbean, Lovelace had acquired a repertoire of island architectural features, including wooden verandas, gingerbread fretwork, a colonnaded greathouse, and brightly colored Dutch colonial facades. These he incorporated into the buildings to reflect the diverse styles and cultures that touched the islands in colonial times.

All work was done by Salt Cay inhabitants using traditional island skills and Lovelace's twentieth-century know-how. None had had prior construction experience. With the exception of the stone, sand, and gravel, all materials were shipped from Miami to Grand Turk and then by small boat to Salt Cay. Stone was quarried and cut by hand. The women of the island smashed rocks with hammers to make gravel. Men who had no experience with electricity or running water became electricians and plumbers.

They constructed a greathouse, servants quarters, boat shed, sail loft, overseers cottage, and other buildings that now house the dining room, bar, and eight luxury suites. The buildings form a U around a sandy garden and open onto a 50-foot lap pool with a colonnaded walkway to a weathered boardwalk leading to the beach and a whale watch pavilion. No kidding.

All rooms are individually and distinctively decorated in the fine style of the late eighteenth century, with Caribbean wicker and reproductions of English antiques. They have four-poster beds, antique wicker, hand-carved Haitian beds, and bamboo furniture.

The greathouse has four suites, all with sitting rooms and verandas. The two ground-floor suites have king-size four-poster beds. A courtyard in the rear has a private plunge pool. The second-floor suites have cathedral ceilings, louvered windows, and ceiling fans, and are furnished with queen four-poster beds. The Quarters and Sail Loft have two bedrooms each. Those in the Quarters have an 18-foot high cathedral ceiling.

Steve and Diane Newcomb, the managers, will greet you with a welcome drink, and you may help yourself at the open bar anytime. Guests gather at the bar around 7:00 P.M. for cocktails and dine on the porch by the garden or in the dining room by candlelight. Everyone sits at one large table, unless they prefer a separate one. Meals and wine are served casually—very casually—family style. The cuisine, like the buildings, represents the Caribbean islands and is made up from creole recipes collected by the Lovelaces.

The Newcombs say most guests, arriving exhausted and stressed out, are content to sit on their veranda or at the whale-watch hut, sipping a cool drink, or lie in a hammock reading a book from the inn's library. Others walk along the beach, watch birds, or float on the crystal-clear water over the unspoiled reefs in front of the inn. Snorkel gear is provided. A day sail to a deserted nearby cay with picnic lunch is also included. Steve Newcomb is a certified PADI instructor and will teach you to dive for a fee; island men will take you fishing or sailing for a fee.

The resort takes its name from the windmills that once powered the island's salt industry. The old salt pans and machinery ruins can still be seen. Exploring the island is fun: The people—all two hundred inhabitants—tend to be friendly, courteous, and helpful. You can hike, explore on horseback, or take an island tour by Land Rover with the Newcombs.

Without being there, it may be impossible to imagine the tranquillity of The Windmills' setting—probably *too* serene for many people. Restless folks, television or telephone addicts, and anyone allergic to cats should stay away. (Six fluffy felines have the run of the place.)

Address/Phone: Salt Cay, Turks and Caicos Islands, B.W.I.; Phone and Fax: (809) 946–6962

Owner: Guy Lovelace

General Manager: Steve and Diane Newcomb

Open: Year-round

Credit Cards: American Express, Visa

U.S. Reservations: Direct to Windmill or (800) 822–7715; Fax: (407) 845–2982

Deposit: $100 for each night reserved; 30 days cancellation, less $50

Minimum Stay: 3 days

Arrival/Departure: Transfer service is arranged from Grand Turk, 9 miles on north, via 8-passenger DeHaviland Islander; cost US $100 per flight, paid with cash or credit card. Flying time to Salt Cay is 5 min. From Provo, 75 miles west of Salt Cay, Charlie Air flies 5-passenger Aztec direct to Salt Cay, 30-minute flight, $50 per person. The hotel manager meets arriving guests at Salt Cay "aerodrome" (1,800 feet of hard-packed gravel).

Distance from Airport: (Salt Cay Air Strip) quarter-mile; taxi one-way, $5

Distance from Balfour Town: 1 mile; taxi one-way, $5

Accommodations: 8 deluxe units with terraces (4 rooms with queens or kings; 4 suites with queens and kings)

Amenities: Ceiling fans, bath with shower, basket of toiletries, saltwater faucets to wash sand off your feet; hot water for showers 5:00–7:00 P.M.; room service on advance notice for additional charge.

Electricity: 110 volts
Sports: Saltwater pool, plunge pool for 2 suites. Snorkeling and equipment, island tour by Land Rover free. Hiking and birding. Scuba, horseback riding, sailing, fishing for fee.
Dress Code: Informal. Shirts with collars and sleeves required for men at dinner; no bathing suits or cutoffs in dining room
Children: None under 12 years
Meetings: Up to 16 people
Day Visitors: Welcome for lunch with 24-hour notice
Handicapped: No facilities
Packages: None
Rates: Per room, double, daily, FAP. *Year-round:* $415–$575. *Low Season:* One night free for week's stay.
Service Charge: 10 percent
Government Tax: 7 percent

ON THE HORIZON

Grace Bay Club

The Grace Bay Club brings to Provo its first truly luxury property. Set in gardens along 750 feet of an exquisite white sandy beach, the hotel/con-dominium resort has an elegant design of three- and four-story, semide-tached buildings in Mediterranean style with white stucco and red roofs. They all have patios or terraces facing the sea.

Designed with European flair and built to South Florida standards, the units include studios, one- and two-bedroom apartments, and du-plexes. They are air-conditioned and have luxurious appointments that include microwave ovens and multichannel cable television.

Grace Bay, which has European owners and management, is de-signed to attract affluent international travelers. It has two swimming pools, lighted tennis courts, Jacuzzi, a restaurant, and gaming tables. The resort will arrange diving and water sports, and Provo's new eighteen-hole championship golf course is nearby.

Address/Phone: P.O. Box 128, Providenciales, Turks and Caicos; (809) 946–5757
U.S. Reservations: (800) 255–9684
Accommodations: 99 units (studios, one- and two-bedroom)
Rates: Per room, double, daily, EP. *High Season* (December 21–March 31): $150–$500. *Low Season:* $100–$350.

The Ocean Club

This is not exactly a new hotel. The Ocean Club opened its first phase in 1989 as Provo's first luxury beachfront condominium. The last section is nearing completion for a total of nine buildings, set in a U shape around a central garden. With the new facilities and services being added, the club will debut this year as a hotel.

Guests have a choice of studios, one-, two- and three-bedroom units, all equipped with large screened balconies and fully furnished with kitchenettes, air-conditioning, ceiling fans, cable television, direct-dial phones, washers and dryers. Rooms are airy and spacious; their high-quality contemporary furnishings in soft colors lend a soothing, tropical feeling.

Situated on seven-and-a-half acres, the Ocean Club is on the beach and directly across the road from the new Provo golf course. The resort has a swimming pool and poolside snack bar and tennis courts. A restaurant is to be added.

Address/Phone: Grace Bay, Box 240 Providenciales, Turks and Caicos Islands, B.W.I.; (809) 946–5880; Fax: (809) 946–5845
U.S. Reservations: Robert Reid, (800) 223–6510; Turks and Caicos Reservation Service, (800) TC–ISLES; in Canada, (800) 424–5500
Accommodations: 77 units
Rates: One or two persons, daily, EP. *High Season* (mid-December–mid-April): $160–$230; 1–6 persons, $465. *Low Season:* $100–$140; $320.

U.S. Virgin Islands

The Buccaneer Hotel, St. Croix (© Carol Lee)

Topside or below, few places under the American flag are more beautiful than our corner of the Caribbean. Volcanic in origin, the Virgin Islands are made up of fifty green gems floating in a sapphire sea; only three are developed. They are only a short distance apart, yet no islands in the Caribbean are more different from one another than are our American trio.

St. Croix, the easternmost point of the United States, is the largest. A low-lying island of rolling hills, it was once an important sugar-producing center. Many plantation homes and sugar mills have been restored as hotels, restaurants, and museums; and Christiansted and Frederiksted, the main towns, are on the National Historic Registry.

St. Croix offers an impressive variety of activity, from hiking in a rain forest to turtle watching, but its most popular sports are snorkeling and scuba diving. The island is surrounded by coral reefs, and off the northeast coast is Buck Island Reef National Monument, the only underwater park in our national park system.

St. John, the smallest of the trio, is truly America the Beautiful. Almost three-quarters of the mountainous island is covered by the Virgin Islands

National Park. Around its edges lovely little coves hide some of the most alluring porcelain white beaches and aquamarine waters in the Caribbean.

The National Park Service Visitor Center in Cruz Bay schedules ranger-led tours, hikes, and wildlife lectures and publishes a brochure outlining twenty-one trails. Cruz Bay, the island's main town, is booming with new popularity and rapidly losing its tiny-village charm to traffic and tacky T-shirt shops. The island is reached by ferry from St. Thomas in twenty minutes.

St. Thomas floats on a deep turquoise sea with green mountains and an irregular coastline of fingers and coves sheltering idyllic bays and pretty white-sand beaches. Only 13 miles long and less than 3 miles wide, it seems larger because of its dense population and development. Its capital, Charlotte Amalie, is the busiest cruise port in the Caribbean.

St. Thomas offers good facilities for water sports, and tennis and golf, but it is best known for its smart boutiques with clothing, accessories, perfumes, and jewelry of world-famous designers.

The Virgin Islands, as United States territories, have a special tax status that gives returning United States residents a $1,200 exemption from customs duty rather than the $600 applied to other places.

Information

U.S. Virgin Islands Division of Tourism, 1270 Avenue of the Americas, New York, NY 10020; (212) 582–4520

St. Croix

The Buccaneer Hotel ▣▣▣ ✿

At The Buccaneer you could roll out of bed to play golf, or take a swim at one of the two pools before breakfast, explore some of the Caribbean's best reefs fronting three white-sand beaches before lunch, and then enjoy a game of tennis before dinner—all within eyeshot of the pink palazzo whose history stretches back three hundred years.

Spread over three hundred tropical acres near Gallows Bay on St. Croix's north coast, The Buccaneer was opened in 1948 as an eleven-room inn in a seventeenth-century estate house by a family whose origins on the island date from the same period. The building's thick walls and graceful bonnet arches are still visible in the French Wing; the Cotton House serves as a theater and meeting space; and the eighteenth-century sugar mill is the

venue for the manager's weekly cocktail party (and makes a romantic setting for weddings).

Now greatly enlarged and developed into a complete resort, the main
building sits on a rise with commanding views. The roadside entrance
passes along a drive lined with royal palms and manicured gardens bright
with bougainvillea and a great variety of tropical trees. The hotel interiors
are sporting a new look by well-known interior designer Carleton Varney.

Some of the accommodations are in the main building, while others
are housed in a variety of cottages and bungalows near the fairways and
tennis courts and in terraced gardens cascading from the main building to
the sea. All have terraces. If you are a beach body, you may prefer the cottages that snake along the seashore. They have high, cedar-beam ceilings
and stone terraces overlooking the sea and pretty sunsets. The newest,
most luxurious accommodations are in the two suites, Ficus and Frigate,
each with two bedrooms furnished with four-poster beds, two baths, and a
living room. These also rent as one-bedroom suites.

The Buccaneer's tennis complex is the largest on the island. The
eighteen-hole golf course (6,268 yards; par: 71) dips and dives from hilltops
to the water's edge; and a 2-mile, eighteen-station parcours jogging and exercise path winds through the hilly terrain. At the health club you can iron
out the kinks, enjoy a massage, sauna, seaweed wrap, and other pampering
while your kids participate in a free program that includes crafts, supervised
snorkeling, singalongs, parties, and their own daily newsletter.

One of The Buccaneer's two pools is by the main building, set into
seventeenth-century foundations. The second, added in 1991, is a free-form
pool with a small waterfall and a tiny island with palm trees. It is located on
quiet Beauguard Beach by The Grotto, where burgers and snacks are available during midday.

The Beach Shack, the water-sports center, is on Cutlass Cove. Its proprietor, Charlie Groder, is a PADI-certified dive instructor and an ordained
minister who officiates at the frequent weddings held at The Buccaneer.
Lunch is served daily here at The Mermaid restaurant, which is also the setting for the weekly evening Cruzan buffet, featuring local specialties and
steel-band music. A third strand is Whistle Beach, favored for privacy.

At breakfast on the open-air Terrace, you'll enjoy views of the fairways
and the sea, at dinner the lights of Christiansted twinkling in the distance.
Dinner offers a continental menu with West Indian selections. The Brass
Parrot, a separate air-conditioned restaurant beyond the Terrace, has a
more elegant setting than its casual counterpart; the menu stresses more
gourmet fare. Nightly the Terrace bar has live musical entertainment by different combos.

The Armstrongs, now the third generation to operate the hotel, are a family of naturalists. Elizabeth Armstrong leads free weekly nature walks for guests. The Buccaneer's golf course is a popular birding spot.

A quiet self-contained, family-owned and -operated resort with a casual and friendly ambience, The Buccaneer is suitable for all ages and all situations, from singles to families. It appeals most to travelers who want to have an active vacation with a wide range of sports. Many guests are repeaters; some are from families that, like the owners, are into the third generation.

Address/Phone: Box 25200, Gallows Bay, St. Croix, U.S.V.I. 00824-5200; (809) 773–2100; Fax: (809) 778–8215

Owner: The Armstrong Family

General Manager: Robert D. Armstrong

Assistant Manager: Elizabeth Armstrong

Open: Year-round

Credit Cards: All major

U.S. Reservations: Direct, or Ralph Locke Islands, P.O. Box 800, Waccabuc, NY 10597; (800) 223–1108; Fax: (914) 763–5362

Deposit: 14 days summer, 21 days winter; 30 days Christmas and February

Minimum Stay: 2 nights

Arrival/Departure: Transfer service included in some packages

Distance from Airport: 10 miles (40 minutes); taxi one-way, $11.50 for one or two persons

Distance from Christiansted: 2 miles; taxi one-way, $3; hourly hotel shuttle to town, $3 per person, one-way

Accommodations: 150 rooms and suites (32 in main building; 118 in villas/bungalows; 90 double with queen beds, 47 with kings; 13 suites), all with terraces, in either oceanfront, ocean view, fairway view, tennis, or ridge cottages

Amenities: Air-conditioning, ceiling fan, safe, telephone, refrigerator, cable television, dressing area, bath with tub and shower, basket of toiletries, most with hairdryer; ice service, nightly turndown service; room service at specific hours; boutiques, health spa

Electricity: 110 volts

Sports: 2 freshwater pools, 8 Laykold tennis courts (2 lit), pro shop. Fee for courts, lessons, equipment. Golf: greens fees, charge for equipment, caddies, carts, lessons. Sunfish and windsurfers, hourly rental fees. Snorkeling: lessons, equipment fees. Charges for sports facilities and equipment generally waived in packages. Scuba and snorkeling outings depart daily from hotel dock. Day and evening cruises, deep-sea fishing, horseback riding arranged. Parcourse exercise path; health club.

Children: All ages; free activities program; cribs, baby-sitters

Meetings: Up to 50 people

Day Visitors: Yes

Handicapped: Limited facilities

Packages: All-inclusive; golf, tennis, honeymoon; wedding; family; water sports

Rates: Per person, daily, EP. *High Season* (December 20–March 31): $92–$162.50. *Low Season* (April 1–December 19): $70–$105.

Service Charge: None

Government Tax: 7.5 percent

Villa Madeleine ◉◉◉

A hilltop frothing with lemon chiffon came to mind as my car climbed the steep hill to this luxury retreat high above Teague Bay near the eastern end of St. Croix.

Wedged into the ridge that separates the north and south coast at the narrowest part of the island, Villa Madeleine is a hotel-villa condominium complex with great style—outstanding enough to catch the eye of *Architectural Digest,* which featured it in a cover story almost before the paint was dry.

Intended for sophisticated, affluent travelers for whom privacy and all the comforts of home hold a greater priority than does a pretty beach, the luxurious villas are terraced in flowering gardens down the south side of the hill to catch the prevailing trade winds. They enjoy a wide panorama of the St. Croix sea and landscape from almost every turn. The fact that they are a half-mile from the nearest beach hardly seems to matter, since each villa has its own private swimming pool.

Opened in 1990, Villa Madeleine is the brainchild of Greg and Marcia Roncari. Connecticut transplants who came to the Caribbean in 1982, the young couple spent half of those years on St. Thomas polishing their hotel skills, planning, and searching for a spot to build their nirvana.

The centerpiece of the resort is the two-story Great House, a replica of a West Indian plantation house crowning the top of the ridge. Designed by architect William Adams, it resembles the manor houses that once dotted the St. Croix countryside. It has high ceilings, French doors, wide verandas, gingerbread trim, and a red roof. Its mellow yellow exterior even replicates the "official" color used on historic buildings throughout St. Croix.

The interiors of the Great House as well as the villas in the rental pool (normally about thirty) were designed by Carleton Varney, a New York decorator for whom St. Croix has been a second home for two decades. The Varney style is unmistakable throughout, with his signature fabrics of strong, rich colors and floral patterns and his furniture of classic design.

Varney's involvement with the total complex, part of the Roncaris' plan to maintain continuity, has enabled Villa Madeleine not to fall victim to the policy that often defeats condominiums operated as a hotel: allowing owners to decorate their villas. That distinction led me to break my own rules; Villa Madeleine is the only condominium complex in this book.

The architectural details of the villas match the Great House: red roofs and gingerbread trim, French doors and verandas, and pale yellow exteriors. Three villas have one bedroom; all the others have two bedrooms positioned at each end of the living room, whose French doors open onto a private terrace and a pretty tiled pool. Each bedroom has a separate living room entrance as well as doors to the terrace.

Although each villa's decor is a little different, they all have the same basic features: living room with a large L-shaped sofa piled with large pillows, Mexican terra-cotta floors, French doors, polished chrome fixtures, large pink marble baths, well-equipped kitchens, cable television and VCR, and king-size beds, some with giant bamboo four-poster beds.

The Roncaris work as a team; and along with another team—Asti and Spumanti, their cats—they are seen nightly working the crowd that comes up from town to dine along with the villa owners and guests at Cafe Madeleine. The restaurant has been one of St. Croix's best, and certainly most fashionable, since opening day. Dinner is served on the terrace, and the dinner menu, created by veteran chef David Stottz, who attended the Culinary Institute of America, offers contemporary cuisine based on Italian classics with New Caribbean touches. The pièce de résistance is the cafe's famous "Death by Chocolate."

While Villa Madeleine is operated as a hotel, you are left mostly to your own devices; there's no staff to pamper you. The hotel has two tennis courts and provides snorkel gear for those who want to explore some of St. Croix's beautiful reefs. The front-office staff can arrange almost any sport.

In the winter season you can have breakfast at Cafe Madeleine, or prepare it yourself with supplies from the pricey grocery down the hill. With advance notice, the management will lay in supplies for you, and the kitchen will prepare box lunches if you want to go off exploring St. Croix. You will need to rent a car; convenience is definitely not one of this resort's assets. But then, Villa Madeleine is not about activity.

Villa Madeleine is named after Greg's mother, who upon hearing the news, replied, "If it has my name on it, you'd better get it right." He did.

Address/Phone: Box 24190, Gallows Bay, St. Croix, U.S.V.I. 00824; (800) 548–4461 or (809) 773–8141; Fax: (809) 773–7518
Owner: Gregory and Marcia Roncari and villa owners
General Manager: Gregory and Marcia Roncari

Open: Year-round
Credit Cards: All major
U.S. Reservations: Direct to hotel
Deposit: 3 nights; 30 days cancellation, less 10%
Minimum Stay: None
Arrival/Departure: Transfer arranged for fee.
Distance from Airport: (St. Croix Airport) 14 miles; taxi one-way, $16
Distance from Christiansted: 8 miles; taxi one-way, $12
Accommodations: 43 villas with patio and private pools (3 one-bedroom; 40 two-bedroom with twins or kings); 25 to 30 available for rent
Amenities: Air-conditioning, ceiling fans, telephone, cable television, VCR, clock-radio, safe; bath with large marble shower, hairdryer, basket of toiletries; kitchen with microwave and dishwasher, iron, maid service, fresh flowers daily; no room service
Electricity: 110 volts
Sports: 43 private pools; tennis courts; snorkel gear. Water sports, golf, horseback riding, deep-sea fishing arranged.
Dress Code: Casual by day; elegantly casual at Cafe Madeleine for dinner
Children: Under 6 years of age discouraged
Meetings: Up to 40 people
Day Visitors: With reservations for dinner
Handicapped: No facilities
Packages: Honeymoon, summer
Rates: Per room, daily, EP. *High Season* (mid-December–mid-April): $425–$575. *Low Season:* $300–$400.
Service Charge: 10 percent
Government Tax: 7.5 percent

⌐⌐⌐⌐⌐ ON THE HORIZON ⌐⌐⌐⌐⌐

Hibiscus Beach Hotel

Situated on a 2,000-foot white-sand beach, the new Hibiscus is the best value to appear on this island in years. Three miles from Christiansted, the small resort is made up of two-story buildings—hibiscus pink with white gingerbread trim—clustered around an open-air pavilion/bar. To one side is the front office and air-conditioned dining room; to the other is a swimming pool.

Guest rooms are air-conditioned and have seaview terraces. They are furnished in bright, cheerful colors with king or two double beds, mini-bar, safe, telephone, television, and ceiling fan. Bathrooms are small and have shower only. Two rooms are designed for disabled persons and each has an adjoining guest room for a traveling companion. The buildings, connected by wooden boardwalks at ground level, are fully ramped for wheelchair accessibility. There is one two-bedroom suite with a kitchenette. Packages are available.

Address/Phone: 4131 La Grande Princesse, St. Croix, U.S.V.I. 00820; (800) 442–0121; (809) 773–4042; Fax: (809) 773–7668
U.S. Reservations: Direct to hotel
Accommodations: 38 rooms; two-bedroom suite
Rates: Per room, single or double, daily, CP. *High Season* (mid-December–mid-April): $145–$215. *Low Season:* $90–$150.

St. John

Caneel Bay ▣▣▣▣ ✿

Consider these numbers: 171 rooms on 170 acres and a staff of 450. Not bad odds, you could say. But these are only some of the elements that have made Caneel a legend.

Opened in 1955 as Laurance Rockefeller's first Caribbean venture, Caneel was the first of the ecologically built hideaways of the Rockresort style. A horticultural haven within the Virgin Islands National Park, Caneel is built into the ruins of an old sugar plantation. It's sprawled on a peninsula scalloped with seven (count 'em) flawless beaches protected by coral reefs that are also part of the national park. Indeed, the fact that Caneel is framed on all sides by the national park forever ensures its pristine quality.

The Caneel appeal is immediately apparent. Acres of carpetlike meadows and artfully arranged shrubbery are so manicured they could pass for a golf course. Gardens of tropical flowers adorn the walkways. In all, five hundred species of plants, many of them labeled and spotlighted at night, flourish on the gently undulating grounds.

Everywhere strategic benches and hammocks invite long, lazy afternoons for meditation. It's easy to see why Caneel has been a favorite retreat of overcharged VIPs, politicians, and business moguls. It's where Walter Mondale escaped to the day after he lost the 1984 presidential election and where Alan Alda and Diana Ross go to unwind. Although Caneel has been featured on "Lifestyles of the Rich and Famous," the resort protects the privacy of its celebrity guests. Perhaps that accounts for the high number of repeaters.

Guest rooms and suites are clustered in cottages of natural rock and weathered wood. They're all but hidden in the vegetation and are widely scattered. Some cottages are in the hillside tennis gardens, but most are set directly on the beaches.

The Cottage Point area on a bluff facing the water is the most requested honeymoon spot for its seclusion and quiet. Paradise Beach is next to the famous Cottage Number 7, formerly the Rockefeller home and now luxury digs for visiting bigwigs. Scott Beach, where units are in single-story buildings, is popular for its afternoon sun and lengthy beach. And cozy Turtle Bay Beach boasts the best snorkeling.

Regardless of locale, Caneel's rooms are airy and spacious and remain no-nonsense affairs with subdued decor, walls of louvered and screened windows for cross ventilation, and private patios. There are no telephones, television, or artificial sounds—only the twitter of birds, chorus of mating tree frogs, and the rhythmic lull of the sea.

The rooms may reflect the Rockresort philosophy of less is more, but at meals Caneel apparently operates on the notion that more is more. Breakfast and lunch buffets indulge guests with many choices. If you miss lunch there's always afternoon tea in the English manner on the terrace of the Turtle Bay Estate House, an open-air, plantation-style mansion.

Piano music accompanies cocktails in the living room of Turtle Bay Estate House. There are sunset cruises as well as live music on the Beach Terrace on Mondays and at the Caneel Bar on other days.

Caneel is at its most magical at night, when the grounds are aglow with low "mushroom" lamps, and Polynesian-style torches hidden in the thick foliage light the paths near the activities building. A laid-back combo completes the mood with light dance music. Nothing too energizing, mind you.

Dinner is served in three locations, all with a view of the twinkling lights of St. Thomas in the distance: the casual Beach Terrace on Caneel Bay Beach; the Sugar Mill in the flower-festooned ruins of the enormous eighteenth-century mill; and the more formal, romantic Turtle Bay Estate House, where it's time to dress up and sit down to a five-course meal.

Caneel offers a host of water sports and a variety of sail excursions and charter cruises, available from the Beach Hut. You'll find tennis, along with instruction, jogging paths (and hiking trails in the national park), and a changing selection of daily activities. But many guests are content simply to try a new beach each day and explore the technicolor panorama of marine life through a snorkel mask.

With nearly four decades under its cork, Caneel Bay has aged well, like a good wine.

Address/Phone: P.O. Box 720, St. John, U.S.V.I. 00831-0720; (809) 776–6111; Fax: (809) 776–2030

Owner: VMS Realty Partners; Management: Rockresorts, Inc.

General Manager and Vice President: Martin P. Nicholson

Open: Year-round

Credit Cards: All major

U.S. Reservations: Rockresorts, (800) 223–7637, (407) 394–4433; Fax: (407) 368–1946

Deposit: 3 nights; 28 days cancellation, December 19–31; 7 days rest of year

Minimum Stay: 10 days at Christmas

Arrival/Departure: Complimentary transfer on Caneel Bay's cruiser, which ferries between resort and St. Thomas 5 times daily in 40 minutes; and Little Dix in Tortola, twice weekly in 1.5 hours

Distance from Airport: (St. Thomas) 12 nautical miles (see Arrival/ Departure above)

Distance from Cruz Bay: 3 miles; taxi one-way, $2.50

Accommodations: 171 rooms in one- and two-story cottages with terrace (43 ocean view; 56 beachfront; 27 premium junior suites; 7 in Cottage 7; 13 courtside; 27 tennis/garden); 103 rooms with kings, 68 rooms with twins convertible to king

Amenities: Ceiling fans; bath with tub and shower, hairdryer available, basket of toiletries, bathrobe; sodas and ice service, nightly turndown service, room service with service charge for breakfast; no air-conditioning, telephone, television

Electricity: 110 volts

Sports: Freshwater swimming pool; 11 tennis courts (5 lighted); use of tennis and nonconcession water sports included in rate. Deep-sea fishing, boating, golf in St. Thomas arranged. Dive shop offers resort course, certification. Jogging path; hiking trails.

Dress Code: Casual by day. In evening, men are required to wear collared shirts and trousers; from December 19 to March 30, jackets are also required for dinner in Turtle Bay Estate House.

Children: 8 years and older

Meetings: Up to 50 people

Day Visitors: Welcome in certain areas only

Handicapped: Limited facilities

Packages: Dive, tennis, sailing, Island Hopper (with Little Dix), honeymoon, wedding

Rates: Per room, daily, CP. *High Season* (December 20–March 31): $330–565. *Shoulder Season* (April 1–30): $220–$440. *Low Season:* $200–$380.

Service Charge: None

Government Tax: 7.5 percent on room only

Hyatt Regency St. John ◙◙◙◙

It's all so *grand* it looks like a Hollywood film set. Broad steps lined with royal palms leading down through landscaped gardens flow to the resort's centerpiece, an enormous swimming pool with waterfalls and islands under tall, graceful palms.

Tucked in a cove on thirty-four hilly acres, the deluxe resort fronts a 1,200-foot white-sand beach on yacht-filled Great Cruz Bay. Thirteen guest-room buildings are terraced on the hillside between the reception at the top and the pool and beach below. Most guest rooms have a patio or balcony with views of the sea. All have plush, contemporary appointments. Each room has a large bar and marbled bathroom; the one- and two-bedroom suites have marble whirlpool baths—right in the bedroom!

The Hyatt Regency St. John has a variety of restaurants and bars amid its garden splendor. The informal Cafe Grand is the main restaurant, set in a large open-air pavilion by the beach. It serves three meals daily, offering à la carte menus and buffets. Three nights a week the dinner buffets are centered on a special theme, with different types of food and live entertainment as part of the fun. Sunday brunch is popular with town folk as much as with guests. The Cafe Grand Bar, adjacent to the restaurant, makes a pleasant outside terrace setting for predinner cocktails or as a place to linger with friends in the evening.

For the ever-thirsty and casual nibblers, there is the Splash Grill and Bar by the pool for lunches, afternoon snacks, dinner, and drinks daily until midnight. Another unusual attraction is the West Indian Deli, where you can find specialty food, sandwiches, salads, hot food, wines, fresh meat, cold drinks, and ice cream. Box lunches and complimentary coolers are available for day trips and pizza is delivered from 6:00 to 10:00 P.M. nightly.

Chow Bella, the Hyatt's gourmet restaurant, located above the main lobby, has a most unusual twist. It offers two separate menus: Oriental and Italian.

The hotel stages a folkloric show with Mexican music on Thursday evenings, and another show on Fridays highlights West Indian culture. The manager's Wednesday evening cocktail party is a popular occasion for guests to meet and mingle. Most are from the United States, but some—in growing numbers—come from Germany, Italy, South America, and Puerto Rico.

At the Hyatt, the use of tennis courts is free, and regular clinics provide a chance to pep up your game. A full array of water sports includes free snorkeling, kayaking, and windsurfing equipment along with daily lessons. The hotel's dive shop holds beginner courses as well as others for certification at an additional charge. Certified divers can enjoy excursions—one- and two-tank dives, wreck and night dives—departing daily from the hotel's dock.

If you have never snorkeled, you could never find more beautiful waters than those around this island to make your first discovery. St. John's coastal reefs are part of the Virgin Islands National Park. The Hyatt has sailing excursions to secluded beaches where you can snorkel from the boat or shore. Deep-sea fishing, sunset cruises, and private charters are available from the dock, too.

Camp Hyatt, a year round program for children ages three to fifteen, has a center for indoor play with toys, games, movies, and video games, and a playground with a jungle gym and other facilities. Supervised activities include swimming and windsurfing lessons. The program offers special menus and a frequent-stay program just for kids.

The resort complex has an attractive, small shopping center with an art gallery, quality boutiques for resort wear, books, and sundries.

The combination of a casual ambience, a bit of glamour, and its romantic setting makes the Hyatt a natural for honeymooners. At the same time, its services and facilities have much to offer families with children as well as couples of all ages.

Address/Phone: P.O. Box 8310, Great Cruz Bay, St. John, U.S.V.I. 00830; (809) 776–7171; Fax: (809) 775–3858
Owner: The Allen-Williams Co. of Englewood, Ohio
General Manager: Mark Heinzelman
Open: Year-round
Credit Cards: All major
U.S. Reservations: Hyatt Worldwide Reservations, (800) 233–1234 or direct to hotel
Deposit: 3 days within 14 days of reservation; cancellation for Christmas by October 1; 14 days remainder of year
Minimum Stay: 8 nights during Christmas holiday
Arrival/Departure: Guests met at St. Thomas Airport by hotel representative for transfer to Red Hook/National Park dock and boat directly to hotel dock. Fee charged
Distance from Airport: (St. Thomas Airport): 20 miles; taxi to Red Hook dock one-way, $5 shared
Distance from Cruz Bay: 1.5 miles; taxi one-way, $2.50 per person
Accommodations: 285 guest rooms including 7 one-bedroom and 14 two-bedroom suites in 13 two- and three-story buildings, all with 2 double beds or kings, most with terrace and ocean view
Amenities: Air-conditioning, telephone, refrigerator, cable television, in-room movies; bathrooms with tub and shower, hairdryer, deluxe toiletries; coffee maker, mini-bar, safe; nightly turndown service, room service for meals, business services, video camera rental; 24-hour photo processing

Electricity: 110 volts
Sports: Freshwater swimming pool; whirlpool in suites; 6 artificial grass tennis courts; equipment for rent. Resident U.S.P.T.A. pro, private lessons for fee, pro shop. Free water-sports equipment. Diving and sailing excursions; deep-sea fishing, and golf in St. Thomas arranged. Hiking on national park trails.
Dress Code: Casual by day; elegantly casual by night
Children: Camp Hyatt (see text); cribs, baby-sitters; Rock Hyatt
Meetings: Up to 300 people; audiovisual equipment
Day Visitors: Yes
Handicapped: Limited facilities
Packages: Honeymoon, dive, wedding, family, all-inclusive
Rates: Per room, daily, EP. *High Season* (mid-December–mid-April): $305–$895. *Shoulder* (April 15–May 31 and October 1–December 19): $225–$695. *Low Season* (June 1–September 30): $175–$595.
Service Charge: None
Government Tax: 7.5 percent

Maho Bay (S) 🍃

Folks, we're talking camp here. Camp as in camping—no private baths, no hot water, and no running water, except in the communal bathhouses.

This escape to paradise means tented cabins, which you'll probably share with friendly little lizards, mosquitoes, and other bugs. Getting to this heavenly rest takes ten hours or more with a plane ride, taxi, ferry, and another taxi. On the last stretch—a bone-cracking ride on the wooden seats of a converted flatbed truck—self-doubt may set in. At Maho's reception area you are checked in by a friendly attendant who will give you the do's and don'ts about Maho and about protecting paradise. Then you'll lug your luggage up (or down) the hill to your abode.

It's obvious that Maho Bay Camps is not for everyone. What may be less obvious is why I have included Maho in this book in the first place. But, you see, many people think Maho offers the greatest vacation in the Caribbean. They come from all over the country and all walks of life. Maho runs a year-round occupancy of 90 percent, probably the highest in the Caribbean, with a waiting list in winter so long, it turns away business. The majority of guests are repeaters, and the staff is made up mostly of folks who came as guests and decided to stay.

Maho Bay, a private campground in the Virgin Islands National Park, is unique in the Caribbean. It was created in 1976 by engineer-ecologist Stanley Selengut, who now is teaching the world that being an environmentalist can be good business. The camp enjoys a gorgeous setting on a wooded hillside that falls to a small beach and overlooks an exquisite bay of reef-protected turquoise waters and expansive scenery of mountainous green neighboring islands. Maho Bay has none of the amenities of a typical tropical hideaway. On the other hand, true campers call it luxurious.

Accommodations are in tented cabins, all but hidden in the thick foliage that climbs the hillsides, and are connected by a network of boardwalks and wooden steps. The dense woods help insure privacy but sometimes obscure the view. Each cabin, made out of a translucent water-repellent fabric, is built on a 16-by-16-foot wooden platform suspended above the ground on wood pilings, like a tree house. It is surprisingly roomy and quite comfortable.

The tent has a sleeping area with twin beds; a small sitting area just large enough for a trundle couch that sleeps two; a small kitchen unit with a three-burner propane stove, electrical outlet, cooler, dishes, and utensils; and an outside deck, which makes a great perch for watching the sunset or counting the stars. Mosquito netting, for what it's worth, is provided.

If you don't mind the hike to heaven, the seven newest tents are the most desirable, both for their wonderful views and because they have high ceilings with ceiling fans, which stir the air and help keep away mosquitoes. The innovation has been so successful that Maho plans to install more. If you are more a beach person, you might prefer the camp's lower reaches.

There are five bathhouses with wash basins, toilets, and showers at various locations around the property; a grocery store, which is neither nonprofit nor cheap; a multipurpose outdoor community center for meetings, seminars, weddings, and such; barbecue areas; and a cafeteria-style restaurant and bar in an outdoor pavilion with spectacular vistas. All three meals are available in the dining room and offer a varied menu with usually one meat, chicken, fish, and vegetarian selection daily for dinner, which is served early, from 5:30 to 7:00 P.M.

As St. John beaches go, Maho's isn't much, but there are two longer white-sand stretches a short walk or swim away. All three beaches are great for snorkeling. The resort offers scuba, sailing, windsurfing, and kayaking at additional charge. But the highlight is hiking on any of the national park's twenty-one trails.

Maho protects the environment with missionary zeal—and with the national park's rules. Evening programs are usually eco-oriented and may feature presentations by staff from the National Park Service or a visiting expert. Maho also hosts conferences on ecology.

Maho has taxi service, which makes five trips into Cruz Bay during the day, but if you want to take in the town's nightlife, transportation in the evenings can be a problem unless you rent a vehicle. Cab drivers do not like the rough road into the camp, about a half-mile from the main road.

If you understand that Maho is a campground, and that's the type of vacation you want, you will not find better facilities in a more beautiful setting in the Caribbean. Unfortunately, many people not suited for Maho, perhaps having a romanticized notion of what it is, go there anyway, attracted by the low price and the illusion that they can hack it.

Address: Cruz Bay, St. John, U.S.V.I. 00830; (809) 776–6240; Fax: (809) 776–6240

Owner: Stanley Selengut

General Manager: Bobby Flanagan

Open: Year-round

Credit Cards: None

U.S. Reservations: Maho Bay Camps, Inc., (800) 392–9004; (212) 472–9453; Fax: (212) 861–6210

Deposit: Half of reserved stay; 14 days cancellation less 10 percent of reservation cost

Minimum Stay: 7 days from December 15 to April 15

Arrival/Departure: No transfer service; 20-minute ferry ride from Red Hook dock on St. Thomas to Cruz Bay, $3; 45-minute ferry from Charlotte Amalie to Cruz Bay, $7

Distance from St. John Seaplane Pad: 8 miles; taxi one-way, $10 for one, $4 shared; from St. Thomas Airport, 20 miles

Distance from Cruz Bay: 8 miles; taxi one-way, $10 for 1, $5 shared; Maho's service, $4

Accommodations: 114 tent cabins, all with twin beds and trundle couch for 2

Amenities: Fans (7 with ceiling fans), showers in communal bathhouses

Electricity: 110 volts

Sports: Boating, snorkeling, diving, windsurfing, kayaking, deep-sea fishing arranged for fee.

Dress Code: Informal

Children: None under 4 years of age

Meetings: Up to 125 persons

Day Visitors: Welcome

Handicapped: No facilities

Packages: None

Rates: Two persons, daily, EP. *High Season* (December 15–April 30): $80; $10 each additional person. *Low Season* (May 1–December 14) $55.

Service Charge: None

Government Tax: 7.5 percent

St. Thomas

Stouffer Grand Beach Resort ◙◙◙◙

A deluxe, full-service resort on a great beach makes Stouffer grand in the eyes of many. Spread across thirty-four hillside acres on the northeast shore of St. Thomas, Stouffer Grand Beach Resort fronts 1,000 feet of pearly sands, beautiful turquoise waters, and a horizon filled with a host of neighboring islands.

Built in 1984 for fifty-two million dollars, the hotel required thirty million dollars to be put right again after Hurricane Hugo hit in 1989. Every aspect of the resort was improved, markedly raising the level of the resort and enabling it to garner the AAA Four-Diamond, Gold Key Award and several other other awards.

The resort's architecture—straight out of Akron, Ohio—was never one of its strong points. Built in stucco of contemporary design with sharply angled shingled roofs, the structures appear too modern and too massive for their Caribbean setting. Fortunately, the masses of palm trees, oleander, and bougainvillea soften the setting and all but hide many of the buildings. Indeed, the gardens, which Stouffer richly embellished, have given this tropical haven a romantic quality—one of its biggest assets, along with the beach, of course.

Guest rooms and suites are located in two separate areas: beach and poolside or hillside. Bougainvillea, the area by the beach, has seven two-story buildings around the huge, beautiful pool; they are staggered to provide each unit with a garden or sea view. In Hibiscus, the area where most rooms are located, the buildings are tiered up the steep hillsides, and all have grand views of the Caribbean and neighboring Virgin Islands. Golf carts are on call to shuttle you up and down the hills when you prefer not to make the climb.

The decor of the rooms calls on a rainbow of pastels in their floral fabrics and plush carpeting. There are marble foyers and bathrooms, and the master bedrooms of suites and townhouses have whirlpools.

Stouffer Grand has two freshwater pools, one overlooking the beach; complimentary tennis, along with racquets and clinics; a full range of water sports operated from the hotel's private dock; and a dive center offering day and night dives for beginners and certified divers.

To help you keep in shape, the fitness center has six-station Nautilus equipment, Lifecycle, bicycles, and an outdoor whirlpool. The men's and women's locker rooms are each equipped with changing rooms, showers, sauna, and steam bath. An arrival/departure lounge enables you to use the hotel's sports facilities should you arrive early or need to depart late.

Of course, if you have something less taxing in mind, you'll find hammocks (roomy enough for two) stretched between the palm trees.

Dining at Stouffer Grand takes in views and breezes, too. The food is generally good, but the service, sometimes at a stroll, can be uneven. Baywinds, the oceanfront dining room and bar, offers a menu of American cuisine with a Caribbean accent for all three meals. The Palm, a poolside snack bar, serves light meals and drinks in an outdoor setting during the day.

Smugglers Bar and Grill, a casual poolside restaurant for dinner, features grilled specialties, a large salad bar, and an award-winning Sunday brunch. It has an open "exhibition" kitchen where it's fun to watch the preparations. Wednesday nights bring guests together for the always-popular Caribbean Night beach party with a West Indian buffet, calypso music, and a folklore show.

The piano bar is a favorite rendezvous for cocktails, or you can sign up for a romantic sunset cruise. There is also music for listening and dancing nightly.

Stouffer encourages families to bring their children by providing a Kids Club, a year-round program of supervised activities for ages three to twelve. The cost ranges from $7.00 to $13.00 for a half day; $20.00 full day, and includes activity as varied as face painting and iguana hunts to pool games, nature hikes, and limbo lessons. They offer children's menus, a Kids Club room, and a kiddie pool.

Stouffer Grand's facilities and relaxing, casual atmosphere offer broad appeal to honeymooners, couples of all ages, and families. The majority of guests are from the United States, and at least some are part of a group; they are usually people who have been high scorers in their company's incentive program. A week at this resort is considered quite a prize.

Address/Phone: P.O. Box 8267, Smith Bay Road, St. Thomas, U.S.V.I. 00801; (809) 775–1510; Fax: (809) 775–2185

Owner: Stouffer Hotels & Resorts, Cleveland, Ohio

General Manager: James St. John III

Open: Year-round

Credit Cards: All major

U.S. Reservations: Stouffer Hotels and Resorts, (800) HOTELS–1

Deposit: 2 nights in winter; 1 night in summer

Minimum Stay: None

Arrival/Departure: Transfer arranged upon request

Distance from Airport: (Cyril E. King Airport) 9 miles; taxi one-way, $9.

Distance from Charlotte Amalie: 7 miles; taxi one-way, $7.50

Accommodations: 297 rooms including 36 suites; all with terraces (86 rooms in 7 pool/beachside buildings; 211 rooms in one- to three-story hillside buildings)

Amenities: Air-conditioning, direct-dial telephone, safes, cable television, Spectravision movies, stocked mini-bar, bathrobes, hairdryers, bath with tub and shower, basket of toiletries; nightly turndown service, 24-hour room service; shops

Electricity: 110 volts

Sports: 2 freshwater swimming pools; 6 tennis courts (4 hard surface, 2 Omniturf, lighted), free clinics, equipment use; resident USPTA pro, pro shop. Sunfish, snorkel gear, daily snorkel and scuba lessons, wind-surfing free. Sportfishing, golf, day sail arranged. Dive shop. Jogging trails.

Children: All ages; daily supervised activities program; cribs, high chairs, strollers, car seats, baby-sitters

Meetings: Up to 450 people; audiovisual facilities

Day Visitors: Yes

Handicapped: Yes

Packages: Golf, tennis, family, honeymoon, weddings

Rates: Per person, double, daily, EP. *High Season* (mid-December–mid-April): $157.50–$217.50, rooms; $297.50–$447.50, suites. *Low Season*: $125.50–$177.50, rooms; $225–$337.50, suites.

Service Charge: None

Government Tax: 7.5 percent

～～～～ ON THE HORIZON ～～～～

Emerald Beach Resort

The Emerald Beach Resort is located on a white-sand beach on Lindbergh Bay near St. Thomas airport and offers very good value. The hotel is set back from the road in beautiful gardens, and all rooms face the Caribbean (both factors that may account for the surprising lack of plane noise).

All rooms have air-conditioning, ceiling fans, and balconies and are stylishly decorated in quality rattan furniture and fabrics. They have king or two double beds, direct-dial phones, cable television, wet bar/fridge, safe, and posh marble bathrooms with hairdryer. The Palms restaurant and bar, overlooking the water, is set beside a small freshwater pool with a waterfall and beach bar. There is no room service.

The resort offers water sports. Entertainment includes jazz by the pool and a beach party with calypso weekly. There is a small meeting room for fifteen people, but the hotel is geared basically to individual travelers and families.

Address/Phone: P.O. Box 340, St. Thomas USVI 00804; (800) 233–4936; (809) 777–8800; Fax: (809) 776–3426
U.S. Reservations: Robert Reid Associates, (800) 223–6510
Accommodations: 90 rooms
Rates: Two persons, daily, EP. *High Season* (mid-December–mid-April): $220–$240. *Low Season*: $170–$190.

Grand Palazzo Hotel

The British Pemberton group, which has two deluxe hotels in Barbados, recently opened its first United States hotel and St. Thomas's most luxurious resort. Built in Italian Renaissance style, the new Grand Palazzo has a magnificent setting at the eastern end of St. Thomas, commanding expansive views of the Virgin Islands. The developer went to unusual lengths to protect the site's ecology.

Terraced in fifteen acres of lavish gardens, the elegant resort has gracious colonnaded lounges with high arched Palladian windows and a king's ransom of Italian marble. Air-conditioned guest rooms are mostly junior suites in multilevel white-stucco buildings with red-tiled roofs and flower-filled terraces, resembling large villas on the Italian Riveria. All have fabulous views, ceiling fans, cable television, mini-bars, two phones, and marbled baths.

At the top of the hill, the sumptuous Palm Terrace, the gourmet dining room, has a spectacular setting with 180-degree views of the Caribbean. Another restaurant serves light fare. The resort has a health club, tennis courts, and a free-form pool by the beach; nonmotorized water sports are included in the rate.

Address/Phone: Great Bay, St. Thomas, U.S.V.I.; (809) 775–3333; Fax: (809) 775–4444
U.S. Reservations: Pemberton Hotels (ITR), (800) 283–8666; (212) 545–7997
Accommodations: 150 suites with sea-view balconies
Rates: Per room, daily, EP. *High Season* (December 18–January 1; January 30–February 26): $495–$865 and (January 2–29): $450–$785. *Low Season* : Not available.

U.S. Resort
Reservations Offices
and Hotel Representatives

Bel-Air Hotel Company, 12381 Wilshire Boulevard, Los Angeles, CA 90025; (800) 648–4097; (310) 472–1211; Fax: (310) 476–5890

Bitter End Yacht Club and Resort, 875 North Michigan Avenue, No.3707, Chicago, IL 60611; (312) 944–5855; (800) 872–2392; Fax: (312) 944–2860

Caligo Ventures, 156 Bedford Road, Armonk, NY 10504; (800) 426–7781; (914) 273–6333; Fax: (914) 273–6370

Cap Juluca: 26 Broadway, No. 611, New York, NY 10004; (800) 323–0139; (212) 425–4684; Fax: 212–425–6026

Captain Don's Habitat (Maduro Travel), 903 South American Way, Miami FL 33132; (800) 327–6709; (305) 373–3341; Fax: (305) 371–2337

Caribbean Inns, Ltd., Carolina Office Park, Sapelo Bldg., No. 220, Hilton Head Island, SC 29938; (800) 633–7411; (803) 785–7411; Fax: (803) 686–7411

Caribbean World Resorts (Ray Morrow Associates), 4228 Hermitage Road, Virginia Beach, VA 23455; (800) 243–9420; (804) 460–2343; Fax: (804) 460–9420

Cayman Islands Reservations Service: 6100 Blue Lagoon Drive, Miami, FL 33126; (800) 327–8777; Fax: (305) 441–0483

Coccoloba, 640 Whitney Avenue, New Haven, CT 06511; (800) 833–3559; (203) 776–2596; Fax: (203) 772–1287

Curtain Bluff: 68 East 93rd Street, New York, NY 10128; (212) 289–8888

Doral Hotels: 600 Madison Avenue, 10th Floor, New York, NY 10022; (800) 22–DORAL; (212) 752–5700; Fax: (212) 826–9138

E & M Associates, 211 East 43rd Street, New York, NY 10017; (800) 223–9832; (212) 599–8280; Fax: (212) 599–1755

Elegant Resort of Jamaica, 1320 South Dixie Highway, No.1102, Coral Gables, FL 33146; (800) 237–3237; (305) 666–3566; Fax: (305) 666–7239

El San Juan Hotel & Casino (Williams Hospitality Management Corp.), 405 Lexington Avenue, 4th Floor, New York, NY 10174; (800) 468–2818; (212) 755–9030; Fax: (212) 297–0243

First Class Resorts, 1450 Madruga Avenue, No.208, Coral Gables, FL 33146; (800) 424–0004; (305) 669–0646; Fax: (305) 669–0842

Forte Hotels, 5700 Broadmore, Shawnee Mission, KS 66202; (800) 225–5843; (212) 541–4400; Fax: (913) 384–4727

Four Seasons Resort Nevis, 505 Park Avenue, New York, NY 10022; (800) 332–3442 (U.S.).; (800) 268–6282 (Canada); Fax: (416) 445–9106.

FDR Holidays, 147 West Merrick Road, Freeport, NY 11520; (800) 654–1337; (516) 223–1786; Fax: (516) 223–4815

Guana Island, 10 Timber Trail, Rye, NY 10580; (800) 544–8262; (914) 967–6050; Fax: (914) 967–8048

The Hermitage, 129 Kelmar Avenue, Frazer, PA 19355; (800) 862–4025; Fax: (215) 651–0601.

Hilton Reservations Service, Waldorf Astoria Hotel, New York, NY 10022; (800) 445–8667 (U.S.); (800) 268–9275 (Canada)

Hyatt Resorts Caribbean, 341 Madison Avenue, New York, NY 10017; (800) 233–1234; (212) 972–7000

International Travel and Resorts (ITR), 4 Park Avenue, New York, NY 10016; (800) 223–9815; (212) 251–1800; Fax: (212) 545–8467

International Travel Service (ITS), 3332 NE 33rd Street, Ft. Lauderdale, FL 33308; (800) 521–0643; (305) 566–7111; Fax: (305) 566–0036

JDB Associates, P.O. Box 16086, Alexandria, VA 22302-6086; (800) 346–5358; (703) 684–3834; Fax: (703) 548–5825

Jenkins & Gibson Ltd., Box 10685, Towson, MD 21285; (800) 344–2049; (301) 321–1231; Fax: (301) 494–1910

La Samanna: 509 Madison Avnue, No.2004; New York, NY 10022; (800) 854–2252; (212) 319–5191; Fax: (212) 832–5390

Leading Hotels of the World, 747 Third Avenue, New York, NY 10017-2847; (800) 223–6800; (212) 838–3110; Fax: (212) 758–7367

Le Sport (Tropical Holidays), 927 Lincoln Road, No.110, Miami Beach, FL 33139; (800) 544–2883; (305) 532–2591; Fax: (305) 672–5861

Ralph Locke Islands, Inc., P.O. Box 800, Waccabuc, NY 10597; (800) 223–1108; (914) 763–5526; Fax: (914) 763–5362

Maho Bay Camps, Inc., 17 East 72rd Street, New York, NY 10021; (800) 392–9004; (212) 472–9453; Fax: (212) 861–6210

Jane Martin (Sapore di Mare), 2170 Broadway, No.3317, New York, NY 10023; (212) 319–7488; Fax: (212) 879–1276

David B. Mitchell & Co., 70 Old Kings Highway North, Darien, CT 06820-4725; (800) 372–1323; (203) 655–4200; Fax: (203) 656–3475

Ray Morrow Associates—See Caribbean World Resorts.

Marketing Reservations International (MRI), 175 Fountaine Bleau Blvd. Ste 1C, Miami FL; (800) 255–5859; (305) 225–1740; Fax: (305) 225–1647·

Necker Island, BVI, Ltd., 90 Morton Street, New York, NY 10014; (800) 524–0004; (212) 691–3916; Fax: (212) 627–1494

Paradise Found, Inc., 5 Grinnel Court, Rockville, MD 20855; (800) 776–PALM; (301) 309–1698; Fax: (301) 762–7283

Paradores Puertorriqueños, P.O. Box 4435; San Juan, PR 00905; (800) 443–0266; (809) 721–2884; Fax: 809–721–4698

Pemberton Hotels, Travel Resources Management Group, 5201 North O'Connor Blvd. No.500; Irving, TX 75039; (800) 283–8666; (214) 556–2151; Fax: (214) 556–1538

Peter Island Resort & Yacht Harbour, 220 Lyon Street, Grand Rapids, Michigan 49503; (800) 346–4451; (616) 776–6456; Fax: (616) 776–6496

Petit St. Vincent, P.O. Box 12506, Cincinnati, OH 45212; (800) 654–9326; (513) 242–1333; Fax: (513) 242–6951

Pineapple Beach Clubs, 6401 Congress Avenue, No.100; Boca Raton, FL 33487; (800) 966–4737; Fax: (407) 994–6344

Preferred Hotels & Resorts Worldwide, 1901 South Meyers Road, Oakbrook Terrace, IL 60181; (800) 323–7500; Fax: (708) 290–6172

Ramada International Hotels and Resorts/Latin America Caribbean, 4655 Lejeune Road, No.800; (800) 228–9898; (305) 441–1255; Fax: (305) 448–1656

Resorts Management: The Carriage House, 201 1/2 East 29th Street, New York, NY 10016; (800) 225–4255; (800) 331–9154 (Meredian Club); (212) 696–4566; Fax: (212) 689–1598

Resorts Representation International, 901 NE 125 Street, North Miami FL 33161; (800) 321–3000; (305) 891–2500; Fax: (305) 893–2866

Robert Reid Associates: 810 North 96th Street, Omaha, NE 68114; (800) 223–6510; (402) 398–3217; Fax: (402) 398–5484

Resinter, 1500 Broadway, New York 10036; (800) 221–4542; (212) 575–2228; Fax: (212) 719—5763

Rockresorts, Inc., 501 East Camino Real, Boca Raton, FL 33431-0825; (800) 223–7637; (407) 394–4433; Fax: (407) 368–1946

Salt Whistle Bay Club: 1020 Bayridge Drive, Kingston, Ontario, K7P 2S2, Canada; (800) 263–2780; (613) 634–1963; Fax: (613) 384–6300

Sandals/Unique Vacations: 7610 SW 61st Avenue, Miami, FL 33143; (800) 726–3257; (305) 284–1300; Fax: (305) 284–1336

Small Hope Bay Lodge, P.O. Box 21667, Ft. Lauderdale, FL 33335; (800) 223–6961; (305) 359–8240

Smarts Reservations, 7000 Boulevard East, Guttenberg, NJ 07093; (800) 323–5655; (201) 869–0060; Fax: (201) 869–7628

Spring on Bequia: Box 19251, Minneapolis, MN 55419; (612) 823–1202; Fax: (612) 823–9925

Stouffer Hotels and Resorts, 29800 Bainbridge Road, Solon, OH 44139; (800) 468–3571; (216) 248–3600

Superclubs, NY, P.O. Box 534; Freeport, NY 11520; (800) 858–8009; (516) 868–6924; Fax: (516) 868–6957

Swept Away Resort, 12 Harrison Street, 5th Floor, New York, NY 10013; (800) 545–7937; (212) 966–0508; Fax: (212) 925–3063.

Utell International, 810 North 96th Street, Omaha, NE 68114-2594; (800) 448–8355; (402) 398–3200; Fax: (402) 398–5484

WIMCO: P.O. Box 1461, Newport, RI 02840; (800) 932–3222; (401) 849–8012; Fax: (401) 847–6290

Windmill Plantation, 440 32nd Street, West Palm Beach, FL 33407; (800) 822–7715; (407) 845–2982; Fax: (407) 845–2982

The Best of the Best

The chart on the following pages is meant to help readers locate quickly the resorts that might best meet their particular interests. It is *not* intended to be a complete inventory of each resort's facilities. Instead, it indicates the especially strong features of each establishment. For example, most beach-side resorts in this book offer scuba diving or can arrange it, as we have noted in the text; however, the chart notes only those resorts focused primarily on diving or which have a particularly outstanding dive facility.

Caribbean Resorts — Features Comparison Chart

Feature	Four Seasons Nevis (Nevis)	Filao Beach (St. Barts)	El San Juan (Puerto Rico)	Dunmore Beach (Bahamas)	Divi Divi Beach Resort (Aruba)	Curtain Bluff (Antigua)	Cotton House (Grenadines)	Coccoloba (Anguilla)	Cobblers Cove (Barbados)	Casa San José (Puerto Rico)	Caribe Hilton (Puerto Rico)	Capt. Don's Habitat (Bonaire)	Cap Jaluca (Anguilla)	Caneel Bay (USVI)	Calabash (Grenada)	Buccaneer (USVI)	Boscobel Beach (Jamaica)	Bitter End (British VI)	Biras Creek (British VI)	Bluff House (Bahamas)	Blue Waters Beach (Antigua)	Bakoua (Martinique)	Avila Beach (Curaçao)	Asa Wright (Trinidad)	Anse Chastanet (St. Lucia)
Beachside	✓	✓	✓	✓	✓	✓	✓	✓	✓		✓	✓	✓	✓	✓	✓	✓	✓	✓	✓	✓	✓	✓		✓
Hillside						✓														✓		✓	✓	✓	✓
All inclusive				✓	✓										✓		✓								
Budget																					✓			✓	
Value									✓						✓	✓						✓			
Honeymoon		✓		✓		✓	✓	✓	✓	✓	✓		✓	✓	✓	✓			✓	✓			✓		✓
Romantics		✓						✓	✓				✓	✓	✓				✓	✓					✓
Weddings				✓	✓		✓						✓	✓	✓		✓		✓	✓					✓
Children's Program	✓										✓				✓	✓	✓								
Families	✓	✓		✓			✓				✓	✓		✓	✓	✓	✓	✓							✓
Singles										✓										✓			✓	✓	
Sports/Active	✓		✓		✓	✓	✓	✓	✓		✓			✓		✓	✓	✓	✓			✓	✓		✓
Dive												✓													✓
Golf	✓													✓											
Tennis	✓		✓			✓					✓			✓	✓										
Marina														✓					✓	✓		✓			
Spa										✓															
Naure Lovers				✓		✓					✓			✓	✓	✓				✓				✓	✓
Hiking															✓					✓				✓	✓
Birding																								✓	
History									✓					✓											
Cuisine				✓		✓		✓	✓		✓														
Entertainment	✓		✓			✓					✓		✓												
Casino			✓			✓					✓														

Feature	La Belle Creole (St. Martin)	K Club (Antigua)	Jumby Bay (Antigua)	Jamaica-Jamaica (Jamaica)	Jamaica Inn (Jamaica)	Ivor (Jamaica)	Hyatt Regency St. John (USVI)	Hyatt Regency Grand Cayman (Cayman Islands)	Hyatt Regency Aruba (Aruba)	Hyatt Dorado Beach (Puerto Rico)	Horned Dorset Primavera (Puerto Rico)	Hilton International (Trinidad)	Hermitage (Nevis)	Harbour Village (Bonaire)	Hamak (Guadeloupe)	Half Moon Club (Jamaica)	Guana Island (British VI)	Guanahani (St. Barts)	Green Turtle (Bahamas)	Golden Rock (Nevis)	Golden Lemon (St. Kitts)	Glitter Bay (Barbados)	Galley Bay (Antigua)	Galería San Juan (Puerto Rico)	Frangipani (Grenadines)
Beachside	✓	✓	✓	✓	✓		✓	✓	✓	✓	✓		✓	✓	✓			✓			✓	✓	✓		✓
Hillside						✓	✓					✓						✓	✓		✓				
All inclusive			✓	✓														✓					✓		
Budget				✓		✓													✓					✓	✓
Value				✓								✓													
Honeymoon	✓	✓	✓		✓		✓	✓	✓	✓	✓		✓	✓	✓			✓			✓	✓			
Romantics	✓	✓	✓		✓	✓		✓		✓	✓		✓			✓	✓	✓			✓	✓	✓		✓
Weddings			✓		✓		✓			✓								✓			✓	✓	✓		
Children's Program							✓	✓	✓	✓															
Families	✓		✓				✓	✓	✓	✓		✓				✓	✓		✓	✓		✓			
Singles					✓							✓	✓	✓							✓				✓
Sports/Active	✓		✓	✓			✓	✓	✓	✓				✓	✓	✓	✓	✓			✓	✓			
Dive												✓													
Golf			✓					✓		✓							✓								
Tennis	✓		✓	✓			✓			✓							✓								
Marina			✓				✓	✓						✓					✓						
Spa										✓												✓			
Nature Lovers						✓						✓						✓			✓				
Hiking			✓			✓	✓					✓						✓		✓	✓			✓	
Birding			✓			✓												✓			✓			✓	
History													✓						✓	✓				✓	
Cuisine		✓	✓		✓	✓				✓	✓		✓					✓		✓		✓			
Entertainment				✓					✓	✓	✓	✓	✓					✓							
Casino										✓	✓														

	Ramada Renaissance Jaragua (Dominican Republic)	Ramada Renaissance Grenada (Grenada)	Pirates Point (Cayman Islands)	Pineapple Beach (Antigua)	Petit St. Vincent (Grenadines)	Peter Island (British VI)	Pasanggrahan (Saint Maarten)	Parador Hacienda Gripinas (Puerto Rico)	Palm Island (Grenadines)	Otley's Plantation (St. Kitts)	Old Gin House (St. Eustatius)	Ocean Club (Bahamas)	Nisbet Plantation (Nevis)	Necker Island (British VI)	Montpelier Plantation (Nevis)	Meridian Club (Turks & Caicos)	Malliouhana (Anguilla)	Maho Bay (USVI)	Little Dix (British VI)	Lions Dive (Curaçao)	L'Hibiscus (St. Barts)	Les Petits Saints aux Anacardiers (Guadeloupe)	Le Sport (St. Lucia)	La Sirena (Anguilla)	La Samanna (St. Martin)	
		✓	✓	✓	✓	✓	✓		✓			✓	✓			✓	✓		✓	✓			✓	✓	✓	Beachside
							✓			✓	✓		✓	✓			✓	✓			✓	✓	✓			Hillside
			✓	✓	✓				✓				✓		✓									✓		All inclusive
						✓	✓			✓								✓					✓			Budget
		✓																		✓			✓	✓	Value
	✓	✓		✓	✓		✓	✓	✓		✓	✓		✓	✓	✓		✓					✓		✓	Honeymoon
			✓	✓			✓	✓		✓	✓	✓			✓			✓					✓			Romantics
			✓	✓			✓		✓		✓	✓			✓			✓					✓			Weddings
																										Children's Program
	✓	✓			✓				✓	✓		✓			✓	✓		✓	✓					✓		Families
						✓			✓						✓			✓			✓	✓	✓			Singles
	✓	✓	✓		✓			✓					✓	✓		✓		✓	✓				✓			Sports/Active
		✓			✓														✓							Dive
												✓														Golf
	✓					✓							✓					✓		✓						Tennis
						✓												✓								Marina
	✓																								✓	Spa
					✓				✓	✓	✓		✓		✓		✓	✓								Naure Lovers
					✓				✓		✓				✓	✓		✓	✓				✓			Hiking
								✓							✓	✓										Birding
										✓			✓		✓											History
	✓		✓							✓	✓		✓		✓				✓	✓					✓	Cuisine
	✓																						✓			Entertainment
	✓																									Casino

Hotel/resort features matrix (✓ indicates feature present):

Property	Beachside	Hillside	All inclusive	Budget	Value	Honeymoon	Romantics	Weddings	Children's Progra	Families	Singles	Sports/Active	Dive	Golf	Tennis	Marina	Spa	Naure Lovers	Hiking	Birding	History	Cuisine	Entertainment	Casino
Rawlins Plantation (St. Kitts)	✓	✓			✓	✓	✓	✓		✓								✓				✓		
Round Hill (Jamaica)	✓	✓				✓	✓	✓		✓														
Royal Pavilion (Barbados)	✓																							
Royal St. Lucian (St. Lucia)	✓					✓						✓						✓				✓		
Runaway Hill (Bahamas)	✓									✓								✓	✓					
Saltwhistle Bay (Grenadines)	✓						✓																	
Sandals Dunn's River (Jamaica)	✓		✓		✓	✓		✓				✓										✓	✓	
Sandcastle (British VI)	✓		✓			✓	✓				✓	✓		✓	✓									
Sandy Lane (Barbados)	✓					✓	✓	✓										✓				✓	✓	
Sans Souci (Jamaica)	✓	✓					✓	✓				✓					✓						✓	
Sapore di Mare (St. Barts)		✓			✓	✓																		
Small Hope Bay (Bahamas)	✓		✓				✓			✓	✓	✓	✓					✓	✓					
Spice Island Inn (Grenada)	✓				✓															✓				
Spring on Bequia (Grenadines)		✓				✓		✓				✓						✓	✓					
Stouffer's Grand (USVI)	✓	✓				✓				✓					✓	✓								
Sugar Mill (British VI)	✓	✓	✓		✓	✓	✓	✓		✓													✓	
Swept Away (Jamaica)	✓					✓	✓	✓	✓			✓			✓							✓		
Trident (Jamaica)	✓							✓						✓	✓									
Tryall (Jamaica)	✓	✓								✓		✓						✓					✓	
Twelve Degrees North (Grenada)	✓	✓								✓		✓						✓						
Valentine's (Bahamas)	✓			✓						✓	✓	✓	✓					✓	✓					
Villa Madeleine (USVI)		✓				✓	✓			✓						✓								
Village St. Jean (St. Barts)		✓			✓					✓												✓		
Windmills Plantation (Turks & Caicos)	✓		✓				✓																	
Young Island (St. Vincent)	✓	✓				✓	✓					✓						✓	✓					